Theoretical Perspectives on Deviance

THEORETICAL PERSPECTIVES ON DEVIANCE

Edited by

ROBERT A. SCOTT

and

JACK D. DOUGLAS

BASIC BOOKS, INC., Publishers

NEW YORK   LONDON

© 1972
BY ROBERT A. SCOTT AND JACK D. DOUGLAS

Library of Congress Catalog Card Number: 79–174828
SBN 465–08420–6

MANUFACTURED IN THE UNITED STATES OF AMERICA

CONTRIBUTORS

DONALD W. BALL is Associate Professor of Sociology at the University of Victoria, Victoria, British Columbia. His research and writing are in the areas of deviance and qualitative social psychology, and recently he has done work in the social organization of sports and games. He is currently working on two publications: a book on the family in American society and a monograph on social situation and personal space.

DONALD J. BLACK is Assistant Professor of Sociology and Lecturer in Law at Yale University. His areas of interest include general sociological theory, social control, law, and deviant behavior. He is the author of several articles in these fields and is now editing a volume on the social organization of law with Maureen Mileski.

ALAN F. BLUM is Associate Professor of Sociology at New York University. Most of his work has been in the area of sociological theory.

AARON V. CICOUREL is Professor of Sociology at the University of California, San Diego. He is the author of *The Educational Decision Makers, The Social Organization of Juvenile Justice,* and *Method and Measurement in Sociology.* He is also co-author of *Language Socialization and Use in Testing and Classroom Situation,* and is presently working on a book entitled *Interviews as Situated Accounts.* His primary fields of interest are cognitive sociology and ethnomethodology.

JACK D. DOUGLAS is Professor of Sociology at the University of California, San Diego. His teaching and research have been in social theory, deviance, and social problems. He is the author of *The Social Meanings of Suicide, Youth in Turmoil, American Social Order,* and *The Sociology of Social Problems.* He has also edited several volumes of essays in the fields of deviance, social problems, and general sociology.

HORACIO FABREGA, JR., is Associate Professor of Psychiatry and Anthropology at Michigan State University. He is the author of numerous essays in the field of health and mental illness and is currently writing a book on Shamanistic curing in Zinacantan.

JACK P. GIBBS is Professor of Sociology at the University of Texas, Austin, Texas. He is co-author of *Status Integration and Suicide* and editor of *Urban Research Methods* and *Suicide.* He is interested in the fields of deviance, human ecology, and theory construction.

JOHN M. JOHNSON is a graduate student in sociology at the University of California, San Diego. He is the author of articles on social theory, social prob-

lems, and social welfare and is now working on a book on the conduct of
field work in sociological research.

PETER K. MANNING is Associate Professor of Sociology and Psychiatry at
Michigan State University. He is co-editor of *Youth and Sociology* and is
presently writing a book on deviance and change. His research has been
in the areas of deviant behavior, socialization, and crosscultural studies of
health and illness.

RICHARD QUINNEY is Professor of Sociology at New York University. He is the
author of *The Social Reality of Crime, Social Theory in a Radical Age,
Criminal Behavior Systems* (with Marshall B. Clinard), and *The Problem
of Crime.* He is also the editor of *Crime and Justice in Society* and is interested in criminology, social theory, and political sociology.

ALBERT J. REISS, JR., is Professor of Sociology at Yale University. He is the
author of *The Police and the Public, Studies in Crime and Law Enforcement in Major Metropolitan Areas, Treating Youthful Offenders in the
Community, Occupations and Social Status,* and *Social Characteristics of
Urban and Rural Communities.* He has edited many volumes in the fields
of deviance, urban society, and social policy, as well as having written
numerous essays in these fields.

H. DIETER SEIBEL is Associate Professor of Sociology at Manhattanville College
in New York. He is the author of *Industriearbeit und Kulturwandel in
Nigeria* and co-author, with Michael Koll, of *Einheimische Genossenschaften
in Afrika.* His fields of interest include social change in Africa, comparative
sociology, and industrial sociology.

ROBERT A. SCOTT is Associate Professor of Sociology at Princeton University. He
is the author of *The Making of Blind Men* and has written essays in the
fields of deviance, social welfare, and public policy. He is currently doing
a comparative, historical study of deviance and social control in England and
America from 1800 to the present.

ANDREW SCULL is a doctoral candidate in sociology at Princeton University. His
primary interests are in sociological theory and the sociology of deviance.
He is currently studying social control agencies in Britain and America.

CAROL A. B. WARREN is a graduate student in sociology at the University of
California, San Diego. She is the author of a number of essays on deviance
and is at present completing research on identity and community among
male homosexuals.

CONTENTS

FIGURES

TABLES

Theoretical Perspectives on Deviance

INTRODUCTION

The great conflicts within American society in the past decade once again remind us of the problematic nature of social order and its essential role in man's existence. Man cannot live without the order of social relations and yet the great complexities of the world, the conflict over scarce goods, the differences that divide men, and the necessary freedoms borne of man's inherent symbolic capacities ensure that social order will always be uncertain. And so, like men of all ages, we find ourselves struggling to understand how social order is possible and how to preserve it in a manner consistent with the interests and desires of everyone. Because these problems are so basic to human existence and their solutions so essential to its continuance, the sociology of deviance will always be a central concern to the student of human societies.

Man has contrived many ways to ensure social order, running the gamut from gentle persuasion to brute force. One of his most effective devices involves the use of social rules, by which is meant the symbolic criteria that individuals use in their everyday life as guidelines for their behavior. Men have always believed that conduct ought to be governed by rules, not only because this was intrinsically moral but also because it was vitally important in maintaining social order. The man whose conduct is guided by social rules is said to build and preserve the social order; the man whose conduct is not so guided, especially the one who intentionally violates the rules of society, is said to destroy social order. These beliefs have always been powerful, especially in the pluralistic societies of the West in which order has been, and remains, problematic. For this reason, and because legal rules, or laws, have been purposefully constructed to maintain order, obedience to rules and social order has become virtually synonymous in the ancient phrase "Law and Order."

As men in the nineteenth century turned their attention to the development of a science of society, it is not surprising to discover that the nature of social rules and the relationship of rules to social order was uppermost in their minds. They believed that an understanding of these factors would enable them to solve the practical problem of constructing an enduring and just social order. The sociology of deviance, which the nineteenth-century scholars termed "moral statistics" and that subsequent generations of scholars have termed "social disorganization" or "social pathology," is the field that is most centrally concerned with these questions.

Until the decade of the 1950s, the sociology of deviance was dominated by a natural attitude of common sense toward social rules and social order. Most sociologists viewed social rules as absolute, clear, and obvious to all members of a society in all situations. Moreover, the relation between rules and social order was also seen as absolute: "Law and Order" were necessary, desirable, and moral, and the goal of sociology was to help attain and preserve them. Although there had been some significant departures from this general presumption among early French and German sociologists and in the work of the American sociologist Herbert Blumer, it was not until the 1950s that the absolutist perspective underwent serious questioning.

During the 1950s, the works of men such as Frank Tannenbaum, Edwin Lemert, and Howard Becker were synthesized into the labeling theory of deviance. Labeling theory concentrates on the ways in which rules are used in everyday life by laymen and official agents of social control. The studies of deviance informed by this perspective showed that the practical uses of social rules are far more important in determining deviance than are the absolute, codified rules of society. Sociologists recognized as false the ancient idea that social rules have distinctive meanings that are so clear to everyone that unambiguous evaluations of behavior can be made. The social meanings of rules were found to be highly uncertain.

These early formulations said little about the nature of social order itself or of the relationship between the problematic meanings of rules and the construction of social order. Later works in this vein, especially by Erikson and Berger and Luckmann, extended this labeling perspective to consider these issues. By the mid-1960s, labeling theory and the perspective of symbolic interaction from which labeling theory was derived had been assimilated into the mainstream of sociological theory.

Now that the basic insights of labeling theory are accepted, students of deviance are increasingly turning to the problem of critically evaluating and refining these ideas. Some of this work is being done from the point of view of earlier perspectives and some from the point of view of the emerging perspectives on deviance. This volume is a collection of original essays that report some of the most important recent theoretical and research developments in this field.

The volume is divided into six major parts. The first part contains an essay by Scott that deals with the relationship between social order and the problematic character of social rules. The second part contains a group of essays that are critiques of labeling theory. Gibbs examines this body of theory from the conventional and established normative perspective; Johnson and Warren critically evaluate labeling theory from the phenomenological perspective; and Fabrega and Manning attempt to clarify and extend the labeling perspective by applying it to the problem of disease and illness. The third part presents research studies that report on empirical findings of great significance in clarifying various issues and questions about deviance. Black and Reiss report on the results of their study of police detection of juvenile delinquents; Cicourel's essay is concerned with the management of juveniles by social control agents following their public identification as delinquents; and Ball reports on the findings of his research on illegal abortion clinics. The essays in the fourth part by Douglas and Johnson are concerned with the ways in which social rules are used in concrete situations. Both authors are concerned with the relationship between concrete rule uses and the abstract models of rules. The fifth part contains essays reporting on the results of studies of deviance in societies other than our own. Seibel presents an analysis of the use of social rules in small tribal African societies, and Scull analyzes recent developments in the drug problem in England in the light of that government's official policy. The final part, containing essays by Quinney and Blum, is concerned with the implications for sociological theory of recent advances in the study of deviance.

Social deviance has become one of the most creative fields in all of sociology, a fact that should not be surprising in view of its subject matter. Developments in the study of deviance have commonly presaged general theoretical advances in the discipline, a pattern that remains true today. The essays in this volume communicate some of the most vital contemporary ideas on deviance, social rules, and social order. We hope that they will stimulate the creative efforts necessary to reveal the weakness in labeling theory and show the way to a better understanding of these crucial issues.

R. A. S. and J. D. D.

I

Social Order
and Deviance

From the point of view of labeling theory, deviance is a social property conferred on an individual by others. With few exceptions, sociological studies of deviance informed by this perspective have been concerned with the process in which labels are conferred on people, especially as it involves those who apply the labels. As knowledge about this process has grown, sociologists have increasingly come to ask why these deviant labels are "there" to be conferred in the first place. Why does this social property exist at all and what role does it play in the larger social order? Partial answers to these questions are found in the works of several scholars. The names of Emile Durkheim, Kai Erikson, and Mary Douglas immediately come to mind as prominent examples. In the essay that follows, Scott draws upon both the insights and the seminal work by Peter Berger and Thomas Luckmann on the social construction of reality in order to develop a framework for analyzing the role and functions of deviance in the social order. The framework that is developed serves to integrate much of the material presented in the entire volume.

Chapter One

A PROPOSED FRAMEWORK FOR ANALYZING DEVIANCE AS A PROPERTY OF SOCIAL ORDER

Robert A. Scott

There are some social scientists who derive satisfaction out of debunking the common-sense conceptions that laymen have about human behavior and social life. It is my personal, and somewhat jaundiced, view that neither the social scientists nor the laymen whose views he scrutinizes have yet managed to decisively gain the upper hand in this activity. Still, there are some questions on which the sociologist's views do appear to be the more nearly correct of the two. One involves the relationship between deviance (or, in the laymen's terminology, "social problems") and the larger social order.

According to at least one widely shared popular conception about deviance, problems such as crime, mental illness, prostitution, or drug addiction are abnormal social conditions. These are thought of as "soft spots" that have developed on the surface of the society but that have very little to do with its core values, structures, and processes. These soft spots are aberrations that result from characterological defects that are produced by accidents of birth and/or a certain inevitable "slippage" that occurs in the workings of those social institutions such as the family and the school that are responsible for instilling appropriate values and standards of conduct in the young. According to this view, social problems can be solved by correcting these institutional imperfections and either rehabilitating or punishing those who have gone wrong.

There is a great deal of writing and research in the field of social science that indicates that this view about deviance is largely in error. The sociological literature is filled with examples of research in which the investigator began his studies by accepting the layman's explanation for deviance, intending to document and clarify it, only to discover that the deviant behavior he was observing was more a product of the social definitions that were imposed upon the deviant by others than it was a product of any characterological defects and socialization failures that may have occurred. In fact, this basic finding has been confirmed so often that it has given rise to an entire school of thought concerning the interpersonal bases of deviant behavior; namely, the labeling perspective.[1] The basic point of this perspective, that deviant behavior is in part a product of the social definitions that are imposed on a person by others, has its counterparts at the community level as well. Evidence has now been obtained that suggests that under certain conditions of social life ordinary citizens become enmeshed in a cycle of events in which certain individuals in their midst are singled out and forced to the symbolic fringes of the group where they become heretics and outcasts.[2] These processes of exclusion seem to occur at those times in the life of the group when its unique identity as a social unit becomes obscure or ambiguous. This study has led some sociologists to suggest that the deviate may perform an important service to the society by reminding others of the location of the symbolic outlines of the community in which they live.

It has also been noted that there are deviants in all known human societies both past and present. This fact by itself does not negate the common-sense position since it can be argued that no social system ever operates absolutely perfectly, nor is it likely that there will ever be one. Although this is true, sociologists have come to view this argument with a certain amount of suspicion as they have discovered that deviance seems to persist stubbornly even when there have been ambitious and determined efforts to eradicate it. In fact, the more intense these efforts have been, the more that deviance seems to flourish, suggesting that the relationship between these two phenomena is more symbiotic than antagonistic.

Observations such as these have led sociologists to develop a perspective about deviance that is markedly different from those that laymen hold. Far from being abnormal and aberrant, the sociologist looks upon deviance as a central and essential feature of all social systems. Deviance is an inevitable product of the normal operation of any social system and it appears to have an important role to play in maintaining that system. Indeed, there are some who believe that without deviance social order itself would be impossible.

Although sociologists recognize that deviance is an essential feature of all societies, their efforts to develop an explanation for deviance as a property of the social order (that is, why it develops, how it is related to the social order, what functions, if any, it serves) have not been particularly successful. One reason for this failure is that many of the best ideas that sociologists have had about deviance have been proposed in the context of their scholarly attempt to debunk prevailing popular ideas about social problems.[3] Whereas most of their arguments are convincing, when they are taken together they give us only a piecemeal explanation for specific aspects of deviance rather than the kind of coherent, unified theory that is required of an acceptable scientific explanation. Kai Erikson has gone a long way toward remedying this situation by constructing a coherent, if limited theory about the place of deviance in a social community, and then testing it empirically with historical data from the Puritan colonies.[4] I believe that his work has moved us further toward a theory about deviance as a property of the social order than any other single sociological study. Still, there are many questions that are only partly answered in Erikson's approach, and there are others that it does not answer at all. For example, why does deviance persist during periods when the symbolic boundaries of a community are apparently stable and clearly demarcated? And why do we make such determined efforts to reform those individuals in the community who have been designated deviant? These are only a few of the many puzzling questions that must be answered if we are to have an acceptable theory of deviance. The purpose of this essay is to take a step in this direction by presenting a framework for analyzing deviance as a property of the social order. The framework presented is an integration of Erikson's basic approach with the works of a number of other social scientists who have not been concerned primarily with deviance, but whose ideas, I believe, have a great deal to tell us about its relationship to the social order.

The essay is divided into three main sections. In the first section I have tried to describe the characteristics that distinguish deviance as a property of the social order. In the second section an analysis is presented of certain features of the social order, which I believe, help to account for deviance as a property of it. In the final brief section, I have tried to interpret some of the material presented in the first section in terms of the framework that is developed in the second section.

The Social Property of Deviance

For many years sociologists have been trying to construct a definition for deviance, but until recently these efforts have not been very successful. One reason for this lack of success is that until now most sociologists have insisted on treating deviance as a scientific concept, giving it a special, and usually a quite rigid meaning within the broader framework of one or another sociological paradigm. With the development of labeling theory, the recognition has come that deviance is a property that is conferred upon an individual by other people.[5] Seen in this light, deviance is a natural phenomenon; that is, a property that has meaning to "the natives" who employ it in the course of everyday life. Obviously, there are few natives who actually use the term "social deviant" as such; most of them, when they confer this property on others, use labels such as "nut," "queer," "weirdo," "rascal," "pervert," or "loony." I employ the generic term "deviance" to refer to that property that is conferred upon persons whenever labels such as these are used.

In this section of the essay, I try to describe what this property consists of. Before doing so, however, I want to call attention to an important implication that is contained in the point that I have just made. A scientific theory of human society may or may not include the concept of social deviance; that is really a matter that will be decided by the person who constructs the theory. What such a theory must contain, however, is a concept or set of concepts that can account for deviance as a phenomenon of society. The task that the sociologist must confront initially is to discover what he can do about this natural phenomenon: what it consists of, how and when "the natives" use it, what its place is in the life of the community, and so on. As these questions are answered, scientific concepts will then begin to emerge to account for them. For the present, what the sociologist requires is a set of guidelines that he can follow to enable him to identify the phenomenon of deviance. These guidelines must be specific enough to enable him to sort out this particular phenomenon from other social phenomena, but flexible enough so that they impose only a minimum number of assumptions and *a priori* meanings on the social property of deviance.

As far as I know, the guidelines I present are applicable only to American society, since it is from this country that most of our empirical knowledge about social deviance comes. Unfortunately, there are only a few sociologists who have studied deviance in other cultures, and the few good comparative studies that have been done are seldom included as part of the standard repertoire of empirical experiences that come to mind when American sociologists speak about deviance.[6] I believe it is unlikely, for example, that the characterization of deviance that I develop in this paper can be meaningfully applied to Polynesian or African cultures. I say this because I have spent the better part of a summer working with an anthropologist who is a student of Polynesia, who has persuaded me that many social science theories are excessively ethnocentric, making good sense out of life in selected Western industrialized societies but little or no sense out of the social life of Polynesia. It goes without saying, of course, that a complete theory regarding the place of deviance in a social order cannot be finally constructed until sociologists have acquired more and better information about this phenomenon in all known human societies.

I follow Erikson and others in defining deviance as a property that is conferred upon a person by others. If we reflect about the manner in which this property is applied in the course of everyday life, we will recognize several things about it. One is that deviant labels are given to people for many different reasons. In some cases, persons are labeled as deviant on the basis of their behavior. Thieves, perverts, and heretics are three of the many examples that could be cited as illustrations of behavior that is perceived as deviant. But people may also be identified as deviant because of their physical appearance. I have in mind here the various forms of physical impairment such as crippling, grotesque disfigurement, blindness, and certain racial characteristics.[7] Finally, there are people to whom a deviant label is given for reasons that have nothing at all to do either with their behavior or physical appearance. Perhaps the prime examples are the illegitimate child or the orphan. This basic point, that the property of deviance may be conferred on a person for any number of reasons, is one that most sociologists have ignored. By and large, sociological discussions of deviance are expressed only in terms of behavior, implying that a person's actions are the sole basis upon which this property is conferred. (Indeed, the field of study itself is usually referred to as "deviant behavior.") That this is a misleading implication first occurred to me while I was doing a study of blind people.[8] During this study it became apparent to me that there were many blind people who were regarded as social deviants, simply because they could not see; their behavior had nothing at all to do with it. It was as though they had been excluded from participating in the community on the basis of their physical appearance alone, and, in fact, most of them never even had the chance to behave in the company of ordinary people. The point is an important one because it leads us to pose a question that we do not ask as long as we define deviance only in behavioral terms; namely, why individuals should be labeled deviant and excluded from full participation in the community, when there is nothing in their behavior to warrant this kind of treatment?

Second, the social property of deviance is one that is not applied uniformly in all cases. Thus, if we know that a particular kind of behavior or physical trait has been labeled as deviant in the past, we cannot assume either that it will be similarly applied to all such cases in the future, or even that it is applied in all cases in the present.[9] I can illustrate this point with an example. I once asked a group of students to draw up a list of specific types of social deviants. They began by mentioning cases on which there seemed to be fairly complete agreement such as the criminal, the madman, and the pervert. However, we quickly exhausted the list of obvious cases and moved on to other ones that were more ambiguous. One student suggested that homosexuals and lesbians ought to be included in the list, and a discussion quickly developed in the course of which the student was roundly criticized for being intolerant and prudish. Another student nominated cripples, and again an argument ensued that ended on an inconclusive note. The same thing happened as we considered in turn the cases of hippies, alcoholics, juvenile delinquents, "pot heads," "acid heads," neurotics, and so on. Eventually, there were people on both sides of each argument who felt that their position was both correct and incorrect. For example, those who said that cripples belonged on the list justified their position by describing empirical cases in which cripples whom they had known were so regarded by at least some "natives." Those who argued against this position felt equally justified because they could point to cases they had known in which this did not occur. Moreover, each side ultimately admitted that the other had a point. The exercise served to bring home to us the fact that deviance is not a quality that is inherent in any condition but one that is conferred on them by other people in a manner that is inconsistent. The important sociological problem is not to decide *a priori* which phenomena are deviant and which ones are not· but rather to discover why this property is conferred upon a person when it is. Erikson has, of course, shed a good deal of light on this particular question as shall be seen.[10]

There are at least two features of a deviant label that make it distinctive; one is that it carries an imputation of moral inferiority and culpability, and the other, that it is an essentializing label. The person to whom a deviant label has been applied is usually viewed as being morally inferior, and his condition, his behavior, or whatever basis is used for applying this label to him is interpreted as evidence of his moral culpability.[11] The extent of moral depravity that is imputed to a deviant varies a great deal from case to case. As a rule, the criminal and the dissident are viewed as moral monsters of sorts whereas those who are physically disabled or mentally ill as a rule are not judged so harshly. Still, in both cases the implication of moral inferiority is obviously there, a fact that provides us with one criterion by which to distinguish deviance from other social properties.

Deviant labels are essentializing labels that carry certain implications about character that extend to all areas of personality. To call a person "mad" or "criminal" is to imply that he is different in kind from ordinary people and that there are no areas of his personality that are not afflicted by his "problem." This tendency to generalize about a person's entire character on the basis of a single quality, action, or physical characteristic applies as much to deviants toward whom we feel genuine compassion as it does to those for whom we may feel contempt. The statement that someone is crippled implies that he possesses an entire personality, which is complete with special abilities, feelings, needs, and ways of behaving. Evidence for this is found in the tendency we have to link information about an individual's disability with other statements about him (that is, "he is a blind writer") as though the fact of his condition alerts us to look for a special kind of personality. There are few social labels that involve so strong an essentializing tendency as does the property of social deviance.[12]

It would be incorrect to say that deviance is the only social property to which the quality of moral inferiority attaches or that it is the only essentializing label found in our culture. What makes a deviant label distinctive from other properties is the intensity with which these elements adhere to it, and the special way in which they blend together. These two elements provide us then with one criterion for identifying the phenomenon of deviance in our society. Another criterion involves the consequences that follow for persons to whom the property of deviance is conferred.

When a deviant label has been applied to a person, he is often demarcated off from the rest of the group and moved to its margins.[13] As a rule, he is excluded from participating fully in group activities, and he may even be denied the kind of freedoms that are accorded to others as a matter of right. He is sometimes physically confined and denied the sorts of privileges that are routinely granted to people who are considered to be "in good standing." Thus, when a person has been labeled a deviant, he becomes a second-rate citizen, who is in a symbolic sense "in" but not "of" the social community in which he resides.

The person who has been labeled deviant may also be perceived as dangerous in the sense that he is capable of doing harm to other people. There are, of course, some cases in which this fear is quite justified. Men who have committed murder or those who have lashed out violently at others do pose a very real threat to life and limb. However, most people who are labeled deviant are harmless, in the sense that they pose no physical threat to anyone; yet, there are many who continue to regard them as dangerous. We only need to reflect for a moment on the case of persons who are grotesquely disfigured, or lepers, to recognize the validity in this point. Sociologists have tended to ignore this fact about the property of deviance, terming it another one of the misconceptions that laymen have about the deviant. The fact remains that many laymen regard the deviant as a dangerous person even when he is not likely to do them any direct physical harm. This reaction is one that must be taken into account in attempting to construct a sociological explanation for deviance.

Another reaction that commonly occurs when a deviant label is applied is that within the community a feeling arises that "something ought to be done about him." Perhaps the most important fact about this reaction in our society is that almost all of the steps that are taken are directed solely at the deviant. Punishment, therapy, rehabilitation, coercion, and the other common mechanisms of social control are things that are done to him, implying that the causes of deviance reside within the person to whom the label has been attached, and that the solutions to the problems that he presents can be achieved by doing something to him. This is a curious fact, particularly when we examine it against the background of social science research on deviance that so clearly points to the crucial role played by ordinary people in determining who is labeled a deviant and how the deviant behaves. This research suggests that none of the corrective measures that are taken can possibly succeed in the intended way unless they are directed at those who confer deviant labels as well as those to whom they are applied.

Another feature of the "something" that is done to the deviant in our society is that it often involves isolating and confining him in such a way that he becomes invisible to others in the community. This usually takes the form of some kind of physical confinement in an institution located outside of the community itself, or tucked away in an obscure corner somewhere within it.

The criminal, the madman, the heretic, and the cripple usually end up in one kind of an institution or another, along with persons of their own kind, where they are either forcibly confined for long periods of time or at least kept off the streets and out of the way for the better part of the day. If the deviant is a criminal, the rationale for confining him is that he cannot be trusted to be on his own. When, however, the deviant poses no clear and apparent physical danger, a different sort of rationale is employed. It is usually suggested, for example, that the cripple will be "happier with his own kind" and the act of sending him to an institution or a home is seen as part of a rehabilitation effort rather than an attempt to physically confine him. From the point of view of the deviant, however, this rationale may not be very convincing: what is convincing is its consequences for him, namely, to take him off the streets and to keep him out of the way of other people.

In this regard, it is an interesting fact that most of the formal agencies of social control in our society appear to be better equipped for detecting, apprehending, and confining the deviant than they are to bringing him back from the institution to the center of the community. Mechanic has suggested that most social control agencies employ a far larger number of people to process clients into them than they do to process clients back out again.[14] In a similar vein, I found in my research on agencies for the blind that intake procedures were much more highly developed, codified, and professionalized than outtake procedures, most of which were quite haphazard.[15]

Another fact about deviant labels is that those to whom they have been applied elicit anger in other people. This reaction is readily identifiable as such when the deviant is a criminal or a dissident who has violated the moral code, but it is not limited to these cases alone. It may be less evident when the deviant is a cripple or a madman, but for him it is every bit as real. Psychologists have suggested that the pity we often feel toward those who are blind or crippled or mad, is in reality anger and hatred that have been disguised in a form that is more acceptable to us.[16] An illustration of this anger that the deviant often calls out in others came to my attention during the course of a conversation I had with a British woman concerning a recent attempt made by some hippies to occupy a deserted building in downtown London. She remarked that she found the hippies disgusting, and when I asked her why, she replied in an angry voice, "It's shocking and shameful, wasting their lives like that. They should be taken and whipped with the rod." It was as though these young people had hit a raw nerve; and even though they were doing her no harm she was clearly mad at them and very much in the mood for revenge.

This example also serves to highlight another important fact about deviance, namely, that those to whom the deviant label is applied are usually treated in a punitive way. In the case of the criminal, of course, the punishment is justified in terms of retribution for harm that he has brought to other people. But punishment is not limited just to deviants who have inflicted tangible harm on others; it is also given to other kinds of deviants as well. The history of the treatment of people who are physically disabled, illegitimate, allegedly insane, and so on is not a very happy one. It is filled with examples of sadism, brutality, and neglect. To be sure, we become irate when we learn that such persons are being mistreated, and our moral outrage is accompanied by clarion calls for reform. Yet, when the scandal dies down, our system has a curious way of returning to its original (or perhaps "normal") state, leading us to suspect that those who react most strongly "protest too much."

I have no doubt that some sociologists would want other elements to be included in this characterization of the social property of deviance; and that other sociologists would protest that my discussion is not an entirely accurate portrayal of this property as laymen in our society use it. This characterization is an ideal typical one, and the question of whether it should be modified (or perhaps how it should be modified) is a matter that can only be determined as we pool our collective knowledge about deviance. Whatever the outcome of this effort may be, there is one point on which I believe there will be fairly complete agreement. It is that deviance is inextricably bound up with the social order of which it is a part, and that one cannot speak about it in a meaningful way without also considering social order. This suggests, in turn, that the concept of social order may be the most useful place to begin in trying to understand and explain why the social property of deviance takes the form it does.

The Nature of Social Order

The reader who is familiar with the sociological literature on social order will recognize in the discussion that follows many ideas that have been formulated and developed by other people. In particular, I have drawn very heavily on three sources: the essay by Peter Berger and Thomas Luckmann on the social construction of reality;[17] the essay by Mary Douglas on pollution and taboo in primitive religions;[18] and Kai Erikson's chapters on deviance and social order in his book on deviance in the Puritan colonies.[19] In addition to these works, there is one other essay from which I have also drawn many ideas; it is concerned with a subject which, on its face, appears to be quite unrelated to the topic of this paper. I am referring to Thomas Kuhn's provocative analysis of scientific revolutions.[20] As the reader delves into this section, he will see that there are some striking similarities between the ways scientists respond when data are provided that threaten to disconfirm their basic paradigm and the ways in which laymen respond to people whose behavior, appearance, or existence does not "make sense" within the basic paradigm by which the everyday life of a society is made orderly and meaningful.

I want to begin by trying to define the term "social order," but the definition that I give is general and vague. A more precise conception of it will emerge as we go along. By social order I mean the all-embracing frame of reference in a society that its members know as social reality. Through social order, objects, persons, and events are identified, arranged, and interpreted so as to give them meaning and thereby to convey to people a firm sense of the way things are. Along with most sociologists, I assume that this order is a social product in the sense that it is man-made. There are four basic things about social order that must be understood before we can appreciate the relationships of deviance to it. I will phrase them in the form of questions. What is the nature of the social order required by human beings? Why do they require this kind of frame of reference? How does this frame of reference evolve? What does it consist of?

Many sociologists have tried to answer these questions. One of the most systematic efforts has been made by Berger and Luckmann. One answer that has been given to the question of why man requires a frame of reference (I discuss the nature of this frame of reference shortly) is that man is different from other animals because his relationship to the environment is not given in his basic genetic or hereditary make-up. Man has the capacity to apply his basic biological "equipment" to a very wide, continually changing range of activities and experiences. Berger and Luckmann term this quality "world-openness."[21] Because of it, man is a highly adaptable animal, but at the same time he lacks any innate mechanism that can provide him with stability in his relationships with other men. As Berger and Luckmann suggest, "If the human organism had to rely upon its own resources alone for existence, that existence would probably be chaotic."[22] One reason, therefore, why the human animal requires a symbolic framework for ordering social reality is because he is basically an unstable being. What social order does, in effect, is provide him with a stable environment by effectively pre-empting his capacity for world-openness and transforming it into a kind of "world-closedness."[23]

The mechanism that makes the development of social order possible is man's tendency to habitualize his actions. "Any action that is repeated frequently," Berger and Luckmann write, "becomes cast into a pattern which can be reproduced by its performance as that pattern."[24] Habitualization implies direction, and a narrowing of the range of activity; it also implies that at some point in the future the pattern that has been learned can be repeated with an economy of effort. Man's tendency toward patterning therefore enables him to circumvent the problems that inevitably arise because of his inherent capacity for world-openness. Chaos is narrowed, and man is relieved of the burden of tension that would otherwise accumulate if his actions were undirected.

Berger and Luckmann define social institutions as commonly accepted and established ways of doing things, and man's tendency toward patterning is one of the main reasons for their emergence. A pattern that is habitualized is transformed into a social institution when it has been transmitted to the next generation by its inventors. The child who acquires these patterns as established ways of doing things comes to view them as real. They confront him as things that are external and constraining, and they resist his efforts to modify them. Thus, an institutional world is experienced as objective reality by a person who has been reared in it for, as Berger and Luckmann observe, "It has a history that antedates the individual's birth and is not accessible to his biological recollection; it was there before he was born and it will be there after his death."[25]

The generation that has "invented" a patterned way of doing things intuitively understands the utility of that pattern; however, the succeeding generation to whom it is taught may not, because it has not shared the experience that made the patterning necessary. As a result, the patterns must be legitimated in ways that must be found to justify them to the generation to whom they are being taught. In addition to this problem of making the pattern meaningful to those who must learn it, there is the added problem of developing mechanisms of social control that can be employed against members who have failed to learn the pattern, or, although having learned it, have done so imperfectly. "Legitimation" is the term that Berger and Luckmann apply to the process by which moral validity is given to the institutional order.[26]

Legitimation is a process that occurs at all levels of group experience, beginning with group patterns that are specific and simple, and integrating them into successively more complex and abstract justification systems. In theory, at least, there is no reason why the justifications that are constructed for habitualized patterns relating to one area of social life should be consistent or logically connected with the ones that develop in other areas. Yet, as Berger and Luckmann note, empirically it seems to be the case that societies do integrate justifications for all habitualized patterns into a kind of overarching, all-encompassing framework. "In this way," they write, "the group as a whole is made to appear as a system in the sense that the legitimation of any one institutional pattern is tied into a coherent framework that gives it its special place in that group's cosmic scheme of things."[27]

The most abstract level of legitimation entails the effort to integrate the entire institutional order into a symbolic totality. This, Berger and Luckmann have called "the symbolic universe."[28] They write, "In a symbolic universe all the sectors of the established order are integrated in an all-embracing frame of reference, which now constitutes a universe in the literal sense of the word because all human experience can now be conceived as taking place within it."[29] A system of meaning is created in which everything is put into its proper place by providing a comprehensive integration of all discrete institutional processes in which everything "makes sense." This symbolic universe is regarded as valid and true; indeed, it is seen as being reality itself. It is this dimension of social order that I believe is the most important one for understanding the social property of deviance.

I have implied that there is only one symbolic universe in each society; in fact this implication is somewhat misleading. For one thing, societies vary a great deal in terms of the willingness to tolerate a diversity of points of view and the need to presume order. In general, the European cultural heritage is one in which there is a "one truth" conceptualization of reality. In certain Polynesian societies, such as in Rotuma, there are several competing systems that exist side by side, no one of which dominates or imposes quite so rigid a conception of order as we find in most Western cultures.[30] Furthermore, even in societies that conceive of reality in terms of a single set of truths, we find subuniverses of meaning.[31] As a rule, these subuniverses apply only to a limited sphere of activity so that they do not pose a serious challenge to the broader incorporative framework. However, there are cases in which a subuniverse of meaning may represent a genuine counter culture, as some people feel that blacks and student radicals in America do.

The symbolic universe of a society is usually viewed with a bias that is deeply conservative and resistant to change. To most people it is reality and therefore not a thing that is subject to change. A symbolic universe also serves as a kind of "protective cocoon," shielding us from realities that are harsh and even intolerable.[32] There is an understandable reluctance on the part of most people to permit anyone to attempt to alter this cocoon. Moreover, the symbolic universe is resistant to change because it functions in a kind of self-confirming way. Its validity is "proven" each time we use the categories of perception embedded in it to view reality, since that reality is arranged in our minds by the categories with which we view it. These experiences lead us to believe that our way of viewing the world is natural and correct. Finally, the symbolic universe is resistant to change because it is a public order. As Mary Douglas put it:

> It [the symbolic universe] has authority, since each is induced to assent because of the assent of the others. But its public character makes its categories more rigid—a private person may revise his patterns of assumptions or not. It is a private matter. But cultural categories are public matters. They cannot so easily be subject to revision.[33]

Thus, the symbolic universe "hardens" and "thickens," to use Berger's and Luckmann's terms, and gradually assumes the appearance of an objective reality.

We know the symbolic universe as reality; it confronts us as something that is "out there," independent of ourselves and able to prod us into acting and thinking in prescribed ways. The sense of stability that we derive from this knowledge, however firm it may be, does not entirely obscure from us a crucial fact about the symbolic universe; namely, that it involves the creation of a sense of order out of things that are by their nature untidy. "Order," Mary Douglas writes, "implies restrictions; from all possible materials, a limited set has been made and from all possible realities a limi'ed set has been used."[34] Social order then exists in the midst of uncertainty, and this uncertainty is perhaps the most potent of all threats to it.

Uncertainty and diversity are the natural enemies of order because they are potentially more powerful than the order that stands against them. Order suggests restriction, whereas disorder is unlimited, since, as Mary Douglas points out, "no pattern has been realized in it (disorder), but its potential for patterning is indefinite."[35] Thus, the symbolic universe is set in a force that is more powerful than itself, a force that has the capacity to overwhelm it at any moment. We must be clear about the kind of threat that chaos poses to order. The very concept of social order implies that human existence is meaningful and orderly, that everything has its proper place within an overarching system. The validity of the system depends upon its being able to interpret all phenomena; it would no longer be "believed" if phenomena were found to exist that could not be so interpreted. The chaos that surrounds social order is threatening precisely because it has the capacity to "generate" phenomena that the system cannot interpret in a meaningful way. The nature of this threat is a particularly insidious one, for it is not only a matter of some new thing occurring that does not now fit into our world, but that might do so with a slight modification of our conception of reality. It is, in addition, that chaos holds the potential to confront us with things that literally should not exist if the concept of reality that is embodied in our symbolic universe is true. For example, our conception of being and existence implies that ghosts, witches, and other such creatures are not real. If someone were to prove to us that ghosts exist, he would then have shown that a major part of our view of reality is wrong, since there is no logical way to reconcile our basic concepts of being and existence with the fact that there are ghosts.

The reader who is familiar with Thomas Kuhn's essay on scientific revolutions will recognize several points in my discussion that have been made in his analysis as well. According to Kuhn, scientific revolutions occur whenever phenomena are shown to exist that should not exist if the basic paradigm of the science is a valid one. He believes that such events are crucial because there is no way to alter the basic theoretical paradigm of the science in order to include within it an explanation for things that the paradigm itself predicts ought not to exist. In such cases, the paradigm is shown to be utterly and completely wrong.[36] I am taken by this argument that Kuhn has made, and believe that there are some striking similarities between these scientific events, and certain things that can occur when a symbolic universe is empirically tested against the reality of human existence. As Berger and Luckmann tell us, "all social reality is precarious. All societies are constructed in the face of chaos. The constant possibility of anomic terror is actualized whenever the legitimations that obscure this precariousness are threatened or collapse."[37]

Confrontations between the symbolic universe and chaos are inevitable, and the more highly developed the universe is, the more frequent these confrontations are likely to be. Social order involves a system for classifying human existence and the viability of this system ultimately depends upon there being some measure of clarity between the categories that it establishes. Objects, events, and people must conform in some reasonable degree to the class to which they belong and there must be a comparatively simple way for distinguishing between different classes of things. Unfortunately, by its nature, human existence is an untidy affair; as a result no system that attempts to classify it can ever be a perfect one. "There will always be anomalies," Mary Douglas writes, "if only because the act of classification involves imposing a sense of clear ordering on phenomena which by their nature are chaotic."[38] No social order can survive unless it develops mechanisms for protecting the symbolic universe against the threats that chaos and anomaly present to it.

We are now in a position to develop a conceptualization of deviance as a property of social order. This property is conferred upon an individual whenever others detect in his behavior, appearance, or simply his existence, a significant transgression of the boundaries of the symbolic universe by which the inherent disorder of human existence is made to appear orderly and meaningful.[39] More simply, the property of deviance is conferred on things that are perceived as being anomalous when they are viewed from the perspective of a symbolic universe. Initially we can identify at least two different conditions under which this property is likely to be conferred, which conditions can be distinguished in terms of the amount of ambiguity that is found in any part of the over-all outline of the symbolic universe or in the boundaries of categories within it. The first condition arises when the boundaries and outlines are clear and evident, in which case phenomena are easily identified either as anomalous or normal; in the second condition, an event or thing may be labeled as anomalous in order to mark more clearly the outlines of the symbolic universe when they have become obscure or ambiguous. Each of these cases are considered briefly.

At least three different circumstances can be distinguished under which a phenomenon might be labeled as deviant when the symbolic universe is relatively clear and unambiguous. The first involves cases of individuals who at one time have been accepted as ordinary, normal people, but who changed in some dramatic way, and by virtue of that change became "outsiders." An example of such a case would be a person who has gone completely berserk. When he no longer shares the same system of meanings that we use, and when his everyday behavior no longer conforms to the system of common logic by which the actions of other people are governed, we say that he has gone "beyond the fringe," or that he lives "in another world." Such people quite literally depart from our symbolic universe and dwell in another world that is usually private.

A second case involves persons who have never shared in our symbolic universe because they come from cultures that are different from our own. Such people are also regarded as outsiders, but they differ from madmen in at least two respects. For one thing, they have not been "drummed out of the corps," as the madman has been because they have never been in it. For another thing, they participate in another symbolic universe that is public and shared in their culture. It is this last fact that makes them especially threatening to our own symbolic universe for, as Berger and Luckmann suggest, "their very existence demonstrates empirically that one's own universe is less than inevitable."[40] "Moreover," they write, "it raises questions of power since each symbolic universe must now deal with the problem of whose definition of reality will be made to stick."[41]

A third and probably the most common case of all, consists of instances of people who continue to accept the definition of reality contained in the symbolic universe, but who are nevertheless regarded as anomalies within it. These are people who are "in" but not "of" the system. Examples of these are numerous, including individuals suffering from most physical impairments, many common behavioral disorders, as well as a good deal of the deviance that involves violations of commonly held norms.

The property of deviance may also be conferred upon a person during periods when the boundaries of the symbolic universe are blurred and indistinct. As Erikson has shown, the act of defining a particular belief or pattern of behavior as heretical, and transporting those who engage in it from the center of the group to its margins is a powerful and effective way of clarifying where the lines lie between what is acceptable and what is not. Thus, social and historical forces often conspire to obscure the distinctiveness of a group's symbolic universe, or to change the group so much that its boundary lines may actually be erased. When this happens, we often find crime waves and witch hunts occurring, during which some individuals who were previously accepted as part of the group now find themselves run out of it as heretics, "Such occasions," Erikson writes, "dramatize the issue at stake when a given boundary becomes blurred in the drift of passing events, and the encounters that follow between the new deviant and the older agents of control provides a forum, as it were, in which events can be articulated more clearly, a stage on which it can be portrayed in sharper relief."[42] It is by this act of demarcating someone off from the group and labeling him as a heretic that a sharper edge is given to the symbolic boundaries of the group and its distinctiveness as a social order is clarified.

Berger and Luckmann have given us a particularly incisive analysis of the character of the threat that deviance poses to social order. They state that deviant phenomena

> constitute the most acute threat to taken-for-granted routinized existence in society. If one conceives of the latter as the "daylight side" of human life, then (deviance) constitutes a "night side" that keeps lurking ominously on the periphery of everyday consciousness. Just because the "night side" has its own reality, often enough of a sinister kind, it is a constant threat to the

taken-for-granted, matter-of-fact, "sane" reality of life in society. The thought keeps suggesting itself that, perhaps, the bright reality of everyday life is but an illusion, to be swallowed up at any moment by the bounding nightmare of the other, the night-side reality.[43]

I have said that deviance is inevitable because any attempt to impose order on the untidy phenomena of human existence will inevitably result in a certain amount of matter being out of place. I have also said that the basic chaos of human existence, of which any given anomaly is but one example, is perhaps the gravest of all threats to social order. Indeed, no social order can survive without developing mechanisms for protecting itself against the chaos that anomaly implies. Berger and Luckmann have termed these "universe-maintaining mechanisms."[44] There are many different universe-maintaining mechanisms found in each social order. I only attempt to identify and describe the ones that are most commonly found in industrialized societies such as our own.

One of the most elementary of all the mechanisms for maintaining a symbolic universe is misperception, by which I mean the tendency to mistake as normal and ordinary phenomena that in reality are anomalous. Kuhn has suggested that scientists sometimes fail to see in a particular datum the evidence that would destroy their theoretical paradigm.[45] By the same token, laymen also misconstrue as normal, phenomena whose existence undermines their entire world view. I do not believe that misperceptions of this kind are a question of the deliberate and conscious distortion of reality, nor do I regard them simply as psychological mechanisms of defense against a reality that is too harsh to confront. Rather, the misperception is "genuine"; that is, the categories of perception that are part of our symbolic universe lead us to expect to see things in a certain way, and our resulting readiness to find the normal and the expected can cause us not to see the real nature of an event that is anomalous. A certain amount of confrontation between the symbolic universe and the surrounding chaos is avoided by this mechanism of misperception. At the same time it can only be effective as long as the anomalous events that are misconstrued as normal occur only rarely. The more often such events occur, the more difficult it becomes to mistake them for things that are natural and ordinary.[46]

A second way in which a symbolic universe can be preserved against chaos is by debunking evidence concerning the existence of phenomena that threaten it. This mechanism is probably more effective when the phenomena in question is symbolic rather than physical, since it is an easier thing to persuade people that a symbolic event "never actually happened" than it is to persuade them that a physical object that they can see "isn't really there." To take a simple example, when a person claims that he has seen a ghost, one of our first reactions is to debunk him by trying to convince others that he is an unreliable source of information (that is, "he's under a terrific strain, you know." "He's been hitting the bottle pretty hard lately"). This reaction has its counterpart in the response of scientists to reports of experiments the results of which threaten to discomfirm the accepted theoretical paradigms. Frequently the scientists response is to replicate the experiment, allegedly in order to confirm the evidence of the experiments, but in reality in a spirit of attempting to show that the disturbing evidence is not in fact "real."[47] As a rule, it is an easier thing to debunk such evidence when it has been advanced by a single person (witness the case the Catholic Church was able to make against Galileo), or, when several persons are involved, if their social credibility is problematic because of age, past behavior, or general status in the community. Correspondingly, this mechanism is least effective when those who provide us with reports of anomalous phenomena are respected and established citizens, or when these reports come from a large number of persons from diverse walks of life.

Although some anomalies can be ignored or debunked, not all of them can be handled in this way. Each social order must therefore devise other mechanisms as well for dealing with them. One of the most interesting and effective mechanisms is normalization, which involves the effort to force anomalous events to change in such a way as to become more nearly normal. When the anomaly is physical in character, normalization usually takes the form of attempts to remake it into something that corresponds more closely to the category into which it does not quite fit. When the anomaly is behavioral, then normalization involves attempts to alter a person's behavior through therapy, rehabilitation, or coercion. I can illustrate how this mechanism works with a few examples.

In our society, one of the most rigidly defined boundary lines is the one dividing men and women into distinctly different sex groups. Most of us see this demarcation line as a perfectly normal one, as "given in nature," which of course to some extent it is. The hermaphrodite or intersexed person, therefore, poses a special problem in our culture because "it" stands as glaring testimony to the fact that the line between the sexes is not as firm and rigid as we assume it to be. Robert Edgerton has compared the manner in which hermaphroditism is handled in different cultures.[48] He reports that in our society intersexed people are regarded as freaks and are encouraged to assume either a male or a female role. He writes, "All concerned, from parents to physicians are enjoined to discover which of the two natural sexes the intersexed person most appropriately is, and then to help the ambiguous, incongruous and upsetting 'it' to become at least a partially acceptable 'him' or 'her.' "[49] In this particular case, the symbolic universe is protected from anomaly by physically changing the anomalous thing so that it no longer violates, or at least does not violate as sharply, our system of classification.[50]

Other examples of efforts to normalize a physical anomaly are found among persons with certain kinds of bodily impairments. When the nature of the impairment is such as to render the body incomplete, then attempts may be made to replace the missing part with a prosthetic device, or therapy, thereby creating the illusion that the person is really whole. For example, some upper extremity amputees are advised to wear wooden arms and false hands, and blind people who are enucleated are usually encouraged to wear glass eyes for "cosmetic purposes." None of these devices have any great practical value in enabling the person to circumvent the inconveniences that are caused him by his disability. What they do, however, is to modify the physical anomaly and thereby make the person's body more nearly conform to the categories of the symbolic universe from which they deviate.

The mechanism of normalization can also be employed when the deviations that occur are behavioral in character. When an individual, by his actions, transgresses the symbolic lines that govern relationships among people, attempts may be made to get him to change his behavior so that it is closer to normal. Berger and Luckmann have called this mechanism of universe-maintenance "therapy." "Therapy," they write, "entails the application of conceptual machinery to ensure that actual or potential deviants stay within the institutional definition of reality."[51] They continue,

> because therapy concerns itself with deviations from official definitions of reality, it must develop a conceptual machinery to account for such deviations and to maintain the realities that are challenged by them. This requires a body of knowledge that includes a theory of deviance, a diagnostic apparatus, and a conceptual system for the curing of souls.[52]

The function of therapy is to keep people who behave in anomalous ways within the universe by trying to get them to change their ways so that they conform to accepted patterns.[53]

I have suggested that an analogy can be drawn between a culture's symbolic universe and the theoretical paradigm of a science. One point on which they are dissimilar is that a culture's symbolic universe is less easily disconfirmed than is a scientific paradigm, primarily because evidence that may disconfirm the former is more easily "clubbed into submission," as it were, than evidence from scientific experiments. This is particularly true when these experiments involve physical objects that "don't know" what the investigator expects them "to do."

The universe maintaining mechanisms that I have discussed thus far involve attempts to force experience into logical categories of noncontradictions. As Mary Douglas has suggested, however, "experience is not amenable and those who make the attempt find themselves led into contradictions."[54] There will always be some people who cannot or will not change their behavior to conform to accepted standards, and, as we have seen, attempts to alter a person's physical appearance are seldom completely successful. This suggests that social deviance cannot be dealt with solely by attempting to force all anomalies to conform to our basic categories of existence. Other types of universe-maintaining mechanisms are required, mechanisms that can preserve the integrity of a symbolic universe in spite of the fact that deviance persists. One such set of mechanisms consists of techniques of social control that are used against deviants who cannot be changed. The symbolic universe may be threatened by a madman, but its ultimate superiority may nevertheless be reaffirmed if the social order can render him harmless. There are several ways in which the madman can be "defused"; the most common of which being confinement. By putting the madman or the criminal away, a social order removes the symbolically noxious element from its midst, and at the same time demonstrates its capacity to master those whom it cannot domesticate. I believe it is a highly significant fact that few social orders use killing as a mechanism for dealing with recalcitrant forms of deviance. I say this because disposing of the deviant in this manner would be the most effective and least costly technique for dealing with him. That it is not used more often is, I suspect, attributable to the fact that this method for dealing with deviance does not achieve the sense of mastery achievable by controlling such deviants while they are still alive. The argument by analogy is that the whole point of lion taming is destroyed if the tamer kills his animals: mastery implies controlling the animal while he is alive.

There is one other mechanism of universe-maintenance that I want to mention here. Berger and Luckmann term it "nihilation."[55] Nihilation is not aimed at keeping phenomena within the symbolic universe; its purpose is to "conceptually liquidate everything outside of the universe."[56] This is accomplished by effectively denying the reality of anything that does not fit into the symbolic universe. Thus, certain deviants are regarded as subhuman animals, or savages who are unfit for living in civilized society. According to Berger and Luckmann, this particular mechanism is most often used on groups of people, such as foreigners, on whom therapy cannot be applied because they are outside of a culture's normal range of control. By denying validity to their existence, the group is relegated to "an inferior ontological status" in which they are no longer taken seriously.[57] Berger and Luckmann also point out that nihilation involves an attempt to "grapple with the deviant group theoretically," so as to incorporate the deviant conceptions within one's own universe and thereby to liquidate them.[58] "The deviant conception," they write, "must be translated into concepts derived from one's own universe. It is in this manner that the negative of one's own universe is subtly changed into an affirmation of it."[59] Nihilation is not only used on alien cultures; it may also be applied to subcultures that develop within the symbolic universe as well. Perhaps the most striking examples of this are the attempts that have been made to explain the behavior of members of certain minority groups who pose special problems for the dominant society. I have in mind here groups such as blacks in America, whose experiences have not been traditionally regarded in our society as valid ones and whose behavior is ordinarily explained in terms of deficiency models.[60] Explanations that are based on deficiency models involve attempts to account for the reasons that black Americans do not behave like white middle-class Americans. As a rule, these explanations are found by pointing to certain experiences that the white middle-class person has had and the black person has not had. Thus, a deficiency model is an attempt to explain the reasons why a person or group of people do not behave in a certain way in terms of experiences that they have not had. We can view such efforts as examples of nihilation since their goal is not to explain the behavior of blacks *qua* blacks, but to attempt to make their actions meaningful within a frame of reference that is alien to them.

There is, of course, another possibility that may arise whenever deviance occurs within a symbolic universe. The universe itself may change to accommodate the deviant phenomenon. As a rule this is a rare occurrence, since most people cling quite strongly to the reality that they know, and they are extremely reluctant to modify it in any way. When modifications do occur, they are usually minor, leaving the overarching symbolic framework of the society intact. This suggests that only certain kinds of minor anomalies can be assimilated into a symbolic universe. Other kinds cannot be assimilated because their very occurrence negates the validity of the entire system by which reality is patterned and made meaningful. In these cases, there is no way to reconcile the anomaly with the system of ordering that has produced it.

In this discussion of the mechanisms for maintaining a symbolic universe, the impression has no doubt been given that since deviance is a phenomenon that the symbolic universe is continually trying to rid itself of, its relationship to the social order is entirely negative. It is necessary to correct this impression, since, as I suggested at the beginning of this chapter, deviance has a very important place in a social order, so important that order itself may be impossible without it. It is Kai Erikson to whom we are most indebted for this insight.[61] He has shown that deviant behavior may provide the occasion for demarcating the symbolic boundary line between the community and what lies beyond it. "Its function," he writes, "is to keep these boundaries clearly demarcated and to help to clarify them anew when they begin to be obscured. Morality and immorality meet at the public scaffold, and it is during this meeting that the line between them is drawn."[62] Erikson also suggests that a community's boundaries remain a meaningful point of reference for its members only as long as they are repeatedly tested by people who are on the fringes of the group and repeatedly defended by those who represent the group's inner morality. For this reason he concludes that "deviant behavior may be, in controlled quantities, an important condition for preserving the stability of group life. Deviant forms of behavior, by marking the outer edges of group life, give the inner structure its special character and thus supply the framework within which the people of the group develop an orderly sense of their own cultural identity."[63]

There is another aspect to this relationship between the deviant and the community. Community boundaries inevitably shift, and when they do it is seldom an easy thing to locate them anew. Erikson suggests that "one result of the dialogue between the deviant and the agent of the community is to clarify where new boundaries are to be drawn."[64] It is in this sense that deviance has an important function to play within the group, one that is very similar to other group properties such as leadership.[65]

One implication of the position that deviance is an important resource of the group is that forces may operate within the social order to insure that a limited amount of deviance will always be available for public use. If this is correct (and I believe it is) then the statement that deviance is a property that is conferred on an individual by others assumes an additional significance. As Erikson writes, "It suggests that whenever a boundary line becomes blurred, the group members may single out and label as deviant someone whose behavior had previously gone unnoticed."[66]

These are not the only contributions that deviance has to make toward maintaining the social order. Deviance is a rejuvenating force as well. Earlier in this chapter I suggested that a social order is an attempt to create meaning out of a reality that is chaotic. I also stated that chaos is powerful because it has an unlimited potential for patterning. Deviance, then, represents a force that is potentially more powerful than the order standing against it. However, it is this very fact about deviance that can make it rejuvenating for society. To contain and control deviance, and thereby to master it, is to supply fresh and dramatic proof of the enormous powers that are behind the social order. The visible control of deviance is one of the most effective mechanisms by which a social order can tangibly display its potency. The act of harnessing things that are dangerous helps to revitalize the system by demonstrating to those who live within it just how awesome its powers really are.

The Symbolic Universe and Deviance

In this chapter I have proposed a framework for analyzing deviance as a property of social order. If the framework is a useful one it will ultimately enable us to develop a theory to explain deviance. Such a theory would explain which specific behavioral, physical, or other characteristics and qualities fall outside of the dominant symbolic universe of our culture and why. The framework that I have proposed cannot, of course, do this; it only recommends to us the kinds of questions we ought to ask and answer in order to produce a theory to explain this social property. We cannot now determine how useful this approach will be; however, it is interesting to speculate about some of the characteristics of the property of deviance in our society in the light of the framework that I have proposed.

I have defined deviance as a property that is conferred upon an individual by others. The reader will now understand that this definition conceals a double perspective. Some persons may be labeled deviant because they do not fit into "preset" categories of the symbolic universe. Thus, the behavior of those whom we call "mad" is only insane when we evaluate it against the system of meanings that it violates, just as the person who is a cripple can only be regarded as physically anomalous if there is a classification system into which he does not fit. In either of these cases, we may be able to specify, *a priori,* the forms of behavior or the physical traits that will be labeled as deviant, but only if we have member knowledge of the symbolic universe that has made them anomalous. There are other persons who are labeled as deviant as a result of the fact that the boundary lines of the system of classification embodied in a symbolic universe are prone to shift, to become ambiguous, or even to disappear. When this has happened, deviance may be used to establish them anew. In this case, it is not a matter of some form of behavior or physical trait falling outside of a preset classification system, but of the system itself becoming set, as it were, by the act of defining someone as falling outside of it.

I have said that those who are labeled as deviant are viewed as being morally inferior beings. The roots of this moral evaluation may lie in the extremely significant function that the symbolic universe serves in making social life possible. We have seen that human existence is by its nature disorderly and the symbolic universe helps to create for us a sense of certainty and of anchorage. Anything that threatens to strip us of this protective cocoon will inevitably be seen as evil. Evil is a trait that most of us view as being alien to ourselves, and we experience great difficulty in empathizing with those whom we regard as possessed of it. We are easily led to view such people as being different in kind from ourselves, a response that helps us to better understand the fact that deviant labels are essentializing.

There are certain types of deviants who are thought to possess special abilities and power that are not granted to ordinary people. The spirituality that some people believe that the blind or the deaf possess, or the mysterious powers that the madman is thought to have are but a few examples of this belief. One of the sources of this belief is, no doubt, the feeling that these are persons who have dwelled in the disordered regions that lie beyond the ordinary boundaries of the social order, and, as Mary Douglas suggests, those who have ventured beyond the confines of the society bring back with them "a power not available to those who have stayed in the control of themselves and of society."[67] If our speculations on this matter are accurate, we may then suggest that these special powers and feelings are also related to the essentializing quality of deviant labels.

I have characterized the deviant as a person who is demarcated off from the rest of the group, and moved to its margins. This exclusion is a concrete manifestation of the symbolic marginality of those upon whom the label of deviant has been conferred. I have said that the "natives" often regard the deviant as a dangerous person who can bring harm to them. I believe that those sociologists who have argued that the natives are mistaken in their view

ROBERT A. SCOTT **31**

are themselves in error, for the deviant is a person whose existence does threaten to inundate with chaos the symbolic system by which order and meaning are given to human existence. The madman whose rantings challenge our system of meanings is in a sense just as dangerous as the madman who is a threat to our physical being. The practice early in our history of beating and killing heretics is strong testimony to this fact.

From our discussion it is not too difficult to understand why society treats the person who is labeled a deviant as it does. Because he is said to be harmful and dangerous, he is confined; it is because he threatens us and our world view that we treat him in a punitive way. We insist that he change to conform to the established patterns because these patterns involve nothing less than our grasp of reality itself, and we seldom kill the deviant because the act does not reaffirm the "truth" of our world view nearly so effectively as does either changing him into someone who is nearer to normal, or, completely mastering and controlling him while leaving him as he is.

I have said that in our society more effort is expended in detecting deviance and processing the deviant out to the margins of the group than changing him and then bringing him back into its center once again. Judging from what little we know about deviance in other cultures, this is not by any means a universal quality; indeed, it may even be a peculiarity of our own society. Perhaps the American obsession with constructing a paradise on earth has led us to become preoccupied with finding social problems and rooting them from our midst; and perhaps it is related to a deep-seated intolerance of anything that deviates markedly from that conception of the utopian world that we hold.

Finally, I have said that the social property of deviance is one that is not applied uniformly in all cases. By this I mean that all people who transgress the symbolic boundaries of a group are not regarded as deviant. There is no obvious and apparent explanation for this fact suggested in the proposed framework. It might be argued that symbolic boundaries remain viable as long as there is some public reaction at least some of the time when they have been transgressed. I know of no empirical data that bear on this question. Another possibility is that some efforts are made by some people to apply deviant labels to all cases in which symbolic boundaries are transgressed, but these labels "stick" only under special circumstances. Some of these circumstances have been expounded in a recent book by David Matza about the process of becoming deviant.[68] Matza explains the complexity of this process and sensitizes us to the crucial role in it of the subjective meaning of the experience to the actor. The framework that I have proposed ignores this crucial dimension and, I believe, this is one reason why this particular characteristic of the social property of deviance cannot be explained by it.

This chapter can be concluded by returning to the place from which it began; namely, my criticizing the laymen's view that deviance is but an appendage to the society, a matter that is unrelated to the core of its structures and processes. The answer that would be given to this assertion, and the one that is explained in this chapter, has been admirably expressed in another context by Mary Douglas. In her analysis of the conception of pollution and taboo, she writes:

> Dirt, then, is essentially disorder. It offends order and by eliminating or controlling it we are engaged in a positive effort to organize the environment. It is impossible to hold a conception of dirt without also having a conception of a social order into which dirt does not fit. Dirt is matter out of place. This implies two things: A set of ordered relationships and a contravention of that order. Dirt, then, is never an isolated or unique thing. Where there is dirt there is a system. Dirt is simply the by-product of a systematic ordering and classification of matter.[69]

Notes

1. See for example: Howard S. Becker, *Outsiders: Studies in the Sociology of Deviance* (New York: The Free Press, 1963); Edwin M. Lemert, *Social Pathology* (New York: McGraw-Hill Book Company, Inc., 1951); John I. Kitsuse, "Societal Reactions to Deviant Behavior: Problems of Theory and Methods," in Howard S. Becker, ed., *The Other Side: Perspectives on Deviance* (New York: The Free Press, 1964, pp. 87–102); and Thomas J. Scheff, *Being Mentally Ill: A Sociological Theory* (Chicago, Aldine Publishing Company, 1966).

2. Kai T. Erikson, *Wayward Puritans: A Study in the Sociology of Deviance* (New York: John Wiley and Sons, Inc., 1966).

3. See for example: Emile Durkheim, *The Rules of Sociological Method* (New York: The Free Press, 1964), pp. 65–75; and George H. Mead, "The Psychology of Punitive Justice," *American Journal of Sociology* 23 (1918): 577–602.

4. Erikson, *Wayward Puritans*.

5. *Ibid.*, p. 6.

6. One notable exception is Edwin M. Lemert. See for example: "Stuttering among the North Pacific Coastal Indians," *Southwestern Journal of Anthropology* 8 (Winter, 1952): 429–441; "Drinking in Hawaiian Plantation Society," *Quarterly Journal of Studies on Alcohol;* and "Stuttering and Social Structures in Two Pacific Island Societies," *Journal of Speech and Hearing Disorder* 27 (February, 1962): 3–10.

7. The reader may object that a person who is crippled or one who is black is not really deviant in the same way that a thief or a murderer is. When this question is considered, I explain why I believe it is proper to consider such persons as deviants.

8. Robert A. Scott, *The Making of Blind Men* (New York: Russell Sage Foundation, 1969).

9. See especially: Thomas J. Scheff, *Being Mentally Ill: A Sociological Theory,* pp. 47–50, and Thomas J. Scheff, ed., *Mental Illness and Social Processes* (New York: Harper & Row, Publishers, Inc., 1967, passim).

10. Erikson, *Wayward Puritans.*

11. For the most systematic treatment of this aspect of deviance see: Erving Goffman, *Stigma: Notes on the Management of Spoiled Identity* (Englewood Cliffs, N.J.: Prentice-Hall, Inc., 1963).

12. For excellent discussions of this aspect of the property of deviance, see: Erving Goffman, *Stigma,* pp. 4–19; and Thomas J. Scheff, *Being Mentally Ill,* Part I.

13. Erikson, *Wayward Puritans,* pp. 8–19, 27–29.

14. David Mechanic, *Medical Sociology* (New York: The Free Press, 1968).

15. Scott, *The Making of Blind Men,* Chap. 5, pp. 71–89.

16. See for example, Thomas C. Cutsforth, *The Blind in School and Society: A Psychological Study* (New York: American Foundation for the Blind, 1951); Hector Chevigny and Sydell Braverman, *The Adjustment of the Blind* (New Haven: Yale University Press, 1950); and Roger G. Barker, *et al., Adjustment to Physical Handicap and Illness: A Survey of the Social Psychology of Physique and Disability* (New York: Social Science Research Council, 1953).

17. Peter L. Berger and Thomas Luckmann, *The Social Construction of Reality: A Treatise in the Sociology of Knowledge* (New York: Doubleday Company, Inc., 1966).

18. Mary Douglas, *Purity and Danger: An Analysis of Concepts of Pollution and Taboo* (New York: Frederick A. Praeger, Inc., 1966).

19. Erikson, *Wayward Puritans.*

20. Thomas S. Kuhn, *The Structure of Scientific Revolution* (Chicago: The University of Chicago Press, 1962).

21. Berger and Luckmann, *The Social Construction of Reality,* p. 45.

22. *Ibid.,* p. 49.

23. *Ibid.,* p. 49.

24. *Ibid.,* p. 50.

25. *Ibid.,* pp. 56–57.

26. *Ibid.,* p. 58.

27. *Ibid.,* p. 60.

28. *Ibid.,* p. 88.

29. *Ibid.,* p. 89.

30. Alan Howard, *Education in a Changing World* (New York: Columbia University Press) (in press).

31. Berger and Luckmann, *The Social Construction of Reality,* pp. 79–82.

32. D. O. Hebb, "The Mammal and his Environment," in Eleanor E. Maccoby, Theodore M. Newcomb, and Eugene L. Hartley, eds., *Readings in Social Psychology* (New York: Holt, Rinehart and Winston, Inc., 1958).

33. Douglas, *Purity and Danger,* pp. 38–39.

34. *Ibid.,* p. 94.

35. *Ibid.,* p. 94.

36. Kuhn, *Scientific Revolution,* pp. 52–66.

37. Berger and Luckmann, *The Social Construction of Reality,* p. 96.

38. Douglas, *Purity and Danger,* p. 94.

39. I recognize that the term, "significant," is a troublesome one in this definition, if only because it is difficult with our present state of knowledge to provide any concrete guidelines to follow that enable us to differentiate, *a priori,* events or things that are significant transgressions from those that are not. However, some qualifying term is necessary in a definition of deviance because of the fact that not all transgressions result in the application of a deviant label. Until much more is known about the conditions under which these labels are applied, we are forced to accept the term, "significant," vague though it may be.

40. Berger and Luckmann, *The Social Construction of Reality,* p. 106.

41. *Ibid.,* p. 106.

42. Erikson, *Wayward Puritans,* pp. 68–69.

43. Berger and Luckmann, *The Social Construction of Reality,* p. 91.

44. *Ibid.,* pp. 96–118.

45. Kuhn, *Scientific Revolution,* pp. 77–90.

46. Jerome S. Bruner and Leo Postmen, "On the Perception of Incongruity: A Paradigm," *Journal of Personality* 18 (1949): 206–223.

47. Kuhn, *Scientific Revolution,* p. 82.

48. Robert B. Edgerton, "Pokot Intersexuality: An East African Example of the Resolution of Sexual Incongruity," *American Anthropologist* 66 (1964): 1288–1298.

49. *Ibid.,* p. 1290.

50. Edgerton's research also supplies us with an excellent illustration of a point that I made earlier concerning cultural differences in the need to presume order and to be tolerant of a diversity of points of view. Edgerton shows that in the American culture we force the "it" into becoming a "him" or a "her" but that in other cultures, such as the Pokot, the hermaphrodite is permitted to remain an "it," and to live an existence that is not too far removed from the ones engaged by the person who is of a normal sex.

51. Berger and Luckmann, *The Social Construction of Reality,* p. 104.

52. *Ibid.,* p. 104.

53. Elsewhere I have tried to show how the meanings of deviance are being affected by societal experts who are responsible for treating such persons

by means of therapy. See Robert A. Scott, "The Construction of Moral Meanings of Stigma by Experts," in Jack D. Douglas, ed., *Deviance and Respectability* (New York: Basic Books, Inc., 1970).

54. Douglas, *Purity and Danger,* p. 162.

55. Berger and Luckmann, *The Social Construction of Reality,* p. 104.

56. *Ibid.,* p. 106.

57. *Ibid.,* p. 106.

58. *Ibid.,* p. 106.

59. *Ibid.,* p. 106.

60. The term "deficiency model" was first suggested to me by Alan Howard, and it will serve as the basis for a monograph that we will coauthor on social science explanations of behavior among ethnic minorities. The tentative title for this publication is "The Trouble with Them Is . . ."

61. Erikson, *Wayward Puritans.*

62. *Ibid.,* p. 12.

63. *Ibid.,* p. 13.

64. *Ibid.,* p. 7.

65. Robert A. Dentler and Kai T. Erikson, "The Functions of Deviance in Groups," *Social Problems* 7 (1959): 98–107.

66. Erikson, *Wayward Puritans,* pp. 8–19.

67. Douglas, *Purity and Danger,* p. 95.

68. David Matza, *Becoming Deviant* (Englewood Cliffs, N.J.: Prentice-Hall, Inc., 1969).

69. *Ibid.,* pp. 2–3.

| II |

Problems in
Labeling Theory

In the last two decades, the labeling perspective has enlightened a great deal of important research and writing on the subject of deviance. As social scientists have become adept at using the labeling perspective in their work, they have acquired a more mature appreciation of its potentialities and limitations as sociological theory. Each of the three chapters in this part reflects this growing awareness. The first essay, by Gibbs, is a provocative critique of labeling theory from the perspective of normative theories of deviance. The author points out aspects of deviance in everyday life that are ignored, distorted, or unaccounted for in the classical versions of labeling theory presented by Becker, Erikson, Kitsuse, and Lemert. Gibbs then discusses the limitations of normative definitions of deviance and proposes a set of criteria by which to judge the deviancy of a social act.

The second essay, by Warren and Johnson, also contains a critical evaluation of labeling theory, but is presented from an entirely different perspective than that used by Gibbs. These authors suggest that the main contribution of labeling theory has been to serve as a forerunner to phenomenological studies of deviance in everyday life. By using the labeling perspective rather than the more traditional correctional perspective in the study of deviance, sociologists were made more aware of the various meanings of morality and immorality as acted out in everyday life. According to Warren and Johnson, these meanings are the appropriate subject matter of the sociology of deviant behavior. The critique of labeling theory that they offer presents both its contributions toward developing the phenomenological perspective on deviance and its deficiencies as seen from this emerging point of view.

In the final chapter of this part, Fabrega and Manning use the basic insights of the labeling and phenomenological perspectives on deviance in order to clarify an important question about physical illness. Medical and social scientists have long recognized the symbolic and behavioral aspects of physical disorders, and several sociological theories of illness have been proposed. These theories have concentrated almost exclusively on the symbolic aspects of illness, leaving unanswered the question of how such factors interact with the more familiar physical and biological factors in determining the genesis and outcome of illness. Fabrega and Manning present a theoretical framework that incorporates the social, biological, and physical aspects of deviance and illness. In addition, they develop a detailed analysis of the uses of labels of physical and mental illness, showing in the process how recent labeling theorists analyze the situational uses of social categories and rules.

Chapter Two

ISSUES IN DEFINING DEVIANT BEHAVIOR

Jack P. Gibbs

This century has witnessed conspicuous changes in conceptions of deviants and deviant behavior. Few social scientists now entertain the once fairly common notion that deviants (criminals in particular) are distinguished by some biological characteristic, such as body build or facial features. Even the idea that deviant or criminal acts are intrinsically distinctive no longer receives a serious hearing. On the contrary, it may be that no specific type of act (for example, sexual intercourse between siblings) is deviant or criminal in all social units, and the once common assertion that crimes are acts "injurious" to society is also increasingly subject to question.[1] What has emerged is a purely *social* conception of deviation, according to which deviants are merely individuals who have committed deviant acts, and an act is deviant only because it is considered *wrong* by some members of a social unit. Stated in conventional and technical terminology, an act is deviant if it is contrary to a "norm." More than two generations of social scientists have accepted this *normative* definition of deviation, but recently the definition has been either expressly or tacitly rejected by at least three sociologists.

The New Conception of Deviant Behavior

Whereas the concept norm is central in a conventional definition of deviation, the new "school" in sociology abandons that concept. Consider the following illustrative statements by Becker, Erikson, and Kitsuse.

Becker: From this point of view, deviance is *not* a quality of the act the person commits, but rather a consequence of the application by others of rules and sanctions to an "offender." The deviant is one to whom that label has successfully been applied; deviant behavior is behavior that people so label.[2]

Erikson: From a sociological standpoint, deviance can be defined as conduct which is generally thought to require the attention of social control agencies—that is, conduct about which "something should be done." Deviance is not a property *inherent* in certain forms of behavior; it is a properly *conferred upon* these forms by the audiences which directly or indirectly witness them. Sociologically, then, the critical variable in the study of deviance is the social audience rather than the individual *person,* since it is the audience which eventually decides whether or not any given action or actions will become a visible case of deviation.[3]

Kitsuse: Forms of behavior *per se* do not differentiate deviants from non-deviants; it is the responses of the conventional and conforming members of the society who identify and interpret behavior as deviant which sociologically transform persons into deviants.[4]

At first glance these statements may appear consistent with a normative definition of deviation. In declaring certain acts to be wrong, blameworthy, and the like, members of a social unit are reacting, but they are reacting to *types* of acts, or, stated differently, acts "in the abstract." This consideration is evidently crucial for Becker, et al., because they assert that whether a given act is deviant depends upon concrete reactions to it by some member of the social unit and not whether the act is an instance of some particular type.[5] Consequently, an investigator cannot justify classifying an act as deviant without reference to concrete reactions, regardless of opinions voiced by members of the social unit as to types of acts. For example, most Americans would probably denounce "armed robbery" in the abstract; but, according to the argument, knowledge of that "normative opinion" does not justify an investigator's classifying a particular act as deviant, let alone as armed robbery, on the ground that it is an instance of a type of act that is deviant. Again, whether a particular act is deviant depends upon the reaction to it *by members of the social unit,* and whether the act is armed robbery or something else depends upon how the members of the social unit "label" the act.

The word "evidently" appears twice in the foregoing because Becker, et al., have not explicitly and consistently rejected a purely "normative" criterion of deviation. For the most part, the rejection and reasons for it are implicit; but if Becker, et al., concede that a normative evaluation of *types* of acts is the criterion of deviation, then their perspective is not novel and poses no fundamental issue.

Criticism of the New Definition

Two problems are encountered in assessing the notion that only reactions identify acts as deviant. First, it is difficult to distinguish definitions, conceptions, and substantive theory in analyzing statements by Becker, et al.[6] Second, no definition of deviation can be disproven in any sense of the word; accordingly, at best, this critique can only explore certain implications.

Empirical Applicability

If definitions are to be used in research, then the notion of empirical applicability is a central consideration. In this critique a definition is treated as empirically applicable to the extent that independent observers can agree in classifying events, things, or individuals by reference to the definition. Thus, for example, an empirically applicable definition of "upper class" would enable independent observers to agree in identifying residents of a community as to whether they are members of that class. Without the possibility of such agreement, the definition is dubious.

The definition of deviation suggested by Becker, et al., is not empirically applicable because the authors have failed to specify the kind of reactions that identify acts as deviant. To be sure, they suggest the kind of reaction, but the suggestions are vague and ambiguous. For example, Becker refers to deviants as "outsiders," but that term is Becker's, not that of the man on the street or even officials. For that matter, the public may be more familiar with "deviant" than with "outsider."

Turning to reactions supposedly indicative of deviation, curious results ensue. Kitsuse, for example, found the reactions of students to individuals identified as homosexuals to be "generally mild."[7] These reactions may not be representative of the public generally; nonetheless, two questions are posed. First, are we to conclude, because of the mildness of the reaction, that homosexuals are not deviants after all? Second, how "harsh" must the reaction be before an act is considered deviant? More generally, since "mild" and "harsh" judgments are subjective, exactly what *kind* of behavior identifies an act as deviant? In that connection, one of Becker's observations is puzzling. "Whether an act is deviant, then, depends upon how other people react to it. You can commit clan incest and suffer from no more than gossip as long as no one makes a public accusation. . . ."[8] Why does not gossip identify an act as deviant?

The overriding consideration is not just that Becker, et al., fail to specify the kind of reaction that identifies acts as deviant; it is that such specification would also be most difficult. To illustrate, consider a series of questions. First of all, must the reaction be overt? If so, what is the significance of *covert* evaluations of acts as an unquestioned fact of experience? Further, why is the manner of committing an act irrelevant? As a case in point, a married man may attempt to conceal his sexual intercourse with a woman who is not his wife. As observed by Weber, such an attempt to conceal an act is normatively significant, and it remains so whether the act is detected or reacted to by anyone else.[9] This consideration suggests still another general question: Who must react to identify an act as deviant? That question is all the more important because Becker, et al., emphasize those "official" reactions that identify acts as deviant, and they thereby suggest (but not explicitly state) that only reactions by persons in special statuses identify acts as deviant. In any event, a consideration of the identity of reactors generates numerous unanswered questions. For example, can the reaction of the actor to his own act identify it as deviant? The question is particularly relevant in considering expiation and compensation as reactions. Let us consider the following account of a homicide among the Cheyenne.

> Twenty years previously, Little Wolf had ordered Starving Elk to keep away from his wife. Bad feeling had smouldered. Now they were at an army cantonment after the northward flight. Little Wolf's great job was done, but the taste of power lingered. Unchieftain-like, he let himself meddle where he ought not, by trying to stop a card game in which his daughter was playing and gambling for candy. Because it was none of his business, and because he was slightly "full," the players paid him no attention. Enraged, he shot and killed Starving Elk, who was standing by. The act sobered him. "Well," he said, "I am going up on that hill by the bend of the creek. If anybody wants me, I'll be there."[10]

Now ignoring any normative preconceptions of homicide, did Little Wolf's reaction to his own behavior identify it as deviant? If not, why not?

In addition to the identity of reactors, there is the object of the reaction. For example, suppose an individual responds to an act of another by denouncing that act in clearly derogatory terms to a third party, with the matter ending at that point. Would that reaction identify the act as deviant? The more general question is, of course: Must the reaction be such that something is done *to the actor*?

No claim is made that Becker, et al., cannot answer these questions; but they have not done so, and it would be most difficult to avoid arbitrariness in answering. Moreover, even if the requisite reactors and objects of reaction are designated, there is still the question of the "content" of the reactions. In other words, it is not just a question of "who reacts and to whom" but also what the reaction must be. It is not enough to say that "sanctions" identify acts as deviant, because the concept sanction is defined in various ways.[11] Nor can the question of content be answered by saying that a deviant act is an act "so labeled," because the kind of label is left unspecified. With reference to American society, an illustrative list can be readily compiled— theft, lying, robbery, pimping, and the like. But an infinite class cannot be defined by the enumeration of instances, and all the more so if that definition is to be applicable cross culturally. Finally, it is not clear why and how a label in *itself* identifies an act as deviant. Consider a policeman's designation of a particular act as "pimping." In what way does that word in itself identify the act as deviant? Obviously, it does not do so without reference to the normative connotations attached to the word by officials and/or the public. In other words, the label identifies the act as deviant because and only because the label denotes a *type* of act that is evaluated as wrong by some members of the social unit. Note, however, that the evaluation of *types* of acts is central in the normative conception of deviation, which Becker, et al., ostensibly reject.

For the sake of argument, suppose that the kind of reaction that identifies acts as deviant can be specified satisfactorily. The question then arises for a given social unit: What *types* of acts are deviant in that unit? Conceivably, the question could be answered by observing actual reactions to particular acts as instances of types. But what proportion of the acts must result in the designated kind of reaction before the related *type of act* is considered deviant? Fifty per cent? Obviously, any numerical criterion would be arbitrary. As will be seen, a normative definition of deviation also entails arbitrariness, but the new perspective does not escape it either. The only way the problem can be solved by Becker, et al., is to reject the notion of types of acts, and that is where the logical extension of their perspective leads.

Some Inconsistencies

Henceforth, we shall assume a satisfactory specification of the kind of reaction that identifies acts as deviant. The critique then shifts to another question: If the reaction identifies an act as deviant, why is there any reaction and why one kind rather than another? The question suggests that whereas a reaction may identify an act as deviant, it does not explain why the act is deviant. Still another argument makes reference to uniformities in reactions, that is, to the fact that reactions are not idiosyncratic. No one would assert, for example, that reactions to completely naked individuals strolling down a sidewalk would be indistinguishable from reactions to fully clothed pedestrians. Stated more generally, in all social units there is some degree of association between types of acts and types of reactions; indeed, the idea that acts are identified as deviant by reactions to them presupposes that association. But why does it exist?

These arguments do not refute the "reactive" definition of deviation, since a definition cannot provide answers to empirical questions (for example, as to why reactions occur). Nonetheless, these phenomena are much more compatible with a normative than a "reactive" conception of deviation. Since norms are shared beliefs as to what conduct *ought* to be, an act contrary to such a belief is likely to result in a distinctive reaction; but the reaction occurs because the act is deviant and not the reverse as Becker, et al., would have it. Imagine a police officer saying or even thinking: This individual has committed a criminal act because I arrested him.

Just as members of a social unit tend to share beliefs as to what conduct *ought* to be, so do they as to what the reaction to deviation *ought* to be. The latter type of belief is designated as a *reactive norm,* and without that concept or a related notion any uniformity in actual reactions to deviation is inexplicable.[12] Yet, the "reactive" conception of deviation eschews the concept norm.

Still another advantage of a normative over a reactive conception is that it permits research on the *empirical relation* between deviant acts and the character of reactions to those acts. Such research is precluded unless deviant acts and reactions to them are *conceptually distinct.* If an act is deviant only because of a certain kind of reaction to it, then the relation between deviation and reaction is fixed by definition. That point has some inconspicuous implications. The reactive definition leads to a declaration that an act is not a crime unless it is so labeled by officials. Accordingly, the notion of "unreported crimes" becomes meaningless, and along with it, a vast amount of research to determine the extent of criminality (or juvenile delinquency) apart from official records. Indeed, even speculation on the reliability of the crime rate as reported by the police is pointless. If an act is criminal only when labeled as such by the police, then the crime rate reported by the police is absolutely reliable. In other words, the crime rate is what the police report, and the analogous declaration is that intelligence is what intelligence tests measure. Just as one may justifiably ask: Which intelligence test?, so may one ask advocates of the reactive definition: Why the police and not judges or juries?

As has been suggested, the concept norm is not employed in reactive definitions of deviation; but Becker, et al., do not consistently reject it.

> **Becker:** An even more interesting kind of case is found at the other extreme of *secret deviance.* Here an improper act is committed, yet no one notices it or reacts to it as a violation of the rules.[13]

> **Kitsuse and Cicourel:** We wish to state explicitly that the interpretation of official statistics proposed here *does not* imply that the forms of behavior which the sociologist might define and categorize as deviant (e.g., Merton's modes of adaptation) have no factual basis or theoretical importance.[14]

> **Erikson:** There are societies in which deviance is considered a natural pursuit for the young, an activity which they can easily abandon when they move through defined ceremonies into adulthood. There are societies which give license to large groups of persons to engage in deviant behavior for certain seasons or on certain days of the year. And there are societies in which special groups are formed in ways "contrary" to the normal expectations of the culture.[15]

These statements recognize one way or another that deviant behavior can be defined *normatively,* but these authors are not consistent on the issue. Thus, if deviant behavior is defined by reference to reactions, then Becker cannot speak properly of "secret deviance." If behavior defined as deviant by sociologists with reference to norms is "real," then how can one justify maintaining, as Kitsuse does elsewhere, that behavior is deviant only when there is a certain kind of reaction to it? Finally, how can Erikson identify the behavior of "large groups of persons" as deviant when they have been given a "license" to engage in it? To be consistent, Becker, et al., would have to insist that, regardless of normative considerations, an act is not deviant unless it is detected and there is a particular kind of reaction to it. Thus, if a couple engage in adultery but their act is not discovered and reacted to in a certain way, then it is not deviant! Similarly, if an individual is erroneously thought to have committed an act and is reacted to in a certain way as a consequence, a deviant act has taken place! The point is that a reactive definition negates the notion of a "bum rap."

The Issue of Nominalism

Since Becker, et al., have not explicitly stated their rationale for rejecting a normative definition of deviation, one can only speculate as to their objections. First of all, the concept norm is a highly abstract notion. Conventionally, as suggested earlier, it refers to beliefs as to what conduct *ought* to be; and evidence of such beliefs can be gathered systematically only through eliciting statements of opinion from the members of a social unit by posing "normative" questions, that is, asking individuals if they approve or disapprove of designated types of acts. Such questions employ abstract terms (for example, robbery, use or threat of force, adultery, theft, taking valuables without the owner's permission), and the respondents may not interpret those terms in the same way. In effect, then, the "same" questions are not posed for all members. Similarly, in replying to normative questions the respondents will not employ the same terms or, in any case, necessarily "mean the same thing." Finally, assuming that members of a social unit voice disapproval of some type of act, there are problems in classifying actual behavior in terms of that type. For example, suppose the members voice disapproval of "adultery" or, depending upon the way the normative question is posed, "a married person engaging in heterosexual intercourse with someone other than his or her spouse." Subsequently, in observations on actual behavior, it is found that a married man has engaged in such intercourse. But suppose he has lived apart from his wife for ten years and engaged in extramarital relations with his wife's express approval. Now even if it be argued that his act was still "adultery," would the members who disapproved of adultery in the abstract disapprove this particular act? If not, then designation of that particular act as "deviant" would be dubious. Moreover, the members would not be "inconsistent," since the normative question did not specify any contingencies, such as a married man living apart from his wife for ten years and engaging in extramarital relations only with her approval. The point is, of course, that we do not evaluate actual behavior without references to contingencies. To consider another illustration, it is one thing to condemn "speeding" but quite another to judge the action of a motorist who is transporting a seriously wounded individual to a hospital. True, normative questions can be worded to specify contingencies but certainly not all possible contingencies.

Confronted with the complexity of normative phenomena, one possible solution is appealing—identify acts as deviant by reference to actual reactions. In other words, allow the members of the social unit to "decide" whether a given act is deviant. That perspective appears most realistic, but it creates more problems than it solves. Above all, if an investigator cannot justify classifying acts as deviant, how can he "know" when a reaction identifies an act as deviant? In other words, if one cannot justify distinguishing particular acts as to type (deviant or nondeviant), then how can one justify distinguishing reactions as to type (those that identify acts as deviant and those that do not)? Needless to say, to apply a reactive definition, the *type* of reaction that identifies acts as deviant must be specified. However, without employing abstract terms, it is not possible to ask members of the social unit what kind of reaction identifies acts as wrongful or the "appropriate" reaction to such acts. Moreover, as suggested earlier, an investigator cannot "know" that a given reaction (including "labeling") identifies an act as deviant without reference to normative considerations. For example, suppose a clerk approaches an individual in a store and says: "May I wait on you, sir?" only to be pistol whipped by the individual who then takes money from the cash register. The reaction to the statement of the clerk ("May I wait on you, sir?") is definitely coercive, harsh, and punitive, but who would say that the act of the clerk was therefore deviant? Further, who would fail to recognize that the pistol whipping is the deviant act and not the conduct of the clerk? But how would we know? Obviously we would know only by reference to the very normative considerations that are rejected by Becker, et al. Finally, even if normative considerations and the notion of types of acts could be ignored, the study of the particular and the unique cannot escape the problem of "meaning." Thus, returning to the Cheyenne homicide: Did Little Wolf really shoot Starving Elk? The question could not be answered satisfactorily even by a witness, because a phenomenologist could argue that it depends upon how Little Wolf perceived his act and perhaps even how Starving Elk "defined the situation." In any event, since either party would use concepts to communicate his perception, we could not know with certainty what he "really" meant in making a statement. Hence the road to nominalism and on to solipsism.

The nominalistic character of the reactive conception of deviation is manifested both by an emphasis on "meaning" and by the notion that behavior is a response to the "definition of the situation." Even if that notion is something more than a truism, it does not preclude consensus in perceptions of situations, or stated another way, some relation between perception and reality.[16] With reference to the issue at hand, if an act is deviant only when it is perceived as such by the participants (that is, particular individuals) the social quality of deviation is negated. The negation ignores not only obvious uniformities in social life but also the techniques consciously and deliberately employed to create and maintain those uniformities. As a case in point, if the meaning of a "stop" sign is idiosyncratic, then why is it that motorists *do not* respond to the sign in a purely random fashion? If types of acts are not "real," then how and why do individuals anticipate any particular responses to their acts? Needless to say, a motorist who runs a red light (his perception) does not anticipate that a traffic officer will perceive the act as saluting the flag. And why does the traffic officer perceive the act as "wrong"? He evaluates the act as an instance of a type, as does the motorist who refrains from the act. Becker, et al., may insist that not all members of a social unit have the same perception of an act and/or a type of act, and that is why a purely reactive conception of deviation leads ultimately to a rejection of types of acts and an obsession with the particular and the unique.

The rejoinder is not that *all* members of a social unit agree in their perceptions or that they interpret terms that denote types of acts the same way. But less than absolute perceptual uniformity within a social unit does not negate the notion of types of acts. In fact, without that notion, both the fact of social organization and its analysis are inconceivable.

Some perceptual differences among members of a social unit are certain, and their study is both justified and needed. With reference to the issue at hand, it is readily admitted that some acts identified as crimes by members of the public and/or a researcher may not be so perceived or reported by the police. Even some of the acts initially identified by the police as crimes may not, for one reason or another, be reported as such in official statistics. For that matter, there are at least five types of "crime statistics"—(1) complaints to the police alleging the commission of a crime, (2) acts reported as crimes by members of the public in response to questions by a researcher, (3) acts reported by members of the public that the researcher identifies as crimes, (4) acts identified as crimes by police officers in an initial investigation, and (5) the number of crimes reported in official police statistics. There is every reason to believe that the ratio of any one number to any other is not the same for all social units, and the variation in the ratios calls for explanation; but the variation should be treated as an empirical question and not negated by a definition. However, if we follow Kitsuse there is and can be only one crime rate—that reported by the police, which is to say that an act is not criminal if it is not reported as such by the police.

Kitsuse extends his argument to the assertion that "*rates of deviant behavior* are produced by *the actions taken by persons in the social system* which define, classify and record certain behaviors as deviant."[17] If that statement raises any issue, it only does so by implying that whether a social unit has a high official crime rate depends *solely* upon the action of the police rather than upon the behavior of the public. But assuming that assertion to be correct, we should find numerous instances in which the police in a political unit of 5,000 residents report far more crimes than do the police in a political unit of 500,000. After all, even with only 5,000 residents, there are billions of acts during a year, and the police can "label" all or none of those acts as crimes; so there is no reason to expect any relation between population size and the number of crimes reported by the police. But what is the relation? The rank-order coefficient of correlation between number of crimes (1961) and population size (1960) among twenty-one randomly selected Standard Metropolitan Statistical Areas (SMSA's) in the United States is +.91.[18] Surely a coefficient of such magnitude does not just happen.[19] Dare we suspect a conspiracy among *all* police organizations in *all* SMSA's to report only that number of crimes proportionate with population size? Evidence of such a conspiracy would be most interesting, and all the more so since there is also a very close relation between the number of crimes reported in 1958 or 1959 and the population size in 1960. How did the police know what the 1960 population size would be when they reported the number of crimes during the previous two years? Dare we expand this suspected conspiracy to include the Bureau of Census? After all, reporting individuals as residents or nonresidents is labeling, and perhaps the census enumerators conspired to report the 1960 population to produce a correlation with crimes reported by the police in 1958 and 1959. In any event, the control of crime is within our grasp. If the citizenry are concerned by the number of rapes and robberies, the police can eliminate that concern by "labeling" away acts.

A Particular Case of Deviant Behavior

Most of these issues are illustrated by Malinowski's account of an event that occurred among the Trobriand Islanders. The account is especially important because Becker cites it to illustrate his contention that a particular act is not deviant unless it is so labeled.

Reduced to essentials, Malinowski tells of a young man who engaged in sexual relations with his mother's sister's daughter, that is, he broke the "rule of exogamy."[20] There is no doubt that knowledge of the affair was widespread in the local population and, to use Malinowski's own words, it was "generally disapproved." However, nothing was done (evidently for some time) until the girl's discarded lover publicly accused the young man of incest, and subsequently the accused committed suicide.

In his commentary on the Trobriand case, Becker implies that up to the point when a public accusation was made, the sexual intercourse between the young man and his maternal cousin was not deviant, even though Malinowski makes it clear that this type of act was "socially disapproved" and this instance was generally known.[21] If the reactive criterion of deviation is interpreted to mean that something overt, public, and direct must be done to the actor before his act is deviant, then Becker would be consistent in declaring the behavior of the Trobriand couple as nondeviant up to the point of the public accusation. But consider how difficult it is to explain or even understand the accusation and the events that followed without reference to normative considerations, in light of which the behavior was deviant before the public accusation. For one thing, why did the girl's discarded lover select one accusation rather than another? Indeed, how can an accusation have any consequence unless that type of act is evaluated negatively by some members of the social unit? How did Malinowski know that the words spoken by the discarded lover were an "accusation" or an "insult"? In other words, to use Becker's terminology, how did Malinowski know that the words spoken by the girl's discarded lover "labeled" the act as deviant? Why did the young man commit suicide because (ostensibly) of the accusation? Was the "validity" of the accusation irrelevant? If the young man feared that others would reject him because of the accusation, why the fear? Such questions are alien to a purely reactive conception of deviation.

The Question of Deviants

A purely normative definition identifies an act as deviant if the act is an instance of some designated type. However, that characterization does not apply to the identification of a deviant, and the reactive conception is clearly most applicable in that context.

Even if a deviant is merely an individual who has committed a deviant act (a questionable definition since virtually everyone becomes a deviant), a purely normative conception does not enable one to classify deviants as to "type." True, the labeling of someone as an alcoholic, common drunk, psychotic, nut, homosexual, fag, communist, or red, is not unrelated to the fact or suspicion of previous acts by that individual; but a nonarbitrary criterion for identifying a deviant or type of deviant by reference to previous acts is not feasible. Obviously, an individual may not be labeled as a deviant (at least "permanently") on the basis of only one previous act, but it appears impossible to specify any particular number of acts that would "justify" a particular label. To illustrate, with reference to previous acts alone, when does one become a lush or a pimp, and how long does one remain a lush or a pimp? *There appears to be no other standard than the application of labels by members of the social unit.* However, even though the strongest case for the reactive conception is in the identification of deviants, whether a given "label" identifies a deviant (or a type of deviant) depends upon the "normative" interpretation of that label.

Psychiatrists are especially prone to overlook not only the normative aspects of labeling but also the connection between acts and labels. In their study and treatment of individuals who were labeled as psychotic or neurotic, psychiatrists view them as suffering from some "abnormal condition" rather than merely individuals who act "abnormally." Why the acts constitute symptoms of some "abnormal condition" is regarded as a technical question (for example, one answerable only with reference to the concepts of psychoanalysis) and not a normative consideration. Stated another way, normative elements in the psychiatric conception of "abnormality" are left implicit. Further, the labels applied by psychiatrists appear to be explanations of the acts that were the implicit basis for applying the label in the first place. For example, whereas a psychiatrist would be prone to say (or imply) that a certain individual acts the way he does "because he is psychotic," sociologists tend to reverse the syntax—the individual is psychotic because he acts the way he does. The difference is not merely a choice of words; it reflects a basic contrast in perspective. The contrast is well illustrated by the following statement of a New Jersey Supreme Court Justice on a particular case:

> A defense psychiatrist found Lucas to be schizophrenic and irreversibly so, but he added that whether Lucas could live harmlessly within his fantasy of religion depended upon whether in fact he did set fires. If he did, then he should be confined; otherwise he was entitled to his freedom. Another expert, testifying for the state, was satisfied that Lucas was a psychopath, but on cross-examination agreed that whether he was a sexual deviate depended on whether he did in fact deviate and that whether he was a pyromaniac depended upon whether he did in fact commit arson.[22]

The Issue in Relation to Law

Since an "illegal" act is regarded as a special form of deviation, the issue at hand extends to the concerns of jurisprudence. Moreover, although unnoticed in either field, the contending points of view in sociology have their counterparts in jurisprudence. Sociologists who advocate a purely normative conception of deviation find their counterparts in the "analytical" school of jurisprudence. Correlatively, the advocates of a "reactive" conception are philosophically akin to the "legal realists," in that members of both schools adopt a nominalistic conception of normative phenomena. These parallels are revealed best by a consideration of two types of definition of law.

Coercive Definitions of Law

Although "law" may be something more than the aggregate of particular laws, law cannot be defined adequately without first defining "a law." However, one scarcely could find a more controversial issue in jurisprudence.[23] The issue centers largely on a particular kind of definition, variously identified as coercive, analytical, or positivistic; but objections to it by different critics are essentially the same. Indeed, even though the criticism is directed primarily at Kelsen's conception of law, it applies also to definitions by Weber (a sociologist) and Hoebel (an anthropologist), which are given as follows along with some of Kelsen's familiar statements.

> **Weber:** An order will be called *law* if it is externally guaranteed by the probability that coercion (physical or psychological), to bring about conformity or avenge violation, will be applied by a *staff* of people holding themselves specially ready for that purpose.[24]

> **Hoebel:** A social norm is legal if its neglect or infraction is regularly met, in threat or in fact, by the application of physical force by an individual or group possessing the socially recognized privilege of so acting.[25]

> **Kelsen:** Law is the primary norm, which stipulates the sanction . . . If "coercion" in the sense here defined is an essential element of law, then the norms which form a legal order must be norms stipulating a coercive act, i.e., a sanction.[26]

Because criticism is directed against coercive definitions in general, a composite definition of that type is needed as a point of reference. The composite "coercive" definition of *a law* in this instance is as follows:

1. an evaluation of conduct held by at least one person in a social unit, and
2. a high probability that, on their own initiative or at the request of others, persons in a distinctive status will attempt by coercive or noncoercive means to revenge, rectify, or prevent behavior that is contrary to the evaluation, with
3. a low probability of retaliation by persons other than the individual or individuals at whom the reaction is directed.

Rather than employ the terms norm, rule, or order, none of which can be defined with precision or without controversy, the composite definition treats an evaluation of conduct as a *necessary condition* for a law. The concept is thus not purely behavioral, because, regardless of model behavior in a social unit, an act is not consistent with or contrary to a law unless at least one member of that unit *evaluates* that act positively or negatively. But the evaluation need not be collective, which is to emphasize that a law may not have popular support. Accordingly, while the evaluation of conduct may be thought of as a norm, it does not necessarily reflect consensus.

The composite definition can be applied to both literate and nonliterate populations, and for that reason, the term "distinctive status" is used rather than official, court, government, or state. Those terms are not applicable cross-culturally and reflect an ethnocentric conception of law. The statuses are distinctive in two respects. First, they do not include everyone in the social unit, that is, if the persons who "enforce" the evaluation of conduct do not occupy a special status, as opposed to just "anyone," the evaluation is not a law. Second, the statuses are distinctive in that the occupants stand in a universal rather than a particular social relation to the perpetrator of an act or the victim (the individual construed as harmed or the complainant). Accordingly, revenge by kinsmen or friends is not indicative of a law, however regular the revenge and improbable the retaliation.

In reference to cross-cultural applicability, it should be noted that laws need not be written or codified. For that matter, some codified statements may not qualify as a law, because observations of actual behavior are necessary to identify a law. Consequently, the definition differs (as does Weber's) from Kelsen's in one important respect—the emphasis is on what persons in particular statuses actually do, not what they "ought" to do. Finally, unlike most coercive definitions, the composite version treats a low probability of retaliation as no less important than coercion. The variable of retaliation provides a means for specifying the empirical referent of "legitimacy," a concept as vague and controversial as law itself.

Legal Realism

Two features characterize the criticism of the coercive definitions of law. The first is an insistence that such a definition is inconsistent with or does not "explain" some aspect of law. For example, H. L. A. Hart takes issue with the emphasis on coercion, and points out that individuals may conform to laws for reasons ostensibly unrelated to a fear of punishment.[27] The observation is valid, but it is erroneous criticism nonetheless. Hart is demanding an answer to an empirical question from what is nothing more than a definition. Why some but *not all* individuals "internalize" a law to the point that they conform to it without fear of punishment is indeed a significant question. Differences among social units as to the "acceptance" of laws pose still another significant question. But such questions cannot be answered by a definition.

The second feature of criticism of coercive definitions is the absence of alternatives, and that is especially true of critics who would revive "natural law" concepts.[28] They reject a coercive definition but, insofar as they advance any alternative, it appears to be a statement of what positive law should be, not what it is or may be.[29]

But one opposing school—the legal realists—have formulated a distinct alternative to a coercive definition of a law, as suggested by the following.

> Rules, whether stated by judges or others, whether in statutes, opinions or textbooks by learned authors, are not the Law, but are only some among many of the sources to which judges go in making the law of the cases tried before them.
>
> The law, therefore, consists of *decisions,* not of rules. If so, then *whenever a judge decides a case he is making law.*[30]

> This past behavior of the judges can be described in terms of certain generalizations which we call rules and principles of law.[31]

What these officials do about disputes is, to my mind, the law itself.[32]

. . . the theory that rules decide cases seems for a century to have fooled not only library-ridden recluses, but judges.[33]

These statements assert that a law exists *only* in the actions of officials, judges in particular. Stated another way, they assert that law is made by judges in their decisions. This perspective suggests a definition of "legal deviation" akin to that of Becker, et al., in sociology. Whether a particular act is criminal, contrary to law, or illegal, depends upon the actions of officials.

Criticism of Legal Realism

This assessment of legal realism begins with a statement by Justice Holmes, the major figure in the history of that school: "The prophecies of what the courts will do in fact, and nothing more pretentious, are what I mean by the law."[34]

Holmes' statement is contrary to analytical jurisprudence, because Kelsen argues that a court does not and cannot exist without law.[35] However, there are other implications and bases for criticizing legal realism. Note that Holmes did not specify the source of a prophecy. Are we to conclude, therefore, that anyone's prophecy is a "law"? If a jockey predicts the outcome of a litigation, is his prophecy a "law" in the same sense as the prediction of an attorney? If not, why not? If not, whose prophecies are to be treated as laws?

In hailing Justice Holmes' pronouncement, the realists conveniently ignore that a "prophecy" may imply some uniformities in court rulings. Making prophecies on that basis may appear entirely consistent with the principles of legal realism, but if there is no law other than the decisions of judges, how and why would any uniformity be realized in their decisions? The uniformities suggest something that constrains judges and channels their decisions.[36] What is this "something"? It is evaluations of conduct shared to some degree by judges, and accordingly, their decisions reflect law, and do not make it.

Significantly, unlike Holmes, later legal realists are not prone to use the word "prophecy." They are far more nominalistic in their outlook, which explains their preference for "decisions of judges." That preference avoids the difficult question: Whose prophecies? It also allows them to ignore the point that prophecies imply uniformities in rulings of courts. But it does not avoid still another difficult question: Is any decision of a judge "law"? If not, what *kind* of decision? Suppose an American judge sentences a defendant to execution on a conviction for tax evasion? Certainly it would be a decision, but would it be "law"? The legal realists might reply that it is not a law since the sentence will be appealed and overruled. But why the prediction?

Whatever the merits of the legal realists' emphasis on courts and judges as *lawmakers,* the conception poses insurmountable problems when an attempt is made to apply it outside of Anglo-American jurisdictions. If courts and judges are to be defined in cross-cultural terms, reference must be made to the administration of law; but, given the perspective of legal realism, a law cannot be identified without first identifying courts and judges. This is not a problem for the legal realists, because they speak of judges and courts as they know them in Anglo-American jurisdictions. Indeed, their conception of law clearly reflects a preoccupation with case law, despite Weber's demonstration that the "judge-centeredness of the Common Law is not a general feature of all legal systems."[37] What the legal realists provide is a jurisprudence of Anglo-American law. True, some of their observations suggest a universal definition of judges, courts, and officials. The legal realists never tire of stating that the "function" of law is to settle disputes. But even in Anglo-American jurisdictions law is not the only institutionalized means for the settlement of disputes; and certainly judges, policemen, and prosecutors are not the only persons who settle disputes. What, then, is distinctive about a "legal" settlement? Obviously, it is backed by force; yet stress on coercion is alien to the perspective of legal realists; if anything, they find the notion distasteful.

Analytical jurisprudents, Kelsen in particular, insist that law is a system of abstract principles and should be so studied. As such, jurisprudence scarcely is concerned with the actual behavior of citizens or officials. Actions by officials, if considered at all, are viewed as merely the application of abstract principles. Legal realism is primarily a distinctive school because it rejects the "formalism" of analytical jurisprudence. But it is not merely a proposal to consider actual behavior as well as "legal norms"; on the contrary, it is also a rejection of the latter. Thus, to "know the law," one must observe the actual behavior of litigants and officials. This perspective is consistent with all "realisms," but whether the observed behavior confirms the cardinal principle of legal realism—law is nothing more than the decisions of judges—is another matter.

For one thing, the principle is a strange realism if it is contrary to the opinions of some judges, and that it appears to be. By the legal realists' own admission, judges "deceive" themselves in thinking that they *find* law, not make it. One thing is clear—it is not difficult to see why judges deceive themselves. Consider a judge saying (or even thinking) to a defendant in a nonjury trial: "You have committed a criminal act because I find you guilty." The judge's mental process is just the reverse, and his "self-deception" is nothing more than a belief that there are *types* of acts and appropriate *types* of reactions to them. Even if the legal realists should point out that judges must decide whether particular acts and reactions qualify as instances of the types and really "make" law in so deciding, a judge will be concerned by the fact that he did not create statuses or precedents and wonder why the case at hand reached his court in the first place. After all, if a judge *makes* the law for each case, how could a plaintiff or a prosecutor possibly anticipate that he will rule one way rather than another? To be sure, they could anticipate a ruling by reference to past cases, but only the judge can decide what cases are comparable. His Honor probably will be even more concerned with another of his "self-deceptions"—that only some kinds of decisions are legitimate. His turmoil would be resolved by merely taking the legal realists seriously—since any decision the judge makes is law, then any decision he makes will be law. Further, if judicial decisions are dictated by the personalities and ideologies of jurists (a favorite theme for realists), then sentencing a convicted tax evader to execution should not be entirely unexpected, especially since a judge can interpret the statutes in such a way that the tax evasion is really first-degree murder. In any event, he need not fear being overruled by an appellate court. If all cases are unique and judges free themselves of restraints by interpreting statutes, there can be no basis for predicting the outcome of an appeal. Is the illustration preposterous? Of course, but observe why—judges in Anglo-American jurisdictions simply do not sentence individuals to execution on conviction of income tax evasion. The question for the legal realists, then, is why judges do not do so.

Even if it be granted that judges do make law, they are not the only "lawmakers." Specifically, why exclude the police, prosecutors, or even lawyers? They enter more directly into the life of the typical citizen than do judges, if only because their decisions largely determine whether a given case will ever reach a court. It will not do for the realists to argue that actions by the police, prosecutors, and attorneys are dictated by pronouncements from the bench. For one thing, at least in Anglo-American jurisdictions, judges do not command police officers or district attorneys to prosecute cases, which means that the latter officials exercise considerable discretion independently of the rulings of judges.[38] Moreover, judicial pronouncements must be interpreted in application; and if judges make law by interpreting statutes, how is it that policemen, prosecutors, and attorneys do not make law in their interpretations of court rulings?

Just as the preoccupation of legal realists with judges is questionable, so is it, *a fortiori*, when extended to appellate courts. Their rulings cannot possibly be "law" for trial courts in subsequent cases, because by the legal realists' own reasoning, appellate rulings must be interpreted, and each trial judge makes "his" own law in the interpretation. The same may be said for a ruling on any case.[39]

Far from viewing law as abstract principles, legal realists are very much concerned with law as an agency of social control, a mechanism for settling disputes, and a means of promoting public welfare. Is this realistic? It is to be sure, but it does not confirm their conception of law. Even the most opinionated legal realists would admit that law is not and cannot be an effective means of social control unless the citizenry have some basis for knowing what is expected of their conduct. And how do they know for the most part? By following the decisions of particular judges? Incredible! The proverbial man on the street may not even know the name of a local judge, let alone any decision by that judge. And would the citizenry lead more orderly, "law-abiding" lives if convinced that conformity to a law is not a matter of conduct but, rather, only the decision of judges? A strange realism would be required to answer this affirmatively.

Problems Concerning a Normative Definition of Deviation

The critique of Becker, et al., and legal realism is obviously partisan, and it is admitted that the rejection of a reactive definition of deviation does not solve the problems associated with a normative definition. On the contrary, the problems are so vast that the proposed solution is to abandon the concepts of norm and law.

Rejection of the Concept Norm

The subjective dimension of the concept norm refers to the sensed "rightness" or "wrongness" of conduct. Common experiences—feelings of guilt, indignation, pride, and admiration—all are evidence of normative phenomena. True, only individuals evaluate conduct, but such experiences tend to be shared, that is, the act that is admired or abhorred by one member of a social unit tends to produce a similar covert reaction in other members. Nor is a *collective evaluation* restricted to particular acts; *types* of acts are also evaluated, and consensus is often striking. For example, who would expect to find great differences of opinion among Americans in their response to the question: Should a mother engage in sexual intercourse with her son?

Given the reality of normative phenomena, the concept norm should be anything but ambiguous. Unfortunately, that is not so; the concept is controversial and defies adequate definition.

The most conspicuous problem is the diversity of phenomena subsumed under the concept. Although the terminology varies, most definitions emphasize that a norm is a collective evaluation of a type of conduct.[40] However, distinctions among classes of norms clearly suggest that *collective expectations* also enter into the notion. Customs and mores are particularly relevant. If any distinction can be drawn, customs refer to expectations of conduct, not evaluations as do mores. Consider the "custom" of drinking coffee. We expect (in the sense of a prediction) that adult Americans will drink coffee in certain situations, but a sense of "ought" or "should" is not attached to that expectation. Accordingly, a generic definition of norm is incomplete without a recognition of both collective evaluations and collective expectations.

The matter is further complicated by an empirical observation: what an individual thinks conduct ought to be (or will be) may not correspond to his perceptions of the opinions of others. Thus, an individual may feel that pre-marital sexual intercourse is not wrong (his evaluation of conduct), and yet he may perceive the opinions of others as condemning that act. Similarly, a police officer may expect that the typical juvenile will smoke marijuana at least once, even though the officer perceives the "expectations" of the public to the contrary. The distinction between an individual's "normative" opinions and his perceptions of public opinion has been explicated by Scheff.[41] He focuses on alternative measures of consensus, but the distinction is relevant in defining norm. Specifically, in defining norm it is difficult to defend the exclusion of "perceived normative opinions," and all the more so since Scheff argues forcibly that the phenomenon may influence behavior.[42] Thus, one may refrain from smoking marijuana not because he thinks it wrong (his normative opinion), but because he thinks that others view it as wrong (perceived normative opinion). Such perception could influence his behavior even though it is erroneous (that is, other members may not regard smoking marijuana as wrong). Accordingly, a definition of norm should refer not only to collective evaluations and collective expectations but also to *perceived* collective evaluations and *perceived* collective expectations, that is, four distinct phenomena.[43]

Still another consideration expands the range of normative phenomena. No one questions that a law is a type of norm. The conceptual problem is that a law, even though it is an evaluation of conduct, may not have the properties ascribed to norms in general. Specifically, the notion that a norm is a *shared* evaluation of conduct does not "fit" all laws. By virtually any definition, all laws do not have popular support. Social units in which a small class or caste dominates a large majority, as in the Republic of South Africa or in some counties in the Deep South, are likely to exhibit a divergence between "legal" and "extralegal" evaluations of conduct. In what sense then is a law a type of norm? No answer would satisfy all social scientists or jurisprudents, but the argument is that a law cannot be defined without considering actual reactions to actual behavior. Consequently, if a law is a type of norm, it is necessary to expand the definition of the latter concept to include still another distinct class of phenomena—actual *attempts* to prevent, revenge, or rectify instances of a certain type of act (henceforth identified as "negative" reactions to behavior).

The designation of reactions as normative phenomena is necessary for reasons that are unrelated to law. Conceivably, all members of a social unit may voice disapproval of some type of act and yet commit it and/or appear indifferent when others commit it. In other words, individuals may act inconsistently with their expressed normative opinions, and thus the question: In what sense are normative opinions "real" or "viable"? This question probably underlies a preference among some social scientists to identify norms as average or modal behavior. For example, rather than solicit normative opinions to determine if premarital chastity is the "norm" in American society, one may estimate the frequency of premarital sexual experience. If a majority have engaged in it, then that behavior is the norm. But a conceptual problem is posed by the notion that norms *influence* behavior. If a norm is defined by reference to actual behavior, then it is questionable to speak of norms influencing that behavior. For example, if the rarity of brother-sister marriages leads one to declare that such a marriage is contrary to the norm, then it is pointless to say that brothers and sisters do not intermarry because of the norm.

Whereas there are compelling reasons for not defining a norm in terms of statistical standards, the "reality" or "viability" of a norm can be assessed by observing actual reactions to acts that are contrary to the norm. If negative reactions are infrequent, especially when the behavior is highly visible, then there is evidence of no real commitment to the norm. Nonetheless, regardless of reactions to actual behavior, opinions as to what conduct ought to be are still "normative." If the opposing argument is made—opinions are norms only when contrary behavior is regularly subject to negative sanctions—then the regularity of sanctions is *the* criterion of norms, not opinions as to what conduct ought to be. The argument is debatable for two reasons. First, it makes norms and sanctions conceptually indistinct. And, second, any specification of the criterion of "regular" sanctions is bound to be arbitrary.

Normative Elements

Whereas the concept norm suggests some unitary phenomenon, no less than five distinct classes of phenomena may be subsumed under the concept: collective evaluations, collective expectations, perceived collective evaluations, perceived collective expectations, and negative reactions to behavior. Definitions of the concept norm emphasize one or, at most, two classes of phenomena; and the exclusion of others is not surprising. Any definition that subsumes all five classes would be extremely cumbersome and logically questionable. Above all, debates over the inclusion of some phenomena and the exclusion of others are certain to be inconclusive.

The solution is to abandon the concept norm and identify each related class of phenomena as a distinct *normative element*. That strategy is especially desirable because of still another conceptual problem. Superorganic qualities are ascribed to norms and perhaps rightly so. No living individual invented the proscription of incest, nor does one conform to it from a purely personal preference or ignore it with impunity. Further, normative consensus may be so marked that it cannot be attributed to chance, but it is rarely complete and therein lies a crucial question: What should be the statistical "cutting point" for declaring the opinions of individuals to be a norm? The immediately suggested figure is 50 percent (the majority notion); but this or any other figure would be arbitrary. Accordingly, social scientists should cease declaring that some type of act is *the* norm in a designated population; there is only a collective evaluation of that type of act that prevails in the population to some specified degree, depending upon the proportion of the members who approve, disapprove, or have no preference concerning the type of act. What has been said of collective evaluations applies also to collective expectations, perceived collective expectations, perceived collective evaluations, and negative reactions.[44] Thus, each of these five normative elements are *quantitative.*

The proposed treatment of normative phenomena is likely to be rejected disdainfully by those social scientists who are imbued by the word "superorganic." Specifically, they will brand the treatment as "reductionistic" since measures of normative elements would be based on the opinions of individuals. Even the fact that the opinions are *collective* (not in the sense that everyone shares them but in that all members or a sample thereof are questioned) will not blunt the charge of reductionism. The charge will persist because the "superorganic" notion suggests that "norms" somehow exist independently of opinions, but that notion fails to specify any empirical referents, that is, how to demonstrate the existence of a norm. Further, if a norm is something more than "opinions," then exactly what is it? True, one can point to actual behavior as the referent of a norm (that is, a statistical standard), but then how can one justifiably use the concept to explain the behavior?

Rejection of the Concept Law

Just as the concept norm poses insoluble problems, so does the concept law. If one must employ the concept, a coercive definition is preferable, but even that definition is questionable. One problem is empirical applicability. According to the composite definition, a type of act is a law if there is: (1) a high probability of "negative" reactions to contrary acts; and (2) given such reactions, a low probability of retaliation. The only referent for probability in this context is actual behavior; so the question raised is: What proportion of "cases" must result in a negative reaction to satisfy the criterion of a "high" probability? Obviously, any figure would be arbitrary. Consequently, rather than employ an arbitrary concept, the notion of law should be abandoned and replaced by additional *quantitative normative elements.*

Given at least one member of a social unit who evaluates a type of conduct, "enforcement" is the proportion of cases of contrary conduct that result in "negative" reactions *by anyone.* Two additional normative elements follow from recognition of enforcement. Given a negative reaction, the object of the reaction may accept it or respond *refractorily,* that is, attempt to flee, use force to thwart reactors, or seek revenge for the reaction. In any event, with reference to social organization, the crucial consideration is the response of other members of the social unit to a negative reaction. If reaction is highly organized, refraction by the object of reaction is usually of no avail unless others rally to his cause, specifically, to forcibly *retaliate*. Such a "reaction to a reaction" is often conspicuous as the second event in a race riot. [45]

As a normative element, retaliation signifies public denial of the legitimacy of reaction. However, one could argue that frequent refraction by objects of reaction also denies the legitimacy of reactions. If it were necessary to define a law, then the relative importance of retaliation and refractoriness would have to be debated and one would be excluded in favor of the other; but once the concept law is abandoned, both retaliation and refractoriness can be treated as quantitative normative elements, with their relative importance treated as an empirical question.

Designation of enforcement, retaliation, and refractoriness as normative elements rather than as "conditions" of law solve still another conceptual problem. One virtue of the composite definition of a law is that it would exclude unenforced statutes ("dead" laws). However, it could be argued that even an unenforced statute is still a law because officials could "legitimately" enforce it.[46] Rather than enter into a sterile debate on that point, any statute can be analyzed as an evaluation of conduct, with its enforcement treated as a matter of degree and its legitimacy considered in terms of retaliation and refractoriness.

Even without these insoluble problems, the concept law is so controversial that it has no utility. For example, some jurisprudents insist that coercion is the *sine qua non* of law, but others deny it that primacy. There is no conclusive way to resolve the debate. Moreover, even if coercion is the *sine qua non* of law, application of that criterion is difficult. If no "negative" reaction in a social unit entails coercion, is law absent? An affirmative answer would be indefensible because "legal officials" (by any conventional definition) do not always use force. Typically, they use it only after encountering resistance to orders; hence, references to coercion as a legal phenomenon are usually couched in terms of "the potential use of force." But those terms preclude systematic empirical observation and, therefore, it is necessary to consider only the actual frequency of coercion. Yet any statistical criterion concerning frequency of coercion as a necessary condition of law would be arbitrary, which is the rationale for simply designating the frequency of coercive reactions as another normative element.

Most "coercive" definitions of law emphasize not only the use of force but also the social characteristics of those persons who use it. Stated another way, both the character of the reaction and the characteristics of the *reactors* identify law. However, those writers, especially Ehrlich,[47] Malinowski,[48] and Fuller,[49] who do not insist on a distinction between legal phenomena and normative phenomena in general, would question the emphasis on any particular characteristic of reactors. Moreover, designations of the "essential" characteristics of "legal reactors" are so vague as to render them empirically inapplicable, and attempts at greater precision are likely to result in arbitrary and ethnocentric distinctions.[50] Nonetheless, if the concept law is to be applied cross culturally, "legal reactors" must be identified without use of such terms as police, judges, and officials. The vagueness of those terms and their ethnocentric character become obvious when an attempt is made to apply them cross culturally. Any doubts on that score can be eliminated by two steps. Read descriptions of the statuses *tonowi* among the Kapauku Papuans,[51] the *monkalun* among the Ifugo,[52] the "leopard-skin chief" among the Nuer,[53] and the members of Cheyenne soldier societies;[54] and then attempt to answer the question: Which of these statuses represents a police officer, a prosecutor, a judge, or simply a "legal official"? To be sure, occupants of those statuses play a distinctive role in reaction to deviant behavior (however defined); but, nevertheless, an answer to the question is bound to be arbitrary.

Once the concept law is abandoned, there is no need to emphasize any particular characteristic of reactors to the exclusion of others, and certainly no need to employ such terms as police, prosecutor, and judge, which are, after all, peculiar to Anglo-American jurisdictions. Rather, a range of social characteristics of reactors to deviant behavior can be recognized as a generic normative element. Designation of one such characteristic as an illustration must suffice. In some *but not all* social units certain individuals react to deviant behavior as a full-time occupation or an exclusive means of livelihood. Accordingly, the proportion of all reactors who are so characterized is a quantitative normative element—designated as *occupational exclusiveness*. That notion permits comparisons of social units without engaging in the sterile debate over the presence or absence of "legal officials" in social units outside Anglo-American jurisdictions, and particularly among nonliterate peoples.

Codified Evaluations of Conduct

One ostensive referent of a "law" may be a written statement that appears to be an evaluation of a type of act. The evaluative quality of the statement is reflected in the words employed (for example, "ought" or "should"), the penalties stipulated for contrary behavior, or the context. In the latter case, an entire set of statements has an evaluative quality, as in a code or any body of rules.

Whereas a written statement may be the ostensive referent for a particular "law," a definition of laws by reference to written statements is questionable. Such a definition would arbitrarily and ethnocentrically preclude law in nonliterate societies. The definition would be questionable even if applied to Anglo-American political units, where we find both common and statutory law, with only the latter clearly representing "laws" as written statements. Moreover, it is difficult to justify identifying all statutes in all codes as laws, since a statute may be seldom if ever enforced. If so, is the written statement a law? That question reintroduces the issue of "dead" but "legitimately enforceable" laws, an issue that cannot be resolved conclusively.

Further, if a written statement is not a "law" unless it is regularly enforced, the specification of any numerical criterion of "regular" is bound to be arbitrary.

It thus appears that there is no defensible basis for identifying written statements, and statutes in particular, as normative phenomena. However, that is true only insofar as the identification entails an attempt to define law. Once that concept is abandoned, then any written statement that represents an evaluation of a type of act can be recognized as still another normative element. The element is identified as a *codified* evaluation of conduct, but that designation requires qualification. The term codified is used only because we often find an organized set of written evaluations of conduct (for example, a code) rather than isolated statements. Actually, although, with one exception, any written evaluation of a type of act qualifies as a codified normative element. Accordingly, with reference to the United States, codified evaluations include, *inter alia,* not only statutes and ordinances but also some statements in Emily Post's *Etiquette* and in the *Official Chess Handbook*. The inclusive character of the concept codified evaluation stems from the recognition not only that the notion of a legal code is culturally relative and therefore of dubious utility for comparative studies but also that other types of written statements are just as "normative" as statutes.

Only one kind of written evaluation of conduct is excluded as a normative element. If a statement is "alien" to a social unit, it is not a normative element in that unit. Thus, to point to an obvious illustration, the presence of Laurence Larson's *The Earliest Norwegian Laws* in the library of an American city does not mean that all of the evaluative statements in that publication are codified evaluations for that city. However, what is alien to a social unit cannot be specified satisfactorily without invoking a particular criterion—that at least one member of the social unit must subscribe to a written evaluation of conduct before it is a codified evaluation for that unit.

Conclusion on the Subject of Law

All of this comes down to one assertion—there are no laws, only evaluations of types of conduct; but all evaluations of conduct are not the same. They differ as to enforcement, the use of coercion in enforcement, the frequency of retaliation and refraction as responses to enforcement, and the social characteristics of persons who attempt enforcement. Accordingly, all of these variables are *normative elements*.

Deviant Behavior Reconsidered

At first glance, it may appear that abandoning the concepts norm and law negates the notion of deviation. That is not the case, but without those concepts the notion becomes extremely complicated. However, the complexities simply reflect a reality that cannot be described in terms of norms or law.

Of the eleven normative elements that have been recognized, five enter into a definition of deviant behavior—collective evaluations, collective expectations, perceived collective evaluations, perceived collective expectations, and codified evaluations.[55] These are five distinct criteria for assessing the "deviancy" of any act, which is to say that, by definition, there are five standards; and a type of act is deviant *if and to the extent* that it is contrary to one or all of these five standards. If in response to normative questions all members of a social unit (or a representative sample thereof) voice disapproval of some type of act, then that type or an instance of it is *evaluatively* deviant to the maximum proscriptive degree.[56] Similarly, if all members (or a representative sample) predict that no other member will commit the act designated in a normative question, then commission of that act is *expectationally* deviant to the maximum degree. The same characterization of the types of acts would apply if the acts are analyzed in terms of two other standards—perceived evaluative and perceived expectational. Needless to say, regardless of the social unit or the standard, it is probably true that most if not all types of acts are deviant to some degree. However, the deviancy of a type of act is not a matter of degree if a codified evaluation is the standard. According to that standard, a type of act is either deviant or not deviant.

In the light of these complex distinctions, one may well ask: But how is it that social scientists have studied deviant behavior for decades? They have done so merely by leaving the conceptual issues and problems implicit, and they could do so primarily because they focused on types of acts that would be highly deviant regardless of the standard of deviation considered. For example, the criminologist who studies armed robbery in the United States would not be hard-pressed to justify the identification of that type of act as deviant. It is probably highly deviant by virtually any definition or standard. However, insofar as the study of deviation purports to be truly general, it cannot focus on extreme types of acts alone. Indeed, the study of deviation in a social unit should attempt to analyze acts that represent a wide range in type and degree of deviation.

In reference to types of deviation, the distinctions are not limited to evaluations and expectations. Other normative elements can and should be considered. Thus, for example, two types of acts may be deviant to approximately the same degree (that is, with reference to all of the five standards) and yet be quite different with regard to the enforcement, the characteristics of the reactors, the use of coercion by reactors, the frequency of retaliation, and the frequency of refractoriness. Since differences among types of deviant acts are a matter of degree, the distinctions would not be as arbitrary and controversial as the conventional distinction between crime and extralegal deviation.

To be sure, the present perspective entails a host of complicated technical problems, none of which are near solution. For one thing, there is every reason to believe that responses to normative questions are determined appreciably by the way the questions are phrased, for example, merely the choice of "ought" rather than "should" could influence responses to the question. Similarly, the responses may be quite different to a question that employs a label to identify a type of act (for example, homosexual) than to a question that defines the types of act (for example, sexual relations between persons of the same sex). Then there is a choice of asking individuals to evaluate hypothetical or actual instances of a type of act or asking them to evaluate types of acts in the abstract. And, in either case, there is the question of whether and how contingencies should be introduced in posing normative questions (for example, specifying the age of the actors). The point is that we know very little about the way that the wording of a normative question influences the responses to that question, let alone the "best" way. Finally, even if the problems associated with phrasing normative questions should be solved, there would still be at least two additional sets of problems—(1) classifying responses to normative questions and (2) measuring the degree of deviation for the related type of act.

Given all of these difficulties, one may want to settle for a more simple conception of deviant behavior. However, the problems that have been noted are potentially soluble, provided that social scientists are willing to undertake research for the purpose of formulating and perfecting techniques. In any event, social scientists should cease attempting to define deviant behavior by reference to norms or law and, above all, they should confront the issues rather than ignore them.

Notes

1. For elaboration on these points, see Jack P. Gibbs, "Conceptions of Deviant Behavior: The Old and the New," *Pacific Sociological Review* 9 (1969): 9–14.

2. Howard S. Becker, *Outsiders* (New York: The Free Press, 1963), p. 9.

3. Kai Erikson, "Notes on the Sociology of Deviance," *Social Problems* 9 (1962): 308.

4. John I. Kitsuse, "Societal Reaction to Deviant Behavior: Problems of Theory and Method," *Social Problems* 9 (1962): 253.

5. The perspective adopted by Becker, et al., is closely akin to that formulated earlier by Lemert, who is conventionally identified as a member of the "labeling school." However, it is not certain whether Lemert rejects a normative criterion of deviation, since one may focus on the consequences

of labeling without declaring labeling to be the criterion of deviation. For that reason Lemert is not identified here with the "new" perspective of Becker, et al. See Edwin M. Lemert, *Social Pathology* (New York: Mc-Graw-Hill, Inc., 1951); and Edwin M. Lemert, *Human Deviance, Social Problems, and Social Control* (Englewood Cliffs, N.J.: Prentice-Hall, Inc., 1967).

6. For elaboration, see Gibbs, "Conceptions of Deviant Behavior."

7. Kitsuse, "Societal Reaction to Deviant Behavior," p. 256.

8. Becker, *Outsiders*, p. 11.

9. Max Rheinstein, ed., *Max Weber on Law in Economy and Society* (Cambridge, Mass.: Harvard University Press, 1954), p. 4.

10. K. N. Llewellyn and E. Adamson Hoebel, *The Cheyenne Way* (Norman: University of Oklahoma Press, 1941), p. 83.

11. See Jack P. Gibbs, "Sanctions," *Social Problems* 14 (1966): 147–159.

12. For a detailed treatment of the concept "reactive norm" see Alexander L. Clark and Jack P. Gibbs, "Social Control: A Reformulation," *Social Problems* 12 (1965): 398–415.

13. Becker, *Outsiders*, p. 20.

14. John L. Kitsuse and Aaron Cicourel, "A Note on the Uses of Official Statistics," *Social Problems* 11 (1965): 135.

15. Erikson, "Notes on the Sociology of Deviance," p. 315.

16. If the notion of social reality is rejected (as the nominalists are bound to do), then the point can be made in the way of a question: Why is any consensus or uniformity in perception ever realized?

17. Kitsuse and Cicourel, "A Note on the Uses of Official Statistics," p. 135.

18. Source of data: Federal Bureau of Investigation, *Uniform Crime Reports for the United States, 1961* (Washington, D.C.: no publisher, n.d.), Table 4. The "total" number of crimes is actually the sum of seven "major" offense categories as designated by the F.B.I.: murder and nonnegligent man-slaughter, forcible rape, robbery, aggravated assault, burglary, larceny fifty dollars and over, and auto theft.

19. A direct relation between population size and crimes reported by the police would be expected only in a universe of social units with the same or similar criminal laws. Moreover, an absolutely invariant relation would not be anticipated because there is reason to believe that the "true" crime rate does vary among social units, even those in the same legal system. Note again, however, that the "new" perspective denies a "true" crime rate or incidence as a theoretical construct. Indeed, insofar as Becker, et al., do grant even the reality of criminal acts as a type, they write as though the incidence of such acts is a constant from one population to the next, with the only difference being the proportion of acts that are labeled as criminal. But such an interpretation of a crime rate is no less conjectural than the notion of "true" incidence, and it is difficult to see how the coefficient of correlation reported can be explained without entertaining that notion.

20. Bronislaw Malinowski, *Crime and Custom in Savage Society* (Paterson, N.J.: Littlefield, Adams, and Co., 1959), pp. 77–80.

21. Becker, *Outsiders,* pp. 10–12.

22. Quoted in Monrad G. Paulsen and Sanford H. Kadish, *Criminal Law and Its Processes* (Boston: Little, Brown and Company, 1962), p. 340.

23. See Hermann Kantorowicz, *The Definition of Law* (Cambridge, England: Cambridge University Press, 1958) and M. P. Golding, *The Nature of Law* (New York: Random House, Inc., 1966).

24. Rheinstein, *Max Weber on Law,* p. 5.

25. E. Adamson Hoebel, *The Law of Primitive Man* (Cambridge, Mass.: Harvard University Press, 1954), p. 28.

26. Hans Kelsen, *General Theory of Law and State,* trans. Anders Wedberg (Cambridge, Mass.: Harvard University Press, 1945), pp. 45, 61.

27. H. L. A. Hart, *The Concept of Law* (Oxford, England: Clarendon Press, 1961), esp. p. 38.

28. See Philip Selznick, "Sociology and Natural Law," *Natural Law Forum* 6 (1961): 84–108.

29. See for example, Lon L. Fuller, *The Morality of Law* (New Haven, Conn.: Yale University Press, 1964).

30. Jerome Frank, *Law and the Modern Mind* (New York: Tudor Publishing Co., 1935), pp. 127–128.

31. Walter W. Cook, "Scientific Method and the Law," *American Bar Association Journal* 13 (1927): 308.

32. K. N. Llewellyn, *The Bramble Bush* (New York: Oceana Publications, Inc., 1951), p. 12.

33. K. N. Llewellyn, "The Constitution as an Institution," *Columbia Law Review* 34 (1934): 7.

34. "The Path of the Law," *Harvard Law Review* 10 (1897): 461.

35. Kelsen, *op. cit.,* esp. p. 151.

36. For elaboration on the significance of uniformities in judicial decisions, see Morris R. Cohen, *Law and the Social Order* (New York: Harcourt Brace Jovanovich, 1933), esp. p. 242.

37. Rheinstein, *Max Weber on Law,* p. xlvii.

38. For elaboration, see Egon Bittner, "The Police on Skid-Row: A Study of Peace Keeping," *American Sociological Review* 32 (1967): esp. 700.

39. As stated by Lord Halsbury: "A case is only an authority for what it actually decides. I entirely deny that it can be quoted for a proposition that may seem to follow logically from it." Quoted in Benjamin N. Cardozo, *The Nature of the Judicial Process* (New Haven, Conn.: Yale University Press, 1949), p. 32. If Halsbury's assertion is correct, then the study of decisions of judges or, more generally, cases cannot reveal any rules, principles,

uniformities, and the like, which is to say that legal realism would confine "law" to the particular and the unique.

40. See Jack P. Gibbs, "Norms: The Problem of Definition and Classification," *American Journal of Sociology* 70 (1965): 586–594.

41. Thomas J. Scheff, "Toward a Sociological Model of Consensus," *American Sociological Review* 32 (1967): 32–46.

42. Scheff (*ibid.*) insists that consensus (and by implication "norms") should be analyzed in terms of how individuals perceive the normative opinions of other members of the social unit and not in terms of the individual's own normative opinions. The argument pursued here is that rather than exclude "personal normative opinions" (what an individual thinks conduct ought to be or will be) in preference for "perceived normative opinions" (what individuals think other members think about conduct), both should be treated as a distinct normative element.

43. To say that an opinion of a type of act (whether an evaluation or expectation) is "collective" does not mean that it is shared by all members of the social unit. Rather, the term collective signifies that all of the members (or a representative sample thereof) have expressed an opinion concerning that type of act.

44. In the case of negative reactions, the referent is the proportion of instances of a type of act that result in negative reactions (that is, enforcement) *by anyone.*

45. See Stanley Lieberson and Arnold R. Silverman, "The Precipitants and Underlying Conditions of Race Riots," *American Sociological Review* 30 (1965): 887–898.

46. For elaboration on the "reality" of statutes even if unenforced, see Arthur F. Bentley, *The Process of Government* (Chicago: University of Chicago Press, 1908), pp. 282–283.

47. Eugen Ehrlich, *Fundamental Principles of the Sociology of Law,* trans. E. Moll (Cambridge, Mass.: Harvard University Press, 1956).

48. Malinowski, *Crime and Custom in Savage Society.*

49. Fuller, *The Morality of Law.*

50. Reconsider the composite definition of a law and that set forth by Weber and Hoebel. In all three definitions, the designation of the status of a "legal reactor" is very vague.

51. Leopold Pospisil, *Kapauku Papuans and Their Law* (New Haven, Conn. Yale University Publications in Anthropology, No. 54, 1958).

52. R. F. Barton, *Ifugao Law* (Berkeley: University of California Publications in Archaeology and Ethnology, 1919, Vol. 15, No. 1).

53. E. E. Evans-Pritchard, *The Nuer* (Oxford, England: Clarendon Press, 1940).

54. Llewellyn and Hoebel, *The Cheyenne Way.*

55. The other six normative elements: negative reactions to behavior, enforce-

ment (as a special statistical property of negative reactions), coercion, refraction, retaliation, and social characteristics of reactors to deviant behavior.

56. To the extent a type of act is disapproved, commission of it is *proscriptive* deviation; and to the extent it is approved, omission of the act is *prescriptive* deviation. Note, however, that proscriptive and prescriptive deviation are not exhaustive contradictories because members of a social unit may view an act as permissive, meaning that they neither approve nor disapprove it.

Chapter Three

A CRITIQUE OF LABELING THEORY FROM THE PHENOMENOLOGICAL PERSPECTIVE

Carol A. B. Warren and John M. Johnson

Introduction

Since the beginning of the twentieth century, one of the staples of the sociological regime in the United States has been the standard undergraduate course in the sociology of "social problems," affectionately called "Nuts and Sluts" by many of the consumers and by some of the producers. In fact, it could be reasonably argued that courses such as these played important roles in educating the many publics whose support was solicited to transform sociology's claim to a legitimate status within the scientific community into an acknowledged reality. Once the exclusive domain of intellectuals, sociology has expanded its market to the corner drugstore and its jargon has apparently become firmly entrenched as the shibboleth of popular culture.[1] The success of this social movement was achieved only after many decades of political struggles on the part of those involved; furthermore, the many arguments over the scientific status and legitimacy of the field of "social problems" have divided even sociologists themselves. Probably because of the realization that the promise of "scientific" solutions to social problems is tenuous at best (or, as more commonly heard, at least premature), and that the community support for such seemingly "subversive" activity is exceedingly problematic, many sociologists have shunned these efforts to make their discipline "relevant" and "useful." Many others, however, have perceived the field of social problems to hold the key for the promise of the sociological imagination, and have tried to address themselves to "relevant" concerns. Although a concern for image led many of the earlier sociologists to make use of reputable glosses, such as "criminology," "delinquency," "criminalistics," or (more recently) "deviance" to mask their research concerns, many of us have implicitly understood the underlying corpus that provides the major thrust (and popularity, no doubt) of this field as an intellectual enterprise: morality and immorality.

Recently, a small group of scholars increasingly known as "labeling theorists" has been largely responsible for generating much excitement and renewed interest in the sociology of deviance. Although most frequently associated with Howard S. Becker's now famous *Outsiders,* the scholarship of Lemert, Goffman, Scheff, and many others has also been important in establishing the importance of "labeling theory." It is certainly one of the more significant and influential contributions to this field since the appearance of Robert Merton's famous article on social structure and anomie in 1938, and, although it has stimulated a great deal of creative intellectual activity, it has rarely been subjected to critical analysis.[2] This essay (and several others in the volume) represents an initial attempt to institute a critical dialogue between labeling theorists and phenomenological sociologists.

From the phenomenological point of view, the study of deviance is simply the observation of the meanings of morality and immorality as acted out in everyday life. The labeling theorists made several advances from this point of view, over the earlier correctional theorists in the analysis of such meanings. But, at the same time, they created several major types of problems for the ongoing development of the phenomenological sociology of deviance, discussed later under the general headings of problems of fads and foibles, problems of rhetoric, and existential problems.

The advances made by labeling theory over earlier correctional or traditional theory have been cited very frequently by sociologists without much consideration of what deviance theory was advancing to (or in retreat from). From the phenomenological perspective the sociology of deviance is advancing toward a study of the meanings of morality and immorality in everyday life, so that from this perspective, the major advances made by labeling theory are: (1) defining deviance as problematic, (2) recognizing that deviance must be perceived and constructed from someone's point of view, (3) viewing officials' responses to deviance as problematic, (4) stressing description rather than cure as the goal of deviance research, (5) shifting the temporal focus from past to present, (6) allowing for the development of field research methods, (7) acknowledging the importance of the deviant actor's will.

Advances toward Phenomenology

The first three major advances made by the labeling theorists may be conceptually separated, but they are existentially and historically linked. Traditionally, the concept of deviance had not been regarded as problematic, but as predefined or "made ready for the sociologist" by officials of social control such as police and policymakers. As a result of this, the officials' response to deviance was "naturally" not regarded as problematic since it was a "natural" response to a "given" state of affairs; at the same time, the perspective used to define deviance was, "naturally," not at issue. Labeling theory challenged all three elements in correctional theory by *defining deviance as a product of officials' definitions of deviance:*

> *social groups create deviance by making the rules whose infraction constitutes deviance,* and by applying those rules to particular people and labeling them as outsiders. From this point of view, deviance is *not* a quality of the act the person commits, but rather a consequence of the application by others of rules and sanctions to an "offender." The deviant is one to whom that label has successfully been applied: deviant behavior is behavior that people so label [emphasis in the original] . . .[3]

This perspective rendered the concept of deviance problematic rather than "natural," and suggested that deviance must necessarily be perceived from someone's point of view.

A further challenge to the ideas of the traditional school was in the labeling sociologist's definition of his role or tasks. Like traditional sociologists, labeling sociologists accepted the officially defined tasks of locating, diagnosing, and explaining deviance (which will be discussed later), but at the same time they added a significant new goal—to *describe* deviance, and see "what it looked like." Further, the labeling sociologists declined, unlike the correctional sociologists, to propose "cures" for deviance, primarily because of their rhetorical shift in perspective from official "overdogs" to deviant "underdogs."

Because of this new interest in describing deviance, labeling sociologists paved the way for a radical shift in both temporal focus and methodology: from past-oriented hypothetical methods and multivariate analysis to present-oriented field research. To test their etiological theories (and to suggest curative measures based on explanatory research), correctional sociologists sought explanatory variables through the use of multivariate analysis, and the hypothetical method to substantiate previously determined explanatory theory based on previously determined explanatory variables. Participant observation, which was sometimes used instead of or as well as survey methods, tended to introduce "extraneous" difficulties, or "nonfitting" data, into this closed system, as in Thrasher's *The Gang,* which, as a result, is probably the most significant work of the correctional school from the phenomenological perspective.

With the switch from survey to field methods as the "most appropriate," the temporal focus of the labeling theorists shifts from the past (etiological concerns) and future (curative concerns) to the present (descriptive concerns). The stress is on "living with" the deviants, and the phenomenological result is the immersion of the sociologist into the everyday life of his subjects. As Becker states:

> What we are presenting is . . . the reality which engages the people we have studied, the reality they create by their interpretation of their experience and in terms of which they act. If we fail to present this reality, we will not have achieved full sociological understanding of the phenomenon we seek to explain.[4]

By eliminating some of the more deterministic elements of correctional theory, labeling theory came closer to the phenomenological view of man as a real and significant actor on his own social scene, who could have some say in the outcomes of his life. From the correctional perspective, man was a pawn of some aspect of fate—of his biological heredity, the shape of his skull, the amount of fat on his body, his early toilet training, or the area in which he lived—and his deviant act the product not of his being but of factors outside his immediate control. But from the labeling perspective, man was no longer a pawn of fate and of the past, since, as shall be seen, the past was not a major issue for the labeling theorists.

At the same time, the labeling theorists retained the idea of a society that was governed by abstract norms that had the same sort of constraining effect on the "normal" individual as a "pathological environment" had on a deviant one. Thus, whereas the advance toward a conception of man as ruled by his own will was made by the labeling sociologists, the conception of man as partially governed by a series of abstract rules or norms that could usefully be used to make generalizations about deviant action in the real, situational world remained. As a result, the labeling theorists only partially advanced to a phenomenological view of man as an actor.

Problems of Fads and Foibles

The foregoing section on advances made by labeling theory briefly covers some exceedingly significant theoretical ground, but, at the same time, makes far fewer claims than the global or definitive "advances" claimed for labeling theory by many sociologists of deviance. This is because of the sociological "fads and foibles" effect analyzed by Pitirim Sorokin, in which the advances in theory made by each generation or school of sociologists are "buried" under an avalanche of competitive theory developed by the next school:

> the first defect of (sociology) has been a sort of amnesia concerning their previous history, discoveries, and achievements. A second foible is closely related to the first . . . the "discoverer's complex."[5]
>
> (Sociologists) cancel a large part of the knowledge of mental, social, and cultural phenomena accumulated by the experience and study of many generations of observers and thinkers.[6]

In their professional competition for "discovery" and the generation of "new and exciting" theory, sociologists tend to theoretically "throw the baby out with the bath water," or throw *all* aspects of a pre-existing theory into disrepute by "disproving" key aspects and by negative-labeling other aspects of the theory. As this section points out, this is exactly the fate of correctional theory at the hands of the labeling theorists.

These theoretical advances over correctional theory having been made and heralded, labeling sociologists felt free to attack other aspects of such theory without the use of empirical evidence. Nowhere is such a process more in evidence than in the labeling theorists' rejection of the "core values" in American society, which are "taken for granted" by the correctional theorists. Where the correctional theorists assumed that there were core values in American society, labeling theorists assume that there are none—and either assertion is empirically questionable.

Unlike most of the labeling sociologists, however, Lemert does propose an alternative formulation—that there are certain values (or, phenomenologically, key social meanings) that come to be widely shared by most of the members of American society through their socialization experiences, and other, less central values that are more diversely and pluralistically held.[7] This assertion, whereas clearly a matter for extremely detailed empirical research, seems to be more warranted than the more general "no core values" approach of Becker and others. From Warren's research, it appears that certain moral meanings connected with sexuality are so taken for granted by members of society that they constitute, in nonphenomenological language, a set of societal "core values." But, phenomenologically, assertions of taken for granted "core values" and counter assertions of pluralistic values (neither subjected to empirical analysis) tend to obscure the necessity of empirically investigating how "values" are used by, and what their use means to, the members of society in the situated occasions of their use.

Although evidence indicates the use and upholding of "core values" in everyday life by members of society in America, labeling theorists have refused to investigate these matters, or to acknowledge their plausibility, because of the generalized repudiation of all aspects of correctional theory. This process is further apparent in the consideration given by labeling theorists to the question of deviant identity or being, and deviant acts. Since the deviant act, for the labeling theorists, was regarded as a product of others' definitions, the deviant was not regarded, as he was within the correctional perspective, as someone with the special quality of deviance.[8] On the other hand, faced with the fact that some deviants (for example, homosexuals, as shall be seen) do organize their lives around their deviant acts, labeling theory utilized Lemert's distinction between "primary" and "secondary" deviance, which distinguished the origins of deviant behavior from how deviant acts are symbolically attached to persons, and become life-organizing and significant in the generation of subsequent deviant acts.[9] But rather than empirically determining the alleged differences between the "incidence" of rule-violations (primary deviance) and the organization of such activities into stable social roles (secondary deviance), the scholarship within this tradition simply *asserted* that this was indeed the case. Put another way, by stressing the rule-breaking of the "deviants" and the rule-enforcing of "officials" who do the labeling of such actions as the central dialectic of deviance (and the importance of this formulation is great indeed), labeling theory centers its attention on acts to the exclusion of any investigation into the nature of the "being" of the actor. For example, Becker's conception of a deviant career, contains the notion of a progressive identity-transformation, as well as implying that such a transformation is coterminous with a sequence of acts.[10] This focus on acts, however useful it may be with respect to the sociological analysis of everyday definitions of some "deviant" phenomena, for example, marijuana smoking or shop-lifting, has little utility for the substantive investigation of others. For example, Warren's research indicates that among homosexuals, the "deviant" *sex-act* is not the organizing aspect of their lives: the organizing conception is *being* homosexual, in the full sense of a condition, or an identity. Donald Webster Cory (a pseudonym for a psychiatrist-author) expresses this:

> fundamental to all answers is an understanding that the dominant factor in my life, towering in importance above all others, is a consciousness that I am different. In one all-important respect, I am unlike the great mass of people always around me, and the knowledge of this fact is with me at all times, influencing profoundly my every thought, each minute activity, and all my aspirations. It is inescapable, not only this being different, but more than that, this constant awareness of a dissimilarity. . . . An insatiable curiosity grips me as I yearn to know what it would be like not to be a homosexual. . . . But it is all in vain. It is outside the realm of my wildest flights of fancy. I am powerless even to capture a dream image of another world . . . a state of existence in which I would be like others is utterly beyond my conception.[11]

> *I am different.* I am different from all these people, and I must always be different from them. I do not belong to them, nor they to me.[12]

Another homosexual, interviewed during Warren's ongoing research of the gay community, implies his own distinction between "being gay" and "performing homosexual acts" in the following statement:

I: How old are you, John?

S: Forty.

I: Oh?

S: I started kind of late in life (laughing). Not actually started. I started rather late in life as far as leading -er- exclusively (pausing) homosexual (pauses again) -er, not homosexual, but leading the gay life with a particular set of people that I knew where just about everyone was gay.

I: Um-hum.

S: Prior to that time, even though I was a homosexual -I would -my life was strictly based on straight people per se.

In this context, the term "gay" signifies the being or identity aspect of homosexuality, as well as the identity-generating community aspect. "Confirmed" homosexuals, such as Cory and John, perceive themselves as homosexual *beings,* not simply as homosexual *actors.* The labeling perspective, with its unconventionally sentimental rhetoric about rule-breaking and negotiation, is theoretically too misleading, and humanly too bland, to have any direct relevance to the understanding of the social worlds and selves of the homosexual members of society.

This point is further illustrated by the meaning associated with the term "bisexual" by the members of the gay community. In the larger societal context, this word is rather ambiguously taken to mean "one who engages in sexual acts with both males and females." But, within the gay community, the term "bisexual" is used to refer to the state of *being bisexual*—of feeling equally drawn to, or attracted to, the members of both sexes. Thus, the test of being bisexual within the gay community is not the *sexual-act test:* "Would you, or have you ever, had sexual relations with members of both sexes?" Rather, it is perceived in terms of this hypothetical case: "If a man is faced with a beautiful man and a beautiful woman, and cannot decide to which he is most attracted, or which he would have sex with, then he is a bisexual."[13] A *non-act,* or a state of being so profoundly ambiguous that it prevents action, is, for the homosexual, at the core of the bisexual indentity. Similarly, a married homosexual who is sexually active with his wife can say to his male partner, "I am 100 percent homosexual," violating the labeling (and, in this case, societal) act-definition of bisexuality, and at the same time validating the being significance of homosexuality.[14] Again, the labeling perspective of deviance as a product of rule-breaking and rule-enforcing is not a useful distinction within the context of our attempts to understand the gay community or homosexual behavior; the perspective assumes the stance of the omniscient sociologist and ignores the meaning of the deviant status (which is itself problematic) to the subjects themselves.

Regarding the significance of rule-breaking acts for deviance, and the development of deviant identities, then, this analysis appears to suggest the usefulness of the correctional tradition that viewed deviance as a condition of being. Quite correctly, the labeling sociologists rejected the correctional theorists' definition of homosexuality and other deviance as unproblematically "pathological" elements of identity and society, but at the same time they also "threw out" all concern with the deviant being of the deviant and what such a being meant to him, and to those with whom he interacted, in everyday life.

In a similar fashion, labeling theory has focused its attention upon concrete *acts of labeling* (by the rule-enforcers) in the same vein in which it has focused upon *deviant acts* (by the rule-breakers). This is to say, in the works of Becker and Lemert at least, the escalation of the actor from primary to secondary deviance is thought to be brought about through labeling *acts* by the official agents of social control who apprehend, try, and convict these persons through the publicly legitimated and sanctioned ceremonies of degradation. Becker states:

> One of the most crucial steps in the process of building a stable pattern of deviant behavior is likely to be the experience of being caught and publicly labeled as a deviant.[15]

And Lemert:

> Secondary deviation refers to . . . essentially moral problems which revolve around stigmatization, punishments, segregation, and social control. . . . The secondary deviant, as opposed to his actions, is a person whose life and identity are organized around the facts of deviance.[16]

Again, this focus upon the act of public labeling rather than the theoretically and methodologically more difficult idea of "being labeled" (whether public or not), obscures important features for an adequate phenomenological understanding of deviance, at least in the case of the gay community. As Gagnon and Simon point out, relatively few homosexuals are ever prosecuted for homosexual acts, and only an infinitesimal fraction of the homosexual acts committed ever come to a trial, or undergo any other dramatic public ceremony.[17] Most homosexuals live out their lives (certainly all of Warren's research subjects have done so) without their sexual activities ever being made a public issue.

And yet, it is evident that the vast majority of the members of the gay community possess the "attributes" of secondary deviance, a status to which (from the labeling perspective) labeling acts are supposed to have escalated them. Members of the gay community, as has been noted, defined themselves as essentially *being homosexual,* and tend to organize their lives around the fact of possessing this *symbolic* (as opposed to publicly applied) *stigma.* Their deviance is pivotal in terms of how they perceive their "substantial selves."[18] Their social worlds are, to a very great extent, defined by the relevance and revelation of their homosexuality:

> I think so many people in this particular way of life are very well adjusted . . . because of the fact that they have to lead two entirely different social standards, and generally they can adapt themselves to it. You've got to be able to make instant changes. You can be flitting around in one instant, and just absolutely have to stop dead in the next -er- it's like putting on a mask and taking it off, and you have to do it instantaneously.[19]

> Society has handed me a mask to wear, a mask that shall never be lifted except in the presence of those who hide with me behind its protective shadows. Everywhere I go, at all times and before all sections of society, I pretend.[20]

One needs simply to extend Lemert's thesis one step further to explain the escalation of homosexuals from primary to secondary deviation (ignoring for the moment the crucial issues concerning the theoretical validity of these conceptions): homosexuality is *symbolically labeled* deviance. It is suggested that this is primarily so because, even in our immensely pluralistic society, it tends to be the one type of deviance condemned, at least rhetorically, by almost everyone. As a result, homosexuals appear to be largely *symbolically labeled* as deviants in American society; thus, their "escalation" to the status of secondary deviance (with its implications of a homosexual "substantial-self") results *not* from (official) *acts of labeling,* typically at least, but through more informal and amorphous processes of *being-labeled,* or having an identity infused with the cognizance of its public opprobrium. This, in turn, gives some indication of the inadequacies of labeling theory's *implied* pluralism-of-values, and emphasis on "acts," deviant or labeling. "Mundane" events occur throughout the life of the (not-known) homosexual that symbolically label him as a deviant, by denigrating the category of which he is a member. Cory describes one such incident:

> Sometimes I find myself drawn as if into a net by the abuses and sneers of the hostile world, I hear the vile joke or the calumnious remarks, and must sit in silence, or even force a smile, as it were, in approval. A passenger enters an elevator and remarks, "When I come out of a barber shop, I have a feeling I smell like a fag. I better watch out or some goddam queer'll pick me up on the way home." The operator laughs, and I find myself forcing a smile, joining in the humiliating remark, that is, unknowingly, directed against myself.[21]

Through many socialization processes, the mass media, and the typically taken for granted understandings of everyday interaction, homosexuals are symbolically labeled as deviant. There is a widely shared recognition among homosexuals, certainly all of those studied by Warren, that this "state of affairs" causes "troubles" for homosexuals, demanding that he "cope with" them in some manner, although what constitutes the "trouble" for a given individual, how he perceives it, and how he chooses to "cope with" it varies to some extent. The process very rarely consists of a dramatic, official stigmatization through arrest and trial, however, the *potential threat* that this, or other equally "serious" troubles could indeed happen, is not to be underestimated in its symbolic importance. An excellent example of potential "dangerous trouble" is found in Sherri Cavan's discussion of the patronization of gay bars:

> Ego (a homosexual who may put a good deal of effort and energy into maintaining a straight image at work) may, as they say, "let his hair down" in the gay bar, insofar as he anticipates that his behavior will be circumscribed in time and place and will not count outside the bar. Were ego to anticipate otherwise, he might be less likely to undertake the same course of action. Now suppose alter, ego's co-worker, enters the bar, reads the setting for what it is, and furthermore, by virtue of the course of action ego is engaged in, reads ego for what he is. In addition, to provide "reasonable grounds" for alter's subsequent actions, suppose both alter and ego (with his straight identity thus far undoubted) are both likely candidates for a promotion at work. In such a situation it might be naive to expect alter to act upon what might be considered his moral obligation to respect the unserious definition of the bar and hence studiously to ignore the information about ego's identity which he now has.[22]

Another example of the "fads and foibles" effect concerns the question of the etiology of deviant behavior. As we have seen, correctional sociologists were dedicated to the explanation and cure of deviant behavior, and they often sought explanatory variables in the past histories of their deviant subjects. The labeling theorists, however, dismissed all concern with etiology as erroneous, because of the phenomenologically valid question of "filtering the past through the present," or presentations of the past by members that tended to support their present self-images through reinterpretation of biography and "forgetting." David Matza (a sociologist with phenomenological and labeling-theory interests) goes so far as to say:

> The purpose of ridding ourselves of the phenomenon manifests itself most clearly in an overwhelming contemporary concern with questions of causation, or "etiology." The phenomenon itself receives only cursory attention.[23]

From the phenomenological perspective, however, etiology becomes an issue insofar as the members are preoccupied with it, and use it in their every-

day lives. No *prior* assumption of the significance or insignificance of etiological searching can be made. In the case of the homosexual community,
there are few homosexuals who do not regard the etiology of their (and
others') condition as a valid and potentially rewarding locus of research and
study in much the same way that the sociologists of the correctional perspectives viewed it. Furthermore, the recently popular play *The Boys in the Band*
gives some indication that the gay community is one of the major consumers
of etiological research. Many are significantly influenced by the "recent dis-
coveries" in the field, and often reconstruct their biographies in light of them.[24]
In other words, both correctional sociologists and homosexuals regard homosexuality as having a "cause" located somewhere in the past, and both typically
neglect the considerations involving a reinterpretation of the self's biographic.
In this very important sense, "etiological searching" does not always deny the
phenomenological reality of the present, as Matza claims, but it may, in fact,
positively reinforce and legitimate the reality of the present for the actor by
rendering his present "condition" (and/or actions) with "causes" from the
(now) irrevocable past. Speaking to this issue, Cory comments:

> A force that dominates a person's life so much as does the homosexual
> drive compels one to turn inward to answer the question of why he is
> what he is. . . . For a long time the idea of inborn or congenital homosexuality
> was widely accepted both by psychiatrists and social workers on the one
> hand, and by the practicing members of this sexual minority on the other.
> . . . Thus, both homosexuals and heterosexuals developed theories . . . to
> support a conclusion which they sought to reach.[25]

Phenomenologically, then, we have established the need for empirical
investigation of core societal values, the deviant being, symbolic labeling, and
we have indicated the problematic significance of etiological philosophy. A
final "faddish" rejection of valuable aspects of correctional theory by labeling
theorists has occurred over the question of "pathology," a notion rejected out
of hand along with the more significant question of the deviant being as a
whole. As a result of this (sympathetically motivated) rejection, the empirical
question of whether deviants *see themselves* as possessing a "pathological" or
"immoral" condition has been given far less attention than the question of how
officials and "normal" members of society define pathology.

In the case of the gay community, as contrasted with a psychiatrist's
roster of homosexuals seeking "cure," the condition of "being gay" is generally not regarded as being a "pathological" condition. Although, as we have
seen, it is often perceived to have certain "troubles" associated with it, and,
generally speaking, the condition of being gay is not regarded as being "immoral." The following statement, again by John, expresses his sense of these
"troubles," and the typical view that homosexuals are troubled primarily by
the fact that they are rejected (as they perceive it) by the larger society:

I think (homosexuals) are adapting mentally because it can be very much of a mental strain, I think, on a lot of people, because a lot of people have not adj -er- do not adjust themselves to this life -er- mental, because they're still having a feeling, you know, that it's wrong, or (that) they're doing something wrong, and it's hard for them to -to cope with a situation such as this where you're obviously trying to live to your ability, er, comfortable situation in life, and yet you're an extreme minority in a group of people that obviously disapprove of you, which can become a very uncomfortable situation.

Problems of Rhetoric

Problems of rhetoric are in general the opposite of problems of fads and foibles. With problems of rhetoric, certain traditional sociological concepts, methods, statements, perspectives, categories, and the like are *rhetorically* repudiated, but are *empirically* still present within the "new" theory in thinly disguised form. However, the thin disguise is usually not penetrated even by critical sociologists, because of the power and heat of the rhetoric, the *real* theoretical advances made in other aspects of the theory, and the negative-labeling of the remaining concepts and methods, which are still useful.

In labeling theory, there are several significant instances of rhetorical repudiation of aspects of correctional theory, and actual retention of these aspects in disguised (or even undisguised) forms. The most obvious and simplest instance of this is the labeling sociologists' retention of the conventional "deviant" categories used by the correctional sociologists. Despite the rhetoric of locating deviance in the acts of officials, labeling sociologists actually locate it in the traditional "areas," some of which—particularly homosexuality and marijuana smoking—rarely lead to official intervention. Homosexuality, gambling, alcoholism, crime, prostitution, marijuana smoking, suicide—all of these conventional categories have generally been retained (as practicalities?) by the labeling theorist, at the same time as they have been rhetorically repudiated.

Similarly, while repudiating the correctional sociologists' reliance upon officials to predefine the research situation for them in various ways, the labeling theorists have implicitly taken on the traditional functions of locating and diagnosing deviance in society. To a lesser extent, labeling sociologists have also retained the older function of explaining deviance (to the public and to officialdom), although, as we have seen, the function of describing deviance has assumed more prominence than that of explaining it.

Not only have labeling theorists allowed officials to predefine their functions to some extent, they have also taken the perspective of officials on deviance. Rhetorically, the labeling sociologists have claimed the perspective of the deviant or underdog, and have firmly repudiated that of the officials. But *by locating and diagnosing deviance, and by locating deviance in "traditional" areas, labeling sociologists take the perspective of officials.* They further take the perspective of officials by defining deviance as what *officials perceive as deviance* rather than what *various* groups in the society perceive as deviance. Overall, and while ferociously castigating correctional theorists for this very process, labeling theorists, by using the category "deviance" as it has traditionally been used, still align themselves with the absolutist moral meanings of officialdom. To illustrate this, we cite some examples from Warren's research in the gay community.

Among the members of the gay community, there are several typifications of behaviors, and several typifications of "being," which *they* define, either verbally or interactionally, as deviant. For example:

> **Jerome:** I think it's too bad that, that so much of the world judges all gay people and all gay kids, both girls and guys, by a few of the social deviants that, you know, throw a bad light on all of us . . . certain people . . . get carried away with the idea of drag, and they become transvestites, but talking about these people is quite foreign to me because I neither socialize with or know people like this. They're completely in another dimension, you might say, from us.
>
> Well, basically I think you can categorize gay kids the same as you can any other social environment, religion for instance. Because you have, ah, low trashy people that I feel consist of the cruisers, you know, on the streets, um, possible deviants that do prey on younger children, and then you have business people that are really trying to make something out of their life.

In this example, Jerome is expressing a definition of deviance that is commonly expressed among the members of his community, giving an indication that the members of the gay community categorize their social worlds by using the same respectable-deviant labels that are used by the "straight" world to categorize *them,* and that the label used by the omniscient sociologist to categorize these "normal" homosexuals is, in turn, applied by these "normal" homosexuals to those whom *they* consider deviant. But these typifications of deviance (such as transvestism, also defined as deviance from the "official perspective") are not the only typifications of deviance recognized within the gay community. There are other typifications of deviance that would (probably) not be shared by those who were members of nonhomosexual groups in the society. For example, within the gay community, typifications of deviance include people who do not drink at parties, homosexuals wishing to be "cured" by psychiatrists (or other paramedical "experts"), and those wishing to marry in order to construct a front of respectability to present to the larger society. Probably all of these "deviant" typifications would not be socially defined as deviant by many other groups in the society. Labeling theorists recognize rhetorically that deviance is a relative concept that is defined differently by different groups, but they take no account of this in their everyday lives as practical sociologists.

Finally, there is a rhetoric of methodology within labeling theory that is tied to the foregoing rhetoric of theory. According to labeling theory, and also according to phenomenology, phenomena must be described and analyzed through the use of field research methods. But, as has been seen, labeling theory, like traditional sociologies of deviance, allows for the annihilation of members' interpretations of society by the omniscient sociologist who claims to "know" that a given act constitutes (or can be interpreted as an instance of) deviance, independent of actor-perceptions, because it has been labeled as such by officials.

The correctional and labeling perspectives deny the reality of members' social worlds in different but related ways. Specifically, whereas correctional sociologists reinterpreted their subjects' experiences in terms of their *ad hoc* theories of disease or pathology, labeling theorists reinterpret them in terms of their own "official" or professionally sanctioned conceptions and sentiments, albeit the fact that it is typically an "unconventional sentimentality" within the discipline of sociology.[26] This is essentially where a phenomenological perspective differs from the correctional and labeling perspectives. The fundamental datum for a phenomenological approach is the everyday social reality of the individual social actor and his interpretations of that reality in order to address the pre-eminent theoretical problem of understanding how social order is possible. Whereas labeling theory also appears to take this datum as fundamental, and some of its major proponents even explicitly promote the taking of this stance, its presuppositions regarding "labeled deviance" indicate that, in fact, *it takes itself as a datum*. With such a theoretical backing, participant observer methods, although presented rhetorically as necessary, are not phenomenologically necessary, since "all relevant" aspects of the phenomena have been predefined and predetermined.

Existential Problems

Although problems of fads and foibles and problems of rhetoric tend to be easily defined and readily observable, existential problems are more complex and elusive. Essentially, existential questions are those that concern the fundamental nature of sociological research—the basic arguments that have been carried on about the sociological (or literary, or philosophical) experience throughout the development of sociological consciousness. As such, the existential problems in labeling theory as perceived from the phenomenological perspective are more significant and yet more questionable than the other kinds of problems.

The existential problems in labeling theory that are here considered concern two major questions: that of perspective and that of abstraction and situation. The question of perspective has already been touched upon in connection with the rhetoric of perspective but must be further developed in the context of existential theory. It has already been noted that labeling theory does not actually take the perspective of the deviant actor, although it does so rhetorically; we must now consider the existential question of whether or not the sociologist *can* take the perspective of the deviant actor in any sense other than the most general one of "empathy." With the possible exception of those who completely "surrender" to the perspectives of their subjects, to use Wolff's terminology, and hence "go native" (at which point they are lost for the purposes of sociological analysis), the researcher is always an observer. As Schutz has so clearly seen:

> A social scientist . . . must . . . put somebody else instead of himself as the center of this world, namely, the observed person. . . . The first and most fundamental consequence . . . is that the scientist replaces the human beings he observes as actors on the social stage by puppets created by himself and manipulated by himself. What I call "puppets" corresponds to the technical term "ideal types" which Weber has introduced into social science. . . . The puppet called "personal ideal type" . . . strictly speaking . . . has no world at all. His destiny is regulated and determined beforehand by his creator, the social scientist. . . . The scientist distributes his own store of experience . . . among the puppets with which he peoples the social world . . . this social world, too . . . is not centered in the ideal type . . . what counts is the point of view from which the *scientist* envisages the social world.[27]

> There is no warranty that the world as taken for granted subjectively by the actor is in the same way beyond question for the observer. The actor may suppose that what he takes for granted is beyond question also "for everyone belonging to us," but whether this assumption holds good for the particular fellow-man depends upon whether a genuine we-relation has been pre-established between both. Yet, even if this is the case, the biographically determined situation and therewith the selection of the relevant elements among the open possibilities of the actor and the observer must necessarily be different. In addition, the observer does not participate in immediacy in the process of the actor's choice and decision even if some of its phases were communicated to him. *He has to reconstruct from the accomplished overt behavior,* from the act, the underlying in-order-to or because of motives of the actor. Nevertheless, to a certain extent at least, man is capable of understanding his fellow-man. How is this possible? [Emphasis added.][28]

In this existential sense, then, labeling theory's claim to the perspective of the observer is an erroneous one.

In a practical sense, too, it is impossible to exhaust all of those biographical situations that have led a given actor to interpret the social world in the way he does, or takes it for granted in the way he does, but this is an objection only to those who still cling to the hope in the possibility of situation-free knowledge, or Absolute Truth. The phenomenological perspective in the study of deviance approaches this research problem by interacting imaginatively with subjects to reconstruct their experiences, by doing what they do, by listening to what they say, and by attempting to grasp the "essence" of such activity—that is to say, what it means to the members of the group. For phenomenological sociologists, the crucial research problems are not those of "taking the side of" the presumably all-powerful officials, on the one hand, or the underdogs, who are "more sinned against than sinning" on the other: the problems are those of doing imaginative and creative sociology. The phenomenological stance in sociology is that of the *open* observer Here attempting the understanding of the ongoing There of the actors, and how such activity is methodically produced and accounted for by them.[29]

The foregoing sections indicate a further practical and theoretical difficulty with labeling theory as summarized by Becker:

> It is, of course, possible to see the situation from both sides. But it cannot be done simultaneously. That is, we cannot construct a description of a situation or process that in some way fuses the perceptions and interpretations made by both parties involved in a process of deviance. We cannot describe a "higher reality" that makes sense of both views.[30]

But we have seen, in our discussion of labeling theory, that the theory itself is *constructed* on the basis of just this sort of simultaneity—deviance is perceived in a manner that partakes of sympathy for the underdog, of official theories of deviance, and of common-sense everyday uses of the labeling process in everyday life. A theory practically concocted from "both sides" of the question of deviance, and the middle besides, cannot, practically, be used to describe a situation from one side.

Theoretically, also, there is little basis for Becker's comment. It would appear to be true that rule-breakers and enforcers cannot be observed and analyzed simultaneously if, in fact, the observer "took" the perspective of one of the "parties" in the struggle. But this cannot be achieved, as we have seen; the observer is always Here, within himself, his biography, his space and time, while the "parties" are both There—only their *interactions* open to the observer, and his memories of past interactions. So the sociologist is quintessentially an observer, constructing his theory from open observation, and creating not a "higher reality" (a loaded word) but a different, sociological reality that phenomenologically attempts the absolutely impossible, but relatively possible, task of simultaneously understanding the existential interactions between members of society.

One set of existential problems of labeling theory concerns different aspects of perspective; another equally major problem is the abstracting of "deviance" from the context of use in specific situations, coupled with a lack of investigation into how typifications of deviance are used by, and what their use means to, social actors on the actual occasions of their use. For example, data gathered during John M. Johnson's ongoing field research on social welfare indicate the existence of some (possible) number of persons who have been publicly stigmatized through official ceremonies dramatizing their deviance, but who have been "labeled" in the first instance not by officials but by *egos in interaction situations using "labeling rules of thumb" to punish or torment alters.* Thus egos are "escalated to secondary deviance" by a route more problematic than allowed for in abstract labeling theory.

As a concrete instance, excerpts are given of a conversation with a supervisor of social workers in a "Dependency Unit" involving welfare cases where, for any number of reasons, one or more children have been taken out of the home of their parents and defined as "dependents-of-the-court," typically followed by their "suitable placement" in a foster home:

I: What about the cases that involve child-molestation? Are they the same as those? (Referring to the immediately preceding comments about child-battering cases.)

S: Oh no. Absolutely not. The child-molestation cases are completely different than the child-battering, or child-abuse, cases. People quite often make the mistake of lumping the two of them together—I really don't know why—but they are two really different things. For one thing, we get many more child-battering cases than child-molestation cases. They're more rare. I don't know, I'd say (pause), I'd say we only have maybe a half-dozen cases involving child-molestation at any one time, maybe as high as ten or so, but not many more . . . Over the years I've come to see that, oh I'd say in about half of these cases, there isn't really any molestation which has actually taken place. They . . .

I: Really? What do you mean?

S: Well, when you've been through a number of cases involving child-molestation, when you have investigated them thoroughly, and heard all of the different stories supposedly describing what really happened, or had been happening between the various people in the family, then it's obvious that some of them, always the wives, from my experience at least, are just making claims that the father molested little Judy—because they know that that's supposed to be one of the most terrible things in our society—they do it to get back at him for something else he did. Maybe the husband has been drinking and comes home and slaps her around—believe me, some of these people can really be mean. So the next day Mamma calls up the police, or maybe the welfare department, and says that her husband has been playing around with little Judy. She wants to get back at him, and this is the only way she knows how to do it.

I: What are some of the, what are some of the things that happen in these homes that leads to this? Is heavy drinking always involved?

S: Well, it usually is, but, well, it usually is in many of the cases in our files. Many cases not involving any child-molestation at all. No, that's not it— I've seen a couple of cases where I thought that it might have been a drinking bout that brought it about, but that's usually only one of the

problems in these homes. It's really hard to say. I'd say (long pause)—
you really can't say it's any one thing in these cases. It depends on the
cases really, on the total family situation. . . . The last case we had like
this was, oh, I think it was a couple of months ago, the Hamilton case.
Now that was a case! They were really what they call a "multi-problem
family." Everything was a mess! . . . Well, we learned that Daddy liked
to go in the living room after supper to watch TV. He liked to lie on the
floor with little Suzy who I think, oh let me see, who was about six or
seven I think. He was just crazy about her and liked to lie there on the
floor with his arms around her while watching TV. Nothing sexual at all,
although I think that he probably patted her a little. . . . This had been
going on for several years the best we could guess. . . . The mother never
said anything to him about it, although she did tell us that it worried her
from time to time. . . . She said he was really kind and gentle around the
kids, although he had beaten her and several of the kids when he had
been drunk a couple of times. . . . Wasn't ever any serious injury to any
of them, at least not from what the Mother told us, don't know really.
. . . Well, one day Mrs. Hamilton found out, and it was when they were
fighting a lot, she found out that Daddy had been seeing another woman
on-the-sly. Not only that, the woman lived about a half a block away
from them. Well, that was just too much for her to take. . . . So she
called up the police and told them that her husband had been playing
around with her daughter. . . . That's the only way some of these women
think they can fight back, it's the only way they think they can win. It's
hard to believe, but some of these people, even husbands and wives,
can't even talk to each other half the time. And the women are usually
(pause) . .

I: What happened to Mr. Hamilton in that case?

S: The police came and arrested him and took him to jail, but he got out
on bail the same day. Most of the things under 600 and 601 (referring
to the sections of the Welfare and Institutions Code that specify the conditions under which a child may be taken from the home and made a
ward of the court—JMJ) have corresponding sections in the penal code
for charging the parents, but they never stick. It's almost impossible to
prove any of these cases, because of the evidence required—it's usually
only the mother who knows enough, and by the time of the trial she
usually doesn't want to testify even if she could. More often than not
the mothers have a change-of-heart when they see their husband hauled
off to jail. . . . They finally dropped the charges against the Hamilton
father. . . . But the case was referred to Child Protective Services . . .
and they were the ones who filed the Dependency Petition. And that's
how we happened to get it. . . .

I: What do you do in cases like these? I mean, when a case comes to you
that's supposed to be a child-molestation problem, and you find out that
there hasn't been any molesting in the family, what do you do with
them? Do you recommend that the child be returned, or what?

S: Well (brief laugh), incidents like this, like in the Hamilton case, just don't happen in normal families. Most of them involve the whole range of problems, really messed-up homes generally. In some of them, child-molestation would be one of the lesser concerns. The child-molesting incident generally only represents more serious problems that are underlying it. . . . It's really only the symptom of what's wrong with the home. In those few cases we get where we find out that the mother is trying to fight back at the father, and that's why she reported him, well, believe me, we've usually got our hands full with a case like that. . . . In these cases we've usually, we're usually faced with more problems than we can effectively deal with anyway. . . . Sometimes all they need is a mediator, a go-between, so that they can start talking to each other, so that they can begin functioning as a family again. But that's really rare. I've only seen one file like that in all the time I've been at DPSS. Usually these cases have so many problems, and they've been messing up their lives for such a long time, that we've really got our hands full. . . .

This example, and others from Johnson's field research, suggest the possibility of a relatively large group of persons who have been publicly labeled (or stigmatized) as "child molesters" without having previously broken the (child molestation) rules at some previous point in time. That is, these persons are typically escalated to the status of "secondary deviant" (in California, persons convicted of child molestation must register as a "known sex offender" in each community they enter) without having broken these rules in the first place (primary deviance) (a *necessary* condition in accord with the theoretical assumptions of labeling theory). In *Outsiders,* Becker admits of this possibility, but classifies such cases as "the falsely accused." Although the example cited does not deny the viability of labeling theory in this case (perhaps if "seeing another woman-on-the-sly" is seen as the deviance that is being labeled here), or the usefulness of a "falsely accused" category (with Mrs. Hamilton's accusation against her husband perhaps being a false one), it certainly does raise some doubts regarding the usefulness of the official labels for the purposes of sociological theory. Stated another way, these examples suggest that the issue of "who is doing what to whom" is much more problematic than labeling theory would lead us to suspect. The brief example cited here should suffice to suggest that the capacity to label is not one that is the sole and exclusive domain of the official agents of social control, although it is true that they "do it for a living." This does not imply, however, that all persons (or groups) are equally powerful to ensure the success of their efforts, that their labels will "stick."

A second situational challenge to the concept of unilaterally powerful officials occurs in cases where those to be labeled as deviant actively *conspire to negotiate deviant labels for themselves in concert with officials.* As presently and abstractly formulated, labeling theory presumes adequate knowledge of the nature and uses of power, and ignores such situational negotiations of power as might be implied within the negotiation of labels. The omnipotent officials are the powerful, possessing a capacity to use this power unproblematically. The deviants, "those who are more sinned against than sinning," are the powerless. For them, a successfully applied label is a "happening," not an act, something that is seen as being *done to* them independently of their will.[31] A recent sociological work, Jack Douglas' *American Social Order,* develops this idea in great detail.[32] Examples from Johnson's research, however, indicate that such presumptions regarding the nature and uses of power may obscure important features in the study of deviance.

Beginning in 1936, to qualify themselves for the matching grants from the federal government, nearly all states constructed statutes specifying "Aid to the Totally Disabled" (ATD) as one of the official categories of welfare. Between 1936 and 1965 (in California), the eligibility test for ATD was "unemployability." According to one of Johnson's veteran informants: ". . . (this meant) that the people couldn't care for themselves, couldn't even get out of bed in most cases, (and) most of them had to have caretakers before they could become eligible for ATD." In 1965, however, the eligibility requirements for ATD were broadened in California to include a variety of categories relating to mental and emotional "problems" not previously covered under the provisions of the Welfare Code. Even though the criterion remained "unemployability" for ATD eligibility, this categorical aid since 1965 has been *routinely* used by social workers to get financial assistance for those who did not qualify under the provisions of the other categorical aids administered by the Welfare Departments (such as AFDC, or Aid to Families with Dependent Children, AFDC-U, where there is an unemployed father in the family, AB, or Aid to the Blind, MN, or the Medically Needy). To cite an example from Johnson's research, in numerous cases of welfare recipients who have been receiving AFDC monies for many years in order to support the children in these fatherless families, the eligibility for AFDC expires when the children are grown and leave the home. When this occurs, the mothers of such families, typically uneducated and unskilled, are left without any financial support. As a *routine practice* social workers in such cases get together with these clients and devise a strategy whereby the mother may become eligible for another one of the categorical aids, usually ATD. This strategy typically involves instruction of the welfare client (not necessary in some cases of course) in how to present the "symptoms" of "emotional disability" to the psychiatrist at the county psychiatric clinic who certifies such matters for official purposes. Such cases as these involve what could be called a kind of conspiracy between the social worker and the welfare client for the purpose of negotiating a deviant label for the client to receive ATD eligibility.

Sociologist John P. Anderson, who is presently engaged in field research of a psychiatric screening facility in California, comments on such cases:

(The psychiatrists of the screening unit) usually know whether the persons are coming to (the clinic) for ATD eligibility or not. They understand what is involved in these (ATD applicants) cases, and which categories will certify one as unemployable and which will not. The categories have changed over the last couple of years, as the legislators try to tighten up on the residual nature of the "emotional disability" category I suppose, but the psychiatrists all know which categories are working at the time and which are not. . . .

These examples regarding ATD eligibility indicate the existential problem in labeling theory concerning the dialectic of abstraction and situationism. By retaining a commitment to the official categories of deviance, the practitioners of the labeling perspective typically obscure *the context within which these labels are used* by members involved in negotiations of deviant labels. Because these negotiations are often as much a product of those who receive such labels as those who initiate them, it makes little sense, at least for the purposes of sociological theorizing, to contend that such matters are ever "structurally determined" by a given officialdom.

Summary and Conclusions

We have seen that although labeling theory has made several major contributions to the development of a phenomenological sociology of deviance, it has at the same time been treated uncritically with respect to fundamental problems of fads and foibles, rhetoric, and existential grounding. None of these problems should be underestimated in its effect both on deviance theory and on theoretical sociology in general. The problem of fads and foibles is pervasive throughout all of sociology, as Sorokin and Friedman have pointed out, although from opposite value stances. In the particular case of labeling theory, labeling sociologists have paid inadequate attention to the question of "core values" or key moral meanings in American society, and to the empirical relationship between deviant identities, deviant acts, acts of labeling, and symbolic labeling. Furthermore, they have neglected to consider the way "deviant" groups use etiological conceptions in their everyday lives.

The problem of rhetoric is equally pervasive, possibly because it is involved in a dialectical relationship with problems of fads and foibles. It obviously is impossible to create entirely new sociological paradigms out of whole cloth, so that when an entire "traditional" theory is rejected wholesale, certain elements of it must necessarily be retained, despite rhetoric to the contrary. In the case of labeling theory, what has been actually retained while rhetorically repudiated includes the retention of traditional categories of deviance, the use of sociologists to locate and diagnose deviance in society, and, more generally, the taking of an official perspective on deviance. Furthermore, although the labeling theorists adopt the rhetoric of participant observation and understanding the subjects' worlds, they actually use their own theory as the starting point for the analysis of what deviance is, rather than empirically investigating the construction of deviance, or morality and immorality, in everyday interaction.

The existential problems with labeling theory are the most complex, and the most significant, from the phenomenological perspective, since they represent aspects of the epistemological foundations of deviance theory and of sociological knowledge itself. First of all, as has been seen, the labeling theorists' contention that the researcher should and can take the perspective of the subjects is erroneous, since the sociologist is always a sociological observer, creating a world of sociological observations rather than reproducing as a mirror image the worlds of his subjects. At the same time, we have seen that the labeling sociologist's rejection of the attempt to comprehend more than one side of any transaction resulting in a label of deviance—which is, in fact, a rejection of the attempt to understand the process of the transaction itself—is based existentially upon a phenomenological misunderstanding of the sociologist's task and perspective.

But perhaps the most fundamental existential problem with labeling theory is its abstracting of reality from the context of uses and situations, and its neglect of empirical investigation into how typifications of deviance are used by, and what their use means to, social actors on the actual occasions of their use. It is to be emphasized again that the intellectual formulations of the labeling theorists have aided our understandings in illuminating one of the practical methods (labeling) that we use to create and objectivate our social worlds, and our personal realities, but that this has not been the major focus of the theorists themselves, who have lapsed back into the "omniscient" stance of earlier sociologists.

For the sociological analysis of deviance, these comments prescribe the grounding of sociological theories in the everyday phenomenological perceptions of the members of society (of which we are necessarily a part), and call for a description of the methodologies systematically employed by social actors in their attempts to construct, define, and use conceptions of morality and immorality in the situations of everyday life. As Gouldner's critique of American sociology so persuasively indicates,[33] sociology has for far too long been in the business of constructing its *own* conceptions of social reality, rather than researching its preeminent question: how is society possible?

Notes

1. Compare Alvin W. Gouldner, *The Coming Crisis of Western Sociology* (New York: Basic Books, Inc., 1970).

2. See in this volume.

3. Howard S. Becker, *Outsiders* (New York: The Free Press, 1963), p. 9.

4. *Ibid.,* p. 18.

5. Pitirim A. Sorokin, *Fads and Foibles in Modern Sociology and Related Sciences* (Chicago: Henry Regnery Co., 1956), p. 3.

6. *Ibid.,* p. 20.

7. Edwin M. Lemert, *Human Deviance, Social Problems, and Social Control* (Englewood Cliffs, N.J.: Prentice-Hall, Inc., 1967), p. 17.

8. Compare Becker, *Outsiders,* and Lemert, *Human Deviance.*

9. Lemert, *Human Deviance.*

10. Compare Becker, "Becoming a Marijuana User," in *Outsiders.*

11. Donald Webster Cory, *The Homosexual in America* (New York: Greenberg, 1951), p. 7.

12. *Ibid.,* p. 9.

13. This example is summarized from field research notes taken by Warren on several different occasions. It is used frequently by members of the gay community to explicate their conceptions of bisexuality.

14. From Warren's field notes.

15. Becker, *Outsiders,* p. 31.

16. Lemert, *Human Deviance,* p. 7.

17. John H. Gagnon and William Simon, "Homosexuality: The Formation of a Sociological Perspective," pp. 349–361 in Mark Lefton, et al., eds., *Approaches to Deviance* (New York: Appleton-Century-Crofts, 1968), pp. 353–354.

18. For a discussion of the concepts "substantial self" and "situated self," see, Jack D. Douglas, *The Social Meanings of Suicide* (Princeton: Princeton University Press, 1967), pp. 280–283.

19. This and subsequent unfootnoted quotes are taken from taped interviews with homosexuals obtained during Warren's field research of the gay community.

20. Cory, *The Homosexual in America,* p. 11.

21. *Ibid.*

22. Sherri Cavan, *Liquor License* (Chicago: Aldine Publishing Company, 1966), pp. 240–241.

23. David Matza, *Becoming Deviant* (Englewood Cliffs, N.J.: Prentice-Hall, Inc., 1969), p. 17.

24. For a discussion of the phenomenon of reconstructing one's biography, see: Peter L. Berger, *Invitation to Sociology* (New York: Doubleday Company, Inc., 1963).

25. Cory, *The Homosexual in America.*

26. For the original development of this thesis, see: Alvin W. Gouldner, "The Sociologist as Partisan: Sociology and the Welfare State," *American Sociologist* 3 (1968): 103–116.

27. Alfred Schutz, *Collected Papers,* Vol. II (The Hague: Martinus Nijhoff, 1962), pp. 81–83.

28. *Ibid.,* Vol. I, p. 95.

29. For a discussion of the phenomenological conceptions of "Here" and "There," see Schutz, *Collected Papers,* Vol. I.

30. Becker, *Outsiders,* pp. 173ff.

31. Compare R. S. Peters, *The Concept of Motivation* (London: Routledge and Kegan Paul, 1958) for the original development of this distinction. A subsequent development of the same notion may be found in Thomas S. Szasz, *The Myth of Mental Illness* (New York: Dell Publishing Company, Inc., 1961).

32. Jack D. Douglas, *American Social Order* (New York: The Free Press, 1971).

33. Compare Gouldner, *The Coming Crisis of Western Sociology.*

Chapter Four

DISEASE, ILLNESS, AND DEVIANT CAREERS

Horacio Fabrega, Jr. and Peter K. Manning

Introduction

Sociologists of the symbolic interactionist persuasion have assembled a very sound case for the importance of the labeling process in the study of "deviant" behavior. They have argued that deviance is widespread; relative as to time, place, and audience; and also that it is diverse as to form, process, and consequence. They assume initially that what is "made of the deviance"—how it is detected, recognized, defined, and managed—should be the central concern of sociology. This argument is having an important influence in the social sciences generally, in medicine, especially psychiatry, and in related mental health professions.

A number of significant critiques of labeling theory have already appeared and others are scheduled for publication in the near future (Petroni, 1969; Gibbs, 1966; Schur, 1969; Fletcher, et al., forthcoming). These reviews are focused on several issues: the vagueness of the definition of the term "deviance," the looseness of the career concept; the paucity of operational measures and research hypotheses; equivocation about the "location" or substance of deviance (that is, is it merely "fictive," a construction of those who respond, or is it based upon a "real" state of being or action of the "deviant?") and the tendency of labeling theorists to focus upon bizarre or exotic behavior of groups rather than cases chosen solely for their potential value for clarifying sociological questions.

The labeling theory has been most effectively explicated and empirically researched in the study of mental illness (Scheff, 1966; Goffman, 1961; Lemert, 1967). The success of this critical assault on previous psychiatric theory led to attempts at a synthesis of the labeling and the more "traditional" social psychiatric approach (Pasamanick, et al., 1967; Angrist, et al., 1968). The latter approach views psychiatric disability as analogous to the medical problems that are the formal preoccupations of physicians. For example, one of the arguments of Pasamanick, et al.'s studies is that there exists a real, palpable phenomenon called mental illness, that it has organic roots, and that it can most effectively be treated by substances having clearly specified pharmacological properties, the so-called tranquilizing drugs. This research, as well as the implicit assumptions that underlie the early sociological work in psychiatry, raises an issue that has not been explicitly confronted even in the medical sociological work that relies on the labeling perspective. Briefly, the issue to which we refer, and that which is discussed in this chapter, can be stated as follows: What is the role or influence of processes or events that have been termed "biological" in those failures in human adaptation that we term illness? In other words, how do "biological" considerations or phenomena help us to explain the careers of individuals who are labeled as "sick"? In a sense, we are seeking to analyze the features of illness and disease that account for or at least make understandable the unusual social and interactional features of those individuals who are labeled sick.

The nature of the symbolic properties of medical careers that are the concern of sociologists of the labeling interactionist persuasion are believed to be a product of some important interplay between categories of phenomena termed biological as opposed to sociopsychological. Indeed, much of the preoccupation in the sociological literature that is focused on mental illness can be explained from this standpoint. This chapter probes these two systems of meaning and relates them to central issues in phenomenological sociology. The responses that are offered by those around the sick person as well as those he himself engenders and acts upon have an important relationship to that which has been termed the biological domain. The nature of this relationship, however, has not been examined with sufficient clarity nor have the assumptions about the use of this domain been made explicit. In particular, we believe that the category "illness" needs to be viewed as comprising types of social transactions that are (in ways that require explication) related to the sick person and his audience's interpretation and use of knowledge or language about the body. Our goal is to examine the uses and the implications of this type of language in order to explain sociologically that type of deviance that is the concern of the medical profession.

In order to examine this problem with some precision it is necessary to discuss relevant concepts and to present a framework or conceptual model of health and illness. This model or framework is used as a focus for the discussion of relevant theoretical issues. The chapter, in brief, proceeds as follows:

(1) some key concepts as well as the logical structure of labeling theory as it relates to medical concerns are reviewed, (2) previous work and positions in this general area are examined, (3) a general model of health and illness is presented, (4) characteristics of given *types of illness careers* are analyzed, (5) unique sociopsychological and interactional features of mental illness are described, with particular emphasis given to the self concept of the patient and, lastly, (6) some explanation is offered for the relatively unique position occupied by mental illness.

Concepts

Several different but related emphases in the scientific communities deal conceptually with health and disease. All are strongly influenced by the behavioral sciences. Engel (1960) stressed the need for a unified view of disease and has lucidly described the arbitrariness and pernicious consequences of traditional definitions. In his view health and disease, rather than representing discrete states or conditions, are described as phases of the continuously changing multilevel set of processes (for example, cellular, chemical, behavioral) that at any one moment constitute human striving. Feinstein (1967), on the other hand, prefers to conceptualize disease in purely morphologic, physiologic, and chemical terms. What the physician directly observes in his dialogue with the patient that he terms the *illness* consists of subjective sensations (symptoms) and certain findings (signs). The illness is described as the result of the interaction of the disease with the host or person, emphasis being given to the mechanism by which the disease develops and "produces" or is associated with the illness. An implication of Feinstein's conceptualization is that physicians treating a patient are engaged in two related levels of transactions, one dealing with the disease (controlling or eliminating it), and the other with the illness (alleviating its distress). Mechanic (1962) introduced the concept of illness behavior to help explain the diverse ways in which persons behave when they perceive in themselves a condition of health impairment. This behavior is seen as being influenced not only by the meanings and response tendencies that have been learned vis-à-vis intraorganismic sensations but also by the socioculturally determined interpretations that are placed on concepts such as health, disease, and medical care. Substantively, it is clear that these three viewpoints are not mutually exclusive, but have a great deal in common. All are alike in that the cause of the disease or of the illness is seen as multifactorial, with both genetic and environmental factors playing important roles. In these viewpoints the empirically derived and experimentally tested knowledge that is acquired by the various scientific disciplines is used to generate mechanisms that explain the correlates of impaired well-being, these mechanisms being structured in terms of necessary and sufficient conditions.

The value of employing the concept of illness, as distinct from that of disease, can be graphically illustrated by focusing on medical phenomena as it is structured in preliterate settings. It has been amply demonstrated that in these settings illness is interpreted using primarily supernatural and moral symbols (Lieban, 1960; Kiev, ed., 1964; Schwartz, 1969). Impaired well-being is seen as a condition that is brought about (directly caused by) an imbalance or lack of harmony in the person's psychosocial and moral state. A person's relationship to the ancestral gods and to his fellow man, in other words, is critical. Medical treatment in such communities involves a restoration of the sick person's sociointerpersonal and spiritual harmony. The development of a patient's symptoms is conceptualized in terms such as wrongdoing, punishment, envy, and the like. Notions of cause, disease, and illness, which, in the scientific system are logically separated, are fused and condensed. A patient's symptoms or signs such as pain and swelling of the extremities, for example, constitute his disease-illness, and they are both seen as the objectification of spiritual or malevolent agencies. This is quite often a sufficient explanation, and if probed, subjects may state that the disease-illness traveled and entered in the way that smoke or wind spreads and diffuses in and around an object. The notion that the body's functioning has been disturbed might be accepted, but this disturbance is not rationalized in physiological, chemical, or morphological terms; instead, concepts analogous to force, damage, injury, evil, and the like are employed. Health and illness are often defined and acted upon as time-bound, sharply demarcated, and mutually exclusive conditions (that is, one is either sick or one is not sick). This conception is isomorphic with the one that appears to be held about treatment, which is to say that sick persons and their families always seem to be in search of the right curer or the right herb that will remove their illness. The search rests on the assumption that illness simply enters or descends on a person and must be removed for a cure to take place.

In preliterate settings, the notion of a chronic illness that can improve or is subject to remissions and exacerbations does not appear to exist (Frake, 1961; Fabrega, 1970). During a remission one is well and not sick. Subsequent symptoms are viewed as manifestations of a new illness or of the same illness that had been improperly cured. A good cure, in other words, is one that eliminates symptoms permanently (makes one well). The recrudescence of symptoms that are taken to reflect the same illness imply an ineffective treatment and consequently a weak and poor healer. In urban settings, of course, individuals often learn to accept the concept of a long-lasting disease that cannot "be cured" and that requires long term "management." Their subsequent behavior is shaped by the acceptance of this concept.

Medical treatment in preliterate settings follows the dictates of the symbolic traditions (that is, common-sense knowledge) that are used to interpret the illness episode. In certain ways it can be said that diseases do not "exist" in preliterate settings. What do exist, instead, are signs, symptoms, and disabilities that are interpreted and acted upon in terms of the concepts and beliefs of the group. The result is a culturally patterned entity to which are attached unique implications, action imperatives, and behavioral expectations. Treatment may, thus, entail propitiating the gods or counteracting malevolent forces by means of culturally prescribed rules. Native practitioners are consulted and their judgments regarding the type of ceremony that is required may result in the formation of alliances and/or rivalries that can have important consequences for members of the family of the "patient" or for suspected out-group competitors. The point that we wish to emphasize is how varied and unique is the nature of sickness and the behavioral transactions that are a response to it. Whereas we term the units that the scientific medical system categorizes (that is, diagnoses, interprets, treats) as "diseases," we prefer to use the term "illness" to depict the socially and culturally patterned entity that members of a group develop and act upon.

The implications of relying upon the concept of illness, as distinct from that of disease, when dealing with the medically relevant behavior of persons residing in industrialized nations have been lucidly described by Freidson (1960), Mechanic (1962), and Rubel (1960). The labels and interpretations that are placed on perceived bodily impairments or on maladjustments of a sociopsychological nature constitute the illness that actors and their audiences deal with by means of variously socially structured interactions. If the medical categories of the scientific community impinge phenomenologically on the particular experience that is termed an "illness," the social consequences of a person that are differentiated in terms of this label will quite obviously be significant in ways that can be predicted given the meaning or content of the particular categories. We return to these and other points later in our discussion.

The analytic distinction that we have attempted to draw between *disease* and *illness* is fundamental in the discussion in the remainder of this chapter. We feel that this distinction has been at best implicit in previous formulations in labeling theory. Moreover, four other concepts are important: *deviance, labeling, career,* and *self* and *identity.*

The centrality of the self in sociology need not be reiterated. The self is most fruitfully seen as a product of a person's own definitions and evaluations of himself. *Identity,* a social placement, is best seen as the product of the appearances that a person presents to another, or to an audience. Ball writes:

> We present our audience with a self, which is acknowledged by them in the making of an assignment of identity; one can ratify and confirm or deny and disconfirm the other. These identity assignments are based upon presented self, social role, biographical knowledge about the actor and biographical experiences of the audience, and situational meanings available to the presenter and the audience. These identities are then available to the actor, ego, for incorporation or rejection in his definition of self. Self, is then, producer, product and process: presenter and presented to the audience; consumed and reconstituted as an identity; and repossessed—possibly in an altered state—

by the presenting actor, now for his acceptance or denial as a definition of his self. [Ball, 1970.]

However, further specificity is required. The self may be transitory or *situated* (limited to a single physically limited setting) and having limited generality, or it may be ineluctable and semipermanent. The first may be called, following Turner (1968), the *self-image,* whereas the second may be called the *self-concept.* These terms both refer to a person as known by himself. Identity may also have a temporal basis being either *situated* and ephemeral, or *substantial* and lasting. Although sociology must take into account and build on situated events, it must ultimately develop transsituational concepts and theories. In the sociology of deviance, sociologists have to some extent attended to human errors of a passing and transitory sort: the slip of the tongue, the open fly, the confused moment (Goffman, 1967), but they have been primarily concerned with the responses from others that lead to the building of deviant or *substantial identity* and *deviant self-concept* (Lofland, 1969).

Identities mobilized in given situations are the bases for roles. Thus, the ociology of deviance is concerned with deviant identities or assignments that in turn, under given or specified conditions, may result in a deviant self-concept. Matza (1969) describes deviance simply as straying from a path. The straying is of little consequence, except when it is responded to in the form of the assignment of an identity. It is further of little interest as long as it can be accommodated, dealt with, or rationalized by the person. Labeling is considered the primary determinant of lasting or career deviance. Deviance is only interesting insofar as the responses of those around the actor provide him with an identity that becomes the basis for anticipated reaction, response or a self.

Thus, *labeling* is the imputation of an identity to a person; this identity may or may not become the basis, from alter's point of view, of a lasting, or substantial identity, and it may or may not become, from the person's own perspective, the basis for either a deviant self-image or a deviant self-conception. Logically, there are many forms of labeling, many types of deviant identities, and many deviant selves.

Finally, *deviance* in labeling theory is usually viewed as a career. (Lemert, 1967, is an exception). What this means, simply, is that deviant identities, when present in interactional encounters and as transformed by ego into self-statements, have a lasting effect upon the behavior and symbolic meaning of that behavior. The ways in which these meanings are patterned are central to the later sections of this chapter. Several definitions of the term "career" have been suggested. Career in an *individual-objective* sense refers to the actual progression of a person through a series of positions in a social system. The *objective* career is used to refer simply to the existence of change in a series of steps themselves. Finally, the notion of a *subjective* career has been posited by Stebbins as "the actor's recognition and interpretation of past and future events associated with a particular identity . . ." (Stebbins, 1970, p. 34). Stebbins' definition clarifies Goffman's earlier subjective definition of career (1961, p. 127). Goffman's definition points out the association between the person's intimate *personal* definitions of events, attributes, means, and self and objectively defined positions or statuses in organizations or occupations (1961, p. 127).

The deviant identity that arises from the perception of others that an individual is "sick" supplies the person with a label and a set of expectations, a role. If the person continues to view his behavior as others do, and they continue to define him as sick, then he is supposedly launched on a career. Parsons' definition of the sick role (1951) assumes that it is temporary, transitory, and curable deviance and in a large part, a product of motivations on the part of the actor and others that he play the sick role, that is, accept help, try to get well, or get professional assistance. Yet, there are certainly cases where persons do not intend or wish themselves to be ill, and nevertheless have this identity imputed to them by others. The sick role based on a single deviant identity is too broad a notion for understanding illness behavior. Haber and Smith summarize some further relevant weaknesses of the sick role model:

> The sick role model does not differentiate between short-term acute sickness and long-term chronic illness. Twaddle (1969) observed that the sick role model does not account for variations in illness expectations among older people. Kassenbaum and Bauman (1965) found that sick role expectations of the chronologically ill were related to the attributes of the illness as well as the attributes of individual; Gordon (1966:99–100) found distinct and unrelated role expectations for the sick and "impaired" roles. (1969:4)

Just as there are a plethora of selves, so there are many roles. A role is an expectation of others. To speak of *the* sick role, as much previous work has done, is to vastly simplify the nature of responses to bodily processes or social phenomena that are associated in illness behavior.

Illness can lead to a deviant identity, but it need not. It can be normalized in a variety of ways if the imputed deviant adopts conventional expectations (for example, the sick role), if his illness is acute, and if it is seen as curable by others. Although illness is deviance in the sense of violations of norms that may be responded to or labeled, it has a variety of alternative objective and subjective meanings. If the person is seen as curable, if his deviance is seen as *unintended,* he is likely to be treated as "*sick*." But, on the other hand, if his actions are such that he is seen as *responsible* for them, or *relatively incurable,* ne may be either stigmatized (discredited as a viable self) or not, but the ways in which social control agencies treat him will vary accordingly. (Freidson, in Sussman, n.d.)

These definitions of others then are especially important since they are influenced by (and may also influence) the activities of agencies of social control. These agencies may either facilitate the return of the treated to the community, or punish or rehabilitate so inappropriately that "false deviants" are produced. Stereotyping and stigmatization may also occur.

In sum, there are several ambiguities in the present application of labeling theory to illness behavior. One is the failure to adequately distinguish between the influence of social and bodily perceptions, and to keep separate the perspectives symbolized by the terms illness and disease. The second is the failure to separate identity and self. The third is the loose use of the term career. The fact that variable sorts of careers, selves, and identities then can be attributed to differing underlying processes (for example, biological, organic, and mentalistic), or to social contingencies has been obscured by the global use of the terms career and sick role.

Having posed our problem and some relevant concepts, the material is now presented in a somewhat more formal way. The framework on the following pages summarizes the argument thus far presented and provides the basis for the latter sections of the chapter.

A Model of Health and Illness

A. The Categories Normal and Sick

1. The segments of behavior denoted by the terms "Normal" and "Sick" refer to aspects of an individual's continued adaptation to his environment. Although these categories are in many implicit ways acted upon as if they were continuous (for example, as if one can "be" or have "both"), they are in an explicit sense often regarded as mutually exclusive.

2. Normal and sick can be seen as designations of a person's behavior by himself (a self-concept), or as designations by others, that is, as an imputed *identity*. These two, self-designation and other designation, may vary independently in given instances. These designations of identity may be viewed as the bases for a *role,* that is, set of expectations mobilized by an identity in a situation.

3. Given these designations, the investigator must know how they are applied. In other words, how do people become differentiated and individuated over time by means of the categoric designations "well" or "sick"? How do people come to act in accordance with the sick role or how do they cease to act in accord with this role and come once again to be viewed as normal?

4. The designations or labels listed come to be applied as part of an interactional process that is culturally structured. Culture in this context refers in part to such inferences from behavior as values, norms, attitudes and "rules of thumb" or taken-for-granted assumptions.

B. Relevant Behaviors

1. "Normal" and "sick" are both highly abstract terms each of which refer to clusters of behaviors that in a given situation have relevance and validity in terms of the underlying assumption listed in A.4.

2. Clusters of behavior labeled either "normal" or "sick" are located in time, geographical space, and in discernible segments, sections or processes of a given social system. To further simplify our meanings, we claim that the labels are applied in situations. What is described as sick in one time and place and with a given audience may not receive the same response in a different configuration of time, place, and audience.

3. A possibility exists that there is a pattern to the relationship between units of the temporal, spatial, and social systems (B.2) on the one hand, and the identities of the clustered behaviors of the categories of B.1 on the other. This pattern, of course, is actualized by processes alluded to in assumptions A.2, A.3, and A.4.

C. The Bases for Relevant Behaviors

1. The behaviors that are categorized as normal or sick (cf. A.1, B.1) may be traced to *individual actions* (or utterances), *external* (that is, socio-cultural) or *situational* contingencies (A.4, B.2).

2. In a great many instances, medically relevant individualistic actions and utterances may be a result of or be accompanied by the perception (by the self or others) of altered functioning that can be verified by biologically based analyses. It is to be emphasized, however, that sickness need not be associated with biologically altered states.

3. The categories or designations "normal" and "sick" bear an important relationship to the manner in which the members of a sociocultural unit evaluate the functioning of their bodies. By this we mean that the form of the behaviors labeled by these terms are affected by the manner in which persons evaluate and perceive the functioning of their bodies.

4. This evaluation (C.3) is linked to the specific normative range of function (and deviations therefrom) that characterizes the various physiological systems of the body. This in turn is determined by the group's sociocultural patterns, gene pool and breeding history, and ecological characteristics. At the very least, to obtain a multilevel appreciation of the meaning and function of health-relevant transactions, the functional status of the systems of the body need to be specified. (It should be clear that it is against these norms that practitioners of Western scientific medicine base their judgments about disease.)

5. Behaviors described in C.1 may also arise from a perception that the individual is in a state of relational disequilibrium with himself, his family, other primary groups in which he participates, and/or the sacred elements (individuals, religious personages, and the like) of his society.

6. The relationships, implicit or explicit, between A.1, A.2, B.2, C.2 and C.5 are *problematic* and therefore require investigation to discover what criteria or rules are used by people in the culture or situation to judge the health status of comembers.

7. The health relevant conditions delineated by B.2, C.2, and C.5 may exist independently or they may coexist.

8. Only by repeated observations and recording of behavioral events will the investigator be in a position to decide whether C.2 and C.5 coexist or exist separately, and also whether the relationship between individualistically and situationally centered changes is one of logical necessity or of probabilistic association.

D. Judgments of Behavior Segments

1. Individualistic behaviors judged to constitute illness thus probably contain references to disturbed feelings, bodily sensations, beliefs, or convictions and at the same time symbolically communicate the individual's inability to function productively and in conformance with the implicit rules, attitudes, and goals of the group.

2. The elements or segments of the behaviors of A.1 may be reacted to with varying degrees of disapproval and, in some instances, approval. They are judged and interpreted in terms of folk or native medically relevant dimensions, for example, cause, severity, consequences, and implications.

3. The goal the investigator should set for himself is to make explicit the content, form, and duration of those behavioral segments that comprise A.1, the medically relevant dimensions on the basis of which these behaviors are interpreted, and, lastly, the action imperatives that they elicit in the immediate family and elsewhere in the group.

4. The judgments and interpretations that associate with the behaviors A.1, B.1 provide the basis for decisions concerning the different possible action alternatives or imperatives.

E. The Consequences of Judgments of Behavior as Sick

1. In an urban society where rational scientific medicine exists, this type of medical system provides one set of *alternatives* that compete with inactivity, peer advice, family definitions and responses, neighborhood experts and quasimedical personnel (pharmacists), and other lay advisors and religious figures.

2. The action choices available in the various curing or medical systems may involve attempts at (a) eliminating the symptoms, (b) eliminating the perceived causes of the underlying illness, or (c) perpetuating the illness source for purposes of expiation or punishment.

3. The consequences of particular responses (D.2) that are made to behavior judged to constitute illness vary. The sick person, generally speaking, is *affected* by both the *nature* of the responses and the conditions (B.2) under which they are generated.

4. The sick person, as a result of this response and in conformance with implicit rules and values of the culture, will consciously modify, shape, or structure his subsequent behavior in ways that the investigator needs to make explicit.

5. Because the behavioral effects of this modification and shaping have synchronic or cross-sectional properties, they can be grouped and said to constitute a *role* (that is, a set of behavioral expectations or prescriptions) for the sick person.

6. Because the behavioral effects of this modification and shaping have diachronic, developmental, or time-bound properties, they can be seen as a *career* for the sick person.

F. The Career of the Sick Person

1. The concept of a career highlights the truism that the sick person is continually involved in interactional sequences (that is, self versus others). A career implies a potential beginning, intervening stages with distinctive properties, and equally important, an end.

2. The investigator should set for himself the task of delineating in depth the characteristics of the sick person's career. The task involves data bearing on A–E given previously. In a concise fashion, this entails making explicit the interrelationships between features of *disease* (altered functioning of the body as determined by direct evaluation of biological status) and *illness,* the socially structured results of the alternatives chosen in the light of factors A–D and consequences as seen in E.

3. The sick person's behavioral participation in or execution of the action imperatives of D.3 constitute what one could term the *explicit* features of his career.

4. The investigator must also attempt to delineate the *implicit* features of the sick person's career. These may not necessarily be tied to the goals of eliminating or perpetuating the illness, but involve issues such as morality, perceived self-worth, and other symbolically altered interactional sequences that indicate that the sick person's identity has been individuated and differentiated in the social setting.

5. The content, form, and duration of these career features must be delineated as well as their effect on the original illness behaviors of D.1.

G. The Return to Normality

1. The termination of the sick person's career and his return to a nonsick status involves, to some extent, a reversal of these experiential and physiological modes. The exact relationship between these modes, the interactions involved, and the shared meanings that mediate them must be delineated.

2. The investigator should assume that there are definite *behavioral consequences* to having been sick, that is, to have experienced and completed one of the possible symbolic types of illness careers suggested in this scheme.

3. These consequences (G.2) might involve putative residues of the cultural stereotyping that associates with having been at one time sick or deviant.

4. These consequences (G.2) may lead the person to re-enter the illness cycle beginning again with A.1 while carrying the symbolic burden of the initial cycle. The investigator must study the extent of overlap and recycling of illness careers as well as the internal variations in their interactional content.

5. Participation in illness chains, or cycles of health and illness, are unending for the individual and in a given group or culture. It is useful, however, to assume that groups do distinguish end points and that the nature of these culturally defined end points should be explicated by the investigator.

Types of Careers

The preceding model draws attention to and to some extent emphasizes that in certain ways all *types* of illnesses or diseases can be seen as equivalent. To state this succinctly, all medically relevant manifestations may be seen as rooted in (and manifest) actions, states, or processes that are *deviant*. Support for this position is obtained by studies conducted in preliterate settings. For example, judgments regarding what is abnormal social behavior depend upon norms or conceptions (which are shared) regarding how particular individuals or groups ordinarily *do* and *should* behave in specified circumstances. Deviations are noted, labeled, and acted upon. If social behavior is strikingly deviant, it is considered illness. The meaning that is attached to this illness, and the way in which persons are correspondingly treated, however, depend upon the beliefs and values of the group (compare Fabrega and Metzger with Fabrega, Metzger, and Williams). In the same fashion, bodily sensations or perceptions that deviate from those that individuals ordinarily have or expect constitute the salient units or symptoms that often accompany behavior subsequently judged to be illness.

It might be challenged that "biologically" determined illnesses give rise to expressions (symptoms) that differ since they are rooted in bodily sensations that experientially and socially can be separated from the self (that is, can be treated as an object) whereas many mental "symptoms" are not separable in such a fashion. If this is the case, then illness careers of persons with different types of symptoms may also be expected to differ. Some support for this position comes from reports that have shown that in a folk community the distinguishing feature of some "psychiatric" illnesses (illnesses primarily manifested in problematic social behavior and having minimal "physical" symptoms) is that initial treatment is forced on the sick person by his family, that is, it often takes place without his consent (Fabrega, Metzger, and Williams). We lack sufficiently detailed data bearing on the careers of such individuals to be able to say whether the nature of symptoms, or the relationship that symptoms have to the self have important and long-range career implications. We will return to this point in greater detail later when we discuss related phenomena in industrial settings. It is to be emphasized, however, that in preliterate settings there are "psychiatric" illnesses that are treated with a consensus that the self is problematic. That is, there are instances in which both patient and family share the conviction that the social self alone (and not the body per se) is sick and in need of treatment, and the illness careers of these persons are not in any significant way unique.

It is our conviction, in general, that in folk (or primitive) settings by and large all illness, regardless of whether it is associated with detectable pathobiological processes or not, is treated and labeled similarly. In effect, we are saying that there is no "mental illness" in these communities, or more precisely, that what is observed is only one type of illness. Organic symptoms as opposed to mental symptoms, or physical ("biological") illness as opposed to mental illness are not distinguished. We now focus on industrialized settings and point out that in certain ways there is no difference between types of *diseases* in these settings. That is, *all diseases* are alike in that they depend ultimately upon the judgments of a specialized community of individuals. A professional person's judgments about disease depend upon his learned conceptions or norms. He shares these norms with other professionals. These norms dictate how persons or bodies ordinarily do and should behave and he applies his labels (diagnoses) when his examinations show that deviance from these norms is manifest. A more elaborate form of stating this position is as follows: (1) Diseases depend for their existence upon the diagnoses of specialists. (2) Although the source or nature of the data used to reach diagnoses vary, diagnoses are nevertheless *types of judgments made by groups of professionals.* (3) Diagnoses may differ in terms of degrees of reliability. (4) The degree of validity of diagnoses also varies, but ultimately depends upon the drawing of correspondences between the informed judgments of people. The nature of the processes that are involved in the making of diagnoses, thus, may be seen as similar.

In summary, our argument draws us to the position that all illness or disease rests upon the perception, recognition, and labeling of *deviant phenomena,* whether these activities be performed by lay people or by professional people. Given this position—that the processual basis and, to some extent, the epistemological nature of all medically relevant diagnoses or entities are equivalent—we are urged to examine how and why the application of the relevant labels has differing social implications in our own society. Stated more succinctly, we may ask how and why are the consequences of applying "mental" as opposed to "nonmental" illness labels different?

To facilitate examination of this question we propose that four categories or types of disease and illness careers be considered. For each type we discuss a representative or paradigm case. Type I is exemplified by pneumonia (pneumococcal pneumonia) but might just as well have included a "sore throat" (bacterial pharingitis) or infectious hepatitis. We illustrate Type II by diabetes mellitus, although carcinoma of the stomach or myocardial infarction would be equally representative. In Type III, tuberculosis is used as the paradigm. Leprosy would serve equally well. We differentiate mental illness (or disease) as Type IV and use schizophrenia as a paradigm.

Diseases in category I are self-limiting, that is, they are characterized by a relatively *discrete* onset and termination. The long range implications of the disease, viewed from within the perspective of scientific medicine, are usually minimal, in large part because the duration of the disease is short and because the underlying biological process is well understood and/or can be controlled. That is, the disease is characterized by etiological and diagnostic certitude and a relatively effective therapeutic regimen is available. The disease usually does not have significant negative social and physical consequences. The diagnostic label, in effect, is applied only temporarily by the medical community. The medical cost or liability of these diseases is small; that is, the value of the product "degree of involvement with the medical care system" × "duration of involvement" × "entailed modification of life trajectory" is, relatively speaking, low. Characteristic features of the illness career associated with disease of Type I are: (1) variable discomfort and disability lasting a short period of time; (2) prompt and relatively unambiguous recognition that one is not well biologically, that is, the phenomenological experience associated with this disease, generally speaking, contrasts sharply with one's ordinary or usual feeling about himself; (3) the individual is not held responsible for his condition; (4) by visiting a physician a person in the illness phase can gain certitude that his condition is short lasting; (5) should the label illness be applied and accepted, its internalization is usually time-limited although during this "labeling phase" it may be all pervasive; (6) during the illness phase the individual is permitted great latitude and release from many of his usual obligations and responsibilities; (7) the long-range social consequences to the person who has the illness label applied to him appear to be minimal. That is, the application and acceptance of the label does not entail a developmentally significant reinterpretation of the person's concept and evaluation of himself. Thus, having completed an illness chain as a result of developing a disease of Type I (that is, having been defined by self and/or others as ill, being treated and then released or cured) is generally speaking of little social consequence. The illness phase may, of course, have social consequences if it is associated temporally with an important event (that is, a loss of a job), but this is not a necessary or frequent and predictable feature of this disease.

Diseases in Type II typically have potentially important *long-range* medical consequences. Although the onset may be sudden (as in the typical "heart attack"), it is more often slow and insidious. The long-range implications of these diseases, viewed within the perspective of scientific medicine, are considerable. Consequently, if scientific medical categorizations form part of the sociopsychological reality that is the illness, the likelihood is high that the resulting illness career will be importantly affected. The serious diseases in this category never really end. Thus, even though a heart attack itself may be brief, the probability is high that a patient with this type of disease (arteriosclerotic heart disease) will be required to modify his life habits considerably. Family life is likely to be altered significantly, and the patient, of course, will be required to visit the physician regularly. The person with diseases of Type II, in effect, will always be said to be in need of medical supervision because he will be viewed as essentially still having the disease. Diagnostic and etiological certitude in this group of diseases is relatively high. The diagnostic label, as we have implied, is never removed. The medical costs of liability of diseases we call Type II are quite high. That is, the product of "degree of involvement with the medical care system" × "duration of involvement with the medical care system" × "entailed modifications of life trajectory" is very high. The career of a person ill with a disease of Type II is characterized by: (1) long duration with increasing pain and disability ending usually with death; (2) the ease of subjectively experiencing that one is *physically ill* fluctuates and varies through time. That is, the phenomenological experience of illness may be all pervasive and intense (for example, the pain and limitation of a heart attack or of cancer) or nonexistent, as in a properly regulated diabetic who does not feel in any way sick; (3) the individual is not usually held responsible for his condition; (4) by consulting a physician the person may learn that his condition is long lasting; (5) when the illness label is applied and accepted, its internalization is significant in a longitudinal or temporal sense (one is always a "diabetic" or has a "heart condition"), although the extent to which it crowds out other features of the self varies considerably. The individual is in a position to significantly control his career as a sick person, for (6) largely depending upon the extent to which he incorporates the illness label into his self-image he will be released from a varying number of his social obligations and responsibilities, and, consequently, may (7) experience long-range social consequences as a result of the labeling process.

Diseases we have termed Type III, viewed within the perspectives of scientific medicine, are analogous to those of Type II. The bodily components of the phenomenological experience of illness in diseases of Type III are more or less equivalent to those of the diseases of Type II. That is, the physiologically determined symptoms, the general subjective experience that one is "physically" ill, and the experienced disability may be identical for diseases of Types II and III. The illness careers associated with these diseases are likewise analogous of those of Type II, but there are important differentiating features that recommend the creation of a separate category. Being given and accepting the label of a disease of Type III has differing implications, for the individual is considerably discredited and experiences consequent mortification. The role of the medical community in this regard is obvious, yet still requires emphasis. An individual who is differentiated as ill and has a disease of Type III label applied to him experiences considerable social constraints since he and his immediate social group are likely to be stigmatized. Ordinary relations that the individual has with others in his immediate group, in other words, are likely to be significantly affected as a result of the application of this label. The changes that take place are quite different from those that take place in the case of Type II diseases. Needless to say, the medical cost or liability associated with these diseases is rather high.

Thus far, the principal parameters of disease that appear to have important social consequences vis-à-vis the notion of an illness career are (1) the temporal extension or duration of the underlying pathological process, (2) its reversibility or curability, (3) the degree of discomfort, incapacity or disability that it produces, and (4) its potential for self-degradation. Regarding features included in 3, that is, symptoms and disability, it must be acknowledged that, to a large extent, they are modified or affected by the processes of labeling (either by the self or by an audience); in other words, their nature, in certain indeterminate ways, is socially prescribed. By this is meant that not only is the perception and communication of the effects of pathological processes learned, but so are the behavioral consequences (that is, whom to see, what to take, and the like . . .) that follow this perception. We are not able to pursue here in greater detail *the extent to which* disability, symptoms, or simply illness behavior is determined by or stems from alterations made manifest by "biological" analyses. It would appear prudent to acknowledge that there are unmistakable "biological" properties of a disease process that affect the illness behavior of the patient. For example, some micro-organisms are more virulent than others, the immunological responsivity of persons may vary, and the extent to which the normal insulin mechanism is disturbed (or any metabolic process underlying diseases of Type II) may also vary. It is no doubt possible to establish these differences in a behavior-free manner, although how the experiences of socialization and enculturation affect and influence the body's responsivity (and, ultimately, the results of the behavior-free "biological" analyses) is difficult to determine. Our thinking in this general area leads us to emphasize that there are components of disease that set limits and constraints on illness careers. A factor that has been emphasized by others and that is not particularly important in terms of the diseases discussed thus far has to do with the notion of accountability. We will return to this point subsequently.

In certain ways it would appear useful to think of disease manifestations as language or communication that audiences, including physicians, are capable of receiving and understanding. This type of communication is ordinarily limited to the relationship that exists between a physician and his patient. Clinically relevant infections, for example, produce temperature and result from virulent micro-organisms that invade and multiply in the body. Laboratory procedures are required to determine the latter, whereas the former is best determined by a thermometer, although feeling the skin of the person will sometimes be sufficient. Ordinary audiences do not usually learn that an infection has taken place or that a temperature is present. A physician, on the other hand, has access to direct body contact with the patient, and is allowed to touch, feel, smell, uncover, inspect, and listen (unaided or by the use of instruments) to the various parts of the patient's body. This free access that he has and the language and decoding system he has internalized as a result of his training allow him to translate and understand what the body (patient) tells him about disease. Stated more succinctly, the patient and his body communicate to the physician a great deal of information about disease that others do not have access to or cannot understand. Consequently, they (the audience) are not in a position to respond in any unusual way. One might, thus, anticipate that the extent to which disease properties become readily interpretable to an audience is an important factor affecting the illness career of a person. Exposed skin eruptions, visible protruberances, unpleasant odors, or a productive cough are relatively visible signs that readily communicate to physicians, and nonphysicians as well, that "biological" abnormality exists. These manifestations seem to account in part for the discrediting and stigmatization that persons with disease of Type III can experience. It is here that the concept of *disease* becomes equivalent, socially speaking, with that of a handicap. The latter, strictly speaking, is not a disease as we have used the term in this discussion. That is, blindness, amputations, and other disfigurements and handicaps are not so much biological processes that may fluctuate and change and that produce bodily manifestations as they are permanently altered states or conditions of people. Physicians, of course, may be involved in dealing with them, and it may be possible to ameliorate the consequences of these handicaps (for example, hearing aids and artificial limbs) by such consultations. It would appear useful at this stage of our thinking, however, to regard handicaps and diseases of Type III as analogous since they are associated with more or less similar careers. This is precisely the case because of the high visibility or communicability of the condition. The underlying biological determinants of these careers, however, are somewhat different. We cannot pursue here in further detail the sociological value of differentiating between the biological bases of these conditions. However, an analysis would involve demonstrating how the characteristics of visibility and permanency or immutability regarding a bodily "condition" (that is, traditional handicaps as opposed to diseases of Type III with florid stigmatizing properties that may fluctuate) are socially organized.

The crucial value of adopting the previous formulation (that regarding the degree of containment and interpretability of the body's communication about disease) is that it allows us to productively discuss the unusual illness careers of diseases of Type IV, namely, "psychiatric diseases." These diseases may be short lasting, chronic, or permanent and be associated with varying degrees of discomfort or disability. The implications of their manifestations, however, differ substantially from those of Type III. An unsightly skin eruption or a chronic "productive and hacking" cough, in one sense, communicates a similar type of information to a physician as it does to an audience of medically untrained persons. The message is that the person is sick, that something is "physically" wrong, or that an obvious disease or ailment is present. It is the nature and existence of this judgment, this capacity of an audience to explain, attribute, or excuse a manifestation because it stems from "biological" or bodily processes that Goffman has emphasized in his analysis of psychiatric disease (1969). The latter disease, in certain ways, is similar to that of Type II; that is, it is chronic and its manifestations are not clearly communicated and evident but require a special language and decoding system. (Some have termed this system a "third ear," and the nature of this metaphor has interesting implications.) Diseases of Type II and Type IV, in other words, do not readily communicate to an untrained audience that a medical (biological or physical) abnormality is present. In sharp contrast to diseases of Type II, however, psychiatric diseases are constituted of behavioral properties that have striking social consequences. In this sense, they resemble diseases of Type III. Their manifestations, in other words, form part of or visibly intrude in the important social relationships of persons. An important differentiating feature, however, is that it is not possible to disassociate the self from the disease; the manifestations of the disease cannot be encapsulated, bounded, and kept outside of social transactions. The manifestations, as it were, become the self or person. The illness-career problems posed by psychiatric disease stem from the difficulty or inability of developing, between a person and an audience, a shared consensus and then inattention regarding what is socially acceptable versus what is "biologically" unacceptable, what is an articulated and wholesome self versus what is disarticulated and unwholesome.

Some of the implications of this latter observation are revealed in the problem of "therapy" or control of the illness. Since all disease is expressed behaviorally in some way, and is discovered and verified by means of empirical observation, the control of the illness requires an initial agreement between the parties involved and subsequently becomes a matter of determination by these parties. The capacity to control the subsequent behavior of the patient with mental disease differs substantially from that of other patients. That is to say that the ways in which responses of significant others modify meanings, according to the behavioral pattern, into a series of options for ego are very different in Type IV than in other illnesses. With an illness of Type IV, the application of expectations of conformity to social roles (what the person "owes" to people in his immediate network of others), becomes difficult. This is so because mental disease is a product of a discrepancy between the person and his others in definition of the meaning of the person's behavior, namely his self. In his actions, the person expresses his claims to humanity; a failure in consensus on self by those around him is equivalent to a questioning of his humanity, not simply his physical capacity to perform a series of discrete roles. The rules broken or breached are *not* those indicated by society's recognition of the "biological" basis for performance of many roles, but rules about being. Social control cannot be simply used to bring the person back into line with some clearly defined social rule or norm. For it is not single rules that are being breached. In other diseases, the forces of informal and formal social control can be used to isolate, terminate, cure, or manage the disease largely because there is a consensus on meanings (the person is sick means he did not intend it, is currently incapable, and should be permitted some lapses in performance). Illnesses of Type IV in this sense are of an incorrigible variety. The rules broken are rules pertaining to selfhood, or to self-presentation itself, some of which are known only to the person and his closest intimates. The person *is* his expressive action. In this sense, he does not find it possible to separate his "failure" with some set of external ("biological") rules that he and his audience validate or support.

> Mental symptoms, then, are neither something in themselves nor whatever is so labeled; mental symptoms are acts by an individual which openly proclaim to others that he must have assumptions about himself which the relevant bit of social organization can neither allow him nor do much about. [Goffman, 1969: 369]

The resultant careers of the mentally ill, thus, do not grow from the amount known of the "biological" language of the body with reference to a medical diagnosis, but rather from the following social facts: (1) differences in power between ego and those around him; (2) the degree of collusion or covert agreement by definers to convey a particular definition of the situation to ego; (3) the coalitions formed by the relevant parties with outside sources of power and, thus, definitional rights, for example, the police, social workers, and psychiatrists; and (4) the degree of permanence of the family group and their capacity to reinforce their selves. For the failure of the person to live up to the place supplied him in the family unit, to be the person others had assumed and expected him to be, will suggest the arbitrary and shaky nature of their claims to expect social things of others. In contrast, then, to the relative ease with which people cast themselves or are cast into a role by being assigned an identity on the basis of their behavior, persons in Type IV illness careers are engaged in a running adjustment and negotiation of their very humanity.

Summary Comment

One of the logical implications of the model of health and illness that was developed previously is that in a substantive sense there is nothing inherently different about the various types of diseases or illnesses. Illness chains are constituted of symbolically differentiated behavior. Any disease process must ultimately be expressed or evidenced by some behavior. These behaviors can range from the demeanor of a patient who presents certain vague complaints, to the "clinical" symptoms obtained and interpreted by the physician, to reports or complaints made by the family or formal legal authorities about the person's behavior. Specialized examinations may be used by the physician, but the results that are obtained require interpretation. In reaching a decision about illness (that is, applying the illness label) the person is guided to a large extent by phenomenological contrasts, those around him rely on shared standards of behavior, and the physician himself uses normative criteria. All parties must make a judgment on the basis of a varied data base about deviant phenomena. This judgment locates the source, meaning, and significance of the disease or illness. In industrialized societies the primary and most binding illness labels are applied by medical doctors. Through a series of historical developments, they have gained control over the judgment of both physical and mental disease. The central fact, however, should not be overlooked that both the designation of a disease as mental and the designation of a disease as physical are the result of decisions made by physicians based on a series of observations and inferences, regardless of the sources of their data. Physicians validate and label behaviors and in this sense they play an important role in creating disease, and by extension, illness careers.

In spite of the similarity in the mode of identification of the two types of diseases, there are real and significant social and psychological differences in the career lines or illness experiences that result. Deviance from "biological" norms and social norms is treated quite distinctly and differently. The patterning of an illness career is based upon the casting of the person, principally by the physician, into a role, and the person's acceptance of that role or imputed identity. If a medical diagnosis is to be maximally socially constraining, (if the patient is to follow faithfully a medical regimen), there must exist both an agreed-upon series of techniques and diagnostic indicators that are acknowledged by the patient as being legitimately used and interpreted by the doctor. The existence of a consensus on the implications of these findings will have important consequences for the future behavior of the patient. A shared consensus must be developed on the cause, the nature, and the future implications of the physician's findings and interpretations. The degree of consensus about the nature of the illness within the society, within the family, and within the medical profession itself will all have an important effect on the degree, type, and source of the most significant social pressures that are directed toward the patient.

Historically, the medical profession has been granted access to the bodies and minds of its patients, and it has been allowed, with varying social restrictions, to effect the necessary actions to cure, manage, or treat their patients. In the past, this treatment has been at times bizarre when viewed from our present frame of reference, including trephination, prefrontal lobotomies, ice packs and icy baths, blood-letting and leech application, and hemicorporectomies. In the last few hundred years, the germ theory of disease and the ac-cumulated and publicly accepted scientific body of medical knowledge have provided a legitimate mandate for the validation of physical illness. The public consensus and the granting of a mandate to the medical profession are com-plimented by the internal agreement of the medical profession concerning the diagnostic procedures for the identification of disease. Medicine has car-ried out its many follies and numerous successes with the support of a vast majority of American society over the last seventy years at least. Science as a basic undergirding for the clinical art and social transaction that is medical practice, the solid and accepted professional mandate that has legitimated the physician's access and manipulation of the body of the patient, and the his-toric mind-body dualism of Western thought, all permit physicians to fairly readily cast the patient into the role of the physically or biologically ill, that is, he whose body is in disarray. The patient, in his turn, with his faith in the rhetoric of science, in the medical profession, and his own doctor, is inclined to define the physician's efforts as being solely directed toward his own well-being and recovery. He is thus facilitated in his tendency to transform his symptoms into mere physical flaws of varying longevity, and to separate them in turn from his social competence, his soul, and his mind. Although he may be temporarily incapable of performance, he is essentially still social in mind and spirit, even if not in body.

In "mental illness," on the other hand, as has been argued previously, there is little consensus in the society concerning the nature, locus, and cause of the illness. There is, in addition, manifest disagreement within psychiatry itself on matters of etiology, diagnosis, and treatment. The techniques by which the disease is validated as "scientifically" real and real in its conse-quences, in other words, are objects of public and professional disagreement. Furthermore, in mental illness, it can be said that the self is the illness, and there is little consensus between the patient and his significant others regard-ing the nature or definition of the illness. The physician is often called on to provide definitional clarity and to enter the struggle over meanings on one side or the other of the communication battle. Thus, we observe that the mandate of the physician is to treat "biological" illness by "scientific" means, and there exists a willingness on the part of society to accept the specific decisions he makes and applies to given persons. Given the *self-bound* nature of mental illness, however, it is not surprising that issues of diagnosis and validation are problematic and the resultant "deviant careers" significantly different.

There is a further important distinguishing feature about mental illness that influences career lines. We have implied that physicians clearly play an important role as social controllers; they provide legitimate rationales for the alteration of social roles; they have the legal power to allocate people into cure or constraint institutions; they are sanctioned to enter into the daily lives of citizens; they have access to drugs and other euphorics; they can make de-cisions about life and death. Physicians typically make their choice of the mode of the social control they exercise on the basis of the *sample* of information they obtain from the patient's verbal reports, his case history or file if it is available, the reports of his family, and any specialized tests they may wish to collect and analyze. In the case of a physical illness, physicians rely on a few rather well-developed techniques for eliciting the needed information for his diagnosis and prognosis. The range of possible tests has of course escalated in the years since World War II, but there are nevertheless a *finite* number known by most competent physicians, and they are interpreted within an acknowledged range of tolerance. Following his gathering of a limited set of dimensions that are relevant to his diagnosis, physicians restrict their attention or therapy almost exclusively to managing, treating, or curing the identified disease using these dimensions as end points. Ethically, and in some ways legally, physicians must attend only to that aspect of a patient's behavior that is relevant to the cure. Other identities, attributes, immorality, lapses in dress, demeanor and the like are theoretically excluded from relevance. Stated succinctly, in physical or biological *diseases* the segment of information used to make diagnoses and monitor treatment in a very real sense stands outside the patient, that is, it is drawn *from* him, perhaps constitutes a part of him, but *it is not him.* In other words, physicians do not make judgments about *selves,* and, equally important, they enjoy the luxury of being able to draw directly and *completely* on that which they base their decisions *and evaluate their actions.*

   With mental illness, on the other hand, the physician has little "objective" (that is, not of the self) information to draw on. Information for his diagnosis rests on the routines of everyday life. Because the psychiatrist or physician dealing with mental disease lacks specific, parsimonious diagnostic tests, and deals primarily in everyday behaviors as data, his diagnostic information (expressed attitudes, beliefs, feelings or signs and symptoms) should in principle approach being a comprehensive biography of the patient although in practice is likely to constitute but a small (and biased) portion of his social demeanor. The impossible mandate of the psychiatrist appears to be to delve into any and all of the patient's life, public, private, past, present, and future. For without that data, he may never discover that bit of behavior, that experience, that relationship that may be the *sine qua non* for effective therapy. From the point of view of the patient, and perhaps of his intimates, the traditional insight therapy or psychotherapeutic relationship has the effect of significantly altering and illuminating nearly all of his intimate social bonds. Thus, the social control of illness seen as biological is based upon a limited number of validating techniques, generally accepted as legitimate, and directly effects only a relatively small number of social relationships. What is more, the treatment relationship supplies a sick role that offers an account or an excuse for changes in behavior and affect. In mental illness, on the other hand, social control is based on a diverse range of techniques and observational skills, is of questionable legitimacy for significant portions of the society, and tends to effect or rearrange a host of social relationships. It requires control of the person as he carries out his daily round of life, and the things requiring control are the very behaviors he presents while engaged in living. The ironic nature of the process of social control of illness and deviant careers is underscored by these final contrasting points.

References

Angrist, Shirley; Lefton, Mark; Dinitz, Simon; and Pasamanick, Benjamin. 1968. *Women After Treatment.* New York: Appleton-Century-Crofts.

Ball, Donald W., 1970. "Self and Identity in the Context of Deviance: The Case of Criminal Abortion." British Columbia, Canada: University of Victoria. See Chapter 7.

Engel, George L., 1960. "A Unified Concept of Health and Disease." *Perspectives in Biology and Medicine* 3: 459–485.

Fabrega, Horacio, 1970. "Dynamics of Medical Practice in a Folk Community." *Milbank Memorial Fund Quarterly* 48: 391–412.

Fabrega, Horacio, and Metzger, Duane, 1968. "Psychiatric Illness in a Small Ladino Community." *Psychiatry* 31: 339–351.

Fabrega, Horacio; Metzger, Duane; and Williams, Gerald, 1970. "Psychiatric Implications of Health and Illness in a Maya Indian Group: A Preliminary Statement." *Social Science and Medicine* 3: 609–626.

Feinstein, Abram R., 1967. *Clinical Judgment.* Baltimore: Williams & Wilkins.

Fletcher, C. Richard; Manning, Peter K.; Reynolds, Larry T.; and Smith, James O. Forthcoming. "The Labeling Theory of Mental Illness." In Paul Roman and Harrison A. Trice, eds. *Current Perspectives in Psychiatric Sociology.* New York: Science House.

Frake, Charles O. 1961. "The Diagnosis of Disease Among the Subanun of Mindanao." *American Anthropologist* 63: 113–132.

Freidson, Eliot. N.D. "Disability as Social Deviance." Chap. 4 in Marvin B. Susman, ed. *Sociology and Rehabilitation.* Washington, D.C.: American Sociological Association.

Friedson, Eliot, 1960. "Client Control and Medical Practice." *American Journal of Sociology* 65: 374–382.

Gibbs, Jack, 1966. "Conceptions of Deviant Behavior: The Old and New." *Pacific Sociological Review* 9 (Spring): 9–14.

Goffman, Erving, 1961. *Asylums.* New York: Doubleday Anchor.

Gordon, Gerald, 1966. *Role Theory and Illness.* New Haven: College and University Press.

Haber, Lawrence D., and Smith, Richard T., 1971. "Disability and Deviance:

Normative Adaptations in Role Behavior." *American Sociological Review* 36: 87–97.

Kassenbaum, G. G., and Bauman, B. O., 1965. "Dimensions of the Sick Role in Chronic Illness." *Journal of Health and Human Behavior* 6 (Spring): 16–27.

Kiev, Ari, ed., 1964. *Magic, Faith, and Healing.* New York: The Free Press.

Lemert, Edwin, 1967. *Human Deviance, Social Problems and Social Control.* Englewood Cliffs, N.J.: Prentice-Hall, Inc.

Lieban, R. W., 1960. "Sorcery, Illness, and Social Control in a Philippine Municipality." *Southwestern Journal of Anthropology* 16: 127–143.

Lieban, R. W., 1962. "The Dangerous Ingkantos: Illness and Social Control in a Philippine Community." *American Anthropologist* 64: 306–312.

Lofland, John, 1969. *Deviance and Identity.* Englewood Cliffs, N.J.: Prentice-Hall, Inc.

Matza, David, 1969. *Becoming Deviant.* Englewood Cliffs, N.J.: Prentice-Hall, Inc.

Mechanic, David, 1962. "The Concept of Illness Behavior." *Journal of Chronic Diseases* 15: 189–194.

Parsons, Talcott, 1951. *The Social System.* New York: The Free Press.

Parsons, Talcott, 1951. "Illness and the Role of the Physician." *American Journal of Orthopsychiatry* 21: 452–460.

Pasamanick, Benjamin, 1967. *Schizophrenics in the Community.* New York: Appleton-Century-Crofts.

Petroni, Frank, and Griffin, Carol, 1969. "Labeling and Psychiatry: Perspectives in Need of Data." *Social Science and Medicine* 3 (August): 239–247.

Rubel, Arthur, 1960. "Concepts of Disease in Mexican-American Culture." *American Anthropologist* 62: 795–814.

Scheff, T. J., 1966. *Being Mentally Ill: A Sociological Theory.* Chicago: Aldine Publishing Company.

Schwartz, Lola Romanucci, 1969. "The Hierarchy of Resort in Curative Practices: the Admiralty Islands, Melanesia." *Journal of Health and Social Behavior* 10: 201–209.

Schur, Edwin, 1969. "Reactions to Deviance: A Critical Assessment." *American Journal of Sociology* 75: 309–322.

Stebbins, Robert A., 1970. "Career: The Subjective Approach." *Sociological Quarterly* 11 (Winter): 32–49.

Turner, Ralph, 1968. "Roles." *International Encyclopedia of the Social Sciences.* New York: The Macmillan Company, Inc.

Twaddle, Andrew C., 1969. "Health Decisions and Sick Role Variations." *Journal of Health and Social Behavior* 10 (June): 105–115.

Zola, I. K., 1966. "Culture and Symptoms: An Anaylsis of Patients' Presenting Complaints." *American Sociological Review* 31: 615–630.

Situational Properties
of the Labeling Process

Evaluations and criticism of any theory must necessarily occur at two levels. One is theoretical, in which assumptions are examined and theory is scrutinized for flaws in logic, errors in reasoning, omissions, and oversimplification of ideas. The other is empirical, in which the validity of hypotheses derived from the theory is tested in real life situations and new data are collected about aspects of the phenomenon that are poorly or imperfectly understood. The essays in Part II of this volume are evaluations of the labeling perspective from a theoretical vantage point. The essays in this part present data based upon empirical studies conducted in order to clarify different aspects of the labeling process.

In the first study, Black and Reiss distinguish three types of deviance: detected deviance; detected but unsanctioned deviance; and sanctioned deviance. The purpose of their study is to identify factors that determine citizen and police detection of juvenile deviance and the sanctioning of juveniles through arrest in routine police work. Special attention is focused on situational conditions of police work that influence the probability that detected offenses will be sanctioned. These findings bear directly on issues raised by Gibbs and Warren and Johnson in their critiques of labeling theory.

Cicourel's study is concerned with the management of juveniles by agents of social control following their public identification as delinquents. In particular he is interested in discovering how law-enforcement personnel attempt to link abstract legal norms that assume that violators of the law are responsible for their own actions with the more ambiguous lay conceptions of juveniles as people who are not entirely responsible for their actions in order to assign responsibility and, hence, guilt to the juvenile offender. Cicourel emphasizes the developmental character of the process and the manner in which the juvenile's behavior is subtly transformed to fit the legal and bureaucratic categories used by the control agents in everyday work.

The research by Black and Reiss and Cicourel is concerned primarily with deviants who have been apprehended by official agents of social control. Most sociologists agree, however, that the bulk of deviant behavior in our society goes unnoticed. Such behavior represents a significant type of deviant behavior that is rarely studied. In his essay, Ball reports the result of research on the users and operators of an illegal abortion clinic. The essay is of interest not only because of the important light it sheds on this little understood aspect of social life but also because of the unusual methodological problems it poses. Ball discusses how he conducted the research and attempts to abstract from his experience some methodological guidelines of value to anyone studying deviant behavior.

Chapter Five

POLICE CONTROL
OF JUVENILES*

Donald J. Black and Albert J. Reiss, Jr.

Current theory on deviant behavior and social control inquires very little into either the organized processes by which deviance is detected or the patterns by which deviance is sanctioned, countenanced, or ignored once it is found out. Despite a ground swell of concern with *social reactions* to deviant behavior—the core of the labeling approach to deviance—the sociology of social control remains a conceptually retarded body of knowledge. One way of drawing detection and sanctioning differentials into the analytical bounds of theory is to define deviance in terms of the probability of a control response. Thus, *individual or group behavior is deviant if it falls within a class of behavior for which there is a probability of negative sanctions subsequent to its detection.*[1] For any form of behavior to be classified as deviant, the probability of negative sanctions must be above zero when the behavior is detected. The greater the probability of sanction, the more appropriate is the

* The research reported in this paper was supported by Grant Award 006, Office of Law Enforcement Assistance, United States Department of Justice, under the Law Enforcement Assistance Act of 1965, as well as by grants from the National Science Foundation and the Russell Sage Foundation. Maureen Mileski, Stanton Wheeler and Abraham S. Goldstein made helpful comments on earlier drafts of the paper.

Reprinted from Donald J. Black and Albert J. Reiss, Jr., "Police Control of Juveniles," *American Sociological Review* 35, 1 (February 1970): 63–77.

classification as deviant.[2] Therefore, whether or not a given form of behavior is deviant and the extent to which it is deviant are empirical questions.

Detection and sanctioning involve separate probabilities. Some forms of deviance, such as those that arise in private places, have extremely low probabilities of detection. Types of deviance that rarely are detected may nonetheless have very high sanction probabilities. In other cases the converse may be true. Furthermore, the particular probabilities of detection and sanctioning may be closely tied to particular types of deviance. In the case of homicide, for example, the probability of detection is high, as is the probability of some form of negative sanction. The probability of official detection of incest surely is low, while the likelihood of sanctioning may be high when incest is detected. Public drunkenness would seem to have a high detection but a low sanctioning probability. Analogous probabilities could be calculated for types of deviance that fall within jurisdictions other than the criminal law.[3]

A control approach, as here propounded, implies three basic types of deviance: (1) undetected deviance, (2) detected, unsanctioned deviance, and (3) sanctioned deviance.[4] These are the three conditions under which empirical instances of deviant behavior appear in relation to control systems. An instance of undetected deviance occurs if an act or a behavior pattern occurs for which there would be a probability of sanction *if it were detected*. Undetected marijuana-smoking is deviant, for example, since there is a probability of negative sanction when an instance of this *class* of behavior is discovered. When a clearly drunken person is encountered on the street by a policeman but is not arrested, an instance of detected, unsanctioned deviance has taken place. The third type, sanctioned deviance, is self-explanatory.

An elaboration of the analytical distinctions necessary in a control approach would exceed the bounds of this discussion. However, two additional elementary distinctions must be noted. A distinction must be made between official, or formal, detection and sanctioning, on the one hand, and informal detection and sanctioning, on the other. Any approach to deviant behavior that does not inquire into the relations between official and informal control systems is incomplete. In other words, the notion of "social control of deviant behavior" should always have an organizational or system reference. Secondly, it is important to distinguish between the detection of deviant acts and the detection of persons who commit these acts. The general conditions under which persons are linked to deviant acts is a problem for investigation. Informal as well as official control systems involve detective work and the pursuit of evidence.

It should not be surmised from the foregoing that a sociology of the deviance-control process consists solely in the analysis of detection and sanctioning processes. Such would be an overly narrow conception of the subject matter, as well as a distorted analytical description of how control systems operate. The foregoing is oriented mainly to the *case-by-case* responses of control systems to deviant behavior. The framework is not geared to the analysis of control responses that by-pass the problems of detection and sanctioning altogether. For instance, it ignores totally symbolic social control responses, such as may sometimes be found in the enactment of rules where there is no attempt to detect or sanction violations of those rules (Arnold, 1935; Gusfield, 1963). It also neglects the preventive aspects of social control. For example, control systems sometimes take measures to limit opportunities for deviant behavior by constraining the actions of all members of a social category, a tactic illustrated by curfew ordinances, occupational licensing laws, food stamp requirements for welfare recipients, and preventive detention of felony suspects. Thus, an emphasis upon detection and sanctioning differentials should not deflect interest from other important properties of social control systems.

This chapter presents findings on citizen and police detection of juvenile deviance and on the sanctioning of juveniles through arrest in routine police work. It makes problematic situational conditions that increase the probability of sanction subsequent to the detection of violative behavior. Put another way, it makes problematic conditions (besides rule-violative behavior itself) that give rise to differentials in official sanctioning. It is a study of law-in-action. Since all of the data pertain to police encounters with alleged delinquents, the relationship between undetected and detected delinquency is not treated.

The Method

The findings reported here derive from systematic observation of police-citizen transactions conducted during the summer of 1966. Thirty-six observers—persons with law, law enforcement, and social science backgrounds —recorded observations of routine patrol work in Boston, Chicago, and Washington, D.C. The observer training period comprised one week and was identical across the three cities. The daily supervision system also was similar across the cities. The observers rode in scout cars or, less frequently, walked with patrolmen on all shifts on all days of the week for seven weeks in each city. To assure the inclusion of a large number of police-citizen encounters, we gave added weight to the times when police activity is comparatively high (evening watches, particularly weekend evenings).

No attempt was made to survey police-citizen encounters in all localities within the three cities. Instead, police precincts in each city were chosen as observation sites. The precincts were selected so as to maximize observation in lower socio-economic, high crime rate, racially homogeneous residential areas. This was accomplished through the selection of two precincts each in Boston and Chicago and four precincts in Washington, D.C. The findings pertain to the behavior of uniformed patrolmen rather than to that of policemen in specialized divisions such as juvenile units.[5]

The data were recorded by the observers in "incident booklets," forms much like interview schedules. One booklet was filled out for every incident that the police were requested to handle or that they themselves noticed while on patrol.[6] A total of 5,713 of these incidents were observed and recorded. This paper concerns only those 281 encounters that include one or more juvenile suspects among the participants.

The Context

Although large police departments invariably have specialized divisions for handling incidents that involve juveniles, the great majority of juvenile encounters with policemen occur with general duty, uniformed patrolmen, rather than with "youth officers." Youth officers receive most of their cases on a referral basis from members of the uniformed patrol division.[7] Usually these referrals enter the police system as arrests of juveniles by uniformed patrolmen. It will be seen, however, that uniformed patrolmen arrest only a small fraction of the legally liable juvenile suspects with whom they have encounters in the field. Youth bureau officers, then, determine what proportion of those arrested will be referred to juvenile court. The outputs of the patrol division thus become the inputs for the youth bureau, which in turn forwards its outputs as inputs to the court.[8] By the time a juvenile is institutionalized, therefore, he has been judged a delinquent at several stages. Correspondingly, sanctions are levied at several stages; institutionalization is the final stage of a sanctioning *process,* rather than *the* sanction for juvenile deviance.

After the commission of a deviant act by a juvenile, the first stage in the elaborate process by which official rates of delinquency are produced is detection. For the police, as for most well-differentiated systems of social control, detection is largely a matter of organizational mobilization, and mobilization is the process by which incidents come to the initial attention of agents of the police organization. There are two basic types of mobilization of the police: *citizen-initiated,* or "reactive" mobilization, and *police-initiated,* or "proactive" mobilization, depending upon who makes the original decision that police action is appropriate. An example of a citizen-initiated mobilization occurs when a citizen phones the police to report an event and the radio dispatcher sends a patrol car to handle the call. A typical police-initiated mobilization takes place when a policeman observes and acts upon what he regards as a law violation or, as in the case of a "stop-and-frisk," a "suspicious" person or situation.

Popular and even sociological conceptions of the police err through an over-reliance on proactive imagery to characterize police operations. Although some specialized divisions of municipal police departments, such as traffic bureaus and vice units, do depend primarily upon proactive mobilization for their input of cases, in routine patrol work the great majority of incidents come to police attention through the citizen-initiated form of mobilization. The crime detection function is lodged mainly in the citizenry rather than in the police. Moreover, most police work with juveniles also arises through the initiative of citizen complainants. In this sense, the citizen population in good part draws the boundaries of its own official rate of juvenile delinquency.[9]

Detection of Juvenile Deviance

Observation of police encounters with citizens netted 281 encounters with suspects under 18 years of age, here treated as juveniles.[10] The great majority of the juveniles were from blue-collar families.[11] Of the 281 police-juvenile encounters, 72 percent were citizen-initiated (by phone) and 28 percent were initiated by policemen on patrol. Excluding traffic violations, these proportions become 78 percent and 22 percent, respectively. The mobilization of police control of juveniles is then overwhelmingly a reactive rather than a proactive process. Hence it would seem that the moral standards of the citizenry have more to do with the definition of juvenile deviance than do the standards of policemen on patrol.[12]

Moreover, the incidents the police handle in citizen-initiated encounters differ somewhat from those in encounters they bring into being on their own initiative. (See Table 5-1.) This does not mean, however, that the standards of citizens and policemen necessarily differ; the differences between incidents in reactive and proactive police work seem to result in large part from differences in detection opportunities, since the police are limited to the surveillance of public places (Stinchcombe, 1963). For example, noncriminal disputes are more likely to occur in private than in public places; they account for 10 percent of the police-juvenile contacts in citizen-initiated work but for only 3 percent of the proactive encounters. On the other hand, the "suspicious person" is nearly always a police-initiated encounter. Traffic violations, too, are almost totally in the police-initiated category; it is simply not effective or feasible for a citizen to call the police about a "moving" traffic violation (and nearly all of these cases were "moving" rather than "standing" violations). In short, there are a number of contingencies that affect the detection of juvenile deviance in routine policing.

A broader pattern in the occasions for police-juvenile transactions is the overwhelming predominance of incidents of minor legal significance. Only 5 percent of the police encounters with juveniles involve alleged felonies; the remainder are less serious from a legal standpoint. Sixty percent involve nothing more serious than juvenile rowdiness or mischievous behavior, the juvenile counterpart of "disorderly conduct" or "breach of the peace" by adults. This does not mean that the social significance of juvenile deviance is minor for the citizens who call the police or for the police themselves. It should be noted, moreover, that these incidents do not necessarily represent

Table 5-1: Percent of Police Encounters with Juvenile Suspects according to Type
of Mobilization and Race of Suspect, by Type of Incident.

Type of Incident	Citizen-Initiated		Police-Initiated		All Citizen-Initiated	All Police-Initiated	All En-counters
	Negro	White	Negro	White			
Felony	10	—	10	—	5	5	5
Misdemeanor:							
Except Rowdiness	18	11	5	14	15	9	13
Misdemeanor:							
Rowdiness	62	77	40	33	69	37	60
Traffic Violation	1	—	26	28	*	27	8
Suspicious Person	—	1	17	22	*	19	6
Non-Criminal Dispute	8	12	2	3	10	3	8
Total Percent	99	101	100	100	99	100	100
Total Number	(109)	(94)	(42)	(36)	(203)	(78)	(281)

*.5% or less.

the larger universe of juvenile deviance, since (1) in many cases the juvenile offender is not apprehended by the police, and (2) an unknown number of delinquent acts go undetected. Nonetheless, these incidents represent the inputs from which uniformed patrolmen produce juvenile arrests and thus are the relevant base for analyzing the conditions under which juveniles are sanctioned in police encounters.

Another pattern lies in the differences between Negro and white encounters with policemen. In the aggregate, police encounters with Negro juveniles pertain to legally more serious incidents, owing primarily to the differential in felony encounters (see Table 5-1). None of the encounters with white juveniles involved the allegation of a felony, though this was true of 10 percent of the transactions with Negro juveniles in both citizen- and police-initiated encounters. Apart from this difference between the races, however, the occasions for encounters with Negro and white juveniles have many similarities.

It might be noted that the data on the occasions for police-juvenile encounters do not in themselves provide evidence of racial discrimination in the selection of juveniles for police attention. Of course, the citizen-initiated encounters cannot speak to the issue of discriminatory *police* selection. On the other hand, if the police tend to stop a disproportionate number of Negroes on the street in minor incident situations, we might infer the presence of discrimination. But the findings in Table 5-1 do not provide such evidence. Likewise, we might infer police discrimination if a higher proportion of the total Negro encounters is police-initiated than that of the total white encounters. Again the evidence is lacking: police-initiated encounters account for 28 percent of the total for both Negro and white juveniles. More data would be needed to assess adequately the issue of police selectivity by race.

Incidents and Arrest

Of the encounters patrol officers have with juvenile suspects, only 15 percent result in arrest.[13] Hence it is apparent that by a large margin most police-juvenile contacts are concluded in the field settings where they arise.[14] These field contacts, 85 percent of the total, generally are not included in official police statistics on reported cases of juvenile delinquency, and thus they represent the major invisible portion of the delinquency control process. In other words, if these sample data are reasonably representative, the probability is less than one-in-seven that a policeman confronting a juvenile suspect will exercise his discretion to produce an official case of juvenile delinquency. A high level of selectivity enters into the arrest of juveniles. This and subsequent sections of the paper seek to identify some of the conditions which contribute to that selection process.

A differential in police dispositions that appears at the outset of the analysis is that between Negroes and whites. The overall arrest rate for police-Negro encounters is 21 percent, while the rate for police-white encounters is only 8 percent. This difference immediately raises the question of whether or not racial discrimination determines the disposition of juvenile suspects. Moreover, Table 5-2 shows that the arrest rate for Negroes is also higher within specific incident categories where comparisons are possible. The race difference, therefore, is not merely a consequence of the larger number of legally serious incidents that occasion police-Negro contacts.

Apart from the race difference, Table 5-2 reveals that patrol officers

Table 5-2: Percent of Police Encounters with Juvenile Suspects according to Type of Incident and Race of Suspect, by Field Disposition.

Field Disposition	Type of Incident and Race of Suspect													All Negro	All White	All Encounters
	Felony		Misdemeanor: Ex. Rowdiness		Misdemeanor: Rowdiness		Traffic Violation		Suspicious Person		Non-Criminal Dispute					
	N	W	N	W	N	W	N	W	N	W	N	W				
Arrest	73	—	36	20	13	8	8	—	—	(1)	—	—	21	8	15
Release-in-Field	27	—	64	80	87	92	92	100	(7)	(8)	100	100	80	92	85
Total Percent	100	—	100	100	100	100	100	100	—	—	100	100	101	100	100
Total Number	(15)	—	(22)	(15)	(85)	(84)	(12)	(10)	(7)	(9)	(10)	(12)	(151)	(130)	(281)

make proportionately more arrests when the incident is relatively serious from a legal standpoint. The arrest rate for Negro encounters is twice as high for felonies as it is for the more serious misdemeanors, and for encounters with both races the arrest rate for serious misdemeanors doubles the rate for juvenile rowdiness. On the other hand, policemen rarely make arrests of either race for traffic violations or for suspicious-person situations. Arrest appears even less likely when the incident is a noncriminal dispute. The disposition pattern for juvenile suspects clearly follows the hierarchy of offenses found in the criminal law, the law for adults.

It is quite possible that the legal seriousness of incidents is more important in encounters between *patrol* officers and juveniles than in those between *youth* officers and juveniles. As a rule, the patrol officer's major sanction is arrest, arrest being the major formal product of patrol work. By contrast, the youth officer has the power to refer cases to juvenile court, a prosecutorial discretion with respect to juveniles that patrolmen in large departments usually do not have. Whether he is in the field or in his office, the juvenile officer plays a role different from that of the patrolman in the system of juvenile justice. For this reason alone, the factors relating to the disposition of juveniles may differ between the two. The youth officer may, for example, be more concerned with the juvenile's past record, a kind of information that usually is not accessible to the patrolman in the field setting.[15] Furthermore, past records may have little relevance to a patrol officer who is seeking primarily to order a field situation with as little trouble as possible. His organizational responsibility ends there. For his purposes, the age status of a suspect may even be irrelevant in the field. Conversely, the youth officer may find that the juvenile court or his supervisor expects him to pay more attention to the juvenile's record than to the legal status of a particular incident. In short, the contingencies that affect the sanctioning of juveniles may vary with the organizational sources of the discretion of sanction.

Situational Organization and Arrest

Apart from the substance of police encounters—the kinds of incidents they involve—these encounters have a social structure. One element in this structure is the distribution of situational roles played by the participants in the encounter. Major situational roles that arise in police encounters are those of suspect or offender, complainant, victim, informant, and bystanders.[16] None of these roles necessarily occurs in every police encounter.

In police encounters with suspects, which account for only about 50 percent of all police-citizen contacts, particularly important is the matter of whether or not a citizen complainant participates in the situational action.[17] A complainant in search of justice can make direct demands on a policeman with which he must comply. Likewise a complainant is a witness of the police officer's behavior; thus he has the ability to contest the officer's version of an encounter or even to bring an official complaint against the officer himself. In these respects as well as others, the complainant injects constraints into police-suspect confrontations. This is not to deny that the complainant often may be an asset to a policeman who enters a pre-existing conflict situation in the field. The complainant can provide what may be otherwise unavailable information to a situationally ignorant patrolman. The patrol officer is a major intelligence arm of modern police systems, but he, like other policemen, must live with a continual dependence upon citizens for the information that it is his allotted responsibility to gather. Furthermore, when a suspect is present in the field situation, the information provided by a complainant, along with his willingness to stand on his word by signing a formal complaint, may be critical to an arrest in the absence of a police witness.

The relationship between arrest and the presence of a complainant in police-juvenile encounters is shown in Table 5-3. It is apparent that this relation between situational organization and disposition differs according to the suspect's race. Particularly interesting is the finding that when there is no citizen complainant in the encounter the race difference in arrest rates narrows to the point of being negligible—14 percent versus 10 percent for encounters with Negro and white juveniles respectively. By contrast, when a complainant participates, this difference widens considerably to 21 percent versus 8 percent. This latter difference is all the more striking since felony situations and traffic and noncriminal dispute situations, which may be regarded as confounding factors, are excluded from the tabulation.

Table 5-3: Percent of Police Encounters with Juvenile Suspects according to Situational Organization and Race of Suspect, by Field Disposition. (Table Excludes Felonies, Traffic Violations, and Non-Criminal Disputes.)

Field Disposition	Situational Organization and Race of Suspect				All Suspect Only	All Complainant and Suspect	All Encounters
	Suspect Only		Complainant and Suspect				
	Negro	White	Negro	White			
Arrest	14	10	21	8	11	16	13
Release-in-Field	86	90	.79	92	89	84	87
Total Percent	100	100	100	100	100	100	100
Total Number	(66)	(93)	(48)	(26)	(159)	(74)	(233)

It also should be noted that as far as the major citizen participants are concerned, each of these encounters is racially homogeneous. The comparatively rare, mixed race encounters are excluded from these computations. Thus the citizen complainants who oversee the relatively severe dispositions of Negro juveniles are themselves Negro. The great majority of the police

officers are white in the police precincts investigated, yet they seem somewhat more lenient when they confront Negro juveniles alone than when a
Negro complainant is involved. Likewise, it will be recalled (Table 5-3)
that the arrest difference between Negro and white juveniles all but dis-
appears when no complainant is involved. These patterns complicate the
question of racial discrimination in the production of juvenile arrests, given
that a hypothesis of discrimination would predict opposite patterns. Indeed,
during the observation period a strong majority of the policemen expressed
anti-Negro attitudes in the presence of observers (Black and Reiss, 1967:132–
139). It might be expected that if the police were expressing their racial
prejudices in discriminatory arrest practices, this would be more noticeable
in police-initiated, typically by the complainants then by citizens. But the
opposite is the case. All of the encounters involving a citizen complainant in
this sample were citizen-initiated typically by the complainants themselves.
Proactive police operations rarely involve complainants. To recapitulate: the
police are particularly likely to arrest a Negro juvenile when a citizen enjoins
them to handle the incident and participates as a complainant in the situational action, but this is not characteristic of police encounters with white
juveniles. Finally, it is noteworthy that Negro juveniles find themselves in
encounters that involve a complainant proportionately more than do white
juveniles. Hence, the pattern discussed has all the more impact on the
over-all arrest rate for Negro juveniles. Accordingly, the next section examines
the role of the complainant in more detail.

The Complainant's Preference and Arrest

If the presence of a citizen complainant increases the production of
Negro arrests, then the question arises as to whether this pattern occurs as a
function of the complainant's mere presence, his situational behavior, or
something else. In part, this issue can be broached by inquiring into the
relationship between the complainant's behavioral preference for police action
in a particular field situation and the kind of disposition the police in fact
make.[18]

Before examining this relationship, however, it should be noted that a
rather large proportion of complainants do not express clear preferences for
police action such that a field observer can make an accurate classification.
Moreover, there is a race differential in this respect. Considering only the
misdemeanor situations, the Negro complainant's preference for action is unclear in 48 percent of the police encounters with Negro juveniles, whereas the
comparable proportion drops to 27 percent for the encounters with white
complainants and juveniles. Nevertheless, a slightly larger proportion of the
Negro complainants express a preference for arrest of their juvenile ad-
versaries—21 percent versus 15 percent for whites. Finally, the complainant

prefers an informal disposition in 31 percent of the Negro cases and in 58 percent of the white cases. Thus white complainants more readily express a preference for police leniency toward juvenile suspects than do Negro complainants.

Table 5-4 suggests that white juveniles benefit from this greater leniency, since the police show a quite dramatic pattern of compliance with the expressed preferences of complainants. This pattern seems clear even though the number of cases necessitates caution in interpretation. In not one instance did the police arrest a juvenile when the complainant lobbied for leniency. When a complainant explicitly expresses a preference for an arrest, however, the tendency of the police to comply is also quite strong. Table 5-4 includes only the two types of misdemeanor, yet the Negro arrest rate when the complainant's preference is arrest (60 percent) climbs toward the rate of arrest for felonies (73 percent, Table 5-2). In no other tabulation does the arrest rate for misdemeanors rise so high. Lastly, it is notable that when the complainant's preference is unclear, the arrest rate falls between the rate for complainants who prefer arrest and those who prefer an informal disposition.

Table 5-4: Percent of Police Encounters with Juvenile Suspects that Involve a Citizen Complainant according to Race of Suspect and Complainant's Preference, by Field Disposition. (Table Excludes Felonies, Traffic Violations, and Non-Criminal Disputes.)

Field Disposition	Race of Suspect and Complainant's Preference						All Negro Encounters	All White Encounters	All Encounters
	Negro			White					
	Prefers Arrest	Prefers Informal Disposition	Preference Unclear	Prefers Arrest	Prefers Informal Disposition	Preference Unclear			
Arrest	60	—	17	(1)	—	(1)	21	8	16
Release-in-Field	40	100	83	(3)	100	(6)	79	92	84
Total Percent	100	100	100	—	100	—	100	100	100
Total Number	(10)	(15)	(23)	(4)	(15)	(7)	(48)	(26)	(74)

These patterns have several implications. First, it is evident that the higher arrest rate for Negro juveniles in encounters with complainants and suspects is largely a consequence of the tendency of the police to comply with the preferences of complainants. This tendency is costly for Negro juveniles, since Negro complainants are relatively severe in their expressed preferences when they are compared to white complainants vis-à-vis white juveniles. Furthermore, it will be remembered that it is in encounters with this situational organization rather than in those with suspects alone that the race differential is most apparent. Given the prominent role of the Negro complainant in the race differential, then, it may be inappropriate to consider this pattern an instance of discrimination on the part of policemen. While police behavior follows the same *patterns* for Negro and white juveniles, differential *outcomes* arise from differences in *citizen* behavior (cf. Werthman and Piliavin, 1967).

Another implication of these findings is more general, namely, that the citizen complainant frequently performs an adjudicatory function in police encounters with juveniles. In an important sense the patrol officer abdicates his discretionary power to the complainant. At least this seems true of the encounters that include an expressive or relatively aggressive complainant among the participants. To say that the complainant often can play the role of judge in police encounters is tantamount to saying that the moral standards of citizens often can affect the fate of juvenile suspects. Assuming that the moral standards of citizens vary across social space, i.e., that there are moral subcultures, then it follows that police dispositions of juvenile suspects in part reflect that moral diversity. To this degree policemen become the unwitting custodians of those moral subcultures and thereby perpetuate moral diversity in the larger community. Assuming the persistence of this pattern of police compliance, then it would seem that police behavior is geared, again unwittingly, to moral change. As the moral interests of the citizenry change, so will the pattern of police control. Earlier it was noted that most police encounters with juveniles come into being at the beckoning of citizens. Now it is seen that even the handling of those encounters often directly serves the moral interests of citizens.[19]

Situational Evidence and Arrest

Another variable that might be expected to affect the probability of arrest is the nature of the evidence that links a juvenile suspect to an incident. In patrol work there are two major means by which suspects are initially connected with the commission of crimes: the observation of the act itself by a policeman and the testimony by a citizen against a suspect. The primary evidence can take other forms, such as a bloodstain on a suspect's clothing or some other kind of physical "clue," but this is very unusual in routine patrol work. In fact, the legally minor incidents that typically occasion police-juvenile contacts seldom provide even the possibility of non-testimonial evidence. If there is neither a policeman who witnesses the incident nor a citizen who gives testimony concerning it, then ordinarily there is no evidence whatever in the field setting. Lastly, it should be emphasized that the concept of evidence as used here refers to "situational evidence" rather than to "legal evidence." Thus it refers to the kind of information that appears relevant to an observer in a field setting rather than to what might be acceptable as evidence in a court of law.

In about 50 percent of the situations a police officer observes the juvenile offense, excluding felonies and traffic violations. Hence, even though citizens initially detect most juvenile deviance, the police often respond in time to witness the behavior in question. In roughly 25 percent of the situations the policeman arrives too late to see the offense committed but a citizen gives testimonial evidence. The remaining cases, composed primarily of non-criminal disputes and suspicious-person situations, bear no evidence of criminal conduct. In a heavy majority of routine police-juvenile encounters, the juvenile suspect finds himself with incriminating evidence of some sort. The low arrest rate should be understood in this context.

On the other hand, it should not be forgotten that these proportions pertain to misdemeanor situations and that the arrests are all arrests without a formal warrant. The law of criminal procedure requires that the officer witness the offense before he may make a misdemeanor arrest without warrant. If the officer does not observe the offense, he must have a signed complaint from a citizen. Such is the procedural law for adults. The law for juveniles, however, is in flux as far as questions of procedure are concerned.[20] It is not at all clear that an appellate court would decide on a juvenile's behalf if he were to appeal his case on the grounds that he was arrested for a misdemeanor even though the arresting officer neither witnessed the act nor acquired a formal complaint from a citizen. Even so, it might be expected that the rate of arrest would be higher in encounters where the act is witnessed by a policeman, if only because these would seem to be the situations where the juvenile suspect is maximally and unambiguously liable. But this expectation is not supported by the observation data (see Table 5-5).

Table 5-5: Percent of Police Encounters with Juvenile Suspects according to Major Situational Evidence and Race of Suspect, by Field Disposition. (Table Excludes Felonies and Traffic Violations.)

| Field Disposition | Major Situational Evidence and Race of Suspect | | | | | | | | All Negro Encounters | All White Encounters | All Encounters |
| | Police Witness | | Citizen Testimony | | No Evidence | | Not Ascertained | | | | |
	N	W	N	W	N	W	N	W			
Arrest	16	10	22	14	—	4	(2)	—	15	9	12
Release-in-Field	84	90	78	86	100	96	(7)	(2)	85	91	88
Total Percent	100	100	100	100	100	100	—	—	100	100	100
Total Number	(57)	(69)	(36)	(21)	(22)	(28)	(9)	(2)	(124)	(120)	(244)

In Table 5-5 it is shown that in "police witness" situations the arrest rate is no higher but is even slightly, though insignificantly, lower than the rate in "citizen testimony" situations. It is possible that some or all of these arrests when the major situational evidence lies with the testimony of a citizen would be viewed as "false" arrests if they involved adult suspects, though this legal judgment cannot be made with certainty. It is conceivable, for example, that some citizen complainants signed formal complaints at the police station subsequent to the field encounters.

The low arrest rate in "police witness" situations is striking in itself. It documents the enormous extent to which patrolmen use their discretion to release juvenile deviants without official sanctions and without making an official report of the incident. Official statistics on juvenile delinquency vastly underestimate even the delinquent acts that policemen witness while on patrol. In this sense the police keep down the official delinquency rate.[21] One other implication of the low arrest rate should be noted. Because the vast majority of police-juvenile contacts are concluded in field settings, judicial control of police conduct through the exclusion of evidence in juvenile courts is potentially emasculated. Police control of juveniles—like that of adults (Reiss and Black, 1967)—may be less prosecution-oriented than the law assumes. In other words, much about the policing of juveniles follows an informal-processing or harassment model rather than a formal-processing model of control.[22] From a behavioral standpoint, law enforcement generally is not a legal duty of policemen.

On the other hand, the importance of situational evidence should not be analytically underestimated. Table 5-5 also shows that the police very rarely arrest juveniles when there is no evidence. In only one case was a juvenile arrested when there was no situational evidence in the observer's judgment; this was a suspicious-person situation. In sum, then, even when the police have very persuasive situational evidence, they generally release juveniles in the field; but, when they do arrest juveniles, they almost always have evidence of some kind. When there is strong evidence against a suspect, formal enforcement becomes a privilege of the police officer. This privilege provides an opportunity for discriminatory practices (Davis, 1969:169–176).

The Suspect's Deference and Arrest

A final factor that can be considered in its relation to the situational production of juvenile arrests is the suspect's degree of deference toward the police. Earlier research on police work suggests a strong association between situational outcomes and the degree of respect extended to policemen by suspects, namely, the less respectful the suspect, the harsher the sanction (Piliavin and Briar, 1964; Westley, 1955). In this section it is shown that the observation data on police-juvenile contacts draw a somewhat more complex profile of this relationship than might have been anticipated.

Before the findings on this relationship are examined, however, it should be noted that the potential impact of the suspect's deference on juvenile dispositions in the aggregate is necessarily limited. Only a small minority of juveniles behave at the extremes of a continuum going from very deferential or very respectful at one end to antagonistic or disrespectful at the other. In most encounters with patrolmen the outward behavior of juvenile suspects falls between these two extremes: the typical juvenile is civil toward police officers, neither strikingly respectful nor disrespectful. The juvenile suspect is civil toward the police in 57 percent of the encounters, a rather high proportion in view of the fact that the degree of deference was not ascertained in 16 percent of the 281 cases. The juvenile is very deferential in 11 percent and antagonistic in 16 percent of the encounters. Thus if disrespectful juveniles are processed with stronger sanctions, the subpopulation affected is fairly small. The majority of juvenile arrests occur when the suspect is civil toward the police. It remains to be seen, however, how great the differences are in the probability of arrest among juveniles who display varying degrees of deference.

The relationship between a juvenile suspect's deference and his liability to arrest is relatively weak and does not appear to be unidirectional. Considering all of the cases, the arrest rate for encounters where the suspect is civil is 16 percent. When the suspect behaves antagonistically toward the police, the rate is higher—22 percent. Although this difference is not wide, it is in the expected direction. What was not anticipated, however, is that the arrest rate for encounters involving very deferential suspects is also 22 percent, the same as that for the antagonistic group. At the two extremes, then, the arrest rate is somewhat higher.

Table 5-6 shows the arrest rates of suspects, excluding felony situations, according to their race and degree of deference toward police. The bi-polar pattern appears in the encounters with Negro juveniles, though in the encounters with white juveniles it does not. In fact, the number of cases where a white juvenile is extreme at one end or the other, particularly where he is very deferential, is so small as to render the differences insignificant. Likewise, there is a case problem with the Negro encounters, but there the differences are

Table 5-6: Percent of Police Encounters with Juvenile Suspects according to the Suspect's Race and Degree of Deference toward the Police, by Field Disposition. (Table Excludes Felonies.)

| | Race and Suspect's Degree of Deference | | | | | | | | |
| | Negro | | | | White | | | | |
Field Disposition	Very Defer- ential	Civil	Antago- nistic	Not Ascer- tained	Very Defer- ential	Civil	Antago- nistic	Not Ascer- tained	All Encoun- ters
Arrest	20	15	24	—	10	9	13	12	12
Release-in-Field	80	85	76	100	90	91	87	100	88
Total Percent	100	100	100	100	100	100	100	100	100
Total Number	(20)	(72)	(21)	(23)	(10)	(76)	(23)	(21)	(266)

a little wider, especially between the encounters where the suspect is civil as against those where the suspect is antagonistic. Overall, again, the differences are not dramatic for either race.

Because of the paucity of cases in the "very deferential" and "antagonistic" categories, the various offenses, with one exception, cannot be held constant. It is possible to examine only the juvenile rowdiness cases separately. In those encounters the arrest rates follow the bipolar pattern: 16 percent for very deferential juveniles, 11 percent for civil juveniles, and 17 percent for the encounters where a juvenile suspect is antagonistic or disrespectful. When felony, serious misdemeanor, and rowdiness cases are combined into one statistical base, the pattern is again bipolar: 26 percent, 18 percent, and 29 percent for the very deferential, civil, and antagonistic cases respectively.

Nothing more than speculation can be offered to account for the unexpectedly high arrest rate for juveniles who make an unusually great effort to behave respectfully toward policemen. First, it might be suggested that this finding does not necessarily conflict with that of Piliavin and Briar (1964), owing to an important difference between the coding systems employed. Piliavin and Briar use only two categories, "cooperative" and "uncooperative," so the "very deferential" and "civil" cases presumably fall into the same category. If this coding system were employed in the present investigation, the bipolar distribution would disappear, since the small number of "very deferential" cases would be absorbed by the large number of "civil" cases and the combined rate would remain below the rate for the "antagonistic" cases. This, then, is one methodological explanation of the discrepancy in findings between the two investigations.

One substantive interpretation of the pattern itself is that juveniles who are and who know themselves to be particularly liable to arrest may be especially deferential toward the police as a tactic of situational self-defense. After all, the notion that one is well-advised to be polite to policemen if one is in trouble is quite widespread in the community. It is a folk belief. These findings might suggest that this tactic is by no means foolproof. In any event the data do not provide for a test of this interpretation. It would seem that a good deal more research is needed pertaining to the relations between situational etiquette and sanctioning.

Overview

This chapter examines findings on the official detection and sanctioning of juvenile deviance. It begins with a conception of deviance that emphasizes sanctioning *probabilities,* thereby linking the empirical operation of social control systems to the analytical definition of deviant behavior itself. In the present investigation, the central concern is to specify situational conditions that affect the probability of sanction by arrest subsequent to the mobilization of policemen in field settings. It is a control approach to juvenile deviance. Simultaneously it is a study of interaction between representatives of the legal system and juveniles—a study of law-in-action.

Several major patterns appear in the finding from the observation research. It would seem wise to conclude with a statement of these patterns in propositional form. Observation of police work in natural settings, after all, is hardly beyond an exploratory phase.

I: Most police encounters with juveniles arise in direct response to citizens who take the initiative to mobilize the police to action.

II: The great bulk of police encounters with juveniles pertains to matters of minor legal significance.

III: The probability of sanction by arrest is very low for juveniles who have encounters with the police.

IV: The probability of arrest increases with the legal seriousness of alleged juvenile offenses, as that legal seriousness is defined in the criminal law for adults.

V: Police sanctioning of juveniles strongly reflects the manifest preferences of citizen complainants in field encounters.

VI: The arrest rate for Negro juveniles is higher than that for white juveniles, but evidence that the police behaviorally orient themselves to race as such is absent.

VII: The presence of situational evidence linking a juvenile to a deviant act is an important factor in the probability of arrest.

VIII: The probability of arrest is higher for juveniles who are unusually respectful toward the police and for those who are unusually disrespectful.

Collectively the eight propositions, along with the corollary implications suggested in the body of the analysis, provide the beginning of an empirical portrait of the policing of juveniles. At some point, however, a descriptive portrait of this kind informs theory. This paper proceeds from a definition of deviance as any class of behavior for which there is a probability of negative sanction subsequent to its detection. From there it inquires into factors that differentially relate to the detection and particularly the official sanctioning of juveniles. Hence it inquires into properties that generate a control response. This strategy assumes that sanctioning probabilities are contingent upon properties of social situations besides rule-violative behavior. Since deviance is defined here in terms of the probability of sanction, it should now be apparent that the referent of the concept of deviance may include whatever else, besides rule-violative behavior, generates sanctioning. The present analysis suggests that sanctioning is usually contingent upon a configuration of situational properties. Perhaps, then, deviance itself should be treated theoretically as a configuration of properties rather than as a unidimensional behavioral event. A critical aspect of the sociology of deviance and control consists in the discovery of these configurations. More broadly, the aim is to discover the social organization of deviance and control.

The topic at hand embraces a good deal more than police encounters with juveniles. There is a need for information about other contexts of social control, studies of other detection and sanctioning processes. There is a need for comparative analysis. What is the role of the complainant upon comparable occasions? Is a complainant before a policeman analogous to an interest group before a legislature? Little is known about the differences and similarities between legal and nonlegal systems of social control. What is the effect of evidence in nonlegal contexts? How is a policeman before a suspect like a psychiatrist before a patient or a pimp before a whore? Are there varieties of procedural control over the sanctioning process in non-legal contexts? To what extent are other legal processes responsive to moral diversity in the citizen population? The intricacies of social control generally are slighted in sociology. Correspondingly the state of the general theory of deviance and control is primitive.

Notes

1. This conceptualization consciously bears the imprint of Max Weber's work. For example, he defines "power" as "the probability that one actor within a social relationship will be in a position to carry out his own will despite resistance, regardless of the basis on which this probability rests" (Parsons, 1964:152). Weber defines "law" as follows: ". . . An order will be called *law* when conformity with it is upheld by the probability that deviant action will be met by physical or psychic sanctions aimed to compel conformity or to punish disobedience, and applied by a group of men especially empowered to carry out this function" (Parsons, 1964:127). Cf. the translation of this definition in Max Rheinstein (1966:5).

2. This does not, of course, preclude a probability of positive sanctions for the behavior. Some forms of deviant behavior are encouraged by subcultures that bestow positive sanctions for behavior which is handled as deviant in the wider community. One interesting but untouched problem in deviant behavior theory is that of the relative effects of joint probabilities of positive and negative sanctions in producing behavior of a given class.

3. One consequence of following this approach is that a control system can be examined from the standpoint of the deviant who is concerned with calculating his *risks* in the system. Oliver Wendell Holmes (1897) proposed this perspective as an approach to the legal system: "If you want to know the law and nothing else, you must look at it as a bad man, who cares only for the

material consequences which such knowledge enables him to predict, not as a good one, who finds his reasons for conduct, whether inside the law or outside of it, in the vaguer sanctions of conscience."

4. The definition of deviance presented above excludes what may appear to be the fourth logical possibility, i.e., undetected, sanctioned deviance.

5. Very little research on the police has dealt with the routine work of the uniformed patrol division. For a review of investigations on the police see Bordua and Reiss (1967). A recent exception is James Q. Wilson (1968); his study, however, relies primarily upon official statistics.

6. These booklets were not filled out in the presence of the policemen. In fact, the officers were told that our research was not concerned with police behavior but, rather, that we were concerned *only* with citizen behavior toward the police and the kinds of problems citizens make for the police. In this sense the study involved systematic deception.

7. In two of the cities investigated, however, aggressive youth patrols ("gang dicks") are employed in the policing of juveniles. Most youth officers spend much of their time behind their desks dealing with referrals and work relatively little "on the street."

8. Most research on the control of juveniles begins at stages beyond the police field encounter. (Examples are Goldman, 1963; Terry, 1967; McEachern and Bauzer, 1967; Cicourel, 1968; Wheeler, 1968).

9. Even in proactive police work, police initiative may be in response to citizen initiative. Proactive police units often are highly dependent upon citizen intelligence, though the dependence usually is once removed from the field situation (see Skolnick, 1966). For example, citizens occasionally provide the police with intelligence about *patterned* juvenile behavior, such as complaints provided by businessmen about recurrent vandalism on their block or recurrent rowdiness on their corner. These may lead the police to increase surveillance in an attempt to "clean up" the area.

10. The relatively rare police encounters with suspects of mixed age status—adults and juveniles together—are excluded from this analysis. Further, it should be emphasized that the unit of analysis here is the encounter rather than the individual juvenile. Many encounters include more than one suspect.

11. It sometimes is difficult for a field observer to categorize a citizen according to social class status. During the observation period two broad categories were used, blue-collar and white-collar, but observers occasionally were unable to make the judgment. The precincts sampled were mainly populated by lower status citizens; so, not surprisingly, the vast majority of the citizen participants were labeled blue-collar by the observers. This majority was even larger for the suspects involved. Consequently, there are not enough white-collar suspect cases for separate analysis. However, the small number of juveniles of ambiguous social class status are combined with the blue-collar cases in this analysis.

12. Some police-citizen conflict may be generated when citizens view the police as reluctant to respond to their definitions of deviance. Citizens regard this as

"police laxity" or "underenforcement." This complaint has lately been aired by some segments of the Negro community.

13. The concept of arrest used here refers only to transportation of a suspect to a police station, not to the formal booking or charging of a suspect with a crime. This usage follows Wayne R. LaFave (1965).

14. The arrest rate for adult suspects is somewhat higher than that for juvenile suspects. For findings on the policing of adults see Donald J. Black (1968: 170–262). The present analysis is similar to that followed in Black's study.

15. In a study of youth bureau records, it was found that past record was an important factor in the referral of juveniles to the probation department and to the juvenile court (Terry, 1967). Past record was also found to be an important factor in the sanctioning decisions of youth officers in the field (Piliavin and Briar, 1964).

16. For a discussion of the pivotal roles of lay persons in the control of mentally ill persons, see Erving Goffman's discussion of the complainant's role in the hospitalization of the offender (1961:133–146).

17. Less than 50 percent of the citizen-initiated encounters involve a suspect. Police-initiated encounters, by contrast, typically do result in police-suspect interaction. However, almost nine-in-ten encounters patrol officers have with citizens are initiated by citizens. In the modal police encounter, the major citizen participant is a complainant (Black, 1968:45, 92, and 156).

18. Jerome Hall (1952:317–319) suggests several propositions concerning the probability of criminal prosecution. One of Hall's propositions is particularly relevant in the present context: "The rate of prosecution varies directly in proportion to the advantage to be gained from it by the complainant or, the rate is in inverse proportion to the disadvantages that will be sustained by him."

19. Paul Bohannan (1967) notes that a core function of legal institutions is to *re*institutionalize the normative standards of nonlegal institutions. In other words, the legal process represents an *auxiliary* control resource for *other* normative systems. (Also see Bohannan, 1968.)

    The patterned compliance of the police with citizens may be understood partly as an instance of the reinstitutionalization function of the legal process. Police control of juveniles, for example, is partly a matter of reinforcement of the broader institution of authority based upon age status. The police support adult authority; in parent-child conflicts the police tend to support parental authority.

20. This has been all the more the case since the U.S. Supreme Court decision in 1967, in *Re Gault,* 387 U.S. 1. The *Gault* decision is a move toward applying the same formal controls over the processing of juvenile suspects as are applied in the adult criminal process. For an observation study of juvenile court encounters see Norman Lefstein, *et al.* (1969). This study includes a discussion of constitutional issues relating to the processing of juveniles.

    It might be added that from a social control standpoint, neither police deviance from procedural law, in the handling of juveniles or adults, nor the low rate of detection and sanctioning of this deviance should be surprising. Rarely can a law of any kind be found without deviance, and equally rare is the detection rate or sanctioning rate for any form of legal deviance near the 100 percent level. Curiously, however, social scientists seem to take for granted low enforcement of substantive law, while they take low control of deviance by the agents of law, such as policemen, to be an empirical peculiarity. Much might be gained from an approach that would seek to understand both forms of legal deviance and control with the same analytical framework. Moreover, substantive control and procedural control can be profitably analyzed in terms of their inter-relations (cf. Llewellyn, 1962:22). Procedural control of the police—for example, limitations on their power to stop-and-frisk—can decrease detection and sanctioning probabilities for certain forms of substantive deviance, such as "possession of narcotics."

21. Citizens do not necessarily perceive the "delinquency problem" as a function of official delinquency rates and are probably more concerned with what they know about patterns of *victimization* in their communities or neighborhoods. Many citizens may be inclined more to a folk version of the control approach than a labeling approach to delinquency. Their very concern about "the problem" may be partly a dissatisfaction with the existing detection and sanctioning probabilities they divine about juvenile deviance.

22. Michael Banton (1964:6–7) makes a distinction between "law officers," whose contacts with citizens tend to be of a punitive or inquisitory character, and "peace officers," who operate within the moral consensus of the community and are less concerned with law enforcement for its own sake. He suggests that patrol officers principally are peace officers, whereas detectives and traffic officers, for example, are more involved in law enforcement as such. Banton's distinction has been elaborated by Bittner (1967) and Wilson (1968). Except when patrolmen handle felony situations involving juveniles, the policing of juveniles is mainly a matter of maintaining peace.

References

Arnold, Thurman N., 1935. *The Symbols of Government.* New Haven, Connecticut: Yale University Press.

Banton, Michael, 1964. *The Policeman in the Community.* London: Tavistock Publications Limited.

Bittner, Egon, 1967. "The Police on Skid-Row: A Study of Peace-keeping." *American Sociological Review* 32: 699–715.

Black, Donald J., 1968. Police Encounters and Social Organization: An Observation Study. Unpublished Ph.D. Dissertation, Department of Sociology, University of Michigan.

Black, Donald J., and Reiss, Albert J. Jr., 1967. "Patterns of Behavior in Police and Citizen Transactions." Pp. 1–139 in President's Commission on Law Enforcement and Administration of Justice, Studies in Crime and Law Enforcement in Major Metropolitan Areas, Field Surveys III, Vol. 2. Washington, D.C.: U.S. Government Printing Office.

Bohannon, Paul, 1967. "The Differing Realms of the Law." Pp. 43–56 in P. Bohannon, ed. *Law and Warfare: Studies in the Anthropology of Conflict.* Garden City, New York: The Natural History Press.
1968. "Law and Legal Institutions." Pp. 73–78 in David L. Sills, ed. *International Encyclopedia of the Social Sciences,* Vol. 9. New York: The Macmillan Company, and the Free Press.

Bordua, David J., and Reiss, Albert J. Jr., 1967. "Law Enforcement." Pp. 275–303 in Paul Lazarsfeld, William Sewell, and Harold Wilensky, eds. *The Uses of Sociology.* New York: Basic Books, Inc.

Cicourel, Aaron V., 1968. *The Social Organization of Juvenile Justice.* New York: John Wiley and Sons, Inc.

Davis, Kenneth Culp, 1969. *Discretionary Justice: A Preliminary Inquiry.* Baton Rouge, Louisiana: Louisiana State University Press.

Goffman, Erving, 1961. *Asylums: Essays on the Social Situation of Mental Patients and Other Inmates.* Garden City, New York: Anchor Books.

Goldman, Nathan, 1963. *The Differential Selection of Juvenile Offenders for Court Appearance.* New York: National Council on Crime and Delinquency.

Gusfield, Joseph R., 1963. *Symbolic Crusade: Status Politics and the American Temperance Movement.* Urbana, Illinois: University of Illinois Press.

Hall, Jerome, 1952. *Theft, Law and Society.* Indianapolis, Indiana: The Bobbs-Merrill Company.

Holmes, Oliver Wendell, 1897. "The Path of the Law." *Harvard Law Review* 10: 457–478.

LaFave, Wayne R., 1965. *Arrest: The Decision to Take a Suspect into Custody.* Boston, Massachusetts: Little, Brown and Company.

Lefstein, Norman; Stapleton, Vaughan; and Teitelbaum, Lee, 1969. "In Search of Juvenile Justice: Gault and its Implementation. *Law and Society Review* 3: 491–562.

Llewellyn, Karl N., 1962. *Jurisprudence: Realism in Theory and Practice.* Chicago, Illinois: University of Chicago Press.

McEachern, A. W., and Bauzer, Riva, 1967. "Factors Related to Disposition in Juvenile Police Contacts." Pp. 148–160 in Malcolm W. Klein, ed. *Juvenile Gangs in Context.* Englewood Cliffs, N.J.: Prentice-Hall, Inc.

Parsons, Talcott, ed., 1964. *Max Weber: The Theory of Social and Economic Organization.* New York: The Free Press.

Piliavin, Irving, and Briar Scott, 1964. "Police Encounters with Juveniles." *American Journal of Sociology* 70: 206–214.

Reiss, Albert J., Jr., and Black, Donald J., 1967. "Interrogation and the Criminal Process." *The Annals of the American Academy of Political and Social Science* 374: 47–57.

Rheinstein, Max, ed., 1966. *Max Weber on Law in Economy and Society.* Cambridge, Mass.: Harvard University Press.

Skolnick, Jerome H., 1966. *Justice Without Trial: Law Enforcement in Democratic Society.* New York: John Wiley and Sons, Inc.

Stinchcombe, Arthur L., 1963. "Institutions of Privacy in the Determination of Police Administrative Practice." *American Journal of Sociology* 69: 150–160.

Terry, Robert M., 1967. "The Screening of Juvenile Offenders." *Journal of Criminal Law, Criminology and Police Science* 58: 173–181.

Werthman, Carl, and Piliavin, Irving, 1967. "Gang Members and the Police." Pp. 56–98 in David J. Bordua, ed. *The Police: Six Sociological Essays.* New York: John Wiley and Sons, Inc.

Westley, William A., 1955. "Violence and the Police." *American Journal of Sociology* 59: 34–41.

Wheeler, Stanton, ed., 1968. *Controlling Delinquents.* New York: John Wiley and Sons, Inc.

Wilson, James Q., 1968. *Varieties of Police Behavior: The Management of Law and Order in Eight Communities.* Cambridge, Mass.: Harvard University Press.

Chapter Six

DELINQUENCY AND THE ATTRIBUTION OF RESPONSIBILITY

Aaron V. Cicourel

The use of terms such as "deviant," "delinquent," "child," and "immature," implies a lack of competence and responsibility in discharging what sociologists term "institutionalized roles" and their attendant normative tasks. Global theoretical depictions have been unsuccessful in confronting the empirical problem of how persons come to be labeled as "strange," or "different," and how behavioral displays are recognized as "odd," or "deviant." Nor do abstract theories specify how the socially organized daily activities of agencies of social control come to produce the cases that ultimately find their way into official rates of deviance. The labeling, the interpretation of behavioral displays, and the daily activities and judgments by social control personnel all constitute ideal normative as well as practiced and enforced decisions that index cultural attributions of deviance. Global theories (Parsons 1951; Merton 1957) do not specify how the researcher, much less the layman, decides on adequate performance in institutionalized roles, and, therefore, these theories can only discuss deviance in a behavioral vacuum.

Theories of deviance seldom provide a developmental context within which to describe how behavioral displays are identified as warranting attributions of rule violation. This chapter imposes a developmental perspective on recent work (Cicourel, 1970) to outline how law-enforcement personnel attempt to link abstract legal norms with ambiguous lay conceptions of institutionalized roles, and thereby assign responsibility and hence guilt or aberrant imputations to juvenile behavior. It focuses upon how lay conceptions of "right" and "wrong" and legal norms are generated in order to first identify and then locate the relevance, and hence socially acceptable meaning, of juvenile conduct so as to justify calling behavioral displays "delinquent."

The Developmental Problem

The sociologist's notion of institutionalized roles (Goode 1960) presumes that there are markers for signaling the transition from some state, whereby a role is seen as "less institutionalized," to some point where "complete" institutionalization occurs. The developmental stages presumably follow a chronological ordering and have been reported in Western and non-Western studies. Yet despite ritualistically punctuated ceremonies attendant to a coming of chronological age, recent studies of child-bearing practices by anthropologists (Whiting 1963) reveal important variations in how different groups assign responsibility within a culture area. For example, in some groups a child may be assigned responsible tasks (such as caring for a smaller sibling or watching a fire) between the ages of four and six, whereas other groups seem to assign complex tasks when the child reaches eight years of age.

I find it significant that variations in cultural attributions of responsibility can be independent of chronological age; daily attributions of competence may vary independently of ideal normative designations of what is expected from occupants of institutionalized roles. The problem can work both ways: a person can be deemed eligible to occupy an abstract or gross institutionalized role or status, but judged by behavioral or performance standards to be "lacking" in observed displays; or a person can be accorded responsibility despite his not having been assigned a normatively defined institutionalized role that presumably accompanies or defines such responsibility. If the anthropologist-sociologist's notion of institutionalized role or status is to have meaning at the level of everyday social interaction, the researcher's model must provide for cultural notions or behavioral criteria in use by the native for attributing status characteristics, as well as theoretical and methodological grounds for claiming that in everyday activities responsibility is assigned and sanctioned despite a lack of ritual designation. Thus the researcher must show the Member's grounds for assigning responsibility under ideal normative and practical circumstances, as well as specify the researcher's grounds for independently observing behavioral displays that he could designate as Member-recognizable role behavior or responsibility.

Lay members of a group are assumed to assign responsibility according to common-sense knowledge that is normative when divorced from action scenes, and emergent (that is, context-bound and immediate) when dealing with unfolding social interaction. The Member's theory of social control, therefore, consists of typical persons to whom responsibility (competence) is assigned routinely because of presumed normal appearances and action, according to unstated rules assumed to be shared with other Members, and that others assume of themselves and him. Members, therefore, typically are sensitive to responsibility (and complaints about discrepancies) in situated or context-restricted displays that require practical judgments about what is presumed to be "happening." Personnel from agencies of social control, however, combine lay schemas with ideal normative rules (such as legal norms) when making attributions of responsibility (or lack of responsibility or deviance). A legal order, therefore, rests upon the ways in which laymen and personnel from agencies of social control depict responsibility and deviance to each other and others (such as layman to police officer, officer to officer, police officer to a jury or judge) so as to justify attributions of "normal" or "strange" behavior.

In North American legal arrangements there have been laws for some time designating when (chronologically) a person can be viewed as responsible for his acts (Platt 1966). But the implementation of the different legal statutes around the country has not been studied vis-à-vis how police officers decide a juvenile's responsibility when observing or told by neighbors or witnesses about behavior said to be in violation of existing legal rules. We have not studied variations in attributions of responsibility over time, although Platt's (1966) work reveals such changes. But I am actually implying at least two problems here:

1. Legal statutes are designed to stipulate the boundaries of responsibility by establishing laws pertaining to "minors" as opposed to adults. Limiting our discussion to children below the age of eighteen, legal statutes presumably would apply uniformly to persons described to, or seen by, the police as guilty of some act defined as a misdemeanor or felony (by adult standards). The stated intention of these laws is to take cognizance of the suspected wrongdoing in the context of the person's age, and not view the act or acts as equivalent to adult behavior vis-à-vis the consequences stated by law. Recent Supreme Court rulings have complicated Juvenile Court laws because it is presumed that such laws provide the child with "sympathetic" justice, yet a few of the rulings imply that the juvenile laws have served to restrict and endanger the child's access to the rights normally accorded adults. The child, therefore, has been treated unfairly by the very Juvenile Court laws that were designed to protect him.

2. The legal issues are further clouded by behavioral variations in how juveniles are "discovered" to be "delinquent," how they are subsequently processed, and how such cases are finally terminated. I am saying that the attribution of responsibility by policemen (or private citizens who call in the police and make the original attributions) is problematic to police departments and different neighborhoods and situated encounters. From my field observations (which can only be called impressionistic for present

purposes) I find that police officers will differentially ignore small children (ages five to seven or eight), and not bother to write up reports requiring the child's parents to come to the station, but will often handle the case individually, and hence not take the legal statutes as seriously encompassing the particular case in point. When the officer does make a case out of a suspected six-year-old, for example, there will usually be other circumstances such as a "history" of incidents, or the child's behavior will be viewed as "too much." Thus justifying a particular case as delinquent is ambiguous at the lower ages, but routine at the older ages (fifteen to eighteen), while context-bound factors loom very important for cases falling in between.

The attribution of responsibility is, of course, a general phenomenon that is critical when deciding how to present oneself before others. Initial appearances become important in establishing some definition of the situation so as to choose among possible courses of action. Context-bound cues interact with socially distributed knowledge for locating the sense of the environment of objects confronted. The police officer's attribution of responsibility presumes a more general conception of competence and some way of evaluating the performance upon which attributions are made.

The attribution of responsibility or competence is basic to the idea of a legal order, and crime and delinquency theories have always contained implicit notions about the presumed relevance of developmental factors in producing later behavioral displays that are termed aberrant. A central theme seems to be that the child should have been exposed to a "better" neighborhood, "better" or more "understanding" parents, a home life where the parents were "stable" and "happily" married, a community where the child was "accepted" and not discriminated against so as to spoil his identity and relations with others, or a community where the child can perceive his future as being hopeful and justly rewarded, all of which means that the juvenile's problems stem from a lack of responsibility or competence and the causes can be found in environmental and genetic factors emergent from some developmental sequence. To comprehend the officer's treatment of the juvenile (or in general terms the mother's or any Member's treatment of another object in socially defined settings) we need some idea of how the officer goes about recognizing phenomena he considers to be "deviant" or in violation of the law, and how such information is processed so as to transform it into "evidence" that can then be described to others by the officer and accepted as "fact" or indices of "real or actual" events. The model we need, therefore, would help fill an embarrassing gap in ambiguously described behavioral displays (or their complete absence) in police reports, and statements by witnesses and juvenile justice personnel when decisions are made to arrest, detain, decide guilt, or commit a juvenile to lengthy incarceration. The entire process, from initial encounter to disposition, requires a model for understanding how reports and statistical materials are produced and understood. What is critical about such a model is that it must explain how the police (or observing researcher) locate phenomena labeled "delinquency" from remarks by witnesses, their observations of juveniles, and interrogating witnesses and juveniles. Unless we have such a model we cannot understand how legal rules said to be integral to a legal order can be articulated with a perceived environment of objects.

Structural interpretations of legal processes presume implicitly that the legal rules are articulated with actual scenes by "reasonable" men, but what constitutes a "reasonable" man is precisely what our model must specify and not leave this notion ambiguous or irrelevant to an explanation of how deviations from legal limits are decided, and how the administration of justice is accomplished. Our model must explain how Members assign meaning to events so as to locate observed (or described) events in a legal context. The articulation of the behavioral activities with legal rules (the articulation of actual scenes with abstract rules) is similar to Rawls' (1955) and Hart's (1961) notion of general rules or policies or practices, and the decision that a particular case (in the present instance rule violation) falls under a general rule or policy (statute).

To summarize our discussion thus far, I have argued that we need essentially two related models that converge at some unspecified point in developmental time (which can be only linked to clock-time in correlational terms): the first model would specify stages at which we might claim that the child has acquired the ability to satisfy standards of language competence and a sense of social structure that permits him to understand differences in clock-time, and increasingly complex rules governing social relationships; the second model, a special case of a more general model of adult competency in language and rule comprehension, must explain how legal personnel utilize interpretive rules to decide rule violations and arrive at dispositional decisions when handling juveniles. I assume that tacit notions of competence or responsibility are being employed to arrive at the articulation between day-to-day activities called to the officer's attention as potential or actual violations of legal rules, and the legal statutes and common law procedures said to cover the location of the day-to-day activities in a generic legal order. The essential point of this chapter is that unless we have an explicit model of how Members assign cultural significance to everyday events as they are perceived over time, we cannot explain the meaning of indexical materials such as arrest reports, court proceedings, dispositional frequencies, and summary statistics about crime and delinquency (Garfinkel 1967). Without a model of this type our research indexes take on "structural meanings" that are *ad hoc* or dependent upon tacit notions about everyday interaction; that is, the "structural effects" are explained by implicit tacit assumptions about the interactional antecedents that led to the structural indexes. The first model must specify cross-culturally free developmental stages whereby the child requires language competence and use, as well as the ability to recognize culturally defined rules and meanings employed by adults, and thus organize his own activities. The central assumption here is that culture-free developmental stages would intersect with culture-restricted (or attributed) stages of development. The researcher must have the first model available if he is to explain the relevance of the second model, whereby adults (particularly parents and law-enforcement personnel) invoke interpretive rules to decide rule violations. The second model presupposes that adults employ a tacit or implicit model of "appropriate" developmental stages of childhood when deciding that rule violations have occurred. The adult must make attributions of responsibility and "reasonableness" in deciding that there has been a violation, as well as deciding what sort of disposition is to be implemented. In recent court rulings on juvenile cases the issue has not been how competence and responsibility have been attributed "correctly" according to developmental and situational circumstances, but whether or not the juvenile's rights, as a person entitled to legal protection considered "minimal" in a democratic society, have been satisfied. The concern with protecting the juvenile's rights from law-enforcement abuse tends to force the case into the use of adult standards for attributing competence and responsibility.

I want to stress that the specification of models of competence and responsibility vis-à-vis the child's developmental stages, and the adult's attributions of competence when making decisions about rule violation and disposition, are basic to all activities whereby deviance is said to occur or stable features of the normative order said to be threatened. The very notion of stable social structures presupposes that we can specify how day-to-day activities continually generate "normative stability." Yet the literature on deviance seldom specifies how the researcher (much less the abstract theorist) identifies "deviant" or "normal" behavioral displays, or how the persons involved in social control identify "deviant" or "normal" behavior. I am insisting that research on how day-to-day activities come to be recognized as "deviant" or "normal" must proceed by identifying a model of the developmental acquisition of competence and performance, and a model of how adults in a given society or group utilize developmental notions of "adequate" competence and performance to decide rule violation and disposition; in short, developmental limits of deviance and normality. Calling deviance that which agents of social control label "deviant" begs the problem of how inferences are made, and leaves social meanings assigned to a neglected residual category.

The Acquisition of Social Structure

A concern with how social order is possible, how stable social organization is maintained or social control achieved, presupposes that children can be socialized so that some continuity can be recognized over different generations.

In the present work I am not concerned with the complex problem of how we identify and measure social changes over generations, but that basic to social change is how adults (particularly parents and law-enforcement agents) recognize "adequate" socialization processes; and by implication, what turns out to be more of a child-rearing task, recognize rule violations and apply correctives. Adults, on the basis of partial information and rather spotty implicit theories of "adequate" character and general physical development, must routinely decide that children, at different developmental stages, are making "normal" progress. These stages are often marked arbitrarily by familial demands (toilet training and the arrival of another child or the mother returning to work), community bureaucratic or administrative arrangements (kindergarten begins and certain tasks must be mastered), and so on. The progression toward adulthood implies that the child gradually acquires or develops *a sense of social structure* or some basic rules that would enable him to use general normative rules on how to "pass" as a "boy" or "girl" and someone's "son" or a "normal six-year-old," and the like. Cultural attributions of an adequate developmental sense of social structure presume that the researchers must examine the varieties of socialization activities that take place in countless settings we term "households," but not simply to measure their ecological representation, but primarily to construct a model of socialization that includes invariant properties to be found in all socialization experiences, as well as properties that adults substantively identify and treat as relevant for claiming that "normal" progression is occurring.

The invariant properties would constitute a "deep structure" (in the sense of deep-structure grammar consisting of phrase structure rules and transformational rules for generating an explicit underlying process and transforming the underlying structure into a surface structure that can be observed [Chomsky 1965] but not a latent structure in the sense of *ad hoc* statistical classes into which public opinion or attitude data are placed, often without an explicit or even implicit theory [Lazersfeld 1950]), while the substantive displays identified by adults as relevant for "normal" or "deviant" socialization would constitute "surface structure" features. In the linguistic formulation the researcher must make his theory explicit by specifying rules and showing how they generate and transform utterances into recognizable sentences by competent adults. In the case of latent structure analysis no such rules or theory are clear or even present, for the analysis is designed to reduce manifest data (opinion polls or attitude surveys) into statistical classes and more facile quantitative analysis. There is no explicit sociological or psychological theory that is basic to the use of latent structure analysis; the only thing that is required are materials or data that have been coded so as to yield appropriate entries for the desired data reduction and manipulation. In latent structure analysis the object is not to generate, with explicit rules, and hence a theory, the rationale for the manifest responses, but to explain the manifest responses through their reduction to a few latent classes that are said to be the "underlying" kernel meanings of not-to-be-trusted manifest responses. Whereas the latent structure analysis technique of data reduction and manipulation could probably be transformed into a model similar to the linguistic model proposed by Chomsky, its original and present use has never reached the intentions, elegance, or success of the linguistic model.

The notion of acquiring social structure assumes that the child develops two parallel competences necessary for producing adequate (from the adult point of view) performance. The initial competence (including phonological and syntactic competence that I assume occur simultaneously) involves the basic rules or interpretive procedures necessary for sustaining a cultural orientation to his environment; locating objects and events in his immediately experienced consciousness, but where the idea of normative comprehension is negligible. The second competence presumes that the child can comprehend the relevance of normative rules as general policies that must be applied "appropriately" to a wide range of activities. The child's use of normative rules is dependent upon interpretive rules in order to decide which general rule or norm is relevant for a particular Here and Now or action scene. Around the age of two years, therefore, the child begins to show some definite language competence (through behavioral displays), and the beginnings of basic and normative rule development. The child's conceptions of social structure emerge developmentally and are partially indexed by parents through the child's use of language and his ability to follow verbal instructions. But parents begin to make attributions of social responsibility even before the child reaches one year of age. These attributions are usually highly context-bound and seldom include prolonged sanctions of a verbal or nonverbal sort. As the parents begin to add toilet-training practices to daily activities, the attributions of responsibility become more pronounced, depending upon parental conceptions of "proper timing" for such practices.

I am proposing that as the child is pushed (however gently or roughly) into activities wherein he is expected to assume more and more self-control such as in eating practices, toilet training, and the handling of objects within and then outside of the home, the parents begin to attribute more responsibility during actual interaction, despite reflections after the fact whereby a decision can be reached that the child probably did not understand, or the parent felt he or she was overly harsh, and the like. A more dramatic observation that can be made frequently has to do with parental reflection after attributing responsibility and enacting some form of punishment on the child, and noticing that someone else or others observed the event. Parents often feel obliged to justify the reprimand or punishment to the observer and the child appears as rather helpless and incapable of the responsibility attributed to it. Yet when a child is viewed as having a "tantrum" and the parent attempts to placate the child with little or no success, it is the parent who looks helpless and at fault despite feelings on the part of the observer that perhaps the child deserves strong punishment. But my point is that adult attributions of responsibility begin early in the child's life, and it is the fact that the child appears to be capable of assuming responsibility that leads the adult to overgeneralize the child's capacity of competence and leap to adult-type standards of evaluation. Most of our admonishments to the child about not doing "something" are couched in futuristic language that the child cannot comprehend in the same sense as adults.

The parent, although aware of the lack of adult competence in the child, nevertheless attributes responsibility in the course of everyday social interaction because there is a growing dependence placed upon the child's ability to perform various tasks. Hence the adult utilizes adult basic rules or interpretive procedures and finds it difficult to sustain a suspension of adult rules when perceiving and interpreting the child's behavioral displays. We have little or no knowledge about the developmental sense of social structure acquired by the child over time. I do not, therefore, attempt to suggest through further anecdotes what the basic or interpretive rules are like for the child, but instead I present a few rules or properties that I assume are integral to an adult sense of social structure in order to indicate what the child must gradually acquire if we are to assume that "adequate" socialization has occurred. The few rules or properties I outline are intended as preliminary elements of a model of the actor needed for any study of social interaction in organized social settings, including fleeting encounters that do not refer to highly routinized activities that are governed by general rules such as laws in a private or public code. Hence the policeman, the probation officer, the judge, and the teacher, attribute competence to the juvenile by utilizing these elements during the administration of juvenile justice or in classroom evaluations of behavior.

A central assumption in generative-transformation grammar and in the social interaction theory assumed in this chapter is that the actor's intentions are basic for understanding his actions, and that the interpretation of action by the speaker and hearer or observer is always accompanied by a reconstruction of the actor's intentions. The reflective ability of the actor, during all phases of interaction, is central for understanding how a sense of social structure develops over time, and essential for our understanding of how an adult attributes responsibility to the child. Some essential elements of basic rules are as follows:

The Reciprocity of Perspectives

The acquisition of this rule enables the child to elaborate the surface utterances of others so as to reconstruct their intentions and to assume that a fellow participant to interaction does the same with the utterances of the child. Thus both participants can assume they would have the same experiences of an immediate action scene if they were to change places. The adult presumes that he and an immediate partner perceive and interpret their environment in essentially the same way such that their personal differences will not alter the way they assign meaning to objects and events (Schutz 1964). The adult speaker-hearer presumes that his utterances will be intelligible and recognizable to others in an "obvious" way so that each lexical item does not have to be explained on each occasion of use. This means, however, that the adult treats lexical items and phrases as indexical expressions (Bar-Hillel 1954; Garfinkel 1967; Cicourel 1970); a lexical item or phrase will be interpreted in a larger context that the particular item indexes, thus permitting the retrieval or construction of information assumed to be relevant for understanding the item or expression. When adult A asks adult B a question, A's message carries an unstated portion that A assumes B will recover and use for understanding the intent of the surface utterance. B, meanwhile, must incorporate the intent or elaborated version of A's message into his answer. The interaction sequence not only locks the speaker and hearer into a series of unstated assumptions about the meaning of the surface utterances, but also presumes that they are referring to a similar oral (stored and/or written) dictionary. When an adult speaks to a child it is not at all clear what each can presume about the other, but based upon my earlier remarks, I would claim that under conditions of rule violation the adult will tend to use an adult version of this rule to assign competence to the child, and thereby expect performances the child cannot deliver.

Immediate and Retrospective-Prospective Uses of the Et Cetera Assumption

The reciprocity of perspectives automatically leads to subroutines that can be described as an additional rule whereby the speaker-hearer must learn to "fill in" constructions "appropriate" to the immediate scene. The "filling in" presumes the existence of common understandings despite their possible ambiguity or vagueness. The idea of common understanding does not intend "agreement" on the part of the participants, but rather a willingness to impose a taken-for-granted meaning or to improvise or let things go until further clarification. The presence or absence of a given lexical item or phrase may be held in suspension or "frozen" until a later part of the exchange, or the item may be assigned provisional meaning according to the context, but altered later in the conversation with new information. The rule instructs the actor to treat objects and events in typified ways, as obvious in meaning, or to prospectively delay passing judgment, or retrospectively reconstruct past assignments of meaning. The "filling in," however, means that the actor invokes normative attributions to decide the larger set of meanings that a given lexical item or phrase indexes or is assumed to index. Over the course of interaction, therefore, the actor must rely upon short-term and long-term stores of information or socially distributed and accepted knowledge (Schutz 1964) when elaborating items embedded in larger networks of meaning. But the invocation of stored information is always subject to context-restricted conditions of the immediate scene; a general normative rule is invoked under the assumption that the particulars of the present context fall under the general rule.

Normal Forms

When the actor subsumes particulars of context-restricted action scenes under more general normative rules he must rely upon typified recognition of his environment. Certain normal forms of acceptable talk, the appearance of objects, and the structure of events are presumed in linking immediate scenes to larger networks of meaning in a normative sense. Self-identification, for example, includes the use of particular lexical items with which the speaker intends to notify the hearer of more general sets of meanings with which the hearer can locate the speaker. The use of normal form typifications is like the construction of common-sense ideal types whereby the actor can readily assign meaning to appearances and presume that others assign similar or identical meanings. When discrepancies arise, the actor attempts to normalize the environment of objects to enable him to decide the relevant general normative rules that should be invoked. Thus, the articulation of particulars in immediate action scenes with general normative rules involves the actor in the creation or construction of a bounded set of related meanings. The construction of the set of meanings permits a decision as to the inclusion or exclusion of a context-restricted object or event within a more general normative or surface rule. The more general rule is presumed to be known in common with others and thus permits concerted action without having to continually define terms during the course of the interaction. But the articulation of the general rule with the particular case can only occur if the actors participating in the interaction have acquired the basic or interpretive rules and their sub-routines as previously described.

Interaction between adults and children or juveniles cannot occur unless both participants have acquired basic or interpretive rules. A number of problems arise here. Can we assume that all adults routinely suspend the attribution of adult competence to children or juveniles when giving instructions, asking for information, and describing presumed violations of surface rules? How do adults make allowances for children or juveniles of different ages? I have argued that we know little or nothing about such problems, yet it is clear that all everyday exchanges between adults and children or juveniles presume that some sort of "solution" to these problems is achieved in every-day behavior. Earlier I asserted that adults invariably treat children and juveniles with adult basic rules of competence in day-to-day social interaction when rule violations are suspected or when unstated (and unclear) attributions of responsibility have been assigned to the child or juvenile. Such assignments of responsibility occur in immediate interaction scenes. The child's or juvenile's demeanor and appearance evoke a sense of adult responsibility that the parent, teacher, and police officer find difficult to suspend. This difficulty frequently arises when the adult senses that the child or juvenile "knows" or "know" that what he was "doing" was "wrong" and hence feels that some form of blame and punishment is justified.

Our juvenile court laws do not distinguish adequately between children age nine or age fifteen when attributing responsibility for acts considered to be rule-violations by adults. The suspension of adult civil rights when juvenile cases come before the courts has been a long political and judicial battle in the United States, and has been criticized precisely because many studies have shown that the child's rights are violated severely when the consequences of the violations are examined; indefinite incarceration, stigma within the community, potential difficulties throughout an adult occupational career, and separation from one's family and community. With the present trend toward providing the juvenile with adult civil rights, the likelihood of attributing adult responsibility increases because adult criminal rules of evidence may be necessary to "convict" the juvenile and enable the court to send the suspect to juvenile installations.

Throughout four years of research on the social organization of juvenile justice (Cicourel 1968), I witnessed countless cases in which the problem of attributing responsibility to the child or juvenile was critical in the decision to arrest, or to file a petition requesting a court appearance, the probation officer's decision to recommend probation or incarceration, the decision to send a child or juvenile to a foster home, and the like. My observations revealed that the attribution of responsibility was linked to the appearance of the juvenile, his demeanor before the officer, his past record or history as known (or discovered) by the officer, and the seriousness of the charge. The combination of appearance, demeanor, and information on the income level or neighborhood of the family was critical in attributing responsibility irrespective of the charge, and this neutralization or escalation of negligence, depending upon the particular combination, was basic to decisions made at all steps in the administration of juvenile justice. The lower the income level of the juvenile's family, the greater is the likelihood that the alleged rule violation would be viewed within the context of adult criminal imputations. The higher the income level of the juvenile's family, the greater is the likelihood of viewing the case as falling under particular clinical criteria of responsibility.

For law-enforcement officials to label a juvenile as "bad" or a "punk" as opposed to "sick" means that behavioral displays enacted by the suspect must be recognized by the official as typical or "appropriate" for invoking a general rule, or that the official be told or convince himself of the necessity of suspending his interpretation of appearances or additional information about the home. My research revealed that the police are less likely to differentiate between different income levels when the demeanor is seen as "offensive" or there is a serious charge and a long record. Under these conditions distinctions between "juvenile" violations of rules and adult violations collapse to a standard language used for adult criminal suspects. I want to argue that the use of language categories taken from the adult penal code and an emphasis upon appearances and demeanor lead officers to attributions of adult responsibility regardless of the age of the juvenile suspect.

A standard interrogation procedure of the police is to force the juvenile into a contradictory set of statements under the assumption that his guilt is obvious. If the officer becomes convinced the juvenile is lying or has lied about his explanations, then the attribution of adult responsibility is felt to be warranted because the officer reasons that the juvenile "knew" what he was doing, "knew" he was not supposed to engage in the alleged rule violation, and hence deserves to be punished. A confession that the juvenile "knew" he was "wrong" is taken as documentary evidence of adult responsibility. A suspension of this responsibility requires an imputation of illness. I am assuming, therefore, that an age range of ten years (eight to eighteen) is not a developmental variable for the officer in attributing responsibility, but instead the officer uses adult *qua* adult criteria based on atemporal (nondevelopmental and hence adult) reasoning; to wit, either obtaining a confession stating the child or juvenile "knew" right from wrong at the time of the alleged violation, or simply satisfying himself that this knowledge is warranted, leads the police officer to divorce developmental considerations or emergent interactional influences from his attribution of responsibility. Thus the officer could use context-restricted evidence stemming from appearances and demeanor that signified the juvenile was a "good kid" or "scared" and misguided by others, to alter the atemporal reasoning derived from a belief that *a priori* knowledge by the child or juvenile of the wrongfulness of a projected action warrants the attribution of adult responsibility. But notice that I am saying that the officer uses the interrogation strategies and language categories at his command to "prove" what he already believes to be "true." A juvenile must be exceptionally convincing before a well-informed juvenile officer to alter the officer's standardized adult-derived reasoning by which attributions of responsibility are made. The officer's reasoning is not a function of ideal legal rules of evidence or ideal normative general rules about children, but stems from his use of basic or interpretive rules in context-restricted settings. The later invocation of a general norm or law in justifying his action in a particular case enables the officer to connect his impressions with a larger community of colleagues or cobelievers.

The officer, in short, attributes adult basic rules to the child or juvenile when deciding the relevance of rule violations. And like the parent, who, in the heat of disconcerting impatience or annoyance with the child or juvenile, cannot suspend the use of adult basic rules, the officer justifies his adult-imposed view of the particular case by invoking general rules from the penal code that was designed to judge adult competence. If an officer is questioned about juveniles, he invariably makes reference to the "obvious" lack of familial training that must have "caused" the alleged rule violation, but his encounters with juveniles assume that it is not the training that is at fault, but a child or juvenile responsible for his own acts vis-à-vis adult standards. Blaming the parents is usually added after the fact. I am not saying that the juvenile's acts could not be viewed as falling under a general rule of the penal code, but that he is accorded adult responsibility irrespective of the provisions of the juvenile court law. It is difficult for the officer to suspend the common-sense reasoning he uses with adult suspects. The interrogation may be more tailored for a young child to make some allowances for vague notions about the necessity of simplifying the structure and context of questions, but the officer seeks to establish guilt or innocence under the same assumptions he would use with adults. In order for the officer to suspend or neutralize the attribution of adult competence, the child or juvenile would have to exhibit stereotyped behavioral displays that the officer could assume were typical of someone who is "confused," "upset," "remorseful," "psycho," and the like. Children and juveniles from lower income families who "answer back" and return the raised voice of the adult (teacher or officer) provide documentary evidence that they are troublemakers by design rather than responding normally or saddled with emotional problems. The attribution of adult responsibility to the child or juvenile begins with the use of basic or interpretive rules that lead to the assignment of typical intentions or motives. The child's or juvenile's appearance, demeanor, and police knowledge about past behavior provide situated grounds for treating a suspect as a competent adult. The invocation of general laws from the penal code to describe the alleged rule violation then provides the officer a basis for justifying his interpretations of "what happened" in the writing of an official report and the possibility of later testifying as a witness. The officer's reasoning or arguments do not make problematic the possible conflict between the general ideology of the juvenile court, the use of adult basic rules, and penal code statutes for justifying the description of the particular case. The officer's interrogation forces the juvenile's remarks to be scrutinized within the framework of the adult's basic and normative rules. And if the child or juvenile is not using adult basic rules, then how can he be said to comprehend the adult meanings of normative rules?

Concluding Remarks

Communication exchanges between adults and children or juveniles can include marked differences in phonological and syntactic comparability particularly if there are discrepancies in educational background (Bernstein 1964) and family socialization experiences. The problem of semantic comparability is more complicated because it can be masked by the appearance of phonological and syntactic competence and performance. If the adult assumes that the child or juvenile is capable of "understanding" what is "right" and "wrong," then a kind of blanket attribution of responsibility is imposed. This attribution of responsibility presumes a recognition by the child or juvenile of "normal forms" of appearances and answers to questions about immediate and past activities. The interaction is governed by adult basic and normative rules. The semantic elaborations (the imputation of typical intentions or motives) that are an integral part of the verbal-nonverbal features of exchanges will be those of normal form adult interpretations.

The general issue is as follows: How do we assume that a ten-year-old or a fourteen-year-old or a sixteen-year-old child or juvenile "knows" or "understands" the consequences of his acts? The problem is compounded if we admit the obvious possibility that during the course of interaction with peers, or even alone, the activities later labeled as rule violations by adults were emergent products of unfolding action scenes that could be described as "one thing led to another." My research on delinquency and juvenile justice convinced me that there are many juveniles who seemed to plan rule violations rather consistently; yet I would argue that police encounters with juveniles, and my analysis of their files, primarily reveal cases that could be best described as "minor." The very nature of group interaction that occurs under collective behavior conditions (for example, social parties, "cruising" in a car at night, gatherings at restaurant drive-ins, street-corner congregations) is most susceptible to emergent outcomes that could not be anticipated and labeled as "planned" rule violation. The after-the-fact interrogation by the police and probation officials or judge, however, is removed from the contingencies of the emergent interaction as it unfolded, but instead concentrates upon a logical (from the adult point of view) reconstruction of "what happened." The reconstruction is not designed to establish the legal possibility that fortuitous emergent conditions produced acts considered rule violations, with the assignment of responsibility tempered because of context-restricted or extenuating circumstances. The interrogation attempts to show that the gathering or activity should have been avoided in the first place and that the rule violations could have been stopped during the interaction. A careful review of the "facts" of the event by legal personnel seeks to establish grounds for assigning guilt to the participants, but the after-the-fact or reconstructed logical constructions that are applied to activities are governed by logic-in-use (Kaplan 1964) procedural rules. The possibility of a developmental discrepancy vis-à-vis syntactic and semantic competence and performance is never a serious issue.

Our treatment of children and juveniles (and the issue could be extended to adults *qua* adults) begins with a vague knowledge about the differences between adult and juvenile basic and normative rules, but when rule violations are suspected, adults are likely to assume that children and juveniles "see" the world as adults see it. This is particularly true vis-à-vis the adult's assumption that warnings about what present violations will do for one's "future" are comprehended as meaningful by the child or juvenile. The child's or juvenile's social horizons cannot be understood by simply forcing adult basic and normative rules upon exchanges between different generations. This difficulty, however, first requires that the behavioral scientist working within the area of social control and rule violation make the study of basic or interpretive rules an integral part of his research on what is to be called deviance and conformity. Some formulation of basic rules is indispensable for understanding everyday social organization and the occasions that are labeled rule or normative violations of the social structures.

References

Bar-Hillel, Y., 1954. "Indexical Expressions." *Mind* 63: 359–379.

Bernstein, B., 1964. "Elaborated and Restricted Codes: Their Social Origins and Some Consequences." In J. J. Gumperz and D. Hymes, eds. "The Ethnography of Communication," *American Anthropologist* 66: 55–69.

Chomsky, N., 1965. *Aspects of a Theory of Syntax.* Cambridge, Mass.: The M.I.T. Press.

Cicourel, A. V., 1968. *The Social Organization of Juvenile Justice.* New York: John Wiley & Sons, Inc.

Cicourel, A. V., 1970. "The Acquisition of Social Structure: Towards a Developmental Sociology of Language and Meaning." In J. Douglas, ed. *Understanding Everyday Life.* Chicago: Aldine.

Garfinkel, H., 1967. *Studies in Ethnomethodology.* Englewood Cliffs, N.J.: Prentice-Hall, Inc.

Goode, W. J., 1960. "Norm Commitment and Conformity to Role-Status Obligations." *American Journal of Sociology* 66: 246–258.

Hart, H. L. A., 1961. *The Concept of Law.* Oxford: Oxford University Press.

Kaplan, A., 1964. *The Conduct of Inquiry.* San Francisco: Chandler Publishing Company.

Lazersfeld, Paul F., 1950. "The Logical and Mathematical Foundation of Latent Structure Analysis." In S. A. Stouffer, et al., *Measurement and Prediction,* Vol. IV of *Studies in Social Psychology in World War II.* Princeton: Princeton University Press, 362–412.

Merton, R. K., 1957. *Social Theory and Social Structure.* Rev. ed. New York: The Free Press.

Parsons, T., 1951. *The Social System.* New York: The Free Press.

Platt, Anthony, 1966. *The Child Savers: The Emergence of the Juvenile Court in Chicago.* Berkeley: School of Criminology, unpublished doctoral dissertation, June.

Rawls, J., 1955. "Two Concepts of Rules." *Philosophical Review* 64: 3–32.

Schutz, A., 1964. *Collected Papers: II,* M. Brodersen, ed. The Hague: Nijhoff.

Whiting, B., ed., 1963. *Six Cultures.* New York: John Wiley & Sons, Inc.

Chapter Seven

SELF AND IDENTITY IN THE CONTEXT OF DEVIANCE: THE CASE OF CRIMINAL ABORTION*

Donald W. Ball

I

The following deals with some aspects of criminal abortion: practitioners, patients and their companions, and the place of such illegal work. More particularly, it is concerned with the management of respectable appearances in such an unrespectable situation—the problematic selves and identities of the actors so located, the presentational strategies and rhetorical devices, and the cooperative evasions used by these participants—to create and sustain legitimizing definitions of themselves and their audiences.

In this theoretical perspective self and identity are not synonyms, but differentiated conceptions. One may distinguish between *self,* ego as known to ego, and *identity,* ego and his self as he appears to alter, his audience (Stone, 1962). The coincidence of these two or the lack thereof is one of the central problems facing social actors in everyday life. We present our audience with a self, which is acknowledged by them in the making of an assignment

* For help with this material, over a period of years, I am grateful to my wife, Donna, and to Stanford M. Lyman. To the anonymous contacts and informants who by now may have forgotten this episode in their lives, I can only say thank you again.

of identity; one can ratify and confirm or deny and disconfirm the other.

Identity assignments are based upon presented self, social role, biographical knowledge about the actor and biographical experiences of the audience, and situational meanings available to the presenter and the audience. These identities are then available to the actor, ego, for incorporation or rejection in his definition of self. Self is then producer, product, and process: presenter and presented to the audience; consumed and reconstituted as an identity; and repossessed—possibly in an altered state—by the presenting actor, now for his acceptance or denial as a definition of his self.

And the stuff of such continual negotiations is symbols: words, phrases, gestures, postures, dress, and other communicative acts, including the ecological and physical settings in which social actors situate and locate themselves. We may refuse our identities, reject them, and present selves that are otherwise; but we cannot ignore them. For they are the materials that structure our audiences' expectations about us, and their responses to us. For any line of action for our selves requiring the actions of our others, our assigned identities must at least overlap, if not coincide with our presented selves.

Central to the notion of defining one's self is the definitions of one's others, their identities. If one is known, given an identity, by the company one keeps, this knowledge is available to oneself, about one's self, to construct a definition of self, as much—if not more—than it is to anyone else. And if we get our identities and thus know ourselves, at least in part, by the company we keep, then in a sense we owe our selves to our others.

Such a model of self, identity, and others is not limited to the "straight" world of fathers and mothers, sisters and brothers, enemies and friends alone, but is also applicable to those situations and settings typically categorized as socially wrong, immoral, illegal, deviant, and the like.

Abortionists get clients, clients get abortions, and in and from the process of these transactions, they both give identities and get selves. It is with such matters that this chapter is concerned: the selves that eventuate from a particular kind of sexual outcome: an unwanted pregnancy and its illegal termination by a criminal abortionist.

An important *caveat* is in order. The data reported here were collected in 1965 and first described two years later (Ball, 1967). The kinds of identities, the attitudes, considerations, and definitions of normality and morality available to social actors *then* are not necessarily the same construction materials for the building of selves that are available today. However, I have tried to maintain faithfulness to the historical reality that was then available to the participants' experience.

To the extent that the problems and dilemmas of self and identity presented herein may seem dated to the reader, that is what social change is all about. Empirically, I have no evidence that that which was either still is or now isn't. All social phenomena are rooted in time and space: so too should be their analyses.

II

A Methodological Excursion: Problems of Research Strategy

Since criminal abortion is just that, illegal, it is a form of deviant conduct; rule-breaking activity officially labeled as morally wrong, and on that basis punitively sanctioned. Thus, there is good reason for persons so involved to hide their involvement, or deny it if accused. It is not, then—as is the difficulty with most hidden or secretive endeavors—amenable to study by constructing questionnaires, sampling, and ringing doorbells to ask people about their participation in this activity. This is a problem that plagues the study of most kinds of deviant conduct, not just abortion; as well as other activities that are considered personal and private, such as sexual relationships. Before turning to abortion, then, it seems advisable to consider some general issues and problems in the study of deviance.[1]

Typically, the study of deviant conduct, at least that which has the potential of evoking formal legal sanctions such as criminal abortion, has suffered from a dearth of primary data. Those materials most readily available and thus most often examined by students of deviance have usually, in some significant degree, been removed from the actual phenomena that are ultimately of basic interest.

Thus, all too frequently, sociological reports dealing with the deviant or unconventional in social conduct have been based upon (1) the official statistics issued by variously concerned control agencies; and (2) self-reports, often by the apprehended violators of formal rules and regulations of conventional society. Such a collection of data has disproportionately represented the technically unskilled and the politically unconnected; and neither of these sources is of the sort that is likely to aid in the constitution of a representative picture of deviant actors, their actions, or the social organization of such phenomena, let alone the selves and identities involved.

By now the sources of inaccuracies in official statistics have become legendary: differential administrative practises and applications by agencies of social control, class biases, unreported violations, lack of uniformity in the definitions of offenses, and so forth. Such statistics are, as Cicourel (1968) and Kitsuse (1963) have pointed out, *products manufactured by the organization issuing them.* And as regards self-reports, even when collected from other than only those actors whose contingency sequences have led them, through organizational differentials, to become labeled as "official" deviants (Becker, 1963), that is, when gathered from unapprehended rulebreakers located in the conventional culture—they are still inadequate data.[2] If more interesting as to their implications regarding actual rates or incidences than the "official statistics," such self-reports tell us little about the structure and process of deviant activities, that is, their social organization as contrasted to their simple statistical distributions, or the selves and identities of the persons involved. Such descriptive materials about people and their rates are only a first step toward sociological analysis of the persons and their social actions implicated in these rule-breaking modes of conduct.

For criminal abortions, frequently sought, frequently gotten, and almost always without legal complications, the biases of conventional data are particularly acute. And there is no evidence that recent changes in legislation regulating abortion (liberalization, tokenism, moral decadence—depending upon your viewpoint) have significantly altered the incidence of illegal pregnancy-terminations; an unascertainable matter anyway.

Alternatively, a less conventional method for pursuing the study of deviance such as abortion, but one which has, to date, unfortunately, been only rarely utilized, is the developing of contacts with unapprehended deviants themselves, that is, going directly to unconventional actors and their cultural milieux. Such a procedure ignores questions about rates, but it is only with such a procedure that the natural, the routine and everyday, the mundane context of deviance and deviant actors can be captured; this, rather than the typically biased picture provided by the conventional data for which we all too often settle. Such common strategies may be safer and easier, but they involve at best a serious compromise with accuracy, and all too frequently a degree of data distortion beyond utility for anything save the sociologist's own *vita* enlargement.

In recent years a few students of deviance have made use, either through design or circumstance, of the more direct approach involving actual observation, if not participation, in deviant subcultures: Becker's (1963) work on marijuana users, Hooker's (1963) studies of male homosexuals, and a few others. Most often, however, the direct method has been applied by sociologists to the study of only marginally or potentially deviant actors, their actions, and their settings, for example, Scott (1968) on horse racing, Polsky (1967) on pool hustlers, Cavan (1966) on bar behavior—topics where the risks and hazards are ordinarily relatively smaller.

We would argue that this less traditional, essentially *ethnographic approach* to the collection of sociological data on deviance is superior, particularly in terms of completeness, to the more conventionally used official statistics and self-reports; *especially as regards hidden deviance* (Becker, 1963:19–20) such as rarely legally acted-upon criminal abortion. However, it should be obvious that this research strategy is not without its own attendant problems and dilemmas; the remainder of this section deals with some of these issues.

Ethics:

First of all, there is the ethical problem. The investigator is, irrespective of any degree of personally experienced cultural integration or alienation, a member of the society that creates, maintains, and applies the definitions of who and what is or is not deviant, as well as the attendant penalties. As Ned Polsky has cogently noted:

> If one is to study law-breaking deviants as they engage in their deviance in its natural setting, i.e., outside the jail, he must make the moral decision that in some ways he will break the law himself. He need not be a [participating observer] and commit the deviant acts under study, yet he has to witness such acts or be taken into confidence about them *and* not blow the whistle. That is, the investigator has to decide that when necessary he will "obstruct justice" or be "an accessory" before or after the fact, in the full legal sense of those terms. He will not be enabled to discern some vital aspects of criminally deviant behavior and the structure of law breaking subcultures unless he makes a moral decision, makes the deviants believe him, and moreover convinces them of his ability to act in accord with his decision.

Polsky goes on that, concerning the placing of the norms of science above those of the community, that is, its laws:

> The last mentioned point can perhaps be neglected with juvenile delinquents, for they know that a professional studying them is almost always exempt from police pressure to inform; but adult criminals have no such assurance, and hence are concerned not merely with the investigator's intentions [and discretion], but with his sheer ability to remain a "stand-up guy" under police questioning. [Personal Communication, cited in Becker, 1963:171, note 7][3]

Thus, for the researcher interested in criminal abortion, direct contact must involve getting his hands dirty, going to abortionists in their natural habitat such as abortion clinics or mills, and compromising himself legally if not morally and sticking to his commitment as he violates the formal prescriptions of the culture vis-à-vis activities defined as deviant. Such a dilemma can only be personally resolved, for there are neither shortcuts nor handy rules for such situations.

Sources:

Another dilemma is the problem of obtaining and maintaining contacts with the worlds of deviants. It may—or may not, and probably should not—surprise us to find how rich our own acquaintances may be as sources or leads to various rule-breaking actors and their subcultures. This is especially true of the more widespread criminal service and supply networks such as abortion, prostitution and other sexual services, soft (if not hard) narcotics, and gambling. Alternatively, habituation of known resorts for such deviant endeavors and/or their products may ultimately lead the researcher to the acceptance that is necessarily adequate to generate access to the relevant actors and their activities. More succinctly, if we don't already know, we probably know who or where to ask (see Manning, forthcoming, and Howell, 1969, on the strategies for finding an abortionist).

Disclosure:

Once contact has been established, the investigator faces the usual problem inherent in the observer role, that is, how much of one's own purposes, motives, and role to reveal to one's subjects (Gold, 1958). While ignoring, but not unaware of the problem of potential physical danger or violence in some settings, the degree of revelation is methodologically still a particularly crucial issue—since in studying deviance *in situ* one's legitimacy in the dominant law-abiding culture may be a discreditable stigma (Goffman, 1963:41–62) in the view of one's subjects. Parenthetically, this may be less of a problem regarding abortion than for many other *organized* criminal activities, since most persons seeking criminal abortions are otherwise conventional (Section III, of this chapter). Again, the general problem probably must be solved by the individual investigator, weighing his own values, the maximization of an efficacious research strategy, and the consideration of an evaluation of his subjects as persons in some form of Benthamite moral calculus.

Reactivity:

Yet, the dilemmas are still more complex, with other issues coexisting with, if not transcending, those of ethics, sources, and access. There is the problem of reactivity (Webb, et al., 1963): the effect of the process of investigation upon that which is being investigated; not just the more or less straightforward one of subjects not talking or dissembling in the presence of an alien researcher, but a much more subtle one, best introduced by way of example:

About fifteen years ago, a young doctoral candidate at a Midwestern university decided to do for his dissertation an observational study of juvenile gangs. To this end the student, who looked less than his years, drifted into a predominantly blue-collar steel mill town and began hanging around a local pool hall frequented (just as folk-lore would have it) by delinquent adolescents (a site identified to him by local police, who were cooperating with the study). In relatively short order he made contact with members of an appropriate gang and was accepted into it by the members. The gang itself fell some place between the negativistic, vandalistic gangs delineated by Cohen (1955) and the instrumentally oriented theft-for-gain criminal gangs described by Cloward and Ohlin (1960).

It was as regards these latter kinds of activities that the researcher had his greatest problems in trying to avoid reactively influencing his subjects. As the gang members would formulate and discuss plans for their next adventure, usually on the order of knocking over a candy store while the proprietor was in the back room, the investigator—who was, after all, not unintelligent or lacking in analytical ability—would see flaws in these schemes; flaws serious enough to make apprehension an all-too-real probability. Needing to keep his subjects on the loose and unfettered by involvement with legal authorities, he would as gently as possible try to mend the holes in the gang's plans, but with an unanticipated consequence. In a short time the gang members began to defer to the investigator's organizational ability and to treat him as a leader. His desire to keep his subjects in a viable state, i.e., uncaught and routinely engaging in their usual deviant activities, which in turn led to his forced demonstration of planning and administrative competence, reactively affected the gang. Having gained access and acceptance, the researcher then faced a new and unexpected dilemma: avoiding the creation of a gang to study which was actually being led by a young Ph.D. candidate.[4]

The object of this little cautionary tale is simple. The reactivity problem, in the study of deviance and other areas as well, is not exhausted merely by the avoidance of having one's subjects "clam up" or deceive in hopes of misleading, or alternatively, pleasing the investigator. Since deviant subjects in particular seem less likely than others in more conventional settings to learn or be informed as to the researcher's true intentions or identity, their direct study appears likely to magnify the dangers of reactivity even more than usual; both the investigator and his subjects are restricted, by a blanket of secrecy, from making the adjustive compensations necessary to assure "normal" conduct in the field.

Scientific Status:

Finally, there is a collection of issues that may be subsumed more generally as the "Scientific Problem." It is frequently if not usually the case that for one reason or another the directly observing student of deviance will feel honor-bound not to reveal his sources or the specifics of his data-gathering procedures. Motivations for such strictures may range from moral obligation regarding the protection of subjects to a more mundane unwillingness to implicate one's self as a participant in, or an accessory to, deviant activities; especially if such disclosure is likely to invite criminal investigation. Until such time as some form of legal recognition of confidentiality, that is, privileged information and communication, and thus immunity is extended to sociologists and others investigating deviance in a manner analogous to that enjoyed now by physicians, lawyers, and clergymen, the risk of criminal prosecution will remain a very real hazard for those going directly to the source.[5] However, for whatever the reason, the *in situ* observation of the deviant and his milieu often precludes the complete reporting of method and the possibility of exact replication ordinarily demanded by the rules of scientific rigor.

Thus, the gemini issues of validity and reliability are raised—and as regarding the study of deviance to a much greater extent than is true of observational research in general. By its very nature, any kind of direct observation is open to question as to *validity,* for example, is what is reported an accurate account of events and relationships; and *reliability,* or would other observers and their observations generate the same set of data, always keeping in mind the dubious *ceteris paribus* qualification. Such problems are difficult enough to answer when the observations are drawn from nondeviant settings and methods are carefully described; they become even more important when full disclosure of procedural minutiae is deemed impossible, as in the following material on abortion—as is usually the case when the data concern deviant actors and actions and their organizations.

We would like to suggest, however, that important as these traditional methodological questions are, they should not be allowed to obscure the central issue. Although conventionally aggregated data may satisfy rigid criteria for statistical manipulation, they do so at the cost of a misleading, even atypical, portrait of the deviant actor—what might be called "the-unable-to-make-the-fix-incompetent"—and that furthermore ignores the structural and situational context of such conduct. In studying nondeviant conduct, at least the central tendencies are frequently known or relatively easily determined; deviance such as criminal abortion, almost by definition is secretive. So too is much, if not most sexual conduct; often legal only if private and hidden. Readily or easily collected data on such phenomena are analogous to the exposed portion of the iceberg, and just as unrepresentative of the whole.

Basically the fundamental issue is age-old; one that has haunted sociology since its empirical beginnings divorced it from social philosophy and criticism. This is the ever-present dilemma of resolving, in some form of compromise, the mutual *desiderata* of richness and rigor; polarities for which a maximization of one can occur only at the expense of the other alternative. Although the phenomenological school—the ethnomethodologists *inter nos*—would argue that the richness-rigor dichotomy is a false one, they especially would also recognize its hoary existence as part of the folkloric sociological tradition. Unfortunately an examination of this debate is beyond the scope of this chapter.[6]

Since the moral statisticians, Durkheim (see Douglas, 1967:3–76) and Lombroso's early study of the physiological characteristics of imprisoned criminals (summarized, with others, in Vold, 1958:43–74), the sociology of deviance has historically stressed conventional methodological rigor at the sacrifice of substantive richness; even to the extent of utilizing data that are trivial if not completely misleading. Ultimately, sociologists seek maps and models of human social conduct, conventional and otherwise, not merely data that conveniently fit existing statistical models.

This should not be taken as a criticism of statistical method *per se.* Rather, it is a plea for a recognition of the unique, hidden character of much that is defined and responded to as deviant, and its lack of ready accessibility as data when compared with other areas of sociological inquiry. To repeat, almost by definition deviance is secretive; that which falls into the net of public information may be considered in a sense almost incidental, and certainly not a true picture of the state-of-affairs as it actually exists and is experienced by actors so situated.

To properly understand their selves, then, we must share their experiences, and learn what identities are available to them as well as what are their presentational resources. Remarking generally about the study of the self, Goffman's comments seem particularly cogent when the subject is involved in deviant doing:

> Little help has been provided by paper and pencil students of the self who start with a subject's verbal description of himself, often based on his selection from verbal trait-lists, instead of starting with *the serious ethnographic task of assembling ways in which the individual is treated and treats others,* and deducing what is implied about him through this treatment. [Goffman, 1969:361, note 5, emphasis added]

III

The Data: An Abortion Clinic Ethnography[7]

What follows is an effort to utilize direct contact with deviant actors in their natural habitat, to describe ethnographically certain aspects of a particular abortion clinic, especially as such data may illuminate the presentational strategies employed by a habitually deviant establishment in its dealing with a situationally deviant clientele. All of the methodological drawbacks discussed apply to this material; hopefully, so too do some of the substantive benefits.

For an abortion clinic's staff, participation in an action legally defined as deviant, that is, criminal abortion, is habitual. That is to say, it is regularly repeated on a routine, businesslike basis; it is a part, the occupational part, of their everyday world. For patrons, such involvement is at most occasional; if that, irregular; and for most, by contrast, however, a once-in-a-lifetime engagement in this form of deviance.

Furthermore, most patrons are members of otherwise law-abiding cultures. Unlike the staff, their involvement in this deviant setting is not an aspect of a career, but an accidental consequence of an unwanted pregnancy. And it is probable that in most cases abortion is the most serious, that is, legally and socially penalized activity in which they will be criminally implicated.

In the context of an abortion clinic, therefore, the deviant transaction ordinarily is enacted by two kinds of actors: those *habitually* involved in such exchanges, that is, the *staff;* and those only *situationally* deviant, the otherwise conventional actors in their clinic-related roles as *patrons.*[8] It becomes of some interest, then, to consider how an abortion clinic manages and fosters impressions for an audience of patrons constituted of actors drawn from outside its habitually deviant, abortion-oriented subculture; how patrons are similarly involved in impression management; and some of the characteristics of such strategies used by each. Stated differently, the focus will be upon (1) techniques used by the clinic to key itself to the demands and expectations of a patronage drawn from the conventional culture, (2) the devices used by patrons to deny the legal if not moral realities of the solution to their predicament, and (3) the consequences of these strategies for the selves and identities of both patrons and staff.

Suffice it to say (see Section II), strictures of confidence prevent any elaborate discussion of method, problems of access, and the like. Let it be noted, however, that the materials reported and interpreted herein are based upon: (1) sufficiently lengthy observation of a clinic's routine (exclusive of specifically medical procedures that are not strictly relevant to the problem) to establish the patterns of its everyday functioning, (2) extensive interviews with a necessarily small number of its patrons, some of whom were also observed within the clinic, and (3) limited discussions with some of the clinic's nonmedical staff. Additionally, supplementary and confirmatory data have been drawn from interviews with individuals who have utilized other, similar facilities. Unfortunately, any more detailed methodological description would, not surprisingly, violate promises of anonymity guaranteed to the persons involved.

Background:

The clinic studied was located, along with several similar establishments, in a border town along the California-Mexico line. Its staff included two practitioners—abortionists—ostensibly physicians, the younger of whom was in an apprentice relationship to the senior man; a practical nurse, a receptionist-bookkeeper, a combination janitress and custodian, a chauffeur-errand boy, and a telephone-appointments secretary.

As costs for such procedures go, the clinic was a relatively expensive one, with fees averaging $500 per abortion. The rate, however, would be somewhat less for other medical personnel and students, who were eligible for a discount; and more for persons desiring postoperative overnight observation, as well as those beyond the tenth week of pregnancy. In terms of finances, the clinic studied was probably representative of others catering to a middle- and upper-class clientele at that time. Its patients were usually married; if single, they were the daughters of well-to-do parents. The few single adult females could be better categorized as "career women" rather than "working girls."

In order to obtain a better picture of the establishment, a brief natural history of a typical involvement between clinic and patron is useful at this point. Preliminarily though, it should be recognized that the ideal-typical practitioner-patient model of the medical sociologist is not appropriate for the analysis of abortion. Like veterinarians and pediatricians, abortionists frequently have *patients* for whom financial if not moral responsibility is an obligation of the role of some other person, that is, a *client*. For abortionists these clients include boyfriends, husbands, and parents. Along with persons such as accompanying friends, they comprise for the patient what might be classified as *supportive others:* persons attending the clinic along with the patient in order to provide psychological support and reinforcement in this crisis situation. Not surprisingly, it is rare for a patient to go to the clinic completely alone, without some morally supportive other.[9] Thus, within the context of abortion, the typical practitioner-patient dyad usually becomes a triad, comprising practitioner, patient, and supportive other; these last two constituting the clinic's *patrons.*[10]

A Natural History:

After referral, usually by a legitimate physician, less often by a friend or an acquaintance, a patron would make original contact with the clinic by telephone. The typically tentative, noncommittal, but implicitly urgent communication of the patron was immediately treated in a matter-of-fact manner by the telephone girl.

> **Girl:** Hello, Doctor —————'s office. Can I help you?
>
> **Patron:** Yes, I, er, uh, would like to make an appointment with the Doctor.
>
> **Girl:** How long has she been pregnant?

The fact of pregnancy was thus immediately introduced by the staff-member. And in appropriate middle-class speech patterns she quickly and efficiently asked the length of the pregnancy, extolled the skills of the staff, set up a tentative appointment, and discussed the fee and its mode of payment by the patron. This treatment of the patron's problem as *routine* helped to minimize the anxiety inherent in such situations.[11] Parallel to this was a "medicalization" of the situation, also helping to disarm the patron vis-à-vis the deviant nature of the proposed transaction; practitioners were always referred to as doctors, and at all times the terminology was that of conventional medicine and surgery. Later, ordinarily two or three days prior to the appointment, the patron again called the clinic, this time to get confirmation of date and time.

Patrons would usually spend the night before their appointment at a hotel or motel near the clinic. Early in the morning of the scheduled date they were to call the clinic once again, this time to get directions to the only then revealed place of rendezvous where they were picked up and transported to the clinic by one of the staff members in a large, late model station wagon.

It was at this time that the patrons would first find that they were not alone in their dilemma; for there would also be several other patrons picked up at the rendezvous site, filling the station wagon to capacity. Although propinquity seemingly might argue for it, there would be little deliberate interaction among patrons during the ride to the clinic; uncertainty, anxiety, and felt stigma, effectively socially immobilizing these situational deviants in the ambiguous situation into which they had placed themselves.

Upon arrival at the clinic, where the station wagon and all related cars of the staff would be hidden from street view, the patrons were ushered into a large, well-furnished waiting room. The clinic itself most resembled an extremely roomy private home, both externally and internally—in its non-medical areas—and was located in a prestigious residential neighborhood on a hill overlooking the community.

Once inside, the patrons would find seats for themselves and settle into a waiting period of hushed expectancy. Conversation was limited to patients and their respective supportive others, that is, only to those sets of persons previously known to one another. After a short interval of perhaps five minutes, the receptionist would appear and call out the name of the first patient. The pair, patient and receptionist, would then retire out of sight of the remaining patrons into the medical wing of the clinic.

The first stop in the medical wing was an office. After first explaining the procedure in explicitly medical terminology, the receptionist would shift to her bookkeeper role and request the fee (in cash or traveler's checks only) from the patient; frequently finding that it was being held by an accompanying supportive other still in the waiting room. Following this discussion and the collection of the fee, the patient was then sent to a bathroom, well appointed in terms of luxury rather than gynecology, to remove her street clothes and put on a surgical gown. Once gowned, the patient would be directed to the room where the actual abortion would take place.

Those specifically involved in this procedure included, in addition to the patient, the two practitioners, senior and apprentice, and the practical nurse. Although a spinal anesthetic was administered, at no time would the patient be allowed to lose consciousness; a necessity born of the possible need for quick removal in the event of visitation by legal agents. Immediately, upon completion of the procedure, the patient would leave the table and then be sent to another room to rest for from fifteen minutes to an hour-and-a-half. Finally, after receiving medication and instructions regarding post-operative care from the receptionist, the patient and any supportive others would be returned by a staff-member to the site of the original rendezvous and thus sent on their way back to their conventional worlds.

Description and Analysis:

With this brief, oversimplified picture it is now possible to turn to more specifically sociological concerns: the aforementioned presentational strategies that make up what may be called, for the clinic, a *rhetoric of legitimization,* and the selves and identities for staff and patrons so generated and cooperatively sustained.

Rhetorics:

Sociologically, a rhetoric may be considered as a vocabulary of specific purpose; that is to say, as a limited set of symbols functioning to communicate a particular set of meanings, directed and organized toward the representation of a specific image or impression. Such vocabularies are not only verbal but also include visual symbols such as objects, gestures, emblems, and the like.

As a theoretical point it should be noted that rhetorics are not necessarily the same thing as ideologies, although empirically they may coincide. The conceptual difference between the two is that whereas rhetoric speaks to communication, both style and content (Simmel, 1950:22–23, 40–43; Wolff, 1959, several papers, especially those by Levine, Weingartner, and Tenbruck), ideology refers to perception and justification in terms of the ideologue's conception of relevant portions of his world. It is conceivable that individual actors, groups, or establishments will utilize a rhetoric without any ideological convictions as regards its validity, but with a recognition of its pragmatic efficacy. Similarly, ideological dedication does not automatically assume a developed rhetoric to attempt its maintenance or furtherance. The former may be illustrated by much of Madison Avenue advertising; the latter by the unarticulate responses frequently elicited by this form of commercial persuasion.

Returning to the case of the clinic: basically its rhetoric operated to subvert the conventional world's view of abortion, and to generate a picture of legitimate activity. Fundamentally, the question thus becomes: what techniques were utilized via this rhetoric to *neutralize* the context of deviance in which the clinic operated so as to enhance parallels with conventional medical and social situations and thus derive a kind of "rightness" or legitimization?[12] How, in other words, were milieu and actions *qua* impressions manipulated in order to maximize the clinic's image over and above the successful performance of its task; and to contradict the stereotypic stigma of deviance? Particularly, how did the clinic (1) minimize the possibilities of trouble with frightened or recalcitrant patrons and thus maximize ease of work-flow, (2) generate the patron satisfaction necessary for referral system maintenance, and (3) present an image that would provide the most favorable selves and identities possible for the actors involved, whether patron or staff?

The second and third problems are, in effect, special cases of the first. Minimization of trouble was not motivated so much by fear of patron complaints to legal agents, which would involve the complainants in admitting complicity, but more by a desire to (a) maintain referrals and (b) maintain or enhance self-definitions.

Only additionally such minimization produced a smoother, easier work-flow for the staff. A similar rationale in conventional medical settings some-times dictates the use of general anesthetics when, in terms of patient pain, locals would be adequate.

For analytical purposes, the clinic's rhetoric of legitimization may be conveniently conceptualized by employing Goffman's (1956:13–14) delinea-tion of front and its constituents of setting, appearance, and manner. This scheme formed an observational framework for data collection as well as a perspective for then analyzing it. Originally a framework for analyzing the presentation of a single self in interaction, this scheme seems extendible to the strategies of establishments and institutions as well; and thereby the selves and identities situated, developed, and given meaning within them.

Essentially, *front* consists of those communications that serve to define the situation or performance for the audience: standardized expressive equip-ment including (1) *setting,* the spatial/physical background items of props and scenery in the immediate area of the interaction, (2) *appearance,* the sign-vehicles expressing the performer's social status or type, and (3) those expressions that warn of a performer's demeanor, mood, and the like, that is *manner.*

Examining each of these elements for evidence of how they were manipu-lated to constitute a rhetoric allows the identification of the central themes and dimensions of the clinic's presentational strategies. Although the combina-tion of the conceptions of rhetoric, neutralization, and front and its elements produces an admittedly loose theoretical scheme, the character of the data does not suggest the utility of further rigor in this case.

Setting:

A paramount feature of the clinic's rhetoric was its physical and spatial characteristics. Especially important for patrons generally was the stereotype-contradicting waiting room, the first impression of the clinic itself—and the dominant one for supportive others. This waiting room was likely to be the only room in which supportive others would be present during their entire visit to the clinic, save for the possibility of a short interval in the office if they happened to be holding the fee (a frequent occurrence, especially if the other was also a client).

Spatially, the waiting room was L-shaped and extremely large; approxi-mately seventy-five feet long and fifty feet wide at the base leg. Its size was accentuated by the fact that most of the room was sunken about three feet below the floor level at its perimeters. Fully and deeply carpeted, well fur-nished—with several comfortable couches and armchairs, large lamps and chandeliers, coffee and end tables—the room spoke of luxury and patron consideration. These were also implied by the presence of a television set, a small bar, and a phonograph; such items of decor in addition to the usual magazines present in more typical medical waiting-room situations.

I knew, for the first time, really, that the whole thing might work out after all. I mean when I saw those crystal chandeliers hanging there, and all that carpeting, I thought that I could come out of it O.K. It reminded me of what I imagine those clinics in Switzerland must look like.

Thus commented one patient about her first reaction upon stepping into the room and seeing it for the first time. It served to reduce anxiety for her, providing for the first time in her patient experience with the clinic the suggestion that she would be all right, that is, physically; while at the same time implying the definition of herself as similar to the persons to be found at legitimate Swiss clinical establishments, such as motion-picture stars, statesmen (Presidents' widows), and other celebrities.

Space was structured so as to create withdrawal niches for each set of patients and their others. Both the size of the room as well as the placement of the furniture functioned to isolate sets of patrons and provide them with private islands; islands that needed not to be shared with others. Couches and chairs were arranged along the walls of the room rather than centered, maximizing distance between groupings and minimizing the possibilities of direct, intergroup eye contact between the various patron-sets who, despite an awareness of their shared problem and the recently experienced forced propinquity of their ride to the clinic, tended to keep their anxieties private. Thus, interaction among patrons in the waiting room was closed within rather than between groups; confined to patients and their own accompanying supportive others alone.

The picture of the medical wing was a far cry from the shabby and sordid image of "kitchen-table abortion" drawn in the popular press. Rather it was one of modern scientific medicine; and with it came comfort and assurance to the patient. The setting symbolized her role, and thus identified her self, as patient rather than criminal conspirator. This close congruence between self and role (or position) has been succinctly summarized by Goffman:

A self, then, virtually awaits the individual entering a position [or performing a role]; he need only conform to the pressures on him and he will find a *me* ready-made for him. In the language of Kenneth Burke, doing is being. [1961:87–88, emphasis in the original]

Once the patient had donned a gown, her next step was to the operating room, a designation used without exception by the staff. In addition to a gynecological table, the room contained familiar (to the lay patient) medical paraphernalia: surgical tools, hypodermic syringes, stainless steel pans and trays, bottles and vials enclosing various colored liquids, capsules, pills, and the like—props for effectively neutralizing the negative "butcher" stereotypes associated with abortion as portrayed in the mass-media version.

After the procedure had been completed, the patient would be moved

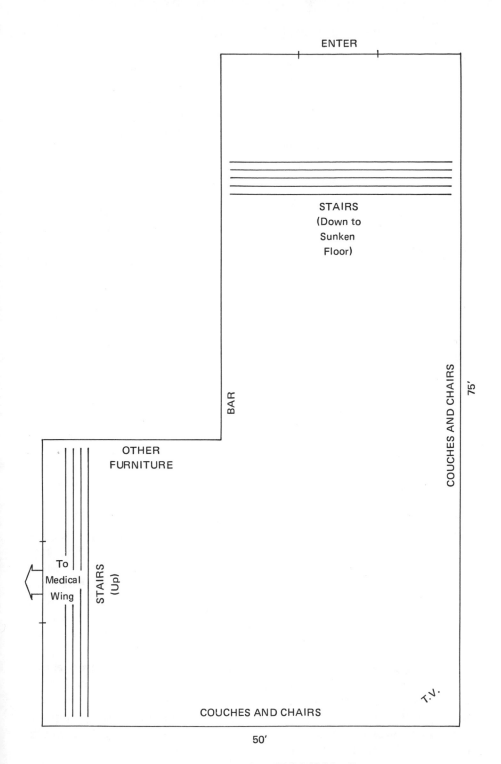

Figure 7-1: The Ecology of the Clinic's Waiting Room.

from the scientific arena of the operating room and back again into luxury. As was the waiting room, the rooms in which the patients spent their short period of postoperative rest were expensively furnished.

Ultimately, after resting, the patient returned to the waiting room, and for most to supportive others, received a final postoperative briefing before being returned to the rendezvous site. Parenthetically, it may be noted that throughout the entire episode music had been piped into every room in which patrons, both patients and their others, were present.

In terms of setting, the clinic presented itself as not unlike a small hospital, albeit with a decorator-designed interior. For patient and supportive others the scenery and props functioned to communicate an image of assurance and protection through the devices of cost and luxury along with that of scientific medicine; to minimize the deviant nature of the transaction, to emphasize positive cultural values, thus efficiently counteracting stereotypic images, and thereby provide for the possibility of positively valued selves and identities for staff and patrons alike.

Appearance and Manner:

A widespread device for visibly differentiating various social categories or types is clothing (Stone, 1962; Roach and Eicher, 1965; Ryan, 1966). Items of dress may function as insignia or uniforms to label the persons so garbed as members of particular social groups, occupations, or the like. Such institutionalized symbols act as both identifiers and identities; to be attired in certain ways is to be a certain kind of person, thus to have a certain kind of self, not only in the identifying eyes of the audience, but also in terms of the actor's perception of himself. Dress is, then, an integral aspect of social identity and experienced self.

So it was with the clinic: practitioners, patient, nurse—all wore from the layman's point of view, the appropriate symbols of dress for surgically centered roles. White tunics were worn by the practitioners; patients were surgically gowned; the nurse and even the janitress wore white uniform dresses. This element of the rhetoric would be especially highlighted at the beginning of the procedure when both practitioners ostentatiously donned surgical gloves, visibly emphasizing their, and the clinic's, concern with the necessity of asepsis. This ritualistic activity also served to forcefully identify these actors in their medical roles as defined by the rhetoric, and thus the patient in hers.

The medical model was further underscored by the preoperative medical history that was taken and recorded upon a standard, multicarboned form (the destiny of these duplicate copies was never made known to the writer). Actions such as this, along with other aspects of appearance such as dress, provided major modes of keying symbols and stressing the medical legitimacy of the clinic, its staff, its task, and thus its clientele.

From the receptionist on up through the clinic's hierarchy, behavior, particularly verbal, emphasized medical and professional aspects of the clinic's operation. Nowhere was this more apparent than in the area of vocabulary; it was strictly medical, with no effort either made or implied to speak down to the less knowledgeable lay patron. It is also noteworthy that at no time was the word abortion *per se* used in the presence of a patron; rather, references were to the operation, the procedure, or a "D and C" (dilation and curettage). Similarly, as noted, the room in which the procedure took place was at all times designated by members of the staff as the operating room.

Other elements of staff behavior that furthered the medical impression were (1) the postoperative consultation and medication that effectively contrasted with the popular view of abortion as an "off-the-table-and-out" procedure, and (2) the presence of an apprentice practitioner and its obvious analogy, at least for the medically sophisticated, with a teaching hospital. For the patient, the teaching aspects of the senior practitioner's role helped to generate confidence in his skill, a matter that was also verbally reinforced by other staff members in their interactions with the patrons.

As with appearance, the manner of the staff was essentially directed toward the medical elements of the clinic's rhetoric; their demeanor was professional at all times, with one exception. This exception was the receptionist-bookkeeper, whose role was, by definition, outside the strictly medical aspects of the clinic. As a result, freed of the obligations of professional mien, the receptionist was able to interact with patrons in a reassuring and supportive manner; in effect, her presentation of the rhetoric was through expressive strategies of nurturance, whereas the manner of other staff members was more instrumentally oriented.[13]

Before turning to central symbolic themes appealing to the patrons that were engendered by the clinic's rhetorical strategies, it might be well to at least take note of some flaws in the presentation, even though they may have escaped the usual patron's attention. These may be considered under the general rubrics of pseudosterility and miscellaneous delicts.

Pseudosterility:

Although ostentation was the rule as regards the emphasis of aseptic and antiseptic precautions, there were also omissions less readily obvious. It will be recalled that measures apparently designed to minimize infection and also at the same time maximize parallels with legitimate medicine included (1) the wearing of tunics by the practitioners, (2) their donning of surgical gloves prior to the procedure, and (3) the display of the tools and paraphernalia of medicine and surgery in the operating room.

It should be pointed out that, aseptically, tunics are no substitute for full surgical gowns, that full precautionary tactics would also include items such as face masks, caps, and the like; and that it is highly irregular for an operating room to lack an autoclave (for the sterilization of instruments) and

changeable covering for the table, which that setting did; or for surgical instruments to stand on exhibition, exposed to the air for long periods of time,
like a sales display at a medical convention. Additionally, it may be noted
that those portions of the preoperative medical history that were taken by the
senior practitioner were recorded by him—*after* his elaborate display of putting on the surgical gloves; a less than ideal practice for sterility.

These breaches of standard surgical procedure suggest that much of
what passed for the lay patron as concern with aseptic and antiseptic
practices was actually a calculated rhetoric, designed to communicate to the
audience a sustained standard of professional medical rigor that did not in
fact exist.

Miscellaneous Delicts:

Within this category are included additional practices at variance with
the fostered medical impression, but not directly involving matters of sterility.

Perhaps the most glaring of these was the lack of privacy afforded the
patient in comparison with more conventional surgical settings. The fact that
patients were handled in groups and moved and serviced in what in comparison with a hospital was a small and not systematically designed space, led
to a good deal of enforced contact between patients and staff involved in
various stages of the process. Of necessity this led to frequent invasions of
privacy, at least as open to perception and definition by patients accustomed
to more traditional medical situations. Thus, for instance, the room used as
the business office also doubled as a resting room, and a patient lying there
for postoperative rest might suddenly find herself witness to a financial
transaction as a later-scheduled patron made payment of the fee. The resting
patient was thus treated, in effect, as an object, becoming, in Goffman's
phrase, a *nonperson* (1956:95–96), that is, an actor not accorded the usual
deferences given as minimal acknowledgment of a person's moral worth,
simply by virtue of the fact of that person's being human.

Also of interest was the function of the *music,* piped into every room
including the one for the procedure. When the patrons first arrived at the
clinic the music would be quiet, soothing, and relaxing in style; but with the
entrance of the first patient into the medical wing, the tempo and timbre both
increased markedly. The volume of the music then effectively operated to
drown out any untoward sounds that might emanate from the medical wing
and alarm those patrons still in the waiting room.

Another delict involved the marked contrast in *vehicles* used in picking
up and returning patrons to the rendezvous. In keeping with the symbolism
of cost and luxury presented to the prospective patron, the station wagon
which would bring them to the clinic was an expensive new model. By contrast, for the return to the rendezvous, which was not done *en masse* as was
the initial pick up, and by which time presentational strategies were less

necessary—the car driven by the chauffeur-errand boy was an old, rather decrepit foreign sedan of low cost and questionable reliability.

Still another item at variance with traditional medical procedures was the emphasis, especially by the practitioners, on the necessity of the patient's cooperation to assure the procedure's success. The patient was in effect invited, if not commanded, to become an active participant in the ongoing activity.[14] She would be told, for instance, of the desirability of her concentrating on other matters, for example, "think of something else and all will go smoothly and rapidly." This assigning of an active role of the patient stands in marked contradiction to her objectification as regards matters of privacy, and implies expediency as a more central concern of the clinic's operation than patient welfare.

Finally, it may be noted that although the practitioners were verbally represented by others on the staff as physicians, gynecologists in fact, no evidence of medical training in the form of certificates or diplomas was displayed and available for patron scrutiny.

Discussion:

From this selective ethnographic description of various aspects of the clinic's front, two broad dimensions appear essential to its rhetoric of legitimization: (1) luxury and cost, and (2) conventional medical practices and procedures. It is these two themes that were most emphasized in the clinic's efforts to neutralize its aura of habitual deviance before an audience of only situationally deviant patrons drawn primarily from the world of conventional society. Thus, the rhetoric sought its vocabulary in meaningful and positive values of the patron's culture.

Within these master themes, four elements may be specified as contributing to the two broader dimensions of luxury and cost and conventional medicine: cleanliness, competence, conventionality, and concern for the patron.

Cleanliness and *competence* are both elements of the instrumental aspects of medicine. Albeit with significant flaws, unrecognized by most lay patrons, the clinic's presentational strategies enhanced these impressions, if not to the same extent their actualities. The obvious symbols of dress and equipment were presented to the patient in the medical wing of the clinic where anxiety and uncertainty were likely to be high. These symbols were readily recognizable and implied the normality of the situation; they provided, in effect, the cues for a set of familiar expectations drawn from past experience with legitimate medicine. In a similar allaying manner, the practitioner's skill and competence were repeatedly voiced by the staff from the time of the initial telephone contact until the beginning of the actual abortive procedure itself.

Conventionality here means a realization of the middle-class values of most patrons. One of these values is, of course, a positive view of professional medicine, a view that the clinic attempted to exploit. Throughout the patron's experience with the clinic, parallels with this model were highlighted; but it is in another area that this element of the rhetoric functioned most effectively —the waiting-room setting.

The obvious expense, comfort, and general decor of the waiting room were such as to disarm all but the most fearful and suspicious patron, as the earlier quotation implied. This room and the first impressions it presented were such as to immediately link the clinic to the safe, known world of respectable middle-class conventionality. In the process of this linkage, the clinic was, in the patron's perception, divorced from the usually illicit image conjured by abortion; if not rendered totally conventional the clinic was at least brought within the context of their definitions and expectations from more mundane, everyday experience. Because of its crucial location in the process, being the patron's first direct exposure to the clinic milieu, it is fair to say that this room was the most successful presentational strategy in the clinic's legitimizing rhetoric.

The comfort of the waiting room was but one of the forms of expression of *concern for the patron* that helped to create a legitimatizing presentation. Other strategies included the telephone girl's supportive routinization of the patron's problem at the time of the initial contact; the similarly solicitous demeanor of the receptionist; and the postoperative consultation. This involved not only the dispensing of drugs to facilitate the patient's convalescence but also a brochure specifically detailing an expected course of progress and steps to be taken in case of complications.

By demonstrating concern, the clinic affirmed its subscription to the values of its patrons, and thus asserted its basically conventional nature, that is, the congruence of its operation with the norms of those upon whom its income relied.

All of these factors combined to help construct a rhetoric of legitimacy: a set of presentational strategies that allowed the clinic to minimize problems inherent in typically anxious and fearful patrons, and thus to function more effectively. And in addition, to generate the reputation necessary for an establishment of its kind, dependent upon referrals from legitimate physicians (or satisfied patrons).

IV

Self, Identity, and Deviance

Additionally, whether manifest or latent, the rhetoric also had consequences for the selves and identities of the actors involved. Both habitual deviants, the staff, and situational deviants, the patrons, were able to partake of the rhetoric so as to enhance their own self definitions. The rhetoric helped the staff to define their participation in the clinic's habitually deviant activities, despite the occasional flaws, as involvement in a professionally functioning establishment with the trappings of legitimate medicine. For patrons, although they too were admittedly involved in a deviant situation, the rhetoric blunted this hard truth. By accepting the presentational strategies as part of the clinic's reality, the patron was allowed to define the situation through symbols drawn from his conventional everyday experience. Thus, for both patron and staff alike, the rhetoric allowed for a minimization of the threats to experienced self and imputed identities that were built into their illicit transaction.

Fundamentally, both patrons and staff were involved, at the inter-personal level, in mutual "face-work," each building images of self delineated in terms of approved social attributes (Goffman, 1955:213). To do so required each team, one the patrons the other the staff, to cooperatively evade certain matters. This *cooperative evasion* took the form of the mutual disattending of information available to each; acknowledgment that could only eventuate in less desirable, actually less respectable selves and identities.

As the rhetoric highlighted certain themes such as luxury and conventional medicine, so too the participants had to look the other way, had to ignore blunt facts in order to make it work. Patrons cooperated with staff by evading or ignoring information in contradistinction to the medical model that the staff emulated; similarly, the staff treated the patrons "as if" (Vahinger, 1927) they were persons with or with persons with a legitimate medical complaint seeking a conventional, a legal course of treatment for their dilemma.

Respectability:

Through mutual evasion of some information and the presentation and acceptance of a rhetoric involving other versions of their shared task, patrons and staff converted, at least for the moments of their face-to-face (or voice-to-voice in the case of telephone conversations) involvement, a context of illegality and deviance into one of respectability.

Sociologically, to be *respectable* is to be a person:

1. perceived-to-be-normal, thus possessing moral worth,
2. the appearance of which is thereby accorded through deferential displays, i.e., signs of person appreciation from others,
3. in socially situated encounters. [Ball, 1970:332]

Briefly, from a sociological perspective, respectability is not an attribute of persons but a relational category. Persons become respectable by virtue of the responses of others to them, at particular times and in particular places; they are seen as normally situated, and therefore moral, and thus respectable.

Thus, therapeutic abortions are respectable and criminal abortions aren't—even though the same medical procedures are employed in both.[15]

The rhetoric rendered an illegal abortion clinic into a normal, respectable medical setting; and what the rhetoric couldn't completely hide: the provision and utilization of a criminal service; *cooperative evasion* served to deny. If one is given identity by the company one keeps, the more respectable the company, the better and more respectable the self available. If one's company is "patients," then self can be more medical than criminal—and if company is "medical," then self can be that of patient rather than law-breaking client.

The clinic setting merely highlights two fundamental characteristics of respectability: (1) as a fundamental dimension in the definitions of selves and identities, it is actively sought after rather than simply passively bestowed; and (2) it is always problematic, its presence is not automatically warranted; it is always contextually given meaning—whether in confirmation or denial.[16]

Temporal Dimension:

A pair of useful distinctions, these concerning the temporal dimensions of self, and perception of identities too—have been made recently by Turner (1968:94) concerning the former, and Douglas (1967:280–283) regarding the latter. Although we have referred to self and identity throughout in a gross, temporally undifferentiated manner, this is not experientially the case: they are both momentary and transitory as well as enduring and persisting over time.

The self, ego as known to ego, is known both as a stable, basic entity, the "Real me"——— "I-myself as I really am" (Turner, 1968:94). This Turner calls the *self-conception,* which he contrasts with the self of immediate experience, the *self-image*—the picture ego has of himself in the immediate present, specifically located in time and space. The relationship between these two is interdependent. The self-conception is the result of the accretion of a life-time of self images, gradually building up a biographical self for the person. And as these images contribute to the more basic self-conception, this latter forms a baseline for comparison and evaluation of momentary images. These are judged as true or false, desirable or undesirable as they contrast or compliment the actor's conception of himself as a self, as an object-to-himself as well as an acting subject. Images too dissonant for incorporation in existing conceptions exert pressure toward change. Such change may, of course, be readily accepted or actively fought depending on the valence of the emotional freight it bears.

A similar distinction can be made regarding identities: they are both *situated* and *substantial.*[17] That is, identities are situated in time and space, and given meaning by that contextual location. At the same time there is, in North American Society

a general, implicit, non-theoretical assumption made in everyday communications (with oneself and with others) that each individual has, or is,
a substance. This substantialist meaning of persons leads to judgements of
persons as wholes . . . independent of time, place, and situation. [Douglas,
1967:281–282]

These substantive judgments are definitions, demands, and expectations about
persons—they are assignments of a substantial identity, against which situated
identities play and reinforce or alter, just as do self-images with self-conceptions. The distinctions made by Turner and Douglas are, then, opposite
sides of the same coin. Schematically, their relationship can be shown in a
paradigm.

Temporality:	Perceptual Source:	
	From Ego (actor)	From Alter (audience)
Transient	Self-*Image*	*Situated* Identity
Enduring	Self-*Conception*	*Substantial* Identity

Thus, the mutual face-work of patrons and staff is designed to keep
negative self-images and situated identities from intruding upon more enduring self-conceptions and substantial identities. Cooperatively, positive situated
identities are imputed to one another, and thus positive self-images derived.
This is not, of course, to construe a rational bent to these phenomena, but
a functional one; although calculation is much more a part of the staff-
mounted production of the rhetoric of respectability than is the patrons'
response to it.

Finally, another useful distinction is the one that has been made by
Lemert (1951; 1967:40–64) between primary and secondary deviation,
which seems particularly useful here. Broadly, *primary* deviation refers to
the *act* of deviation; in this case, performing and procuring criminal abortions.
Secondary deviation, on the other hand, refers more to the deviant actor:
specifically to his acquisition of an identity—and thus potentially a self—as a
deviant. It is the function of the rhetoric of legitimization and the operation
of cooperative evasion to minimize the vividness of the primary deviation in
order to avoid the problems, both interpersonal and intrapersonal, associated
with deviance of the secondary order. If the primary deviance of illegal
abortion cannot be denied completely, it can at least be disguised. And it is
to such concerns that the rhetoric speaks and is attended to by both patrons
and staff.

Unfortunately, the confidential and historical nature of this data and interpretation do not allow one of the usual canons of science to be met, that regarding exact replication; and no claim regarding the typicality of the clinic described herein can be formally made. Thus, if generalizations can be derived, they are of a conceptual rather than a statistical nature. Hopefully, however, the materials have shed some light on a relatively little-known area of social conduct.[18] Given the incidence of criminal abortion, it may be hoped that similar analysis can be conducted by others. Lastly, it may be suggested that hopefully the concept of rhetoric provides a useful tool for examining the dramas of social life and the selves and identities so implicated, whether these be deviant or conventional, spontaneous or routine, unusual or mundane.

Notes

1. Portions of this section are based upon a paper originally presented as "Conventional Data and Unconventional Conduct: Toward a Methodological Reorientation," Section on Deviance, Pacific Sociological Association, Long Beach, California, March 1967 (Ball, 1967b).

2. For self-reports of women seeking and obtaining abortions, both therapeutic (legal) and criminal, see Gebhard, et al. (1958:189–214).

3. For an extended statement by Polsky, see "Research Method, Morality, and Criminology" (1967:117–149).

4. The following two paragraphs are drawn from a class lecture by Donald Bowlus given in 1960. For examples and discussions of reactivity, even within the context of carefully controlled experimental research—involving both infrahuman and human subjects, see Rosenthal (1966) and Friedman (1967).

5. This legal problem is also sometimes encountered by journalists.

6. Among others, see Natanson (1963), Schutz (1962; 1964), Garfinkel, (1967), Hill and Crittenden (1968), and most recently Nicholson (1969).

7. The material in this section has been revised (from Ball, 1967), primarily by a shift in tense to the "ethnographic past."

8. For the *habitually deviant,* their deviance takes on the aspect of a *career* (Becker, 1963:24–25, 101–102), for the *situationally* deviant, their deviance is an *event.* For a similar interpretation of the contrasting Mertonian (Merton, 1938) and Durkheimian (Durkheim, 1951 edition:241–277) views of anomie, see Scott and Turner (1965).

9. Only one exception was observed, and she stayed overnight.

10. This triad, practitioner-patient-client, is probably much more common and the doctor-patient dyad much less common than the use of the latter as the "typical model" by medical sociologists would suggest. See, for instance, Bloom (1963:40–42, 52–58).

11. Garfinkel (1963 and 1964) discusses and demonstrates the importance of routine in interaction, and the tension and anxiety its absence promotes.

12. Compare Sykes and Matza (1957) and Matza (1964), where the analysis is individual rather than institutional, also Lofland (1969).

13. Excluded from the consideration is the telephone girl who was never in face-to-face, but only voice-to-voice interaction with patrons, but who was both medical-professional and supportive in her verbal demeanor. I have dealt with some of the contrasts between face-to-face and voice-to-voice interaction brought about by telephones, particularly opportunities for deceit, in Ball (1968).

14. By way of contrast, see the discussion of the patient as basically passive and helpless in Parsons (1951:439–447).

15. Technically, this is not true. Some criminal abortions may involve techniques other than the dilation and scraping of the uterus. This procedure is the safest though, and most probable technique for the "better" abortionists.

16. The sociology of respectability is more thoroughly explored in "The Problematics of Respectability," as well as other papers in *Deviance and Respectability: The Social Construction of Moral Meanings,* Jack D. Douglas, editor (New York: Basic Books, 1970), pp. 326–371.

17. In his original discussion Douglas referred to situated and substantial *selves,* meaning *ego* as known to *alter.* This kind of terminological imprecision is common in the literature, with a consequent blurring of the important difference between alter's and ego's perspectives. We have, therefore, substituted the term identity in interpreting his discussion.

18. For a relatively recent summary which demonstrates how little is still actually known, see the excellent review of the literature by Schur (1965:11–66).

References

Ball, Donald W., 1967a. "An Abortion Clinic Ethnography." *Social Problems* 14 (Winter):293–301.

    1967b. "Conventional Data and Unconventional Conduct: Toward a Methodological Re-orientation." Presented to the section on Deviance, Pacific Sociological Association, Long Beach, March.

    1968. "Toward a Sociology of Telephones and Telephoners." In *Sociology and Everyday Life,* Marcello Truzzi, ed. Englewood Cliffs, N.J.: Prentice-Hall, Inc., 59–75.

    1970. "The Problematics of Respectability." In *Deviance and Respectability: The Social Construction of Moral Meanings.* New York: Basic Books, Inc., 326–371.

Becker, Howard S., 1963. *Outsiders.* New York: The Free Press.

Bloom, Samuel W., 1963. *The Doctor and His Patient.* New York: Russell Sage Foundation.

Cavan, Sherri, 1966. *Liquor License: An Ethnography of Bar Behavior.* Chicago: Aldine Publishing Company.

Cicourel, Aaron V., 1968. *The Social Organization of Juvenile Justice.* New York: John Wiley & Sons, Inc.

Cicourel, Aaron V., and Kitsuse, John I., 1963. *The Educational Decision-Makers.* Indianapolis: The Bobbs-Merrill Co., Inc.

Cloward, Richard A., and Ohlin, Lloyd E., 1960. *Delinquency and Opportunity.* New York: The Free Press.

Cohen, Albert K., 1955. *Delinquent Boys: The Culture of the Gang.* New York: The Free Press.

Douglas, Jack D., 1967. *The Social Meanings of Suicide.* Princeton: Princeton University Press.

Durkheim, Emile., 1951. *Suicide: A Study in Sociology.* New York: The Free Press.

Friedman, Neil., 1967. *The Social Nature of Psychological Research: The Psychological Experiment as a Social Interaction.* New York: Basic Books, Inc.

Garfinkel, Harold, 1963. "A Conception of, and Experiments with, 'Trust' as a Condition of Stable Concerted Actions." In *Motivation and Social Interaction.* O. J. Harvey, ed. New York: The Ronald Press, 187–238.

1964. "Studies in the Routine Grounds of Everyday Activities." *Social Problems* 11 (Winter):225–250. Reprinted in Garfinkel, 1967:35–75.

1967. *Studies in Ethnomethodology.* Englewood Cliffs, N.J.: Prentice-Hall, Inc.

Goffman, Erving, 1955. "On Face-Work: an Analysis of Ritual Elements in Social Interaction." *Psychiatry* 18(August):213–231.

1956. *Presentation of Self in Everyday Life.* Edinburgh: Social Sciences Research Centre, University of Edinburgh.

1961. *Encounters: Two Studies in the Sociology of Interaction.* Indianapolis: Bobbs-Merrill Company, Inc.

1963. *Stigma: Notes on the Management of Spoiled Identities.* Englewood Cliffs, N.J.: Prentice-Hall, Inc.

1969. "The Insanity of Place." *Psychiatry* (November):357–388.

Gold, Ray, 1958. "Roles in Sociological Field Observations." *Social Forces* 36 (March):217–233.

Hill, Richard J., and Crittenden, Kathleen Stones, eds., 1968. *Proceedings of the Purdue Symposium on Ethnomethodology.* Lafayette, Indiana: Purdue Research Foundation (Institute for the Study of Social Change, Department of Sociology, Purdue University; Institute Monograph Series, Number 1).

Hooker, Evelyn, 1963. "Male Homosexuality." In *Taboo Topics,* Norman Farberow, ed. New York: Atherton, 1963, 44–55.

Lemert, Edwin M., 1951. *Social Pathology.* New York: McGraw-Hill Book Company.

1967. *Human Deviance, Social Problems, and Social Control.* Englewood Cliffs, N.J.: Prentice-Hall, Inc.

Lofland, John, with the assistance of Lyn H. Lofland, 1969. *Deviance and Identity.* Englewood Cliffs, N.J.: Prentice-Hall, Inc.

Manning, Peter K., Forthcoming. "Fixing What You Feared: Notes on the Campus Abortion Search." In the *Sociology of Sex,* James M. Henslin, ed. New York: Appleton-Century-Crofts.

Matza, David, 1964. *Delinquency and Drift.* New York: John Wiley & Sons, Inc.

Merton, Robert K., 1938. "Social Structure and Anomie." *American Sociological Review* 3(October):672–682.

Natanson, Maurice, Ed., 1963. *Philosophy of the Social Sciences: A Reader.* New York: Random House, Inc.

Nicholson, Robert F., 1969. "Sociological Homunculi: Professional Dilemmas in Taking Alfred Schutz Seriously." Presented to the Second Annual Conference on Existentialism and the Human Sciences. San Jose, California, November, 14–16.

Parsons, Talcott, 1951. *The Social System.* New York: The Free Press.

Polsky, Ned, 1967. *Hustlers, Beats, and Others.* Chicago: Aldine Publishing Company.

Roach, Mary Ellen, and Eicher, Joan Bubolz, Eds., 1965. *Dress, Adornment, and the Social Order.* New York: John Wiley & Sons, Inc.

Rosenthal, Robert, 1966. *Experimenter Effects in Behavioral Research.* New York: Appleton-Century-Crofts.

Ryan, Mary Shaw, 1966. *Clothing: A Study in Human Behavior.* New York: Holt, Rinehart and Winston, Inc.

Schutz, Alfred, 1962. *Collected Papers, I: The Problem of Social Reality.* The Hague: Martinus Nijhoff.

1964. *Collected Papers, II: Studies in Social Theory.* The Hague: Martinus Nijhoff.

Scott, Marvin B., 1968. *The Racing Game.* Chicago: Aldine Publishing Company.

Scott, Marvin B., and Turner, Roy, 1965. "Weber and the Anomic Theory of Deviance." *The Sociological Quarterly* 6(Summer):233–240.

Simmel, Georg, 1950. *The Sociology of Georg Simmel,* Kurt H. Wolff, ed. New York: The Free Press.

Stone, Gregory, 1962. "Appearance and the Self." In *Human Behavior and Social Processes,* Arnold M. Rose, ed. Boston: Houghton-Mifflin, 86–118.

Sykes, Gresham M., and Matza, David, 1957. "Techniques of Neutralization: a Theory of Delinquency." *American Sociological Review* 22(December):664–670.

Turner, Ralph H., 1968. "The Self-Conception in Social Interaction." In *The Self in Interaction,* Chad Gordon and Kenneth J. Gergen, eds. New York: John Wiley & Sons, Inc., 93–106.

Vaihinger, Hans, 1927. *The Philosophy of "As If."* New York: Harcourt Brace Jovanovich.

Vold, George B., 1958. *Theoretical Criminology.* New York: Oxford University Press.

Webb, Eugene; Campbell, Donald T.; Schwartz, Richard D.; and Sechrest, Lee, 1966. *Unobtrusive Measures: Nonreactive Measures in the Social Sciences.* Chicago: Rand McNally.

Wolff, Kurt H., Ed., 1959. *Georg Simmel, 1858–1918.* Columbus: The Ohio State University.

| IV |

Using Rules for Practical Situations

The sociology of deviance is concerned with the relation between social rules and social order. Recent research and writing by labeling theorists have demonstrated as untrue the absolutist assumptions that rules and social order are nonproblematic. In their place has emerged a perspective based upon phenomenological studies of rule use in everyday life. Both of the essays in this part constitute extensions of this emerging perspective.

In the first chapter, Douglas outlines the essential details of the absolutist perspective on rules. He then goes on to consider the uses of rules in everyday life situations in order to show why this perspective is incorrect. He shows that the most elementary assumptions contained in the absolutist perspective on the uses of rules are violated by the ways in which people actually think, feel, and act. Finally, Douglas considers the implications of the uses of rules in everyday life for our understanding of social order.

The second chapter, by Johnson, contains a detailed case study of the everyday uses of social rules on a Navy destroyer. He shows that although the rules are codified and publicly represented as absolute, the practical tasks required to run the ship could never be accomplished if the codified rules were obeyed. Johnson shows how crew members construct special meanings for the rules in order to cope with the practical situations that they face. Finally, he shows that members cannot decide what rules "really mean" until they use them in concrete, practical situations.

Chapter Eight

THE EXPERIENCE OF THE ABSURD AND THE PROBLEM OF SOCIAL ORDER

Jack D. Douglas

Man is necessarily free. Man is necessarily constrained. The degree of each necessity varies with the situation he faces, but each is present in any situation and each is always in partial conflict with the other. This coexistence and conflict are basic to the human condition and determine many fundamental aspects of human society.

Man is necessarily free because he can only exist by *creating* means of meeting his animal needs, means that have not been provided us by instinct or imprinting. He is necessarily free as well because he can only do this creative work by using his immensely developed symbolic intelligence, his consciousness; the ability to stand back from and abstract from concrete situations and to consider alternative symbolizations of those situations is the very essence of consciousness.

Man is necessarily constrained because he lives in a world of harsh physical realities that thus far in human history have set definite limits to the creative paths he may choose in meeting his animal needs. He is constrained as well by his necessary dependence upon his fellow human beings for his survival and for the fulfillment of his few distinctively human urges.

The necessary conflict between freedom and constraint produces one of the crucial problems of human existence—the *problem of social order*.

Whereas the degree varies greatly, most (nondomestic) animals are reasonably social and depend in part on their fellows for their survival in a world of predators; but few animals other than man experience a problem of social order. Their social life is instinctual. These social instincts lead them to act toward each other in certain very stable ways in given situations, so any problems that arise are simply the result of changes in the environment or of mutations, and both are solved by the natural selection of instincts. Man's social life is probably built on instincts of sex, parental love, and general fellow-feeling but even these are so flexible and so affected by his symbolic life that he finds great variation in them. And the only social relations that are immediately derived from these are the family ones, which are not sufficient for our survival. Man must depend upon a wider network of human relations, and the further out he goes the less instinctually based his relations with his fellows are; the more he must work consciously to create them. Man's dependency constrains him; his consciousness makes him free to create these relations and even to choose alternatives to his few instinctual urges. The choices in these social relations must be made to partially coordinate with the choices of the other human beings on whom he depends, yet instinct does not dictate how these orderings of relations will come about, and the necessary freedom of consciousness assures him that there will necessarily be some conflicts and disorderings in the choices made. The ordering of his relations with his fellow human beings thereby becomes a necessary problem of all human existence. How is the problem to be solved?

The Problem of Social Order and Social Rules

No human being has ever discovered a simple or sure answer to this fundamental problem of social order: for this reason, *social order always remains necessarily problematic.* But a vast number of different solutions have been proposed and attempted over the eons of human life. Chiefs, kings, despots, tyrants, presidents, generals, executives, organizers, parents, and all men who seek in any way to order their social relations have used physical force, financial reward, promises, threats, pleadings, persuasion, inveiglement, and moral exhortations to construct the order they desire in the relations among their fellows.

Regardless of their particular methods, *men have always found social rules a necessary component in any successful attempt to order social relations beyond immediate situations.* At their most general level, *social rules are the abstract, symbolic criteria normal members of a given society or group are expected to make sincere use of in deciding what to do in any situation for which the rules are seen as relevant.* The general strategy of rule use seems relatively simple: if each member of society shares with all other members a symbolic criteria for action in any given situation, and makes sincere use of that criteria in deciding how to act in the situation, then the actions of individuals will be patterned; if the rules are "wisely" constructed so that patterns of actions flowing from them will be well coordinated with each other, rather than conflicting with each other, then the actions of the members of society can be expected to be coordinated or ordered—the problem of social order will be solved.

Some social rules involve nothing more than "expectations of sincere use." These are *unsanctioned rules* and are commonly found in rules of "good taste" or "sensibility," but even include certain kinds of laws, such as the *factum valet laws* of the English common law, which specify what should not be done but whose violations are understood not to produce any negative consequences for the violators. However, few would-be-common-sense engineers of social order have ever found "expectations" sufficient in producing the "sincere" use of the rule-criteria that they desire. Instead, they have commonly believed it necessary to associate rule uses and nonuses or misuses (both of the latter being violations) with certain kinds of rewards and punishments, or positive and negative sanctions. The vast majority of these sanctions are unformalized and are administered without any formal organization. This is clearly the case, for example, in most uses of rules in family or friendship groups. But some of these rules, especially in the complex civilizations, have been carefully spelled out, formalized, written, and administered by organized groups who are specifically charged with formalizing and administering such rules. These formalized and organized rules are legal rules or *laws*.

The close relation between social rules and attempts to construct social order, or to "maintain order," as men of common sense generally state it today, is seen in the clichés about "Law and Order," which are based upon ideas that go back at least as early as Plato's *Laws* and Saint Augustine's *City of God*.[1] The original idea of this cliché, and the one still generally found in legal treatises, is that obeying the laws produces social order, whereas disobeying them produces social disorder. But the relation between the two is so close in common-sense thought about society that they are commonly treated as being identical. That is, obeying the law comes to be seen as a form of social order, whereas disobeying the law comes to be seen as a form of disorder. (This same confusion is seen in the works of the Chicago sociologists in the 1920s and 1930s who argued that social disorganization causes deviance, but who also commonly used rates of deviance as indices of social disorganization.)

The sociology of deviance has been called many different things, but it has always been either explicitly or implicitly concerned with the nature of social rules, the uses of social rules, violations of social rules, and the relations of social rules and their violations to social order (and disorder). Because social order is such a basic problem of all human societies, and because men have everywhere used social rules as one of the most important components in their attempts to solve this problem, the sociology of deviance has always been one of the most important fields of sociology.

The Absolutist Perspective on Social Rules

Until recently, few men of common sense have been willing to allow all social rules to be subject to the discretion of individual choices. (Although most men of common sense have never been conscious of this as a choice, but, rather, have simply believed that social rules could not by their very nature be subject to individual choice, there have always been some men, such as Plato and John Adams, who were aware of the manipulative or social-engineering aspects of the choice of social rules.) The reason, whether conscious or not, for making some social rules independent of individual choice seems fairly clear now: if individuals can choose what the rules are to be, how they are to be interpreted, when they are to be seen as relevant to a situation, who is to be subject to them, what their limitations are to be, and so on, then the element of freedom is reintroduced and the rules cannot be as effective in producing the constraint believed necessary to construct social order. Because of this, both by purposeful planning and by trial and error, almost all societies arrived at an absolutist perspective on those social rules that were most important to them, especially those that were believed to be important in producing social order or preventing social disorder. These rules were commonly believed to be derived directly from an Absolute Being (God), often in mysterious circumstances that inspired awe (as in a whirlwind on the top of a mountain), were given to man in such a fashion that no one could reasonably believe that some individual human being simply made them up (such as being written in stone), were stated simply and learned through endless repetition (as can be seen in the teaching of the Ten Commandments), were sanctioned with extreme promises of bliss and suffering (such as eternal heaven and hellfire), and were surrounded in this world with extreme sanctions that tied their violation in with injury to everything of value to anyone (such as ostracism, excommunication, or execution).

These *absolute rules,* which have most commonly been called *moral rules* (morality) or moral principles in Western societies, have a number of essential properties that make them *object-like* or thing-like and that, therefore, make them necessarily independent of individual free choices: (1) they are necessary, or they necessarily apply to and are necessarily applied by all individuals; (2) their meanings for any situation are always certain, or unproblematic; (3) they are supposed to provide a *complete ordering* among all potential situations and actions; (4) they are universal or do not vary in their applications with any situations; (5) they are timeless (eternal) and unchanging; and (6) they are imposed and sanctioned from outside the individual members of society, or are a part of Being (Reality) itself. These properties of absolute rules, which are also found in the uses of other kinds of social meanings (such as ideas), constitute the properties of the absolutist perspective on social rules and social order, that have dominated common-sense thought about social rules and social order in the Western world since the earliest historical records.

There have probably always been some men who were led by their experiences with social rules and with those who tried to enforce them to believe that no rules are really absolute and that this whole absolutist perspective on rules is really a rhetorical device used by men of power to maintain their own power and to construct social order according to their desires. After all, although the scriptures speak of many men who followed Abraham in their absolute submission to the absolute rules, never questioning their authority even when they led to conclusions or actions that would otherwise seem absurd, they also teach us of men such as Job whose experiences led them to believe that things that were supposed by the absolute rules to be impossible did in fact happen, and who thereby were led to doubt the rules and their creators. But it was not until the nineteenth century that European thinkers began to seriously consider the possibility that these rules might not be absolute and might, rather, be the creation of men themselves, perhaps even cynical creations intended to keep other men in submission.

Probably because of the great social changes resulting largely from industrialization and the growing complexity of their societies, European social thinkers by the nineteenth century had become very aware that the absoluteness of moral rules was a question. However, this does not mean that they had doubts about it or that they recognized the problematic nature of all social rules. Most of those who dealt with the question took the position that has since been labeled the "conservative position." Dostoevski is probably the most famous representative of this point of view. His novels *Crime and Punishment, The Possessed,* and *The Brothers Karamazov* all deal in one way or another with the question of whether social rules can be considered to be "relativistic" or whether they are necessarily considered to be absolute. In each case he tried to show that any relativism, or personal interpretation of moral rules leads inevitably to murder and suicide. Without the constraint of absolute rules, men are at war with all other men and with themselves; society cannot exist without the constraint on human passions provided only by absolute morality that is imposed by God and the Church. (As one of his characters insisted, "All things are permitted if there is no God.") But there were also the revolutionary theorists, especially the Marxists and the anarchists, who actually raised the whole question in the first place that led the conservatives to try to show that their position would inevitably produce chaos and destruction. The revolutionaries argued that the moral rules of the ancient regime were not absolute, but were in fact used cynically, as an "opiate," by the dominant classes and the Church to keep the lower classes in submission to them. But this does not mean that the revolutionaries rejected all absoluteness in social rules. On the contrary, they insisted with just as much fervor that there was a higher morality—a more absolute morality—that made the actions of the bourgeoisie immoral. This moral right of the producer to the full value of his own product and, thus, the moral right of the proletariat to rule the world, was simply another absolutist morality meant to replace that of the "oppressing classes" who "expropriated" the products of the proletariat. (The anarchist arguments generally appealed to other forms of absolute rights.) Only the early existential writers, especially Nietzsche and Kierkegaard, seriously considered the possibility that all social rules might in fact be problematic for the human actor.

Sociologists almost universally cast their lot, either purposefully or unwittingly, with the conservative social thinkers. Many simply applied the ideas of the philosophers and novelists to the official data on deviance to try to show that the growing relativism of morality in European society, and, especially the growing unwillingness to accept the moral authority of religion as absolute, was producing a veritable crime wave and "suicide mania." Mazaryk, for example, tried to show that increasing irreligiosity was leading to a rapidly growing suicide problem throughout Europe. Durkheim, whose position was to have great consequences for twentieth-century sociology, argued very simply that "We must have either God or society," by which he meant that men must have an absolute moral authority outside of themselves or else social rules will not be obeyed, deviance will increase alarmingly, and social order will become impossible. In all of his works Durkheim treated social rules as being absolute for the members of society and in *Suicide* he argued specifically that the lack of external moral authority over individuals is associated with suicide, especially in the form of *anomic suicide*.[2]

Durkheim's position has been shared by the vast majority of sociologists studying deviance until only quite recently. They have implicitly treated social rules as being absolute for the members of society, have assumed that the members experience no problems in using social rules in their everyday lives, have assumed that they as sociologists have no problems in knowing what the rules are that are being used to decide what to do in concrete situations, and have assumed that such absolute rules and obedience to them are necessary and sufficient explanations of social order.

The assumptions of the absolutist perspective on social meanings and actions in general by men of common sense and by sociologists alike led both to make the *assumption of moral determinism* about acts of deviance. The abstract common-sense view of an immoral act, or any violation of a rule, that comes from the assumption of the absolutist perspective is very simple: a man who commits an immoral act (as defined by the viewer) must be assumed, because of the absolutism of morality, both to know that he is committing an immoral act and to make his decision to commit that act on the basis of moral considerations; consequently, a man who commits an immoral act does so because he chooses to commit an immoral act. Immoral acts are the result of immoral choices or decisions. It is this idea, combined with the assumption that an individual has a unitary (substantial) self that does the choosing, that lies behind the common-sense belief that a man who commits an immoral act is an immoral man and that immoral men commit immoral acts.

The absolutist sociologists, of course, have been overtly opposed to any consideration of such "subjective" phenomena as "intention," so they have excluded it from any overt mention in their works on deviance. In fact, however, because they have implicitly assumed the common-sense perspective of absolutism on morality, they have also implicitly assumed this moral determinism of deviant acts. All of these absolutist sociologists, therefore, have implicitly assumed that individuals who commit acts such as crime or suicide are doing so with the full knowledge that these acts are crimes or suicides. It is this assumption that lies behind the thousands of studies of "criminals" to find out "why they committed the crimes." But this assumption is also implicit in the theories of deviance proposed by structuralist sociologists such as Robert K. Merton and Albert Cohen. Merton's famous theory of anomie and deviance implicitly assumes that the individuals choosing deviant means to lower their anomie are knowingly choosing deviant means.[3] Cohen's argument that lower-class delinquents create counter cultures to oppose the values of the middle classes assumes that they are knowingly rejecting and violating those middle-class rules.[4]

The Necessarily Problematic Nature of Social Rules

Because earlier sociologists believed that social rules were absolute, they saw no need to study the ways in which the members of society actually used social rules in their everyday lives. Because they did not study the actual uses of rules in everyday life, they did not see that the members of society actually experienced fundamental problems in using rules, that these problems produced all kinds of conflicts over questions of morality in most situations faced in everyday life, and that social order is necessarily problematic, whether people "obeyed" the rules or not. As we have done such studies of everyday uses of rules, we have found that the members of society experience two kinds of fundamental problems in using social rules: *abstract problems* and *situational problems*. The problems of abstract meanings of rules are those that exist independently of the situation in which a rule might be used. These are the kinds of problems experienced as a result of experienced vagueness in rules or conflicts between rules. The situational problems exist regardless of whether there are abstract problems. They are the uncertainties about just what a rule means, or just how it is to be applied, in a specific, concrete situation.[5]

These problematic meanings of rules can be found in almost any concrete situation in which members of our society are involved in trying to use social rules. They are most obvious in those situations where a single individual "argues with himself" or "worries" about what he "should do" in a concrete situation, about what is "the right thing to do." But they are also obvious in the interminable moral arguments among individuals and groups that can be observed in our society—arguments over race, arguments over the draft, arguments over taxes, arguments over wars, arguments over dating practices, arguments over child-rearing practices, arguments over educational policies, and so on endlessly.

Rules are necessarily problematic in these ways in American society partly because this is such a complex and pluralistic society, with different values being shared by different ethnic, racial, occupational, and generational groups.[6] But the rules are also problematic because of the social meanings of rules themselves. Ultimately, individuals are believed to have obeyed or violated rules because they are believed *responsible* for actions that are believed to constitute violations. Responsibility is believed to exist only when an individual is believed to have (1) *intended* to commit the action, and (2) *know* the rule involved and the probable consequence of the action. Because intention and knowing are internal states that can never be directly observed in other individuals, and because our fundamental common-sense ideas about truth place greater trust (or truth-value) on externally observable phenomena than on internal (subjective) experiences, intention and knowledge are always problematic; they are always subject to alternative, equally plausible (at least to different individuals) interpretations. This, for example, is why suicide, which is most commonly seen by men of common sense as an "intentional taking of one's own life," is almost inevitably subject to alternative interpretations—as some form of accident, in which the externally observable "facts" may be accepted by everyone, but in which the imputations of meanings, as suicide by some and as an accident by others, are in great conflict.

Some philosophers, especially existential philosophers, have proposed *theories of the absurd* that would lead us to expect that a world in which the experiences of individual actors lead them to believe that they are considered guilty of immoral actions only when the conditions of knowing the rules and the consequences of actions and intending to violate those rules and produce the consequences are met is a world experienced as rational, whereas a world in which the experiences of individual actors lead them to believe that they are considered guilty of immoral actions when they believe (or "know") some of these conditions have not been met is a world experienced as *absurd*.[7] Although we have no comparative studies that could demonstrate this point, it seems reasonable to expect that the more simple, stable, closed and homogeneous society is, the more frequently the conditions of knowledge and intention will be (experienced as) met when individuals are considered guilty of immoral actions; and the more complex, changing, open, and pluralistic a society is, the more frequently these conditions will not be met. In addition, the more fundamentally problematic the meanings of rules and their violations are in a society, the more frequently the conditions will not be (experienced as) met. As a result, the members of such a society may come increasingly to see their social world as absurd. If this is so, and if there is a necessary relation between belief in the rules and social order, especially one in which an absolutism of rules is necessary for order, as Durkheim argued, then a society in which experience with the rules increasingly leads to a sense of the absurdity of the rules could be expected to experience increasing problems of social order.

Since American society appears to be becoming ever more complex, this argument has clear relevance for understanding our society and anticipating its future developments. When we examine the everyday moral experience of the members of our society, we do find plenty of experiences that could produce this experience of the absurd, but we also find that the relations between these experiences and social order are far more complex than this argument would lead us to believe.

Because American society is so complex, open, changing, and pluralistic, and because the meanings of rules and their violations are so fundamentally problematic, we would expect to find that the members of our society often experience the uses of rules as absurd. When we observe the uses of rules in everyday life, I believe we can specify at last three general types of situations that members of our society do at times experience as absurd, although they themselves do not often systematically make these distinctions.

Lack of Knowledge of the Rules:

In a relatively simple society, most individuals probably have a good idea of what the moral feelings and beliefs of their fellow members are. In our complex and pluralistic society, however, all individuals experience many instances in which they are considered to be rule violators by some important groups, and it is a rare individual who is not formally charged at some time with illegal activities against which he did not know there were any laws.

In American society there are many thousands of criminal and civil laws. There are laws concerning almost any realm of life: construction laws, zoning laws, curfew laws, public nuisance laws, fraud laws, vagrancy laws, traffic laws, tax laws, health laws, drug laws, public decency laws, pollution laws, maritime laws, felony laws, marriage laws, child-care laws, labor laws, contract laws, medical practice laws, school attendance laws, blue laws— even laws concerning sex in marriage. These laws vary greatly from one state to another and often from one city or county to another; yet Americans are the most mobile people in the history of the world. There is no statute of limitations on laws themselves, so laws passed in the nineteenth century are still applicable today; yet American society is the most rapidly changing society in the history of the world.

In addition, there are a vast number of different *government regulatory rules* and *private-law rules* that are ultimately backed up by government laws. The government regulatory rules are those of such governmental agencies as the Interstate Commerce Commission, the agriculture department, welfare departments, state equalization boards, and so on across hundreds of different agencies that have the legal power to make rules of their own to govern realms of life that touch all of us either directly or indirectly at various times. The private-law rules are the vast number of different rules used by private corporations, including such public institutions as state colleges and universities and labor unions, to try to govern their massive clienteles.

(In addition to these kinds of rules there are the millions of different "informal rules" used by all groups that deal with the public to handle their relations with an ever-changing clientele. These are the rules concerning seating in theaters, rules about serving, tipping, and dressing in restaurants, and so on endlessly. These are important as sources of "bother" and/or "embarrassment" in everyday life, but they do not possess the importance for us that all rules ultimately backed up by the morally stigmatizing effects of laws do.)

Finally, there are the vast number of different moral rules of various groups and individuals that make up this pluralistic society. There are the basic moral rules concerning eating of the Jews, Mormons, Moslems, vegetarians, organicists, and dieters. There are all the moral rules concerning dancing, smoking, drinking, love-making, and many other more obscure corners of life of the Southern Baptists, Black Muslims, Methodists, prohibitionists, and many others. And there are all the less clearly defined moral rules concerning dress, length of hair, speech (curse words), body motions, and so on that are held in very different ways by all groups.

Because of this vast, unsystematic, changing *conglomeration* of social rules, all individuals inevitably commit actions that could easily be seen as violations of many moral and legal rules of some groups all the time without knowing that there are such rules. More importantly, all individuals inevitably commit actions that could easily be defined as violations of moral and legal rules of the groups of which they are members, and, thus, for which they are potentially held responsible, without knowing that they are doing so; and at some time probably everyone has even unknowingly committed actions that could be defined as felony violations.

That is, individuals of our society are commonly involved in committing certain actions that they themselves and almost anyone else would define as violations of these various moral and legal rules if they were advised of the existence of such rules. Also, inevitably, we are so advised in many different situations. Most commonly, we find that we have unknowingly violated some law concerning the registration of our cars, or unknowingly committed a tri-state auto violation (based on some state laws that forbid registering, insuring, and driving autos in three different states),[8] or unknowingly built a tool shed without "adequate" electrical wiring, or unknowingly put in a fence that is two feet higher than the sales contract on their house allows, or unknowingly let someone read an official file without "proper" authorization. Again, very commonly, we find that we have prepared a dinner for our friends that they cannot possibly eat because of their religious rules against the food or the method of its preparation, or we offer a drink to someone for whom drinking is terribly immoral, or we propose something to a young lady that her religion defines as a mortal sin. But there are also those rarer instances in which individuals do not know that there are laws against the use of certain drugs, or private-law rules against something they have been doing for years—until they are arrested or fired for it.

Unpredictable Enforcement and Interpretive Procedures:

The experiences resulting from a lack of knowledge of rules are all ones in which the problematic nature of social rules are minimal, that is, ones in which the members can agree (for the practical purposes at hand) on the relations between the rules and their actions, once they know what the rules are. But the vast array of different, obscure, and conflicting rules is itself enough to assure us that most of our experiences with rules will be far more problematic than this; and this combined with the necessarily problematic nature of rules leads us to expect that most such experiences will be quite problematic.

Our everyday experiences and all relevant sociological research show that even when we do know what the rules are in the abstract, we cannot predict from this how the rules will be interpreted in any given situation and how the individuals involved will go about trying to enforce or not enforce the interpreted rules. The necessarily problematic nature of rules means that they must always be interpreted, or their concrete meanings constructed, for any concrete situation.[9] There are, of course, various *interpretive procedures,* including, for example, rule-bound procedures of rationality and rules of evidence. But the applications of these procedures, however highly formalized, are themselves necessarily problematic to some degree, so the concrete constructions of meanings of rules always remain problematic to some (and highly varying) degree until a concrete action commits actors to a given construction.

In fact, some of the more basic rules intended to produce rational certainty in our uses of rules, such as the rules of admissible evidence in common law, are themselves important contributors at times to the problematic relations between rules and their practical applications in concrete situations. The rules of evidence, for example, may be interpreted by courts of appeal in such a manner that individuals previously convicted of serious rule violations, perhaps on the basis of their own confessions that they did in fact violate such rules, are now found to be "innocent" of those rule

violations. This has happened, for example, in the case of murder convictions that were later overturned on the grounds that the convicted men
had not been advised of their rights not to confess their guilt or not to give
any testimony without legal counsel. In these cases we find judges deciding
that a confessed rule violation does not warrant the imputation of guilt
because someone else, generally quite unknowingly to the person confessing,
and possibly unknowingly to themselves, had violated legal rules of evidence.
Moreover, we find that the justification for such decisions is based upon the
understanding by the members of society that the truth of evidence and of
the relation between evidence and rules is very problematic: it is precisely
because the members believe that individuals may give false testimony (including false confessions) in some situations and that individuals may falsely
apply rules to defined situations that they believe they are justified in such
ex post facto invalidations of rule imputations. (These events also involve
the members' recognition that there are indeed many instances in which
the members of society will not know what the rules are. Otherwise, it would
not make sense to them to demand that someone be advised of the rules
regarding his situation. We see, then, that the lack of knowledge of rules
has become so "normal" a state of affairs that we have rules concerning the
lack of knowledge of rules.)

Again, individuals may be found guilty of rule violations in which
there has been no denial of the facts of evidence or of the validity of the
enforcement procedures used, but may later be found innocent on the basis
of the ex-post facto invalidation of the rule itself. One of the most common
examples of this in our pluralistic society is the result of the complex and
problematic laws of jurisdiction that are used to try to define which governmental body (if any) has a right to pass laws concerning a given realm of
life. There are many famous cases, such as the "Carol Lane" case, in which
individuals are found innocent of the charges simply on the basis of a
decision that the legislative body that made the laws under which the conviction was achieved did not have the authority to pass such laws in that
particular state (although the comparable body in the neighboring state may
be the only one in that state to have such authority). But there are also the
many cases in which higher bodies, such as the Supreme Court, having the
authority to review the validity of rules passed by lower bodies, decide that
the lower bodies did not have the right to pass such laws. There are even
cases in which the lower bodies apparently expect that the higher body will
invalidate a new law, but in which they decide to pass the law and enforce
it because they believe that the practical situation that the new law is intended
to deal with will no longer be present by the time the higher body makes
the decision invalidating that law.

But the uncertainty or unpredictability of enforcement and interpretive
procedures is not restricted to such relatively infrequent events. On the
contrary, uncertainty is the normal state of affairs. After all, the vast ma-

jority of violations of moral and legal rules, even those that are seen as the most absolute, go "undetected." That is, for all the individuals who consider themselves, or someone else known to them personally, to be guilty of such violations, only a small minority are ever publicly accused of such violations and publicly defined as guilty. (If this were not the case, there would be relatively few people outside of prisons to keep the great majority of the population inside and there would also be vastly fewer cases of unrelieved guilt feelings.) The case of marijuana today is a good indication of this. It is now an "open secret" that anywhere between 20 to 80 percent (with most insiders insisting that the percentage is definitely at the upper end) of today's university students have "knowingly and intentionally" violated the laws against the possession of marijuana. The laws concerning this activity that are still "on the books" treat the possession of marijuana as a very serious violation, in fact a form of "use of narcotics" in spite of the universal recognition that this is not true. There are still sporadic instances in which individuals are subjected to the full force of such laws, which involve sentences of years in prison, but the situation is one mainly of uncertainty about whether there will be any attempt to enforce the rules, whether the rules will be drastically altered, and about what will in fact happen if one is "detected."

This is roughly the situation with most forms of violations. All studies of the police have found that the police do not arrest or bring any charges against the great majority of violators they do detect (that is, people they have good evidence against as violators).[10] They normally give people warnings, turn their heads, talk to the parents of juveniles, and so on. Even when arrests are made, it is highly uncertain whether an individual will be found guilty of rule violation, since two-thirds of those arrested are never formally charged with any crime and some of those charged are found innocent. Of those found guilty of violations such as felonies, the "penalties" are highly uncertain, since one never knows whether he will get a "hanging judge" or a "sympathetic judge." (There are even some cases in which the sympathetic judges attack the victims of crimes such as rape in an attempt to get those found guilty "off easy.") The variability in sentencing is immense, both between states and within states, as the President's Commission on Crime and Justice found. Almost anything *can* happen, from a first offender's getting twenty years to life for armed robbery to a multiple offender for the same offense being placed on probation. As stated by the members of the commission, "It all depends on the situation."

Individuals who (knowingly) violate private laws probably experience even greater uncertainty in the interpretations of the relations between their actions and the rules. Any survey of the interpretations of the rule-meanings of campus demonstrations will show this. Students around the country took part in various reasonably well-patterned activities, such as marching, breaking windows, seizing buildings, forcibly evicting officials, throwing rocks at the police, and burning buildings. In some cases, the authorities who controlled the organizations so attacked joined the demonstrators. In many others they reasserted the rules, but "looked the other way" by refusing to do what "everyone knew" was necessary to get any legal evidence for convictions. In many more cases they "denounced the violations," but "understood the provocations" and "condoned the specific acts." In other cases they found the demonstrators guilty of violating the rules, but declared "amnesty," or changed the rules, or suspended or expelled the students. In a few cases they called in outside forces who shot people they believed to be violators, although it later seemed that some of those shot were not violators, but were, instead, "innocent bystanders," while the violators disappeared.

Individuals who (knowingly) violate private morals probably experience even greater uncertainty over how those violations will be interpreted by the other individuals involved. The "I thought you'd be angry" response, and the "I didn't think you'd really care" response, are both common experiences in any family or among any group of friends. For example, there is apparently a considerable amount of adultery in our society (or any society?). This is an activity that the participants cannot normally indulge in without knowing that there are some rules regarding it. In addition to being included under one of the Ten Commandments, it is also defined as illegal by state laws and as immoral by most individuals (although individual definitions apparently depend a great deal upon who is doing the defining for whom). But the actual responses to concrete instances that are detected vary from "gladness," "relief," and "understanding" to "horror" and "murder."

The uncertainties about the concrete uses of rules, both enforcement and interpretive procedures, are so great that individuals and groups may do something for years in full public view without any idea that anyone would ever find them worthy of anything but praise, only to suddenly discover one day that they are publicly damned by a change in moral interpretations or by a change in the policies of the agents of control. The top executives of the automobile manufacturers, for example, probably felt very proud of their successful production of ever more, ever bigger automobiles; but they suddenly found themselves attacked as "murderers" and "polluters" by a public that had almost overnight become concerned with auto safety and pollution. Even more strikingly, some of the nation's largest corporations had for decades been openly discharging their industrial wastes into rivers and streams, only to find quite suddenly that they were being charged with (civil) violations by the Department of Justice of the Federal Refuse Act of 1899. The law was seventy-one years old and certainly had not been invoked for decades, but one day it was. Such unpredictabilities of interpretations are also seen in the so-called "incredible electrical conspiracy." As Sutherland showed long ago, almost all of the major corporations of the United States have been found guilty of antitrust violations over the past half century.[11] This is one of those violations that can be costly if caught, but that is so rarely detected, or, at least, acted against, that it is profitable for corporations to do it in many situations. For the first half century of legal cases, all charges brought against antitrust violators were civil charges, so there were no apparent risks of being branded a "criminal" by criminal procedures, if one were caught at it. But this was strictly a discretionary decision of the federal government, since the law gives the Department of Justice the power to bring either civil or criminal charges. It was not until the price fixing by all the large producers of electrical circuit-breaking equipment was discovered in the 1950s that the Department of Justice decided to bring criminal charges against the violators.[12] In this case the circumstances of the situation, especially, perhaps, the size of the conspiracy, led members of the administration to bring criminal charges against the main conspirators. A few executives who were "respectable citizens" one day, carrying out price-fixing business as usual, became "criminals" the next.

These kinds of unpredictable relations between one's actions and the concrete interpretations of the rules that will be made in relation to those actions are in general a necessary part of life because of the necessarily problematic meanings of social rules, but they are most directly dependent upon a more specific property of the use of social rules: *in using and constructing concrete meanings for social rules, the members of society rely heavily upon their purposes at hand in the concrete situations.* Whereas it is true that there are generally some members in any situation who are committed to "strict constructionist" uses of the rules as part of their purposes at hand, most members of society in most situations seem far more committed to using the rules to achieve other (nonrule) purposes at hand in the situation, such as "getting ahead in the world," "getting even with your enemies," "putting the bad guys in their places" (when the "bad guys" are defined in more general, trans-situational terms—such as by their membership in a racial category or other hated category), and "saving one's own skin."

Because of this, we find agents of control *starting out with* a goal of controlling some individual or group and then *finding a rule* they can invoke against him to achieve that purpose of control. As all administrators and agents of control understand implicitly, because there are so many rules and so many highly problematic interpretations of rules, "everyone must be guilty of something at some time." For this reason, when someone becomes a threat to what they want to achieve in the organization, or in the society, they "watch him closely," "investigate him," "put a tail on him," or even "frame" him by creating situations in which he will be "tempted" to violate an unproblematic rule and in which they will be able to carefully record the "compromising evidence." The more absolute the social interpretation of the rules he can be "proven" to have violated, the more effective the attempts to "discredit him" and, thus, to control him. Hence, they commonly go for sexual violations and other "stigmatizing violations." This is why a social reformer will sometimes find that the corporations or officials that he is trying to reform have hired private detectives to investigate his private life. This is why members of organizations who tell the public about the (inevitable) violations of various rules that take place in the organizations will find themselves being constantly reviewed and watched by their superiors, until a violation of their own is uncovered that will allow their superiors to plausibly attack them, demote them, transfer them, or fire them. This is why government officials suddenly under attack for "not doing enough about water pollution" will search through "musty law books" to find some statute (anything!) they can use to bring charges against polluters, why "suspicious persons" will find themselves "rousted" on any conceivable "pretext," why police under attack in the newspapers for "not being tough enough on the perpetrators of vice" will suddenly start arresting many times more people for "vagrancy," why civil-rights workers in the South found themselves arrested for all kinds of things they could never anticipate, and so on. (Wise social actors understand this, so they are always very careful to "watch their step" when involved in a fight— and to "cover their tracks" by destroying all records.)

Because the meanings of situations change over time, we find a frequent pattern to the unpredictability of the rule-meanings of actions: *as the situation of the users of the rules change in relation to an earlier situation, we find that they (reflexively) renegotiate the meanings of the rules for the earlier situation.* There are instances in which there was actually a decision at an earlier time that there were no rule violations, but in which changed circumstances lead them to decide there was "in fact, all along," a rule violation. Commonly, the change in the situation is that the rule users, such as the agents of control, find themselves under attack from someone for themselves violating the rules that oblige them to enforce the rules; to "save their own skins," the control agents then go back and find that "new evidence and new interpretations of old evidence show that there were in fact violations by someone else," generally a subordinate. In his study of "gundecking" (or filling out reports not based entirely upon factual accounts) in the navy, John Johnson has argued that this renegotiation of the meanings of rules is quite common, so much so that it is understood by the members of the organization and commonly interpreted as "due to political reasons":

> a report which is deemed sufficient-for-all-practical purposes at one point in time may, at some later date, be re-defined as insufficient. A contemporary example of this phenomenon, which reached the pages of the mass media, were the official reports of what is now called the "My Lai Massacre." In this case, the routine reports which accounted for the military actions at My Lai to those in higher positions were (presumably) sufficient for the practical purposes at that time. Eighteen months later, however, following an entrepreneurial initiative taken by a person who was not a member of the organization, these reports were redefined as insufficient for the practical purposes of the new situation. Members who had demonstrated their organizational competence in the initial issuing of these reports

were subsequently re-defined as "incompetent," and threatened with prosecution. That membership in military organizations often includes an understanding that such re-definitions-of-the-situation may occur is another one of the problematic features of gundecking practices. Members commonly perceive that such actions may happen for political reasons.[13]

Lack of Fit between the Rules and Situations:

Less common, but, nevertheless, relatively frequent in our complex society, are those situations in which the members experience great uncertainties about the meanings of rules and how they should be used in a situation because the rules don't seem appropriate, don't seem to "fit," the situation and yet in which the members are held responsible for using the rules to deal with that situation. Most commonly, the members see the rules as being in conflict with each other or as being simply irrational in their supposed implications for the situation faced. Probably the most common response is for the members to go ahead and apply the rules *in appearance,* but not in fact (as they themselves define it), or to explicitly subvert the rules.

In law these experiences are common enough to have produced special devices for "bridging" the relations between the laws and the situations when the specific laws relevant to a situation seem inappropriate for any reason. One such device is the *legal fiction,* by which the laws are "pretended" to apply to the situation, and are so applied for all practical purposes, even though it is tacitly understood by all parties that the law does not rationally, appropriately fit that situation in the way it is applied. These legal fictions are especially created to deal with new situations for which the old laws were not created but in which the legal authorities seem to be responsible for handling the situations. A famous case was the legal fiction of the "king's two bodies," his temporal body and his eternal body, which was created to "solve" problems concerning inherited rights of kings.

In American society today these experiences of the inapproriateness of rules are common in bureaucratic organizations and might best be categorized as *"Catch-22" situations.* In many instances the rules simply seem to the participants to completely contradict each other. This, for example, was found to be the case in certain instances observed by John Johnson in his study of social welfare case work. One instance of this was the requirement that a person have an address of his residence in order to receive welfare, whereas in some situations the welfare is needed specifically so that the person can get a residence in order to have an address. In these situations the workers "find a way around the rules" by telling the would-be recipient how to "work the system." More commonly, the members see the relations between the rules and their activities as being more in the "gray region" and find "justifications for apparent violations" in the "exigencies of the situation" at hand, that is, they seem to believe that lesser rules are superseded in such situations by more important rules. This, for example, seemed to be the case in most instances of gundecking studied by Johnson.[14]

Unintended Consequences of Actions:

One of the most common experiences members of our society have in which rules are believed to have been violated and individuals are held responsible for that violation (often by themselves), without meeting the ideal requirements of moral responsibility are those in which individuals do not know the consequences of their actions or do not intend to produce them. These experiences range all the way from simple traffic incidents to events involving the killing of many people.

One of the most common experiences in which we know we are performing the act, but neither intend its consequences *nor the act itself,* and one everyone has, is found in certain violations of traffic laws. At some time or other almost everyone knowingly violates traffic laws without intending to do that or, even more importantly, without intending to create the danger and, possibly, the "accidents" that result from those violations. Almost all drivers, for example, know perfectly well what the rules say about stop lights, yet almost all drivers at some time or other will observe the red light and go on through the intersection without the situation being in any way one that might serve as an "extenuating circumstance" (such as going too fast to stop). Drivers will even stop at a red light and then "run" the red light without intending to do so. The common experience in this situation is one of shock. We know full well what the rule is, we remember full well that we knew the light was red, and yet we know we really ran the light. (Less commonly, drivers from a state such as California in which it is legal to turn right on a red light after stopping and checking oncoming traffic may turn right on red in a state where he knows the law forbids it in that state. He simply doesn't "think of it" in the concrete situation.)

Life is full of such incidents. Most of them are relatively insignificant, although they may not be for the individual involved at the time. At some time or other, almost everyone walks out of a store without paying for something he has picked up. We know the laws and their common interpretation. We intend to always pay for what we get in the store, but we "forget" to think about paying in a concrete situation. People often go back and pay for an item or try to forget it as "one of those things." Sometimes, however, people get in very serious trouble for the "simplest things" of this sort, as a former Secretary of the Interior discovered when he "unintentionally" walked out of a store with ninety-cents worth of cigars without thinking about paying for them and found himself arrested for shoplifting and "exposed" in all the mass media. Some other incidents have far more serious consequences. One such instance was described very well by the man who knowingly, but unintentionally, sent out the message of a national emergency to all radio stations:

The error was blamed on an Army civilian technician using the wrong piece of tape during a regularly scheduled weekly test of the nation's defense warning system. The tape used did not signify a test.

The alert was transmitted directly onto the broadcast news wires of the Associated Press and United Press International by technicians at the National Warning Center inside Cheyenne Mountain near here. About 2,500 stations participate in the program.

It came at 6:33 A.M. PST and finally was cancelled at 7:13 A.M. after two attempts to lift it failed because they carried improper codes.

The operator on duty who erroneously sent the alert was W. S. Eberhardt, a 15-year-veteran of the center. He said, "I can't imagine how the hell I did it." Once the cancellation notice was sent, his phones started ringing.

"Everything hit the fan," he said.

"It's something you just can't explain," Eberhardt said. "When I sit back and look at it now, I just can't imagine how the hell I did it. If I could have pulled the tape back, I sure would have."[15]

Other actions of this sort can have disastrous consequences, as when running the red light results in an "accident" that kills one's whole family, or when a copilot who has been assisting in landings in the same way for years without serious incident suddenly, and unintentionally, pulls a lever too early and thus causes a plane crash that kills everyone aboard. As another example we might note that almost any family with several children at some time or another drives off leaving one of the small children at a gas station or a picnic area and only later discovers the "terrible mistake." In almost all such instances the shocked parents discover the mistake in time to rush back and rescue the child or else someone else helps the child to get in touch with the parents. But there are also those instances in which the "terrible mistake" becomes a "tragic act" with immense moral implications for the parents:

As Peterson explained later, he put Tina in the family station wagon first when it was time to go. Then he went for the other children.

Peterson asked, "Is everyone in?" Everyone shouted, "Yes." Neither Peterson nor the others had noticed that Tina had gotten out of the car before the others got in.

She may have been watching as the car drove away. It was 4:30 P.M., a cold day, already getting dark. She was wearing light clothes—low, white saddle oxford shoes, a white sweater, capris.

Tina went to a cabin in nearby Twin Peaks, a community midway between Crestline and Lake Arrowhead, and asked an 8-year-old girl if she could use her telephone to call home.

"My father went off and left me," she told the youngster.

The girl told her they didn't have a telephone.

"Then I'm going to walk to San Bernardino," Tina said.

The 8-year-old didn't tell her it was impossible. Tina walked off down Rim of the World Highway. San Bernardino was 18 miles away.

Peterson, meanwhile, drove all the way to the family's home at 2101

Palo Verde Ave., and, in the turmoil of homecoming, no one noticed that Tina was missing until the next morning.

By then it was too late.[16]

To psychoanalysts and various other theorists of different persuasions, these are seen as examples of "secret death wishes," "secret desires to be punished," "secret desires to escape a hated person," and so on. The psychoanalyst refuses to accept the idea that these acts are not caused by some meaningful state of the social actor, even if it must be an "unconscious" or "unintended" meaningful state or decision. He contrasts this theory of the unconscious motivation, the unintended intention, and the irresponsible responsibility, with the ideal theory of common sense that would classify these as "mistakes" or "errors" because they were not "really intended." But the psychoanalyst fails to see that his own ideas about these kinds of acts are the result of the very common, common-sense experience of them. He fails to see that the members themselves are in various ways and in various situations quite aware of these experiences, regardless of their ideal (absolutist) theories of rule-governed action.

If one followed the common-sense, absolutist theory of moral decision-making, individuals who commit actions without intending to do so, or without knowing about or intending to produce the consequences that actually result from those actions, would not be responsible for such actions and would not, therefore, be morally blameworthy or feel guilty for the acts or their consequences. But *the fact is that the members of society very commonly do experience the most profound feelings of moral blame for others and of moral guilt for themselves for precisely these kinds of actions that they committed without intending to do so and without anticipating or intending their consequences.* There seems to be two reasons for this and, taken together, these have fundamental implications for all of our understanding of moral experience.

First, the members of society not only apply their theoretical moral ideas to the concrete situation-of-action, but also apply these ideas (problematically) to the preceding situations believed to have caused the situation-of-action. The members commonly are not only concerned with what an individual does in one situation but also with what he does across situations; and each concrete situation is always seen to some degree to be related in some ways to other situations. This is to say that actions are almost always seen to be to some degree *trans-situational,* cutting across different situations. (This is so partly because each individual actor is believed to be a *substantial self,* or a self that is absolute, thus at least partially independent of all situations.) Consequently, *even when an individual is not held responsible for an action and its consequences, he may still be held responsible for the situation that is believed to have made that action possible.* Since the degree of intention involved in committing such an action is less direct and the consequences less likely, we commonly, although not always, find the imputation or *reduced intention* and, thus, of *reduced responsibility* or guilt.

The idea of reduced responsibility is, in fact, an ancient principle of Western law, going back at least to Aristotle's argument that, whereas a drunken man may not be responsible for the actions that produce another man's death, he is responsible for becoming drunk and, therefore, can be held responsible to a lesser degree for the resulting death. This is the theoretical principle used in justifying charges of manslaughter against drunken drivers who kill other people. While the application is more problematic, this is also the principle behind the parents' feeling of guilt over having left the child behind, the technician's feeling of responsibility for having put the wrong tape on the teletype, and so on. The principle can even be extended to produce responsibility and guilt for *actions that did not occur.* The common experience involved here is that of "Why didn't I do something" or "I should have known." *Because our absolutist ideas about the relations between meanings, such as rules, and actions is timeless and involves the idea that there should be completely ordered sets of relations among rules and actions, an individual can hold himself or others responsible for not having known or not having done what anyone in that situation should have known or done.* This is what we observe, for example, in the family members and friends of people who have committed suicide.[17] The individuals who were most involved with the "suicide victim" commonly feel that "I should have known he would do something like that" and "I am to blame because I should have foreseen this and stopped him." At the extreme, individuals who hold themselves or the public in general responsible in some way for the general situations of society that they believe lead individuals to commit immoral actions, may come to believe that "No matter who did it, I am responsible" or that "We are all responsible for the sins of every man." It is these ideas that lay behind the Christian ideas of universal guilt (as we find it in Dostoevski) and the modern form of what Ward Eliott has called *over-guilt,* or the blaming of all members of society for the immoral actions of a few. (Because they failed to see how the ideal theory of moral action is applied backward, or reflectively, to the situations that produce the situations-of-action, analysts such as Ward Eliott have failed to see that these experiences of over-guilt do "make sense" in terms of the ancient common-sense theories of responsibility.)

Second, the common-sense theory of absolute morality must itself be problematically applied by the members of society to their experience and is not the only set of ideas about morality that the members make use of in their everyday lives. Whereas it definitely seems to be true that the members do in most situations make exclusive use of their ideas of absolutism of meanings in general, and of moral meanings in particular, to construct the meanings of things, it is not true that they always do. There are even situations in which individuals will openly say that there are real, sincere, fundamental differences in morals, values, or rules and that it is these differences that lie behind some

conflict. Because such admissions that one's own rules are not absolute immediately puts one in a weak position in opposing someone who insists that his
rules are absolute, it seems likely that the private recognition of the problematic nature of rules is far more common than the public admissions of it
might lead us to suspect. Far more commonly, whereas individuals still hold
to their absolutist theory of rules, they also almost universally recognize in
practice various situations that the concrete meanings of rules "depend on the
circumstances," "vary with the situation," are often in a "gray region," may
be "unclear," and so on.

Implications of the Failures of Absolutism for the Construction of Social Order

Although we have no way of knowing precisely how common these experiences of the failures of the common-sense ideal theory of the absolutism
of rules are in our society today, we see that we have every reason to believe
that they are quite common in the lives of everyone. Moreover, because our
society has become increasingly complex, with rules of all sorts proliferating
in all directions as the members try to manage the growing problems of social
order, we expect that these experiences are increasing in our society. In attempting to assess the implications of these facts for the fundamental problem
of constructing social order in our society, we must first consider the direct
effects of these experiences on the members of society: what do the members
make of these experiences and how do they handle them?

We began our discussion of these failures of absolutism with a brief consideration of the philosophical argument that the members of society would
experience such failures as "absurd" because they would not fit the theory of
absolutism held by those members. We have already seen some reasons to
believe that this argument is not justified in this simple form. In general, because of the problematic nature of all imputations of meanings to our everyday experience, we must expect that there will be no such simple relations
between actual experiences and the social definition of them as absurd. This
is, in fact, what we find. Let us briefly consider the alternative meanings that
members give to these experiences of the failures of absolutism.[18]

First, as has already been mentioned in the last section, there are situations in which the absolutism of rules is felt to fail, but in which *this failure
is simply not seen as significant or relevant* because the individual does not
see the need to apply the theory of the absolutism of rules to this situation.
Instead, he applies other ideas about rules. This is the kind of situation that
arises simply as a result of the problematic uses of the common-sense theory
of the absolutism of rules.

Second, it must be remembered that the members of society normally
do not demand complete specifications of the meanings of anything in every-

day life. What we seek is *meaning adequate for the purposes at hand.* There are all kinds of experiences we have in which we fully recognize that we do not have the full meaning that someone is trying to communicate or that could be gotten if we thought about it more. One of the most common and obvious of these is our recognition that someone has said something that we could not even hear clearly. In some of these situations, we ask the person to repeat what he said, amplify, clarify, and so on. But in many such situations we simply *let it pass.* The same seems to be true of experiences of the failure of absolutism. In some fleeting way we may recognize that "something is wrong," that the use of the rules doesn't seem right, doesn't fit our ideas about morality and immorality; but we let it pass. Probably most of the failures that have few practical implications for us are allowed to pass in this way as simply "one of those things." A feeling of "peeve" or a shrug of the shoulders is about all the response that the experience elicits.

Third, an initial recognition of the failure may be followed by a *reassertion of the absolutism of the rules.* There are at least two common devices used to reassert the absolutism that "appears to have failed." We may for one argue that there must have been a "misunderstanding" or a "mistake," perhaps resulting from some "accidental slip-up beyond human control." We may also argue that we simply didn't see what the "real meaning" was because of our situation. The people using the rules must have "known something we didn't," "must have their own reasons for doing it," and so on. These devices are complemented by the possibilities of "letting it pass" and of "bridging the gaps."

Fourth, the "apparent failures" of the rules may be *bridged* by various devices. Various symbols of absolutism, such as those of religion and those that inspire awe, may be used both to mystify those experiencing the failures, thereby leading them to question their own understanding of what actually happened, and promising that apparent failures will be "made up" by some means. Courts thus use symbols of religion to insure the absolute validity of what transpires, regardless of what can be seen and heard in the concrete situation, and to remind anyone that seeming injustices in the here and now will inevitably be "made up" in the hereafter. Again, courts may simply invoke such rules of thumb as "ignorance is no excuse for violating the law" and assert thereby that no failure could have occurred; the person asserting ignorance is presumed to be simply "lying."

But, fifth, there are those times when we take the use of rules very seriously, probably in most situations because their use by someone else poses a very real practical threat (loss of money, stigmatization, imprisonment), and in which we do feel a strong sense that "something is wrong," that the assumptions of our ideal of absolute morality are not met, but in which we do not impute the meaning of absurdity to our sense of this failure. Most commonly, these are the kinds of situations we think of as *unjust.* What seems to distinguish the sense of injustice from that of absurdity is that the something that is wrong is not seen to be the result of something about the rules or the world themselves. Rather, what is wrong is the knowing, purposeful *misuse* of the rules by someone else whom we see as corrupt, evil, sinful, and so on. The rules in this case are divorced from their use, and it is the users, not the rules, that have something wrong with them. In fact, the rules may be even more idealized in our attacks on our attackers. This, for example, was found to be the case in a study of prisoners in a maximum security prison who developed a highly idealized idea of what the laws are and simply attacked their judges and keepers as evil corrupters of the ideal system of law. The sense of injustice seems to be the most common definition given those experiences of the failures of the absolutism of rules that we take seriously.

Sixth, it is only in a minority of cases that individuals experience these failures as *absurd*. These experiences are not always defined specifically by the use of the word "absurd," since there are many related terms in common use, such as "ridiculous," "ludicrous," "insane," and so on. But there seems to be a common meaning, a common recognition that the assumptions of the ideal of absolute morality do not hold where we believe they should hold. Specifically, the assumptions of absolutism seem to fail because there is something about the nature of the rules themselves (such as that they are necessarily problematic, there is not really a God after all, they do not make any specific sense when applied to the real situation we face, and so on), or because of something about the nature of man or society: it is this "something" that gives us the sense of absurdity about the failures of absolutism, rather than leading to a reassertion of the absolutism or any of the other possibilities.

Now, it is only in those instances where the failures of absolutism lead to the definitions of things as unjust or as absurd that the failures raise the possibilities of increases in social disorder, such as would result from rebellions or revolutions. In all of the other situations the failures are ignored or seen as irrelevant or insignificant or as not really being failures. They lead to no attacks and may well lead only to attempts to clarify the absolutism of the rules for future use.

But neither are there any simple and clear relations between the definitions of such experiences as absurd and any attacks on existing social orderings of relations. Any such relations are quite problematic. Most of these definitions of the failures of absolutism as unjust or absurd, in fact, seem to remain isolated experiences. The individuals experience momentary anger or exasperation or despair over what they see as the "injustice" or "absurdity" of this rule, or that rule, of this set of rules, or that set; but they do not generally put all of these together to generalize to "all situations," "all rules," and so on. Such *trans-situational definitions* of social experience would seem to arise only when the experiences are extremely common and/or only when individuals are very consciously comparing situations with each other far more than seems common in the practical activities of everyday life.

However, what we seem to find in American society and other Western societies today is that these trans-situational definitions of such experiences as unjust and absurd are being made available to ordinary members of society by those who spend almost all of their time doing such comparing of situations with each other—intellectuals and scholars. It is the intellectuals and scholars, the people who have least common-sense experience of the direct uses of rules in practical situations, who are providing such trans-situational definitions to the men of practical affairs through the mass media and formal education. But the fact seems to be that the men of practical affairs are finding these proffered definitions more and more fitting to their experiences, presumably because they now have such categories available to use in thinking of their experience, and because their experience has become such that it is now plausible to accept these definitions.

As our society becomes more complex, we could expect for this reason that the failures of absolutist rules will be seen increasingly as unjust and absurd. But, again, we have no necessary reason to believe that this will result in increasing problems of social order. It may simply lead to an increasing rejection of the idea that rules should in any way be absolute. We may, thus, move toward an increasingly *common-sensical existential theory of social rules* that accepts rules as necessarily problematic in concrete situations. It is possible that Dostoevski, Durkheim, and the other absolutist theorists may prove right in arguing that this will inevitably produce more social disorder. This would possibly be the case if, for example, the members decide that "there is really no need to sincerely use rules that are only self-imposed." It could be, however, that they will decide with most of the intellectual existentialists that the acceptance of responsibility for the creation of social rules and for their problematic (free) use entails a greater responsibility for using them sincerely to produce an increasingly worthwhile social order. The outcomes will be decided by the common creative efforts of the members of society.

Notes

1. I have previously considered the relations between rules and social order in great detail in *American Social Order: Social Rules in a Pluralistic Society,* New York: The Free Press, 1971.

2. I have critically analyzed Durkheim's theory in *The Social Meanings of Suicide,* Princeton: Princeton University Press, 1967.

3. Robert K. Merton, *Social Theory and Social Structure,* New York: The Free Press, 1957, Chaps. 4 and 5.

4. Albert Cohen, *Delinquent Boys,* New York: The Free Press, 1955.

5. See my essay in *Deviance and Respectability,* New York: Basic Books, Inc., 1970

6. I have considered the evidence concerning trends toward greater pluralism and trends away from some traditional forms of pluralism in American society today in *American Social Order*.

7. I am using the idea of the absurd in quite a different sense from that in which the term is used in Stanford Lyman and Marvin Scott, *The Sociology of the Absurd*, New York: Appleton-Century-Crofts, 1971. Scott and Lyman use the term "absurd" primarily to refer to the lack of absolute meanings and the consequent need for the members to construct meanings of things for themselves. What I am arguing here is that even when the members do construct the meanings of things, there are still experiences that the members themselves define as absurd (or something else): that is, some of the constructions of meanings by some members are defined as absurd by other members (and sometimes members even see some of their own constructions as absurd).

8. Many of the examples used throughout this chapter are taken from my own experiences, those of friends and colleagues, and from typical reports in the mass media.

9. For a systematic discussion of the principles of the construction of the meanings of social rules see *American Social Order* and *Deviance and Respectability*.

10. See the discussion of police uses of rules in Aaron Cicourel, *The Social Organization of Juvenile Justice*, New York: John Wiley & Sons, Inc., 1967.

11. Edwin Sutherland, "Is 'White-Collar Crime' Crime?" *American Sociological Review* 10(1945): 132–139.

12. Richard Austin Smith, "The Incredible Electrical Conspiracy," *Fortune* (April, 1961), and (May, 1961): 132–180 and 161–224.

13. John Johnson, "The Practical Uses of Rules," University of California San Diego, La Jolla, California, unpublished paper.

14. *Ibid.*

15. Taken from the *Los Angeles Times*, Feb. 23, 1971.

16. Taken from the *Los Angeles Times*, Feb. 24, 1971.

17. For a discussion of cases of guilt feelings over suicides and the ways in which individuals construct meanings to try to prevent such guilt feelings see James Henslin, "Guilt and Guilt Neutralization: Response and Adjustment to Suicide," in *Deviance and Respectability*, pp. 192–228.

18. In his (unpublished) work on social welfare, John Johnson has even reported an instance of response to a new interpretation of a rule in which various members defined the interpretation in some of these alternative ways. My personal discussions with John Johnson about such evidence and ideas have been especially helpful.

Chapter Nine

THE PRACTICAL
USES OF RULES

John M. Johnson

Introduction

One of the notions most commonly used by the members of societies to understand or explain how social order is possible has been that of social rules (see Chapter 8 in this volume). The abstract or theoretical relationships that have been proffered are many and varied, but the general conception that there is *some* relationship between social rules and social order appears to be firmly grounded in members' common-sense discourse about their societies. This appears to be as true for those thought to possess some specialized warrant for manipulating a given society's symbolic universe at a given point in time (who, in an increasingly technological society, typically identify themselves as "scientists") as it is for other members of the society. Within the various American societies, there are many distinct linguistic devices that are used by the members to address their concerns about social rules and social order. One of the more common of the common-sense notions expressed by the members is that of "law and order," although the relations and meanings of these terms appear to be diffuse and not widely shared among various groups of people. Within what is sometimes called the academic community, the interests with social rules and social order are sometimes masked by linguistic devices such as "values," "beliefs," or, more commonly. "norms." Some of those claiming an interest in such matters have observe that this theme recurs throughout the histories of various

Western societies since the time of St. Augustine's *City of God*. Others use the idea of history to present the claim that this interest was first expressed by the Sophists over 2,500 years ago. At any rate, it seems that it may be observed with some certainty that the interest in social rules and social order is a widely shared one, even if there does not appear to be any forthcoming resolution of the many arguments and heated debates on these matters.

Within contemporary sociology, perhaps the two fields that have most directly concerned themselves with the relations between social rules and social order have been the fields of formal organizations and deviance. Researchers in both fields have continually addressed their interests toward explaining "deviations" from what are conceived as commonly shared rules (or, "norms"). Whereas the predominant perspectives of these conventional sociologies have been variously identified as "structural," "functional," or "structural-functional," some exceptions to these have also occurred. A very brief examination of certain features of these conventional sociologies are used to introduce the perspective and concerns of this chapter, the practical usage of social rules by competent members of society.

Few social scientists now disagree with the basic premise that all social action is action that possesses meaning to those engaged in it. As this premise is translated into the theoretical arguments of the structural-functional sociologies, these social meanings are presumed to be stable, unchanging, and unproblematically known either by those engaged in constructing them, or to the sociologists who allegedly "observe" them. Within these perspectives, social order is typically accounted for by using the presumption that the social meanings, typically characterized as social rules, or norms, are unproblematically known by sociologists and the members of society alike. The major theoretical presuppositions of the structural-functional sociologies have been analyzed elsewhere, and will not be presented in detail here.[1] These comments are used here to address the issue of how the members of society (or sociologists) perceive and identify certain social actions as being "in conformance with," "in compliance with," or "a deviation from" social rules.

By using the presumption that social action is normative, or rule-governed, studies of what are called formal organizations have invariably found numerous examples of observed practices within the organizational setting that could not be readily reconciled with the formally instituted rules and procedures of that organization, at least insofar as the researcher had come to common-sensically understand those rules and procedures. In order to preserve their notions of social action as rule-governed, these conventional sociologists studying formal organizations have typically invoked the notion of an "informal structure" with its own "rules" in the terms of which these observed practices may be appropriately "classified." Study after study documents a variety of practices observed during the everyday lives of organizational actors that are perceived (by the sociologist) to be instances of the formal/informal structures of the organization. What is of greater concern for our present purposes, however, is that such everyday activity can only be so identified by the observer through his common-sense usage of the formal plan of a given organization in order to determine the status of such activity. As Egon Bittner states, ". . . the sociologist finds himself in the position of having borrowed a concept from those he seeks to study in order to describe what he observes about them."[2] This has been a subtle tactic indeed; explaining one set of rules by invoking another set of rules.[3]

A similar dilemma is posed by the recent researches in the field of deviance. The brilliant scholarship of Lemert, Becker, Scheff, and many others has recently challenged the conventional notions of "objective deviance," or "objective rule-violations." These scholars, increasingly known as "labeling theorists," have aided our understanding by promoting the argument that what are called "rule-violations" cannot be usefully defined as being ontologically distinct from the reactions of others ("rule-enforcers") directed toward the control of such activities. But the social theorists using the idea of "labeled deviance" have retained the notion of social action as normative, or rule-governed (for further comments on this, see Chapter 3 in this volume). Several have maintained that such a distinction is necessary "for scientific purposes."[4] For example, Scheff in his *Being Mentally Ill,* proposes to conceive as "residual rule-violations" (or, residual deviance) what were previously conceived as violations of various medical, biological, or psychiatric "norms." There appear to be some similarities in the uses of this notion and the uses that students of formal organizations have made of "informal structures." In both cases, one set of rules is explained by the promotion of another set of rules to maintain the theoretical presupposition of social action as rule-governed.

By preserving the (presumed) ontological status of social rules, the conventional sociologies have obscured a wealth of *background information* possessed by the competent users of a society's rules to meet the various practical exigencies arising out of their everyday existences within that society. By presuming to possess technical skills or methods that allow an omniscient observer to know unproblematically which "rules" are relevant for the situation-at-hand, practitioners of the conventional perspectives in sociology have failed to address the issue of how such rules and procedures are used by, and what their use means to, competent members of society on the actual occasions of their use. This chapter seeks to consult such background information for the purposes of investigating the *practical usage* of social rules by social actors authorized to do so (that is, their organizational competence being recognized in the setting).

Perspective

This research reports on one aspect of an investigation of how petty officers and commissioned officers in the United States Navy conduct their everyday practical affairs. More specifically, this investigation is concerned with a description of the ways in which these men use the various features of the rational schema of the formal organizational design to manage the exigencies of their "practical circumstances," and how they determine the operational meaning of the organization's rules and procedures in concrete, everyday situations.[5] To ascertain the actor's methodical use of the rational properties of the formal organizational design in his ordinary, everyday activities, and to insure the relevance of the perspective of the actor in sociological investigations, the recent scholarship of various phenomenologically oriented sociologists will provide a foundation for the perspective to be used.[6]

One of the most prevalent concerns in the contemporary research of formal organizations has been the investigation of the "gap" between the "formal structures" and the "informal structures" of the organization.[7] Some of the more prominent writers have explicitly addressed the various theoretical and/or practical reasons for the "necessity" of this gap.[8] It is *not* the purpose of this research to merely add to the already preponderant literature on the existence of the difference between the literal meaning of a given rule or procedure and the various events that allegedly occur under its jurisdiction. Also, whereas a concern for the "adequacy" or "efficiency" of a given formally organized program, or a concern with the "rule-violations" of organizational personnel in given situations might be appropriate for other researches of formal organizations, these are not among the focal concerns of this research. This report proposes no such remedial interests. Rather, the interest here is with the *contextual determination of the meaning of certain organizational rules and procedures by the organizationally competent actors on the occasions of their actual use in everyday work situations.* The focal emphasis here is upon *what it takes* for these organizationally competent users of the various rules and procedures of the formal program in terms of their practical reasoning and judgmental abilities. These concerns are similar to those explicated by Zimmerman:

> The problem that concerns this paper is how the formal plan of an organization (or some aspect of it) is used by the organization's members to deal with everyday work activities. What are the features of the sanctioned courses of common-sense judgment which members use to recognize, to interpret and to instruct others about the operational intent and behavioral implications of such a plan? Thus conceived, the problem dictates, first of all, that the relationship of the formal plan to actual conduct be investigated

with specific reference to how members of the organization reconcile the two on a day-to-day basis. This approach also leads to revision of the theoretical treatment of the range of practical circumstances typically confronted by the bureaucrat. This revision consists in entertaining the possibility that these circumstances may in fact be consulted by bureaucrats in order to decide what the formal plan might reasonably be taken to mean and "what it would take" to implement it in the first instance.[9]

This research then, informed by Zimmerman's notion of "competent rule-use," seeks to describe, from the perspective of the actor, what is involved in doing the everyday work within the organizational milieu.

The remainder of this chapter is organized as follows. After brief discussions of the setting of the study, the general nature of the everyday activities of the actors of the organization, and the general nature of the phenomenon of "gundecking" (and the extent to which this term is shared within the organization), the remainder of the chapter is devoted to a detailed description of the various work tasks involved in the successful completion of the sonar performance report as one aspect of the routine activities of the "Anti-Submarine Warfare Division" (ASW) aboard a United States Navy destroyer. A concluding section addresses some of the problematic aspects of gundecking as a practical activity of these members.

The Setting of the Study

The materials of this study were drawn from research conducted primarily aboard one U.S. Navy Destroyer, hereafter referred to as the USS *Walden*. Additional interviews and research included personnel stationed on other ships in the same "division" as the USS *Walden,* as well as other persons still on active duty and some who had been separated from active duty.[10] The USS *Walden* was home-ported at a large U.S. naval facility in California between its scheduled cruises to the West Pacific that generally lasted six to seven months in duration. Like most of the World War II destroyers of the same "class,"[11] the USS *Walden* typically carried a complement of two senior-grade commissioned officers, approximately fifteen to eighteen junior-grade commissioned officers, eighteen chief petty officers, and 240 to 260 other enlisted personnel.[12] The USS *Walden* was one element of a "Division" of four destroyers of the same class, and the division was one element of a "squadron," which was composed of four divisions. The ship was under the "operational command"[13] of the admiral in charge of the "Fleet"[14] in which the ship operated; this varied depending upon whether the ship was operating near its home port or deployed to the West Pacific, and, regardless of where the ship was operating, it was under the "type command" of the admiral in charge of the operations of a given class or classes of ships.[15] Like many of the older destroyers, the USS *Walden* had been "modernized" in the early 1960s and refitted with newer equipment and capabilities. Its "primary mission" was said to be that of Anti-Submarine Warfare (ASW). However, since many of the navy ships have been called upon to provide "shore bombardment" in the Vietnam War, as well as several other war-related activities, the priority of this primary capability had been replaced in recent years with that of the gunnery operations for all practical purposes. When the ship operated at sea near its home-port, the time was spent completing a series of various exercises, inspections, reviews, drills, and other forms of training to prepare the crew for the ensuing deployment to the West Pacific. Periods set aside for the maintenance and repair of the ship's equipment, as well as various types of in-port training and inspection, accounted for time when the ship was not at sea. The important "Administrative Inspection" (referred to as "an Admin"), one of the crucial criteria for the determination of a ship's "battle readiness" and "battle efficiency," categories in which ships in the same division and squadron competed with each other for "awards" that carried some amount of prestige for the ship's commanding officer and crew, were generally conducted when the ship was in its home-port, although this was not always the case.[16]

The formally defined objectives of the navy have been reformulated and refined many times, of course, since Article I, Section 8 of the United States Constitution charged the Congress with the responsibility. "To provide and maintain a navy; to make rules for the government and regulation of land and naval forces." The primary set of rules governing the activities of the navy are the *United States Navy Regulations,* although there are many additional regulations. Sufficient for our present purpose here, however, is to note that the USS *Walden* is accountable to two different chains-of-command: the "operational command," or what is called in the sociology literature the "line function," which is a hierarchical arrangement of fleets, squadrons, and divisions controlling the operational movements and assignments of the USS *Walden,* and the "type command," or what would be called the "staff function" in the literature, which is a lateral arrangement of various support functions designed to maintain the readiness of the ship's equipment and personnel training. A type commander, generally a rear admiral, promulgates various "standing instructions" designed to enhance a ship's "battle readiness."[17] A successful meeting of the requirements of these standing instructions, as well as successful engagement of one's "operational commitments," which is evaluated through the operational command, determines which ship or ships will receive various "Battle Efficiency Awards." The winning of this award is one determination of "success" for a given ship, and especially for its commanding officer.

To pursue the organizationally predefined objectives of the type commander and the operational commander, the USS *Walden* was formally organized into three "Departments." These were the Operations Department, the Engineering Department, and the Weapons Department, each possessing specific sets of rules and procedures to be followed in order to carry out its function in the maintenance of the battle readiness and operational capabilities of the ship. Each department was headed by a junior officer, generally a lieutenant, who was directly responsible to the executive officer and commanding officer for the successful performance of these tasks. Each department, in turn, was formally organized into "Divisions" according to the specialized functions of the department, with each division being headed by a "division officer," generally an ensign or lieutenant junior grade, who was directly responsible to the department head for the insurance of the successful completion of the specialized tasks of the various "rated" and "nonrated" personnel in the division in accordance with the relevant rules and procedures governing that department.[18]

Since this chapter is restricted to the consideration of the general phenomenon of "gundecking" as it applies to the Sonar Performance Report, one aspect of the maintenance of the ship's Anti-Submarine Warfare (ASW) capability, it is concerned only with those everyday work situations of the personnel in one division of the Weapons Department.

The Everyday World of Work in the "Tin Can Navy"

Famous historians, popular novelists, and naval folklore recite what are alleged to be the unique characteristics of the "Tin Can Navy" (referring to destroyers and their lack of armor to protect the hull). As the smallest ship classified as a "combatant," it is often contended by organizational members that destroyers possess a certain *esprit de corps* not found on larger ships in the navy, although such claims are always subject to dispute.[19] This is allegedly because the competent performance of the various specialized tasks required on a day-to-day basis makes each person "indispensable" to a certain extent, and also because certain occasions (called "special evolutions") such as replenishments-at-sea, gunnery missions, and hi-line transfers at sea require the services of nearly all of the ship's company regardless of their specialized rating or technical specialty. This is not to say the "goldbricking"[20] or "the philosophy of do the least"[21] (the Navy term being "skylarking") are not present. But, rather, because of the relatively small complement of men on a destroyer, and the limitations on privacy imposed by the physical setting, it is just that these alternative *strategies of compliance* are more difficult to realize, especially during these special evolutions. Also, one of the prevailing folk theories of the navy is that the finest junior officers are sent to destroyers for their first tour of duty. This folk theory contends that it is most advantageous for a junior officer, and especially a neophyte graduate of "the Academy," to begin his career on a destroyer if he is to successfully construct the "career profile" thought to be appropriate for (eventual) promotion to "flag rank,"[22] allegedly because he will be able to attain more "leadership responsibility" on a destroyer than on another type of ship. Shared knowledge of some of these and other features of the "Tin

Can Navy" also accounts for the decisions of many others to avoid an assignment to a destroyer at all costs. At least this is sometimes the case when the persons use the prerogative of choice in such matters.

These brief introductory comments, as well as those to follow, provide ample evidence that the fundamental feature of the socialization processes leading to the development of organizational competence is the learning of the specialized lexicon or vocabulary. This socialization involves learning the vocabulary, typically abstracted from the actual situations of its use for the purpose of training the recruits of the organization, the empirical referents for which the vocabulary supposedly stands as an index, and finally, the situated use of the vocabulary by competent organizational members in actual occasions of the everyday routine of the organization. The various branches of the military, it might be suggested, are subdivisions of what Garfinkel has called a "natural language community," with various masteries of the natural lauguage referring not only to general membership categories within the community (or organization) but also to subdivisions of the membership.[23]

When at sea, during "normal steaming operations," the USS *Walden* typically utilized a three-section watch bill.[24] This meant that at any one given time approximately one-third of the ship's complement designated as "watch-standers" (which excluded such persons as cooks, storekeepers, and yeomen) devoted their time to "standing watch." Watches were typically accomplished in four-, five-, or six-hour shifts, depending upon the type of watch (for example, with watches stood as a lookout typically being four hours in duration and watches in the boiler rooms being six hours in duration, for the very practical reason that boiler room personnel could be seated whereas lookouts could not). This necessitated that the remainder of the ship's complement carry on the everyday working tasks without the aid of those personnel who were "on watch" at that time. All personnel were required to "put in a full working day" between 0800 and 1615, regardless of whether or not one had had "the midwatch" the previous morning (that is, the watch from midnight to 0400). As one might expect from even a cursory review of some of the popular literature on the varieties of military experience, however, there are great variations in individual strategies for constructing compliance with this requirement.

The sequential coordination of the various activities of the "normal working day" were set forth in the ship's "standing instructions." Daily modifications to this formal schema were promulgated in the "Plan-of-the-Day" (called "the Pod"), written daily by the executive officer and distributed in mimeographed form each evening for the following day. The everyday routine working tasks could be modified by "special evolutions" called for in "the Pod" for a given day. The typical working day generally included at least one such evolution, if only for a brief "call to General Quarters" (to familiarize personnel with their assigned "battle stations") for the purposes of training.

The routine working tasks required to maintain and/or repair the ship's complex equipment and machinery were outlined in the "Planned Maintenance System" (PMS). This was initially operationalized as a "quality control" measure to insure that the various "preventative maintenance" tasks required to keep the navy's increasingly complex electronic equipment efficient and operational were standardized and routinized. But, in recent years, PMS had been expanded to include such mundane matters as chipping paint and swabbing passageways. The various tasks were designated, for example, as a "Daily Three," which meant that this routine maintenance task (the exact procedures for accomplishing the task were listed on a separate card that was generally kept near the piece of equipment) was the third maintenance procedure to be completed on a daily basis by a person of a given technical specialty, a "Weekly One," a "Quarterly Two," a "Semi-Annual Two," and so on. Upon completion of a given task the worker was required to fill out a form to his superior, generally a chief petty officer or a division officer. The task was then "marked off" on the "working calendar," which delineated the scheduling of the various PMS tasks to be accomplished within a given technical specialty. These forms would be mailed from the ship to the appropriate facility at regular intervals. Several months later the ship would receive a computer readout of all of its accomplished tasks in order to have an adequate chronology of its maintenance work. Copies of this computer readout also went to the relevant type and operational commanders, and comparisons of "total man hours" of PMS work for a given ship, also broken down into the various technical specialties, and its "sister ships" in the division and squadron were often used as an indication of a ship's "battle readiness" or "battle efficiency." There were, of course, some routine tasks on the *Walden,* as well as many of the repair tasks, which were not covered under the PMS system, but for the purposes of recording the accountability of man-hours, there were a number of general or residual categories under which a given task could be classified for computer coding.

After a brief discussion of the general phenomenon of "gundecking" in the navy, the remainder of this chapter concentrates on the specialized tasks of the ASW Division on the USS *Walden* as they relate to the Sonar Performance Report.

Gundecking

Although there is still some disagreement about the origin of the term "gundecking" in the navy, substantial evidence suggests that its meaning is widely shared throughout the navy as common inside knowledge.[25] Further evidence suggests that its meaning, if not its use, is increasingly being shared by more and more people. Webster's defines the term:

gundeck—to fake or falsify esp. by writing up (as a series of official reports) as if meeting requirements but actually without having carried out the required procedures (e.g., gundecking the daily reports on the night before an inspection).

Although navy personnel are familiar with the "literal meaning" of the concept, there are important qualifications. From a recorded interview with a junior officer:

I: What does it mean to you? How do you define it?

S: Well, gundecking is, ah, the job that you know, but that you don't actually go ahead and perform the job, you just go ahead and write the results down without performing the job. Remember, is that what I said before?

I: Yeah, I think so. Okay, what would be an example from something involved in your job?

S: Let's say I was supposed to go out and check certain areas or talk to certain people, but I already know what the results are going to be, so rather than do that I just go ahead and mark down the results, and then hand in the results. I haven't done the job but I've given you the results.

I: Okay, one thing I wondered about is—are there other times when gundecking is something other than a complete falsification of a report?

S: Oh yeah, probably most of the time gundecking doesn't involve a *complete* falsification—I mean, you generally have a pretty good idea that everything's okay before you gundeck.

I: What would be an example?

S: Well, let's take my Hull Reports for example. In the last three years I've probably gundecked half of the entries—you know—things like the lockers and magazines that I knew were all right anyway. I didn't have to go down into the magazines every week to know that they were okay —you know—what in the hell can change in a magazine in the space of a week? Especially when you're in-port and nobody ever goes down there, except the striker who checks the temperature gauges. If there was any change he'd probably recognize it before I would anyway. On the other hand, it kind of depends on whether or not there's any flack going on about Hull Reports. You know, if you've been in-port for a while and the Old Man's on the rag about something, and the JO's are catching a lot of flack about their jobs, then you have to be a little more careful. But, hell, when you're overseas and doing a lot of operating, then I'm sure that all of the JO's (that is, Junior Officers) gundeck most of the entries on their Hull Reports, because they know there won't be any check because everybody is so busy . . . including the Old Man and the Exec. You know that there isn't any chance of getting caught, you've got nothing to lose by doing it. Some things you wouldn't gundeck are things of major significance.

I: Well what's the crucial variable there, I mean, in other words, why would you gundeck some things and not others?

S: Well it just depends on its significance, you know, it's how you evaluate how important something is. I think that say, ah, a pre-firing check before a gun shoot is more important than a Hull Report, and more, you know, more specifically, some checks are more important than others. It depends on the situation.

Another junior officer on the *Walden* comments:

I: First of all, how would you define gundecking?

S: Umm (short pause) . . . that would be, ah, falsifying a document for the purposes of having the paperwork there, ah, (pause) . . . necessary completion of the paperwork without the corresponding real, the actual work being done.

I: Is it always a complete falsification?

S: No, most of the time you don't go on blind faith. It depends on the situation. It depends. It's not a complete falsification, but it *can* be. It depends.

I: What does it depend on?

S: It depends on, for me, it depends on my judgment, my decision as the real value of the report, or the document.

I: What do you mean by the real value?

S: What I decide the value to be. It really depends on the situation. It's hard to generalize about even one report, because there can be different considerations depending on the situation. Depends on how vital I consider it to be to my job, or whether I think it's just a useless piece of paperwork, and, ah, busy-work type stuff. . . . It's such an individual thing, I don't know. I've never really thought much about it, I just do it.

I: Well, do you think you're the only one who does it?

S: (Laughing) No, I know I'm not the only one, but . . . (pause) I might be the only one who does it the way I do it. Put somebody else in my position and he'd probably gundeck quite a bit, but he might not gundeck exactly the same things I do. In other words, his judgment about what would be necessary and what would be trivial might not be the same as mine.

An electronics technician:

I: Well, do you ever gundeck anything each and every single time?

S: No, I don't really think so. It depends on a number of things, probably one of the most important things has to do with whether or not I think there's any chance of being checked up on. For ET's, the only real sweat is the Chief, 'cause your Division Officer usually doesn't know enough to check on your work.

Evidence seems to be persuasive, then, that gundecking "depends on the situation," and that "the situation" is an important determinant of the "reasonableness" of it, that is, whether or not the situation seems to "call for" gundecking an official report.

Before analyzing some of the important features of "the situation" that warrants the gundecking of the Sonar Performance Report as a "reasonable" organizational activity, here are several members' estimation of the extent to which the knowledge of gundecking is shared in the navy.

> I'd say that before PMS began only the officers and most of the leading Petty Officers knew about it, that, well anyone who had to do a lot of paperwork as a part of his job, or who had to handle a lot of chits on an everyday basis. Since PMS I think probably everyone in the Navy knows what gundecking is, even the lowest Seaman Deuce, that is, anybody who's been out of boot camp for more than a week.

> Hell, I don't know. I assume that *everybody* knows what it is. I don't see how you could be in the Navy for more than a couple of days without knowing what gundecking is.

These comments, and many others, suggest that the notion of gundecking is widely shared among navy personnel of all ratings and rankings, and that it "depends on the situation." The following section details some of the practical reasons that lead to the determination by competent organizational members of the "reasonableness" of the gundecking of official reports.

Practical Reasons for Gundecking

Battle Efficiency and the "ASW E"

As mentioned previously, one of the major criteria of "success" for a given ship was its successful competition for "Battle Efficiency Awards," although, assuredly, the meaning of this criteria of success varied greatly among the variously situated personnel on the *Walden*. The most prestigious of these awards was called the "Battle E" and was awarded to only one ship in the squadron (four divisions of destroyers) during a given "competitive period." A given ship deserving of the "Battle E" was thought to be successful not only in terms of the criteria constituting success for the lesser awards but was also said to be exceptional in meeting her "operational commitments." This meant that the ship had earned a reputation for proficiency in battle-related activities above and beyond the "routine" measures of success as set forth in various administrative instructions. During times of "peace," this "battle-related success" was generally determined through a complex set of at-sea exercises involving all of the ship's battle capabilities. In times of "war," such as during the last few years, this battle-related success generally involved the successful engagement of some unusual or out-of-the-ordinary mission while in or near Vietnam.[26] To a very large extent, at least within the past few years, the opportunity to engage in such an unusual activity was beyond the volition of the ship's commanding officer or operational commander. Since one of the prevailing folk theories of the "Tin Can Navy" was that being a commanding officer of a destroyer was a necessary condition for becoming a "straight line officer" to be considered for flag-rank, being the commanding officer of a ship awarded the "Battle E" was commonly thought to be a sufficient condition for the realization of that goal.[27]

In addition to the "Battle E," however, there were several other Battle Efficiency Awards that were awarded, not to "a ship" as such but rather to the various departments of a given ship indicating proficiency in a specialized area. These awards were the "Operations E," the "Engineering E," the "Gunnery E," and the "ASW E," which were determined on the basis of standardized criterion, although these awards were determined through a "competitive" process. For these awards however, unlike the "Battle E" awarded to only one ship in sixteen, it was theoretically possible for all four ships in a given division of destroyers to be awarded, for example, the "Gunnery E." The awards were based on cumulative "scores" on various types of inspections, of which the administrative inspection entailing a thorough review of all of the records on a ship as well as a personnel inspection was the most important, the scores on a number of exercises designed to prepare a ship for its deployment on operational missions, and a variety of lesser types of inspections and demonstrations of administrative and operational efficiency. Generally speaking, the four destroyers in a given division would "take turns" in administering the administrative inspection to each other, and would subsequently report to the commodore on the results of these activities.

Successful competition for battle efficiency awards on a ship such as the *Walden* necessitated the construction of an immensely complex collection of records the routine collection, production, and use of which constituted one of the essential features of the everyday activities of the organizational setting. These various kinds of records, collected and produced by many people about many different aspects of the organization, provided a basis of demonstrating to the various inspectors of the ship's accounts the fact that the everyday affairs of the organizational activities had been conducted in an efficient manner in accordance with the relevant rules and procedures. That this was in fact the case, the various records were taken to be "facts" supporting the contention that the organization had complied with the relevant rules and procedures. Not all "pieces of paper" were regarded as being of equal importance, as shall be seen, but, in one way or another, all of the paperwork collected and produced on the ship was seen to be a part of the routine everyday "work" of the persons doing it. And, of course, personnel were typically "evaluated" in part by their ability to produce such documentation as an artful accomplishment of their assigned task. That popular common-sense understandings of "the military" often note the great emphasis on the accountability of such organizations, and that popular notions have it that the "successful" military actor of our times is the "paper pusher," would seem to suggest, to some extent, the degree of sharedness of this experience. This research, however, suggests that there are an immense number of strategies employed by these actors in the management of these artful workaday practices, as well as considerable diversity of the social meanings of such activities for those so engaged.

The tasks of the personnel in the ASW Division aboard the USS *Walden* involved the operation and maintenance of all of the equipment associated with the ship's alleged primary battle capability, anti-submarine warfare. This included the ship's two sonar systems upon which the remainder of the equipment systems depended for their effectiveness; the "hull-mounted" sonar, located on the keel of the ship, and the "variable depth sonar," which could be "streamed" at the rear of the ship while at sea at considerable depths to provide a capability for penetrating the various "thermal layers" of the ocean. The maintenance of these complex electronic systems entailed considerable technical expertise. The technical specialty of "sonarmen" charged with these responsibilities was allegedly among the more skilled technicians in the navy. Nearly all of the routine everyday work tasks of these technicians were outlined in the detailed instructions of the "Planned Maintenance System" (PMS) in terms of "steps," theoretically to be completed "by the number," which were supposedly sufficient for insuring the "preventative maintenance" necessary for the continued operational efficiency of the equipment.

The sonarmen and torpedomen composing the personnel make-up of the ASW Division were supervised by the "ASW Officer." This billet was typically occupied by a junior officer with less than two years of active duty service possessing little or no knowledge of the complex electronic systems for which he was formally responsible. His duties also included the artful management of many mundane everyday activities such as, for example, insuring that persons from the ASW Division swabbed a given passageway daily, a task that the sonar technicians typically perceived as "beneath them," as well as a variety of other activities unrelated to his primary assignment as ASW Officer. Generally speaking, the sonar technicians constructed the routine accounts providing demonstration that the various technical aspects of their tasks had been competently accomplished in accord with the relevant rules and procedures of the organization. The routine character of these procedures was established by reference to the various standardized procedures specifying that such activities were called for in the first place. The ASW Officer artfully constructed the accounts required that were of a nontechnical nature.

The temporal coordination of these various routine activities of the personnel of the ASW Division was always difficult and sometimes impossible to maintain in some smooth, consistent fashion. This was the case especially when the *Walden* was at sea and the "normal working day" included so many "disruptions" as to make many of the daily tasks impossible to accomplish (except for all practical purposes that varied greatly in terms of "what anyone knew" to be the situation at that point in time). These other than normal situations significantly altered the tasks of the ASW personnel, especially when the *Walden* was involved in long periods of battle operations in Vietnam when some of the sonarmen and torpedomen were called upon as substitutes for gunnery personnel. From the point of view of the ASW officer, the primary everyday working tasks involved those necessary for constructing the accountability of those tasks; "doing his job" assumed an ability to demonstrate, when called upon to do so, the (recorded) "facts" of this efficient accomplishment for all practical purposes. His knowledge that he was personally accountable to others for this artful accomplishment motivated an interest in maintaining this trouble-free development of this accountability. From the point of view of the sonarmen, the "by the numbers" procedures formulated in the PMS program "was just so much baloney." These procedures were thought to be unrelated to the "real needs" of keeping the equipment in an operational condition that was perceived as being the *sine qua non* for maintaining a "troubleless" relationship with those to whom they were accountable. They perceived their watch-standing duties (especially when they were assigned watches unrelated to the ASW function of the ship), their extratechnical duties (such as their turn to swab the decks), and much of the administrative paperwork to be an infringement on the time needed to "do their job with the gear." Having considerable knowledge of the practical circumstances involved in the ASW officer's tasks, the sonarmen frequently employed strategies of compliance in order to insure a certain "evenness" in the flow of reports of accountability, given their knowledge of the appropriate amount for the situation, which could vary greatly depending upon the degree to which the ASW capabilities of the ship were being emphasized. On the other hand, the ASW Officer often employed his physical absence from the working spaces of the technicians as a kind of "strategy of nonsupervision" to allow them to accomplish their tasks in an unfettered manner. Frequently, for example, he would exempt some of the more skilled and proficient technicians from some of the more mundane tasks required on a day to day basis, allowing them greater freedom to "do their job."

The "authority structure" of these relationships was constructed and reconstructed through a series of mundane give and take exchanges that were realized on a situation to situation basis. Typically, these exchanges insured greater cooperation on the part of the sonarmen in aiding the ASW Officer in "doing his job." The artful management of these "working arrangements," from the perspective of the ASW Officer, was often made to happen by his frequent and observable use of a variety of signs dissociating his situated self from the formal role implied in his daily use of a distinctive uniform symbolizing a substantially different self.[28] These relationships were usually the product of long periods of personal involvement by the participants, the accomplishment of which was referred to by the sonarmen's peers as "getting in tight" with one's division officer. Such accomplishments were not, however, unproblematic. With differing conceptions of "what a good officer should be" existent among the division members, actions by the ASW Officer intending to dissociate his self from his formal role, used for the purpose of constructing cooperation among some, sometimes resulted in a diminution of cooperation with others, at least as perceived by the officer. From the point of view of the sonarmen, the construction of such "working arrangements" sometimes resulted in a decrease in their prestige among their peers, as they perceived it. The threat of the use of power, symbolized in the usage of the different uniforms and insignia by the members, could be made more explicit if the situation called for some "emergency" procedure to restore such social orderings were they to become "too problematic." Given the members' understandings about the use of such explicit power, however, its legitimacy was thought to be safeguarded when left unexplicated.

Although this introduction to the everyday activities of some of the personnel of the ASW Division is all too briefly presented here, the research suggests that the artful accomplishment of these routine tasks involves daily cooperation and negotiation among the parties involved in the construction of the everyday social order of the USS *Walden*. That these are indeed routine matters is established reflexively, by referencing the standardized procedures of the formal organizational schema that call for them in the first place, to provide tangible evidence of compliance with those procedures.

An Important Task for the "ASW E"

Although it is not possible to detail all of the practical exigencies of the everyday working tasks of the ASW personnel in a brief chapter such as this, a more detailed consideration will be given to one of these tasks that is of a somewhat greater importance, *as these persons see it,* the tasks involved in "taking a noise level measurement" of the ship's hull-mounted sonar system. This particular task, while also one of the routine maintenance tasks outlined in the PMS program, assumes this importance because its artful accomplishment requires, in addition to the more routine documentation, the sending of a "Sonar Performance Report" in a classified message format to various persons of higher authority. It is one of perhaps only ten or twelve such reports that *routinely* leave the ship in this fashion, and its routine character is established reflexively by referring to the "standing instructions" of the type commander that requires its routine accomplishment. The importance of this report is said to lie in the necessity for persons in high governmental positions to be "informed" about the operational status of the fleet's anti-submarine warfare capabilities and battle-readiness, much of which depends upon the operational efficiency of the various sonar systems employed on various vehicles throughout the navy as the primary sensors of an enemy submarine threat. Competent organizational actors in the lower echelons of such "record-producing agencies" also understand, however, that these routine reports represent not only the organizational activities that were supposedly "made to happen" in accordance with standardized procedures but also the fact of their very submission in the typical temporal sequence documents the organizational acumen of those persons producing these reports as a matter of their everyday routine. The potential evaluational uses of these documents constitutes an important feature of "what any competent actor knows" about the taken for granted workings of the formal organizational schema. In our present case, involving the complex activities of taking a sonar noise level measurement and documenting such activities in the Sonar Performance Report, it was known by competent organizational actors that the use of this report constituted an important factor in the subsequent determination of battle efficiency, and the awarding of the "ASW E." Competent actors assumed that they would be called upon to document the fact that they had conducted these affairs in an efficient manner at the various times these reports were routinely reviewed in the course of a given "competitive period."

The sonar noise level measurement is an attempt to measure the amount of noise put into the water by the ship's machinery and electronic equipment as a function of a given speed of the ship through the water. This measurement also necessarily includes a certain amount of noise introjected into the water as a function of the many persons moving throughout the ship engaged in their normal everyday working routines, activities that often entail the use of various kinds of electrical and/or mechanical tools. The complex set of procedures promulgated by the formal organizational schema to provide for the accomplishment of this measurement cannot be mentioned in detail here. It is sufficient to mention that the task calls not only for a "by the number" process involving relatively simple readings of electronics test equipment that sonarmen are accustomed to using as a matter of routine in their everyday work, but also many other complex coordinative contingencies involving a number of the ship's personnel to whom this measurement is not a matter of their daily routine (such as many engineering personnel required to monitor the various fuel and engineering systems during the numerous speed changes that are required for the measurement). The procedures also call for, at least in their literal meaning, a stopping of the normal work routines of most of the remainder of the ship's personnel for a matter of several hours. What is of crucial importance for consideration here, however, is that the "routineness" of the artful accomplishment of this measurement must be renegotiated on a situation to situation basis in terms of the reasonable judgments of the variously situated personnel involved in terms of "what anyone knows" to be the "givens of the situation," as is discussed later. This particular task of taking a noise level measurement represents a routine, taken for granted working task, requiring no out of the ordinary efforts on the part of the ASW personnel. From the perspective of the engineering personnel, however, the measurement represents what they term "a real pain in the ass," in spite of its routine happening within the setting. This situation requires that the reasonableness of the various judgments involved within the organization must necessarily involve an understanding of "how it all fits together." This emergent definition of the situation is sometimes made to happen by the commanding officer's usage of tactics of compromise to construct order from the differing social definitions proffered by the ASW Officer and the Engineering Officer. As shall be seen later, these organizationally competent actors must orient their activities to the "negotiable routine" in terms of "what is known" about the ship's operational situation in order to provide a defensible claim that their respective organizational duties and responsibilities were "made to happen" and "objectively reported" in accord with a *mutatis mutandis* understanding of the relevant rules and procedures.

The rules and procedures of the standing instructions informing competent users about this measurement specified that the results of the measurement were to be reported in accordance with a given deadline and were to leave the ship in a classified message format. As the preceding comments suggest, however, a necessary condition for constructing "compliance" with these procedures was that the ship had to be at sea, which was not always the case for a given ship within the specified time period. The formal procedures further specified, therefore, that if the ship was not at sea during the given reporting period, or for some other understandable reason could not accomplish compliance with the formal procedures, then the proper procedure was to submit documentation to that effect in the same manner as one would report the results of the measurement if it had been accomplished. *What is of crucial importance for our present concerns here, is that failure to accomplish compliance with the lexical meaning of the formal procedures was NOT sanctionable in the terms of the formal organizational schema, at least as long as the report was properly submitted detailing this "noncompliance."*

Thus, if the "literal application" of the complex set of rules and procedures informing competent organizational actors regarding the accomplishment and documentation of this important measurement is taken to mean the "normal" or "proper" use of the formal organizational schema, with no considerations of the "extenuating circumstances" of the situation, then other uses of the formal schema would have to be deemed "pathological" or "improper" alternatives. As Bittner so perceptively points out, this determination can only be ascertained by the participant observer by ". . . borrow(ing) a concept from those who seek to study in order to describe what he observes about them." This obscures the fact that such alternatives may be competent uses of the formal organizational schema informed by the "reasonable judgments" of the exigencies of the situation.

The following examples of the "gundecking" of the Sonar Performance Report are analyzed here with an eye to the competent actors' "reasonable judgments" of the exigencies of their practical situations as informing a *competent use of the formal organizational schema.*

"Throwing in a Fudge Factor"

As mentioned earlier, accomplishing the task of measuring the ship's sonar performance, if taken to mean "to the letter" of the various rules and procedures, entailed stopping the "normal working day" of nearly all of the personnel on the USS *Walden* whether or not they were actually involved in the many complex processes of the measurement itself, which most of them were not, in order to reduce to the very minimum the noise on the ship. Given the knowledge of the "disruption" of the practical tasks of so many others, as those others saw it, in the literal application of this procedure, the ASW personnel considered that the measurement task could be accomplished in a sufficient-for-all-practical-purposes manner without the necessity of requesting so many of their fellow shipmates to bring to a halt their practical affairs for a period of several hours. Also, although "the letter" of the formal procedures called for the shutting off of all the electrical equipment in the ship's kitchens and galleys, the ASW personnel considered this unnecessary in order to accomplish their task in a sufficient-for-all-practical-purposes manner. There were other occasions when either the operational commitments of the ship precluded the possibility of making the sonar performance measurements at those speeds that required greater and greater amounts of fuel that might be needed for another occasion, or the requirement for the engineers to "bring all four boilers on the line" would entail a great deal of inconvenience for them, possibly causing serious delays in their everyday maintenance routines.[29] This meant that the measurements were only accomplished for the lesser speeds, with the ASW personnel "sketching in" the measurements for the higher speeds using a common-sense extrapolation based on the measurements taken at the lower speeds. That these practical exigencies of the situation called for relatively minor modifications of "the letter" of the formal procedures reflected the practical interests of the ASW personnel in maintaining a social environment in which they did not "catch flack" from their shipmates for an "inappropriate" disruption of the normal working routines. It also reflected their knowledge that this was indeed an important consideration, given "what anyone knows" about sustaining a cooperative atmosphere for social relationships in such a physically confining setting.

For the purposes of reporting the *Walden*'s sonar performance measurement in the Sonar Performance Report when practical circumstances such as those described prevailed, the ASW personnel would alter the measurement readings in a relatively minor fashion in terms of their common-sense extrapolation of what they thought would be a "reasonable" factor representing the noise put into the water by, for example, the fact that the equipment in the galley was not shut off during the measurement. These persons spoke of these activities as "throwing in a fudge factor," or "fudging," in order that the report would reflect the "real" measurements of the efficiency of the sonar system. As the *Walden*'s ASW Officer stated:

S: And even though it (referring to the noise level measurements) wasn't a particularly difficult job for us—you know, just having a couple of ST's on the bridge with head sets (referring to sound-powered telephones), and a couple of guys in the equipment room reading the test equipment— the coordination of the damn thing was always a hassle. I always wanted to take the readings right up to (the maximum speed of the ship) and Troxell (the Engineering Officer) always seemed to interpret this as if I wanted to sabotage his whole department. From his point of view, the measurements were, well, I must admit that I understood his situation. Bringing four boilers on the line *did* entail a fantastic amount of extra work for his people. And it was work that wasn't too related to his primary jobs. And, not only *that*, you have to understand that this was only one special evolution which involved Engineering. The snipes also ran into the same problems with everyone else who needed their help to do some little measurement or exercise. Seemed like Troxell was always involved with someone in some kind of hassle about his men. That could have been partially because of the kind of guy he was though (both laugh) . . . Let's face it, we all know that nobody's going to find a submarine on sonar at (the maximum speed of the ship) anyway— maybe not even if you'd run over it on the surface—so I was usually happy just to take the readings to (the maximum speed at two boilers). . . .

I: What about the people in the Supply Department? Same story there?

S: Yeah, same thing. The pork chops could really give a big shit about a sonar noise level measurement. Don't blame them really, I know that I don't have much interest in many of the things that go on aboard the ship. All you have to do is ask 'em to shut down the galleys for a couple of hours and they start screaming. Even worse than the snipes, I think. We actually put the Quiet Ship Bill into effect once for the measurements. About a week later we discovered that we were having a little difficulty, you might say, in processing our (forms requesting spare parts from storage), the Sonarmen began getting all of the torn sheets, and our watch-standers were booted from the head of the chow line. . . . You eventually learn all of these things, you learn what it is that other people have to do as a part of their job, and you learn to do your own job in order to avoid a war aboard the ship at the same time you're trying to fight one. . . .

A former Engineering Officer on the *Walden* comments:

S: Sure I knew that the noise level measurements required (the maximum speed of the ship), but I also know that the people at CINCPAC, or Washington, or wherever it is that the report goes, know what the story is with the plants (referring to the engineering equipment) on these old cans. It's not only that (the maximum speed at four boilers) would probably shake these babies apart at the seams, it's also that these plants require many more man-hours for maintenance and repair. . . . I suspect that there are damn few (class of ship similar to *Walden*)—class ships which could put four boilers on the line at any given time, even though there may be only one or two (name of a report used to inform superiors of a major boiler casualty) outstanding in the entire Fleet at any one time. Everybody knows this. I'm sure the guys who read those sonar reports understand the situation with the engineering set-ups on these old cans. They'd have to. The guys who are now on tours in the Pentagon aren't that dumb. They were here doing the job I'm doing not too many years ago.

All of these Tin Cans are different. Take the, well, ah, even though the (*Walden*'s class) and the (another class of Destroyers) come under the same regulations which govern DD's (Destroyers), there's a difference of 25 years there in construction dates, and that means one hell of a lot when you're reading reports that have to do with the engineering plants on these ships. . . . I'm sure that the guys reading the sonar reports understand these things as well as those who are collecting all of our engineering stuff. . . .

It can be seen that the modification of "the letter" of the formal procedures in terms of competent members' sense of maintaining the organizational "normal working day" requires "reasonable judgment" of relevancies for determining *what it takes* to make the measurement while maintaining *business as usual*. The *intent* of the formal organizational procedures for the sonar noise level measurements, then, is thought to be followed *in terms of the members' understandings of what it takes to maintain the "normal working day" for those situated at other positions in the organization.* Viewing these phenomena from the perspective of "compliance" and "noncompliance" obscures the competent organizational members' judgments regarding the *reasonable* use of the formal procedures to account for the exigencies of the situation. When seen in this light, referring these activities to the formal schema and referring the accounts of these activities to the formal schema become the members' efforts directed toward *constructing social order* from the existential situation. The facticity of that order is established reflexively by referring the documents and reports to the formal rules and procedures calling for such constructions.

As indicated in the comments by the *Walden*'s Engineering Officer, the "markings" or "traces" on organizational documentation such as official reports is *not* regarded as unproblematic by these organizational members. This indicates that part of what is involved in the development of organizational competence is *learning how to read such documents,* that is, learning what such markings stand for, refer to, or mean within the context of the report. In this instance, for example, it can be seen that the same "markings" on two pieces of paper presumably representing the "same" report may mean something entirely different, given a member's inside understanding of the class or type of ship involved.

"Juggling the Numbers": Practicalities and Priorities

A division of four destroyers will commonly depart the United States for their six- or seven-month "Westpac Deployment" at the same time. Often ships of the same division will be assigned to the same "operational commitment" once they arrive in the area of Southeast Asia. When this occurs, the commodore of the division typically plays an important role in assigning and coordinating the assignments and operations of the ships in the division.[30] He usually plays an important role in monitoring the effectiveness of "his" ships through the collection of various documents and reports, from both the standardized competitive exercises and inspections as well as those that may originate from other sources relating an evaluation of some battle-related mission, and also, through his own observations. When operating near the land areas of Southeast Asia it is not possible to accomplish the literal compliance with the formal rules and procedures relating to the sonar noise level measurement because the water is too shallow to permit a measurement uncontaminated by the sound reverberations from the ocean floor. The ships will typically be "detached" from their operational duties for as many hours as are necessary for the ship to reach "open sea," conduct the measurements, and return to its former position.

As stated earlier in this chapter, the formal procedures included provisions for submitting an "unable to comply" report as an alternative to submitting the measurements obtained in the required Sonar Performance Report. This alternative would include a brief statement of the "reasons" for this fact, and the submission of such an "unable to comply" report entailed no formal sanctions to any of the personnel involved. It was perceived by the officers and ASW personnel on the USS *Walden,* however, that the submission of a proper report was taken as evidencing a professional concern for, and efficient accomplishment of, the many tasks necessary for maintaining the operational readiness of the ship's "primary capability."

Anti-Submarine Warfare

On one occasion during its deployment the USS *Walden* was the fourth ship of the division to be detached from its assigned mission for a period of several hours to proceed to the open sea to conduct its noise level measurements. Several of the ship's officers possessed the knowledge that the other three ships had successfully conducted their measurements and had reported the results of these measurements to their appropriate superiors with a message transmitted over the radio-teletype circuits. On this occasion the USS *Walden* had a mechanical casualty to one of its boilers. This state of affairs typically required a message report to various superiors, but had not been submitted by the *Walden* because of the perception by the members that such casualty reports were taken as evidence for evaluating the professional competence of the commanding officer, which is not an atypical occurrence. With the knowledge that the present operational commitments usually required no more than the use of two of the ship's four boilers, it was decided that the ship would conduct the noise level measurements at lower speeds, and then "guesstimate," as it was sometimes called, the measurements for higher speeds for the purposes of the report. As the *Walden* began the required procedures for taking the measurements, it was discovered that the electronic test equipment needed to take the readings was not operative, rendering even an approximation of the measurements impossible. It was perceived that the revelation of either of these two facts could possibly cause embarrassment to the commanding officer. Of much greater concern, at least from his point of view, however, was that such a revelation could subsequently occasion a reassignment of the *Walden* to the nearest naval repair facility for repairs to the equipment. This would not only eliminate the ship from its competitive position vis-à-vis the other ships of the division in meeting its battle-related commitments, which was of greatest importance, but it could also entail the construction of documentary evidence possessing a potential evaluational use by those to whom the commodore was accountable for the operational performance of "his" ships. Thus, since there was no evidence or suspicion on the part of any of the ASW personnel that the sonar system was any less efficient than it had been the month before, it was thought that this (potential) "trouble" could be avoided by "gundecking" the Sonar Performance Report. This was accomplished by "juggling the numbers a little" from the previous report, in order to avoid detection, and submitting the figures as if the ship had actually followed "to the letter" the required procedures. As the ASW Officer commented on this situation:

> S: This was unquestionably one of the tighter situations we ever had with the noise levels. There were several other times when we were at sea, about ready to begin the measurements, when we would discover that our test equipment wasn't in calibration, or would discover some other casualty, but, at least when we were steaming in Eastpac (that is, near the United States), that wasn't all that big a deal because we could postpone them to another time. Then we would—
>
> I: Were problems with test equipment common, or uncommon or . . .?
>
> S: Yes, they were fairly common actually. I'd say, well (pause), I guess

that maybe half the time in the three years I was the ASW Officer I had serious reservations about the test equipment. The reason was that it took so long to get it calibrated. You couldn't really afford to send it to the lab unless you were sure that the ship would be in-port for about two months, and nobody on a DD could *ever* be sure of that! (Laughs.) When my leading ST would have some doubts about the gear he'd usually check it out with a similar piece which the ET's (Electronic Technicians) had, but there were a number of times when we couldn't really be sure that some unusually high readings we had taken were due to the sonar system or the test equipment. . . .

That time when we had been detached by the Commodore from our shore bombardment mission to take the noise levels really made me a little nervous, I'm tellin' you. That whole cruise, the one we made with the other ships in our Division, seemed to go like that though, from one crisis to another, with each CO constantly trying to "one-up" the others. The next one we made didn't go anything like that. It was really smooth by comparison. That's because we steamed with (number of another Division of Destroyers) all the time. But that first one was really something. We'd had the "ASW E" for four consecutive years, and were shooting for the gold one (awarded to the ship on the fifth consecutive achievement of a battle efficiency award). The pressure was really on. The Commanding Officer's major concern at the time wasn't the "ASW E" I don't think, in fact, I'm sure it wasn't. He was more interested in keeping us on the Shorebom missions, where the action was so to speak, and not having us transferred back to (the Philippines) for repairs. . . .

From a legalistic or functionalist perspective this example gives the appearance of a cut-and-dried case of rule violation or "noncompliance." In fact, even from the brief description offered here, it can be seen that the competent organizational actors sensed the "deviant" nature of the gundecking practice. It is suggested, however, that the "deviancy" of this instance of gundecking is established only in terms of the perceptions of the competent actors involved. In fact, the gundecking of the official report is judged by these persons to be a "reasonable" course of action in terms of the perceived consequences that might result from another usage of the formal organizational schema. By constructing the appearance of formal compliance in the situation through the use of the formal procedures (the *intent* of which the ASW personnel believed they had accomplished, that is, having maintained an operationally efficient sonar system), the "troubles" that were perceived to potentially follow from a *literal usage* of the organizational schema were avoided in order to get back to the bigger business of meeting its battle-related commitments along the shores of Vietnam. These commitments were considered by most of the organizational members as being the *raison d'être* justifying the sacrifices of such a long deployment.

Covering Your Ass

As mentioned previously the USS *Walden* had two sonar systems. One was mounted on the keel of the ship and the other was located on the main deck at the rear of the ship and could be lowered into the water at various depths while the ship was underway. This provided the ship with a sonar system capable of penetrating the thermal layers of the ocean. The "Variable Depth Sonar," as it was called, was used very infrequently. As a consequence of several collisions in recent years between the sonar being streamed by the destroyer and U.S. Navy submarines, its use has been severely restricted through the promulgation of many official procedures governing its use in recent years. It would be stressing the obvious to note that many of these policies had been promoted by those in the submarine service.

The actual tasks of the sonar technicians accomplishing the successful maintenance of the primary sonar system entailed continual minor repairs and replacement of various parts. These parts, most of which were electrical components, were kept "in stock" on the *Walden,* with the most frequently used parts being stocked in greater numbers, and the less frequently used parts being stocked in fewer numbers. When desiring a given part in order to effect some minor repair to the sonar system, the typical procedures called for the sonar technician to fill out the appropriate form at the supply office, with one of the supply department personnel taking the form and retrieving the requested part from one of the ship's many storerooms. Then the supply department personnel would use this same form to reorder the part from the appropriate facility in order to maintain an adequate stock of repair parts aboard the ship. When the ship was deployed overseas, however, the periods between replenishments (either in port or at sea) often exceeded the frequency with which the sonar technicians needed certain repair parts to meet the practical exigencies of their repair work and preserve their sense of accomplishing their tasks in a proficient manner. To meet the exigent circumstances of repairing the hull-mounted sonar, and to sustain this sense of proficient job accomplishment among the technicians involved in this activity, there was a tacit understanding between the sonar technicians and their division officer to the effect that, if certain electrical parts were needed to maintain the peak performance of the sonar system and these parts were not presently in stock aboard the ship, then parts would be taken from the "Variable Depth Sonar" for use in the primary sonar system. This procedure was called "cannibalizing" by the technicians. Although these persons clearly understood the explicit "unofficiality" of these practices, they were systematically used to manage certain kinds of contingencies with the knowledge that the official restrictions regarding the use of the "Variable Depth Sonar" were so great that the chances were exceptionally small that they would be called upon to account for its operational efficiency. Considerable care was exercised by these persons to keep these practices "under cover," perceiving official sanctions to follow from any public disclosure of them.

While these covert practices were sufficient for all practical purposes most of the time, on one occasion the *Walden* was called upon to conduct a sonar noise level measurement on its variable depth sonar and to submit the results of these measurements in the format of a message report to the commodore of the division. The commodore was then riding on one of the other ships in the division steaming in company with the *Walden*. Since some of the essential electrical components of the VDS had been "cannibalized" to provide repair parts for the other sonar system (although this was not obvious from any outward appearances of the equipment), it was not possible to construct literal compliance with the organizational procedures in the situation. In this situation the ASW personnel "went through the motions" of accomplishing such compliance, and the ASW Officer and the chief sonarman gundecked a sonar performance report based on the figures from the previous such measurement, and submitted the report to the commanding officer who in turn forwarded the information to the commodore of the division.

As the man who was the leading sonar technician during this occasion comments:

> **S:** That was probably one of the funniest noise levels we ever took. Even though I told Nash (the ASW Officer) when we planned this out that there wouldn't be any trouble pulling it off—because I knew (the Commanding Officer) wouldn't come on down to the sonar equipment room, and couldn't even read a voltmeter if he did—he was really sweatin' it out. Nash was running around like a chicken with his head cut off . . . Really incredible, all those people involved in taking the measurements when we were actually covering ourselves for cannibalizing the VDS for the hull-mounted. At that late date in the cruise I wouldn't have been surprised if everyone on the other three ships wasn't doing the same thing. . . . In fact, I later met Erwin off (another ship in the Division) at the EM Club (Enlisted Men's Club) one night after we got back, and he said they'd been doing the same thing the whole cruise. It's the only way you can keep the gear up (meaning operative), with the supply system as (messed up) as it is. . . . We'd never have to do this in Eastpac, because we can always get the parts we need, even if we have to cumshaw them (loosely, "borrow"). . . .

The ASW Officer comments on the situation:

> **S:** That's the only time we ever had to do that, thank God! I mean, we've completely gundecked the reports before, like the other time I told you about, but (the Commanding Officer) was usually in on the situation with us. This was strictly a case where the ST's had been cannibalizing the gear in the VDS for several months, knowing full well that the restrictions on using the goddamn contraption were so fantastic that we

hardly ever got a chance to stream it. I knew about the situation. I knew about it and didn't know about it, know what I mean? (Laughs.) I could've mentioned it to (the Commanding Officer) long ago, but that would have put him on the spot. . . .

I: What do you mean?

S: Well, officially at least, he would have then been forced to submit a (report noting an equipment casualty), and you always try to avoid that unless it's completely impossible. . . . So we had to cover ourselves, just like everyone has to do in this outfit. "Cover your ass with paper," isn't that the old adage? Went smooth as silk too, I might add. . . .

Once again, if one were to use the notion of social action as rule-governed (or normative) activity, which is implied throughout the various structural and/or functional perspectives in studying deviance or organizational behavior, this example might suggest an instance of "rule-violation," or "noncompliance." And again, some merit to that interpretation is even suggested by the covert nature by which the ASW personnel managed these "under the table" practices. To readily dismiss this example as being an "atypical" one, however, only to be found upon rare occasions in formal organizations and having no greater theoretical importance other than being "an interesting exception to the rule," obscures the critical issue of how these organizationally competent actors methodically employ such "unofficial practices" to deal with certain practical exigencies, which, from their point of view, cannot be reconciled through the literal use of the "official" organization schema and its rules and procedures, *at least if they are to preserve their sense of satisfactory accomplishment of their jobs as they see them.* In this example, the ASW personnel perceived the primary consideration in the successful accomplishment of their tasks to be the maintenance of the *Walden*'s primary sonar system. This objective, incidentally, was also regarded with greater importance by others in the formal schema, as well as in the organizational rules and procedures. To avoid the many "troubles" that were perceived to be the potential concomitants of an inability to accomplish this important task, and to avoid the possibility of an imputation of "incompetence" as organizational actors, which entailed some "troubles" in and of itself (for example, "catching a lot of flack," "having someone looking over your shoulder all the time," and so on), the "covert" or "unofficial" practices were employed to avoid the troubles arising out of the exigent situations within the supply system. These exigencies were indeed difficult to deal with through the "normal" use of the organizational routines, at least as seen by the ASW personnel. Utilizing the "unofficial routine" of cannibalizing one piece of sonar equipment to artfully accomplish what they see to be "the more important tasks" involved in the maintenance of the primary sonar system was one method of providing a socially meaningful and orderly routine to which they could orient themselves in order to preserve that sense of accomplishment that comes, for some people, from the knowledge of "doing what it takes" in a given organizational schema so as to be regarded by others as a "competent bureaucratic actor," a "can-do" person.

Viewed from this perspective, the actions of the ASW personnel in this example, including "going through the motions" of literal compliance with the formal organizational procedures and the gundecking of the official report, can be interpreted as an instance of "covering your ass," to use the members' term for it, although its use is certainly not limited to the world of the U.S. Navy. From the actors' perspective, this case exemplifies a competent use of the formal organizational schema of rules and procedures based on an implicit understanding of "what it takes" to facilitate a consistent reconstruction of a "normal routine" to which the members may orient for purposes of accomplishing their practical activities. "Covering your ass," in this example involved the systematic and competent use of the organizational rules and procedures by these members for the purpose of validating and sustaining the "unofficial practices" that were dealing with the exigent practical circumstances that the "official routine" did not seem to be dealing with adequately. It was a routine that "worked" sufficiently for all practical circumstances as they perceived it.

The Problematics of Gundecking

As these data and comments suggest, the gundecking of the Sonar Performance Report may indeed be a reasonable usage of the formal rules and procedures of the organization when seen from the perspective of the members. As they see it, the propriety of the practice is determined by the exigencies of the situation in which they find themselves. These situations may involve the use of a "compromise," or a partial gundecking of the report ("throwing in a fudge factor"), to sustain the "normal working day" for those situated at other positions in the organization. When seen in this light, the methodical use of gundecking by the members is their way of constructing the larger social order of the USS *Walden* when the lexical use of the formal procedures would presumably lead to a disruption of this order. The situations may involve the overt use of gundecking ("juggling the numbers"), as when members' reasoning and judgment lead them to the conclusion that the intent of the organizational schema will be served more effectively by doing what is necessary to remain on a scene (near Vietnam) which is perceived to possess a higher priority among the various organizational goals. In this light, the methodical use of gundecking is a kind of "minimax" strategy to construct the larger social order of the Vietnam War, one determined by the members' reasonable judgments of the priorities of the situation. Or, the situations may involve the covert, or "unofficial" use of gundecking by the members ("covering your ass") to methodically deal with certain practical exigencies arising out of their everyday routines, which, from their point of view, cannot be reconciled through the literal usage of the organizational schema. In such situations, gundecking is seen to preserve the members' sense of satisfactorily accomplishing their everyday work. At any rate, from the members' point of view, the successful accomplishment of gundecking as a practical matter is *not* one of the "givens" of the situation. It is perceived by the members as a largely problematic endeavor. Some of these problematic aspects of gundecking are elaborated in the concluding comments of this paper.

In the situations analyzed here, the practical accomplishment of gundecking was seen to require the cooperation and coordination of teamwork. As such, gundecking could never be one of the givens of the situation, but is instead *fundamentally problematic*. That is, as a product of the members' reasoning and judgment, gundecking must necessarily be negotiated and renegotiated on a situation-to-situation basis in terms of members' (and audiences') perceptions of the relevancies of the situation. Such situations also involve, to a very great extent, considerations of the unique characteristics of the persons engaged in the situation, either as a member of the team or the audience. As situations and persons change over time, the meaning of gundecking practices, and the members' judgments regarding whether or not the exigencies of the situation warrant its use as a reasonable course of action, must necessarily be renegotiated by the members in terms of their knowledge and perceptions of the situation. Because successful gundecking is as much a result of those who receive it as those who initiate it, it makes little sense, at least for the purposes of sociological theorizing, to contend that it is ever "structurally determined."

Gundecking involves, as has been seen, a presentation of the appearance of orderly situations (presumably what the report is taken to stand for) by organizational members. As experienced by these persons, however, these situations often involve contingencies that could not possibly be adequately covered by any set of formal rules and procedures, no matter how complex and intricate the construction may be. Any given instance of gundecking, therefore, is necessarily problematic to its practitioners because of their *incomplete knowledge* of the reactions of the audience (the persons to whom the report is sent); the fact that they can never be sure that those who will receive their gundecked report will understand the situational contingencies of such an activity in the same manner as the members. This is only to say that a report that is sufficient for all practical purposes at one point in the organization may not be sufficient for the practical purposes of others at another point in the organization at the same point in time. Given a conflict of differing perceptions among organizational members in such matters, this may mean that the meaning of the report may have to be renegotiated.

Closely akin to this problematic aspect of gundecking caused by the members' uncertainty of the audience reaction is the members' perception that a report that is deemed sufficient for all practical purposes at one point in time may, at some later date, be redefined as insufficient. A contemporary example of this phenomenon, which reached the pages of the mass media, were the official reports of what is now called the "My Lai Massacre." In this case, the routine reports that accounted for the military actions at My Lai to those in higher positions were (presumably) sufficient for the practical purposes at that time. Eighteen months later, however, following an entrepreneurial initiative taken by a person who was not a member of the organization, these reports were redefined as insufficient for the practical purposes of the new situation. Members who had demonstrated their organizational competence in the initial issuing of these reports were subsequently redefined as "incompetent," and threatened with prosecution. That membership in military organizations often includes an understanding that such redefinitions of the situation may occur is another one of the problematic features of gundecking practices. Members commonly perceive that such actions may happen "for political reasons."

In conclusion, far from being a clear-cut example of "noncompliance" with organizational rules and procedures, the gundecking of an official report may be seen as a competent usage of the formal schema when seen from the members' perspective. Being dependent upon the members' reasonable judgments of the contingencies of the situation, the persons involved, and the reactions of the audience, the practical accomplishment of gundecking is fundamentally problematic.

Notes

1. See, for example: Jack D. Douglas, *American Social Order* (New York: The Free Press, 1971); and, "Deviance and Order in a Pluralistic Society," in John C. McKinney and Edward A. Tiryakian, eds., *Theoretical Sociology* (New York: Appleton-Century-Crofts, 1970), pp. 367–401.

2. Egon Bittner, "The Concept of Organization," *Social Research* 32 (August, 1965): 239–255.

3. For a more scholarly development of this idea, see: Thomas P. Wilson, "Conceptions of Interaction and Forms of Sociological Explanation," *American Sociological Review* 35 (August, 1970): 697–709.

4. Cf. Howard S. Becker, *Outsiders* (New York: The Free Press, 1963), p. 9; and Thomas J. Scheff, *Being Mentally Ill* (Chicago: Aldine Publishing Company, 1966), p. 33.

5. The term "practical circumstances" is Garfinkel's term to refer to the features of "common-sense situations of choice." See, Garfinkel, *Studies in Ethnomethodology*, esp. pp. 96–103

6. Among the more frequently cited works of phenomenological sociologists are: Alfred Schutz, *Collected Papers I: The Problem of Social Reality,* 1962; *Collected Papers II: Studies in Social Theory,* 1964; *Collected Papers III: Studies in Phenomenological Philosophy,* 1966, (The Hague: Martinus Nijhoff); *The Phenomenology of the Social World* (Chicago: Northwestern University Press, 1967); *Reflections on the Problem of Relevance* (New Haven: Yale University Press, 1970); Harold Garfinkel, *Studies in Ethnomethodology;* "On Formal Structures of Practical Action," in John C. McKinney and Edward A. Tiryakian, eds., *Theoretical Sociology* (New York: Appleton-Century-Crofts, 1970), co-authored with Harvey Sacks. This latter article lists twenty-eight other works of those who have worked with Garfinkel in developing what they refer to as the "ethnological program." Also, see: Jack D. Douglas, *The Social Meanings of Suicide* (Princeton: Princeton University Press, 1967); *Understanding Everyday Life,* and, *American Social Order* (New York: The Free Press, 1970). For an approach that is closely aligned, yet distinctive, see: Barney Glaser and Anselm Strauss, *The Discovery of Grounded Theory* (Chicago: Aldine Publishing Company, 1967).

7. Nearly all of the case studies in the field of formal organizations treat the "formal structure" *versus* "informal structure" dichotomy in one way or another: see, for example: Anonymous, "Informal Social Organization in the Army," *American Journal of Sociology* 51 (March, 1946); Peter M. Blau, *The Dynamics of Bureaucracy* (Chicago: The University of Chicago Press, 1963), rev. ed.; Harry Cohen, *The Demonics of Bureaucracy* (Ames, Iowa: The Iowa State University Press, 1965); Melville Dalton, *Men Who Manage* (New York: John Wiley & Sons, Inc., 1959); Charles H. Page, "Bureaucracy's Other Face," *Social Forces* 25 (October, 1946); and Ralph H. Turner, "The Navy Disbursing Officer as a Bureaucrat," *American Sociological Review* 12 (June, 1947).

8. Cf. Philip Selznick, "Foundation of the Theory of Organization," *American Sociological Review* 13 (1948): pp. 25–35.

9. Don H. Zimmerman, "The Practicalities of Rule-Use," in Douglas, ed., *Understanding Everyday Life.* Also, see his: "Paper Work and People Work," unpublished Ph.D. dissertation, University of California, Los Angeles, 1966; "Tasks and Troubles: The Practical Bases of Work Activities in a Public Assistance Organization," in Donald A. Hansen, ed., *Explorations in Sociology and Counseling* (Boston: Houghton Mifflin Company, 1970); and, "Record-Keeping and the Intake Process in a Public Welfare Organization," in Stanton Wheeler, ed., *On Record: Files and Dossiers in American Life* (New York: Russell Sage Foundation, 1970).

10. The research consists of field notes and unstructured tape-recorded interviews with various petty officers and commissioned officers presently on active duty in the U. S. Navy, as well as interviews with various persons having former associations with the navy. Crucial resources for the research were the personal experiences of the researcher and a number of variously situated inside informants that were used to check the validity of the researcher's observations.

11. A "class" of ships generally refers to ships of the same type, such as destroyers, cruisers, and battleships, which have been constructed according to the same design. Thus, there are many different "classes" of destroyers in the navy.

12. The term "senior-grade commissioned officer" refers to those officers at or above the rank of lieutenant commander; the term "junior-grade commissioned officer" refers to the officers below this rank, ensigns, lieutenants junior grade, and lieutenants. The commanding officer on a ship such as this one is typically a commander, and the executive officer is typically a lieutenant commander.

13. The term "operational command" refers to the chain-of-command through which the ship receives its orders pertaining to its operational activities while at sea, which may include training exercises when operating near its home port, or bona fide battle assignments when deployed overseas.

14. The term "fleet" typically refers to all ships, regardless of "class" or "type," presently operating within a given geographical area. For example, those ships presently assigned to operations in the East Pacific Area are under the operational command of one fleet, while those in the West Pacific are in another fleet. As ships transit from East to West Pacific, they are said to "chop" into the new fleet, hence, are then under the control of its commander, an admiral.

15. The term "type command" refers to the lateral arrangement of staff functions serving various types and classes of ships. The "type commander," an admiral, is responsible for ensuring that given types of ships meet the standardized criteria of battle-readiness for that type, but does not control the operational movements or assignments of the ship.

16. The formal procedures for the administration of such an inspection as "the admin" called for a select group of officers and technicians from one ship to administer the inspection to another ship. Typically, although not always, these inspection groups would be drawn from the ships in the same division, thus promoting a certain degree of "fairness" it was contended.

17. The "standing instructions" were typically standardized for a given class of ships, although some of them could be further modified at the will of the ship's commanding officer through the promulgation of a new (or modified) "ship's instruction."

18. The term "rated personnel" refers to petty (or noncommissioned) officers, which means that they have acquired a given technical specialty within the navy. "Nonrated" personnel include seamen recruits (which means that they are either in the process of completing their initial training in "boot camp," or that they are in the stockade), seamen apprentices, and seamen.

19. Ships classified as "combatants" include destroyers, cruisers, battleships, aircraft carriers, and, since Vietnam, gunboats. All other ships are classified as support, amphibious, or auxiliary.

20. Cf. D. F. Roy, "Quota Restriction and Goldbricking in a Machine Shop," *American Journal of Sociology* 62 (1952): 427–442.

21. Cf. Arthur K. Davis, "Bureaucratic Patterns in the Navy Officer Corps," *Social Forces* 27 (1948): 143–153.

22. The phrase "flag rank" refers to two (rear), three (vice), four (full), and five-star admirals. A one-star admiral, or commodore, is a ranking that is used in times of war only. Whereas the commanding officers of divisions and squadrons are called "commodores," these billets are filled by officers with the rank of captain. Hence, in this instance, the term commodore refers to the billet and not the rank of the person.

23 Cf. Garfinkel and Sacks, "On Formal Structures of Practical Actions."

24. The phrase "normal steaming operations" refers to those operations of the ship while at sea involving no occupation of any of the ship's battle stations. When at war, or when there exists a reason to suspect danger (a decision that may be made at the discretion of the commanding officer), the gunnery and/or ASW stations may be manned as a routine matter. In cases such as these, the ship may operate on a two-section watch bill, meaning that watch-standers work every other watch, usually entailing four hours on watch with every four hours off watch.

25. A historian from the U.S. Naval Academy has informed me that the term originates from the days of the "Square-riggers" of the eighteenth century. These ships, according to this account, could have as many as three decks lined with their cannons (or gundecks). They typically trained their crew members in the use of these weapons by employing a thirteen-step exercise that began, as the first step, with a gunner's mate simulating the ignition of the fuse. Following the simulation of this first step, the other crew members would then proceed through the remaining twelve steps as if the cannon had been fired. The term "gundecking," according to this historian, originates from the simulated first step that initiates the remainder of the exercise. There are, however, many other versions of the origins of the term. Whereas the definition cited from Webster's within the chapter more closely approximates contemporary usage, the remainder of the chapter should provide ample evidence that its meaning is not supplied by the literal, or dictionary definition.

26. For example, while engaged in a "routine" shore bombardment mission near the coast of Vietnam, one destroyer came under the attack of several small gunboats and successfully engaged them in battle. Such events were typically perceived as "out of the ordinary."

27. The phrase "line officer" refers to those qualified to take command at sea (or of an airborne unit). The category includes many aviators and former aviators. The phrase "straight line officer" refers to those who are not, or have not been, aviators but still may be qualified to command at sea. Line officers are distinguished from staff officers, which include such specialties as doctors, dentists, chaplains, civil engineers, lawyers, and supply officers.

28. For a discussion of the notions of "substantial self" and "situated self," see: Jack D. Douglas, *The Social Meanings of Suicide*, pp. 280–283.

29. The ships in the same class as the *Walden* possessed four boilers to generate the steam upon which they depended for propulsion. Nearly all of the sea operations in which these ships were engaged required the use of only two boilers that could, if needed, provide enough power for the ship to attain

80 to 85 percent of its maximum speed. Mechanical and fuel economy decreased drastically with the use of all four boilers, and this was rarely done.

30. In this case, as noted earlier (compare fn. 22 *supra*), the term "commodore" refers to the billet and not the rank.

| V |

Comparative Studies
of Deviance

Sociology is the science of all human societies past and present. Sociologists, however, have concentrated virtually all of their attention on American society. One consequence of our parochialism has been a tendency to assume that theories about behavior and social processes in our own society are valid for all societal forms. The chapters that follow will quickly disabuse the reader of this idea.

The first essay, by Seibel, concerns the nature of deviance in small-scale tribal societies of Africa. Seibel shows that deviance and sanctions work to enhance the level of social integration of groups within which deviant acts are committed and that standards for deviance and appropriate sanctions vary depending upon the nature of social relationships between the parties to a controversy. He also shows that many of the concepts discussed in other sections of this volume are not meaningful when applied to these tribal societies.

The second essay, by Scull, involves a different use of comparative materials. By now it is a classic argument in the sociology of deviance that agents and agencies of social control are frequently responsible for creating, rather than solving, social problems. The case most often cited in support of this argument is the drug problem in America. It is argued that the policies and actions of the Federal Narcotics Bureau have had more to do with creating the current drug problem than any other single factor. In this regard the policies of the British government are usually cited as a paragon of enlightened public policy. In this essay, Scull examines developments in the drug scene in England since the late 1950s. He shows that in spite of the difference in official policies, the drug problem in England has grown enormously and has begun to assume the same features as our own drug problem. The chapter provides an excellent basis for assessing the role of social control agencies in the genesis of social problems.

Chapter Ten

SOCIAL DEVIANCE IN COMPARATIVE PERSPECTIVE

H. Dieter Seibel

Introduction

Conventional perspectives have viewed deviance as detrimental for society. Yet, how is the ubiquity of deviance to be explained when it is only detrimental? This question puzzled Durkheim (1951:362–363) who philosophized: "Whatever is an indispensable condition of life cannot fail to be useful, unless life itself is not useful." This is a postulate, derived from the scholastic axiom *omne ens est bonum,* rather than an empirical finding. The function of deviance tantalized Durkheim throughout his works; but nowhere did he give a coherent general theory of deviance. His major contribution was to hypothesize a positive function for deviance: social integration, a proposition that found hardly any adherents among subsequent students of deviance. His further elaborations were quite inconsistent. (1) He was not able to relate deviance and social integration directly. He had to introduce sanctioning mechanisms as an intervening variable: "Punishment and crime are two terms of an inseparable pair," and crime is only useful "when reproved and repressed" (Durkheim, 1951:363). Hence, sanctions rather than deviance are associated with social integration. (2) His presentation of the direction of the causal flow is contradictory. In *De la Division du Travail Social* (1893), deviance, through sanctions as an intervening mechanism, is claimed to be causal to social integration (Durkheim, 1933:108). In *Le Suicide* (1897), the extent of social integration, or, conversely, of *anomie,* is presented as causal to deviance, namely suicide (Durkheim, 1951:209, 299, 306 n.4, 316). (3) His analysis of sanctions as an intervening mechanism is also inconsistent.

Durkheim (1933:108;1951:363) describes sanctions as a requisite for the integrative function of crime in general, while no such requisite is given in the case of the relationship between *anomie* and suicide (1951:209).

Simmel (1908) simply cut the Gordian knot by arguing that conflict itself, irrespective of its concomitants or consequences, constitutes a form of sociation. He left us with the paradox that conflict, which we might have mistaken for a form of disintegration, is to be considered as a form of social integration.

In sum, students of deviance have raised a number of theoretically relevant issues but have not been able to come up with a general theory of deviance. Most theories of deviance are of a relatively low level of generality and present properties of deviance as universal that are in fact limited to the societies in which they were studied. It seems to be mainly a lack of comparative perspective that has led to this narrow perspective. The societies in which the theories of deviance have been developed are so complex that it is difficult to isolate variables and study their relationships in field-experimental situations. What makes the study of deviance particularly difficult is the fact that in complex societies, the functions of deviance overlap with the functions of other institutions.

The following study assumes a comparative perspective that looks at deviance in both complex and simple societies, concentrating geographically on Africa. The emphasis is first on small-scale African societies since they present a setting that allows the isolation of those variables that deviance is directly related to. In a second step, deviance is analyzed in large-scale African societies where deviance and its social concomitants will become increasingly familiar to the Western reader. In a last step, some general propositions are presented about deviance in any society.

I: Small-Scale African Societies

Deviance and the Integration of Social Groups

The basic proposition of this chapter is that *There is a relationship between social deviance and social integration.* Social deviance is a structural device of society geared at a function which is a prerequisite of any society: social integration.

The main characteristics that are of relevance for the study of deviance in African societies are:

1. There is a strong focus on integration.
2. The units of integration are groups rather than individuals.
3. The prime mechanism geared at integration as a process is social deviance.

Ad (1): In American society, an adult may decide for or against being integrated into a family. He may rent an apartment in Manhattan and live a very solitary life. He may even refuse membership in a productive organization by living on inherited property or by stealing other people's purses. If he is caught, it is he and only he who is punished.

There are no such solitary individuals in traditional African society. Everyone is integrated into a family and into other groups. ". . . the unit of an ancient society was the Family, of a modern society, the individual," observed Henry Maine in *Ancient Law* (1861).

> No one can contract out of membership of a lineage: he is born irretrievably into it. By that membership he gets rights in land, enters into social relationships, inherits totemic avoidances, acquires culture itself, and the sentiments on which it is based are formed in the family itself. [Gluckman 1963:72]

Ad (2): The fact that the African is "irretrievably born" into group membership explains a basic difference between the type of integration in African society and in our society. In our society, where a high valuation is placed on individualism, integration is primarily a process of coaxing *individuals as basic units* into group membership. In Africa, where *groups are the basic units,* integration is a process directed at the cohesion of group members within ever-present groups and at the cohesion between groups. In other words, integration is directed at preventing fission, that is, the disintegration of groups into smaller units, and fusion, that is, the combination of groups into larger units.

This group focus has sociolegal consequences, namely, that the parties to controversy and to sanctioning are not individuals but groups—usually bodies of kindred (Redfield, 1967:23; Gulliver, 1963:1). A conception of individual punishment inflicted on the person who committed a deviant act is generally absent. Settlement of a conflict is not an individual affair, but an affair between the family of the wrongdoer and the wronged. "It was not necessary to take revenge on the person of the killer himself; any one of his kinsmen would do instead," found Howell (1954:40) among the Nuer in the Sudan.

Ad (3): It is the *principle of collective responsibility* that is operative *within* social groups in connecting deviance as a cause and integration as an effect. Upon a deviant act, two integrative processes start immediately, both geared at the integration of the social units concerned. For example, after a murder has been committed, one process of integration takes place *within* the family of the victim. It first finds its expression in a reaction of indignation at the personal loss, a reduction in their numbers, and the damage to the continuity of their group. Formal and informal meetings follow at which measures to be taken are discussed. Eventually, some kind of group action is taken against the family of the killer. Another process of integration starts *within* the family of the killer. First, the family demands that, in their joint interest, the killer shall perform those rites of expiation that will neutralize the effects of spiritual contamination emanating from the spirits associated with the dead man's kin (Howell, 1954:207). Formal and informal meetings take place at which the kin assemble to discuss what action the family of the victim is likely to take and how to respond to it. And lastly, the family as a group responds to whatever action the other family takes.

The reason why a process of integration takes place *within* each one of the two groups concerned is obvious: to prepare them for the ensuing dispute or conflict *between* them. That very conflict represents, as postulated by Simmel (1908:247), a form of sociation: it brings two groups into close contact and increases the intimacy and frequency of interaction between them. In simple cases, settlement procedures lead to a reconciliation of the two parties concerned, retributions are designed in a manner to strengthen the relationship between them. In more complex cases, the conflict between two families may activate the whole web of actual or imagined kinship or other group relationships and first lead to an integration of each group or set of groups on a large scale and then to a settlement between the two groups or sets of groups.

The hypothesis of a relationship between social deviance and integration of social groups explains a phenomenon that appeared to be only bizarre, exotic, and inhuman to all who studied it: the widespread existence in Africa of certain societies generally referred to as leopard societies (also known as alligator societies and baboon societies) (Beatty, 1915; Joset, 1955). The manifest purpose of these societies is to produce a medicine that is supposed to give its owner economic and political power. The potency of that medicine depends upon its being frequently anointed with human fat and blood, which are obtained by killing a person, frequently a relative of one of the members. Moreover, anthropophagy is frequently practiced in conjunction with the killing as is apparent in most of the evidence about the activities of these societies (Joset, 1955), particularly in the trials of the colonial government in Sierra Leone between 1903 and 1912 during which 186 persons were charged with murder and 87 convicted and sentenced to death (Beatty, 1915). The latent function of the leopard society is social integration on an interkin group or even intertribal level, the deviant acts of murder and anthropophagy representing most powerful ties binding the participants together. Why lesser crimes are unlikely to suffice to fulfill the integrative function is discussed in the next section of this chapter. Less than twenty years ago (1952–1956), history provided us with a quasiexperimental setting for the study of the relationship between extreme forms of deviance and the extreme need for integration: the

Mau Mau revolt against the colonial government in Kenya. The task was to unite a segmentary society, the Kikuyu, underground with the final goal of overthrowing the colonial government. The main mechanism through which unification and secrecy were to be achieved were oaths administered in conjunction with highly obscene rituals and frequently with elaborate tortures, murder, and extreme mutilation of the bodies of the killed—completely unknown in traditional Kikuyu society where so strong a reason for integration had never before arisen. These extreme forms of deviance did in fact fulfill their purpose: the Kikuyu were integrated into a secret underground organization. The attempt to overthrow the government failed; yet it was one of the major forces that eventually brought about political independence for Kenya.

Social Deviance and Social Sanctions

Social sanctions constitute a structural complement to deviance. Hence, the initial proposition could also read: *There is a relationship between social sanctions and social integration.* In most cases, the two propositions can be combined into one: *There is a relationship between social deviance with its sanctions and social integration.* However, since social deviance and social sanctions are not identical, one may speculate that they are independently variable. In fact, it will be shown that they are distinct.

The main characteristics of the sanctioning process in African societies are:

1. It is directed toward reintegration rather than alienation.
2. It does not attach moral labels to the deviant act.
3. It does not attach moral labels to the deviant person or group.

The emphasis on integration and the use of deviance as *the* mechanism for implementing integration explain a central feature of deviance and its sanctions in African society: that they effectively prevent the alienation of the deviant individual or group. This has two important social consequences; one related to the deviant act and the other related to the deviant person or group.

In principle, the *deviant act* is not considered immoral. Depending upon the circumstances, it may be considered disadvantageous, but no moral stigma is attached to it. The basic attitude to the deviant act is highly utilitarian. Howell (1954:82, 131–132, 206–207) reports that the Nuer do not consider concubinage, illegitimacy, or murder as "evil" although it may be thought of as quite harmful. Schott (1959:123) reports the same about the Kung Bushmen.

The social attitude to the *deviant person or group* corresponds to the attitude to the deviant act. The deviant is not stigmatized, and there is *no secondary deviance.* Instead of alienating the deviant, he is reintegrated and rehabilitated. If any personality problems are at the root of the deviant act, they are dealt with according to all rules of psychotherapy, as Gibbs (1963) and others have shown. Similarly, therapeutic treatment is given if the deviant act has arisen out of group tensions.

The Relativity of Deviance and of Its Sanctions

The hypothesized relationship between social deviance and its sanctions on the one hand and social integration focusing on groups as social units to be integrated on the other allows the following propositions:

1. Standards of deviance and its sanctions are not absolute or universal but are rather relative or particularistic. They vary according to the types of groups and to the types of relationship between the groups to be integrated.

2. At the one extreme, no deviant acts can be committed and no sanctions imposed between groups that do not stand in a meaningful social relationship to each other. Without a social relationship there is no need for social integration, and without a need for social integration, there is no deviance.

3. At the other extreme, wrongs committed within the smallest social unit, the family, and limited to that group, are considered deviant since there is a meaningful social relationship between the two actors; but no sanctions are imposed since there is no need for integrating different groups. Evidence for this assertion would also prove that integration is not a process pertaining to individuals as the units to be integrated but to groups.

On the basis of these propositions, the initial hypothesis can now be specified, operationalizing social integration as intimacy of social relations:

1. *There is a direct association between social integration (or: intimacy of social relations) among groups and the probability of perceiving an act as deviant.*

2. *There is a direct association between social integration (or: intimacy of social relations) among groups and the perceived magnitude of deviance of an act.*

3. *There is a direct association between social integration (or: intimacy of social relations) among groups and the probability of sanctions.*

4. *There is an inverse association between social integration (or: intimacy of social relations) and magnitude of sanctions.*

In other words: the higher the level of integration between groups (or: the more intimate social relations among groups): (1) the more likely is an act to be perceived as deviant; (2) the more seriously is a deviant act viewed; (3) the higher is the probability of imposing sanctions; (4) but the smaller is the magnitude of sanctions. *Intimacy of social relations* refers to structural intimacy (defined as intimacy of actual or mythical kinship and other group ties) and/or actual intimacy of interactions.

From a negative point of view, this means that disturbing relations between two close groups is more serious than disturbing relations between socially more distant groups. From a positive point of view, th   means that

closely related groups do have a certain need for deviance as a form of interaction and a mechanism of integration since intimacy of relations implies, by
definition, certain levels of interaction and deviance is, as shown in the
previous chapter, a central category of interaction and integration. In both
cases, from the negative and the positive point of view, it is more likely that
an act that affects two close groups is perceived as deviant; at the same time,
a given act is considered to be more serious than it would be among distant
groups. Similarly, sanctions are more likely to be imposed when deviant acts
occur between closely related groups than between distant ones: negatively,
because such acts are viewed as more serious, and positively, because there
is a higher need for restitution and subsequent integration, or maintenance of
integration. However, it takes less to restore closely knit relations than loose
ties. In the case of most intimate social relations as found within the family,
the likelihood of perceiving a norm-breaching act as deviant and the magnitude of deviancy of that act are highest, and so is the probability of imposing
sanctions; but the magnitude of such sanctions approximates zero although it
cannot become zero. In the extreme, sanctions are purely ritual.

The converse correlates of more distant social relationships are self-
evident from the preceding analysis. It may be added that the increase in
magnitude of sanctions that parallels the increase in social distance of a relationship is limited by the maximum indemnification that is customary for a
particular deviant act. In the extreme case of nonexistent social relations
between two groups, acts are not considered deviant, and the probability of
sanctions approximates zero. In a situation of change, however, induced, for
example, by migrations, acts may begin to be considered as deviant and sanctions may be imposed, thus signifying the beginning of a social relationship.

Howell, describing Nuer society, gives ample evidence for the relativity
of deviance and its sanctions.

> The significance of the structural relativity of Nuer society is . . . most im-
> portant in a study of customary laws, for although the rules and principles
> which govern the conduct of all Nuer are essentially the same, the extent of
> their application is relative and largely dependent on the social context.
> [Howell, 1954:24]

About the relativity of deviance, he states, giving homicide as an example, that

> The element of wrongness is relative to the relationship in the social struc-
> ture of the parties involved. The killing of a stranger, especially of a for-
> eigner, who does not come within the most expanded form of the social
> structure, is not really wrong at all. It is neither a crime nor a private delict,
> for there is no political sanction involved and no social relationship which
> might demand restitution . . . It is, however, a situation which demands ex-
> piation in the form of ritual and sacrifice . . . [Howell, 1954:207]

About the relativity of sanctions, Howell states, giving adultery as an example, that the

> likelihood of the wrongdoer paying the cattle (as an indemnity—HDS) at all is determined by the relationship of the parties, both in terms of actual kinship and in terms of territorial proximity, in residence and all the sanctions which go with common residence. . . . Between men who are close kinsmen it is rare that anything more than this one cow (which has purely ritual significance; an additional five cows are customary as indemnity—HDS) will be demanded, for not only is the moral indignation much less, but the group of which they are part is sufficiently well-knit to resist the disturbance caused within it. Not only is the wrong a lesser one because the wronged person has other associations with the wrongdoer which mitigate the offense, but social equilibrium has not been disturbed to a degree which other sanctions making for good relations cannot rectify. [Howell, 1954:24]

Gulliver (1963:1) confirms this for the Arusha: "The significant jural factors are not only the kind of injury involved, but the social relationship between the two persons and the position of each in the structure of his society." If the relationship between groups is altered, the standards of deviance and its sanctions are altered too. For example, as long as the communities are in a state of feud, it is unlikely that disputes between families associated with opponent communities would ever be settled; however, the situation is substantially altered if the feud is composed (Howell, 1954:25).

Many writers have reported that acts committed against other tribes with whom there is no recognized relationship are not really considered deviant. About the Nuer, a segmentary society, Howell (1954:25) reports that

> The sanctions for composition operated along lines of social cleavage, being less intense and therefore less effective the greater the structural distance. A man of one tribe could rarely hope to exact compensation for an injury inflicted by someone of another tribe unless there were other links between them that extended beyond the political limits of the tribe. Similarly, an individual living within one primary segment would find it difficult to get compensation from an individual living in another primary segment unless there were other ties between them, usually kinship or marital ties, which made composition mutually advantageous.

About the Barotse, a state society, Gluckman (1965:204) reports that he "heard very few cases arising out of a variety of wrongs committed by people on others previously unrelated to them." Among the Tiv, a segmentary society, it is even considered a serious breach of manners to interfere in the business of anyone with whom one is not acquainted. "The *jir* (court—HDS) often has trouble in getting witnesses of this sort, even though the number of people who have seen an act is legion" (Bohannan, 1957:39).

The theorem that *the more intimate social relations among groups, the higher the perceived magnitude of deviance of an act* (because there is little or no need to mobilize the integrative function of deviance) explains why leopard societies or the Mau Mau employ such extremes of social deviance as described. It takes very little deviance to integrate closely related groups, but very much deviance to integrate socially distant ones.

The other extreme, deviance within the smallest social unit, is considered a serious wrong, actually more serious than any other wrong, but no sanctions are imposed because no relationship between groups has been disturbed; hence the integration effect of sanctions is not needed. For example, patricide or fratricide are acts that are almost on a par with suicide. But no action against the offender is taken because compensation would be given by the same group that receives it. Howell (1954: 62) reports that "in such circumstances the Nuer find the greatest difficulty in understanding why the (colonial-HDS) Government would seek to punish the culprit, and the Nuer court will usually resist an attempt to do so." Similarly,

> breaches of the rules of exogamy and incestuous extra-marital intercourse are not generally the subject of dispute or of litigation in the courts. Both parties are equally guilty, there is no question of compensation, and the spiritual contamination . . . falls equally on both parties and even upon their relatives. [Howell, 1954:82–83]

Sanctions, in these cases, are merely ritual.

Sanctioning Mechanism and Social Integration

As an intervening variable, sanctioning mechanisms may be crucial in the relationship between social deviance and social integration. It has been shown that before sanctions are imposed, it is the expectation of sanctions that leads to the integration process *within* each of the two groups concerned. The actual sanctioning process leads to integration processes *between* two groups.

The literature about the sanctioning process in our society frequently stresses that it is more likely to increase the alienation of the wrongdoer from society than to reintegrate him. Since the sanctioning process in African societies is essentially geared at integration, it may be expected to be governed by different principles.

Proverbially, one may characterize the sanctioning process in our society as being governed by the principle of "a life for a life" (including the case that a life sentence has been substituted for the actual taking of a life), whereas the African sanctioning process may be characterized as being governed by the principle of "a wife for a life." This is certainly an oversimplification but it well illustrates the insensitivity of our sanctioning process to the need for a restoration of social relations that are disturbed by a deviant act—

social relations that may in fact deteriorate further *because* of the sanctions imposed. The African sanctioning process, however, is very sensitive to the need for social integration, and the sanctions imposed may not only restore the web of social relations but may even strengthen it: for instance by linking the families of the killer and the victim by marriage ties knit as a compensation—without payment of the otherwise customary bride price—for the death of a member of one of the two families.

Sanctions Administered through Moots

The two principal sanctioning mechanisms in small-scale societies are indemnification administered by a moot, and retaliation or self-help directed at an indemnity or at life. An indemnity is something of value given by a person or group to another person or group as compensation for a wrong (Radcliffe-Brown, 1952:210). Among the Nuer, for example, the indemnity for adultery is six head of cattle, and for homicide it is forty head of cattle (Howell, 1954:25). The probability that the indemnity is paid in full, in part, or not at all depends upon the kind of social relationship between the two groups concerned. The payment of indemnities aims directly at the restoration and strengthening of the web of social relations that are disturbed by the deviant act. This is discussed in more detail in a later section of this chapter.

The moot as an adjudicative institution relying on indemnification as its main sanction is found in all types of African societies: both state and stateless. In state societies, it is complementary to the formalized court system and may be considered as the major expression of adjudicatory decentralization. In stateless societies, it is either the only adjudicative institution, or it parallels retaliation or self-help. Moots are nothing specific to Africa. In Old English, the term "moot" refers to town meetings, that is, the settlement of disputes by the important members of the village. Bohannan (1964:202) reports that, "Well into the twelfth and thirteenth centuries, Anglo-Saxon communities settled their disputes by meeting outside, under the shade of a tree, in whole communities, in order to discover correct and just solutions to disputes. Such is, in a sense, the origin of the common law." Gibbs (1963) Africanizes the term as "house palaver," that is, an institution for the informal settlement of disputes within or between families or kinship groups using a third party as an adjudicator. Gibbs (1963) has analyzed the moot and its conciliatory and therapeutic functions from a psychoanalytic point of view. Among the Kpelle in Liberia, the moot is "an informal airing of a dispute which takes place before an assembled group which includes kinsmen of the litigants and neighbors from the quarter where the case is being heard. It is a completely *ad hoc* group, varying greatly in composition from case to case" (Gibbs, 1963:3). Gibbs (1963:1) found that it is "based on a covert application of the principles of psychoanalytic theory which underlie psychotherapy." Although Gibbs describes moots mainly in domestic settings, his findings apply similarly to intergroup disputes. Compared with court procedures, the airing of grievances in the moot is more complete and results in a more harmonious solution because of the following factors:

1. The hearing takes place soon after a breach has occurred, before the grievances have hardened.
2. The hearing takes place in the familiar surroundings of a home.
3. Investigatory initiative rests to a large extent with the parties themselves.
4. The range of relevance applied to matters that are brought out is extremely broad: hardly anything mentioned is held to be irrelevant.

Any solution reached is highly consensual, the adjudicator, chosen by the two parties themselves, acting mainly as a mediator. The following factors are responsible for the high probability that the solution is accepted by both parties:

1. There is no unilateral ascription of blame; fault is attributed to both parties.
2. The mediator is not backed by political authority and the physical force that underlies it; hence, decisions are not imposed.
3. Sanctions are not so burdensome as to cause hardship to the losing party or to give grounds for a new grudge against the other party.
4. There is a ritualized apology at the end of the moot symbolizing very concretely the consensual nature of the solution. Both parties publicly offer and accept tokens of apology indicating that each party has no further grievance and that the settlement is satisfactory and mutually acceptable. The parties *and the spectators* drink together to symbolize the restored solidarity of the group (that is, the two parties within the wider social context) and the rehabilitation of the offending party. [Gibbs, 1963:5]

Gibbs (1963:6–8) found that the moot goes beyond reconciliation, it is therapeutic. It involves support, permissiveness, denial of reciprocity, and manipulation of reward that Parsons (1951:314–319) claims are the elements of therapy:

1. *Support:* In the moot, the parties are encouraged in the expression of their complaints and feelings because they sense group support; the very presence of one's kinsmen and neighbors demonstrates their concern.
2. *Permissiveness:* Everyday restrictions on antisocial statements or impulses are lessened. This permissiveness results in *catharsis*. In a familiar setting, with familiar people, the parties to the moot feel at ease and free to say all that is on their minds. Nothing should be left to embitter and undermine the decision.
3. *Denial of reciprocity:* Permissiveness in therapy requires that the therapist will not respond in kind when the patient acts in a hostile manner or

with inappropriate affection. However, the denial is only of congruent response, not of any response whatsoever. In the moot, the parties are allowed to hurl recriminations that, in the courtroom, would be punished as contempt of court.

4. *Reward:* In therapy, the patient is coaxed to conformity by the granting of rewards. The most important reward of the moot is group approval that goes to the wronged person who accepts an apology and to the person who is magnanimous enough to make one.

At the end, the wrongdoer is restored to good grace and is once again acting like an "upright Kpelle" (although he may of course refuse to accept the decision of the moot). He is eased into this position by being grouped with others to whom blame is also allocated; typically, he is not singled out and isolated in being labeled deviant. Sanctions are positive (institutionalized apology, praise, and acts of concern and affection), not negative (fines, jail sentences) as in our courts. That way, the moot avoids the vicious cycle phenomenon that each step taken to curb deviance has the effect of driving the deviant further into deviance (Gibbs, 1963:6–9). Gulliver (1963:2) found similar principles operative in Arusha society.

Sanctions Administered through Self-Help

Retaliation or self-help as a sanctioning mechanism is found predominantly in societies without legal process, that is, without a formal court system. Retaliation in these societies is not as Durkheim assumed a system of blind revenge in which two parties inflict the maximum injury they can on each other. Rather, there are "socially approved, controlled and limited acts of revenge" (Radcliffe-Brown, 1952:209) that are "reduced to system" (Redfield, 1967:11). In his study of African sociolegal systems, Carlston (1968:412) found that, "Measures of self-help, including the blood feud, tend to be subject to procedural rules designed to limit the retribution or reparation which is exacted so that it is proportionate to the injury offered. Measures of self-help directed to inflicting violence upon the group to which a wrongdoer belongs may be subject to procedural rules designed to control the weapons employed so that less dangerous weapons are used for less serious offenses." Two types of self-help or retaliation may be distinguished; one directed against the property and the other directed against the life of the members of another group. In both types, success depends largely upon the extent to which the wronged and the wrongdoer are supported by their respective groups (Gulliver, 1963:2). If an action is considered justified and the group decides to seize a certain number of cattle from the other group, then

the wronged may receive the assistance of their own kinsmen and neighbors, who will overwhelm any attempt at resistance. This applies to groups of indi-

viduals in relations to other groups in the same way, and is expressed in the
balanced opposition of tribal segments and kinship groups. A Nuer may owe
one of his kinsmen a cow and refuse to pay it. His kinsmen will take the
cow by stealth or wrest it from him by force, and the success of this action
will depend on the extent of the non-intervention of other relatives. [Howell,
1954:23]

Similarly, a Tiv who seized a goat will be defended by his kinsmen if the
others try to retaliate; however, if he has taken the goat inappropriately,
that is, if he has a "bad case," his kinsfolk will not risk their hides and their
reputations for him (Bohannan, 1964:204). It must be stressed that this type
of licensed seizure is fundamentally different from theft for which the thief
can produce no customary justification. Howell (1954:199) even asserts that
"a man will never steal a cow from a fellow tribesman merely because he
wants one." It is only from persons belonging to neighboring tribes that he has
no hesitation in stealing cows; but this is not considered in any way wrong—
because of the relativity of deviance that limits wrongness to acts between
groups in a meaningful social relationship to each other. On principle,
retaliation directed at property serves the same purpose as the payment of a
compensation and can be interpreted as being geared at social integration the
same way (see: "Social Deviance and the Web of Obligations" in this chapter).
At the first look, retaliation directed at life seems to fall into a different category because, "To kill a person of the other group restored the balance by
reducing their number proportionately, but it was a negative way of dealing
with a situation which required more positive action if a permanent feud was
to be avoided" (Howell, 1954:41). What are the conditions, then, that
determine which one of the two alternatives is chosen? The discussion of
the relativity of deviance hypothesized: the larger the social distance between
groups, the lower then is the probability of imposing sanctions, but the
greater is the magnitude of sanctions. This theorem answers the question:
a feud, that is, a sanctioning mechanism directed at a maximum magnitude of
sanctions, namely life, is more likely to arise between socially distant groups
for whom the need for integration is low. A conflict between closely related
groups is more likely to be settled by retaliation directed at property that
implies that a smaller indemnification than life is sufficient to restore the
relationship and that the probability of imposing sanctions is higher. The
reason for a high need for and a high probability of sanctions between closely
related groups is obvious: "Two tertiary tribal segments, for example, previously hostile might have to settle their differences because of the threat of
violence from another and less closely related segment of the tribe" (Howell,
1954: 41). However, if it is correct that deviance in African societies has
such a strong integrative function as claimed, one may wonder why there
are any feuds at all directed against the life of members of other groups. A
feud has an integrative function in a double sense. Anascopically (Geiger,

1962: 147–150), it is a powerful integrative force *within* a segment because the threat to life is more likely to unite the members of a group into a closely knit unit than the threat to property. From a catascopic point of view, however, integration may not only be seen as a process that welds the segments of a society into solid units but at the same time as a process aiming at the maintenance of the general integration level of the whole society. This means that segments in a given social distance from each other are to be kept at that distance and prevented from merging. Without a mechanism directed at that goal, segmentary societies would very soon change into centralized states. Hence the dual integrative function of the feud: it integrates segments and keeps society segmented. Howell (1954: 40) observed this among the Nuer: ". . . the spread of a state of feud follows . . . generally the lines of social cleavage, and gives emphasis to the segmentation of the tribe."

Retaliation and indemnification are the main sanctioning mechanisms for deviant acts committed between different groups in segmentary societies. These societies are politically decentralized and do not recognize any central authority, neither in the political nor in the judicial realm. Political and judicial roles are typically performed on an *ad hoc* basis. That is, as the need for the exercise of political or adjudication roles arises, a person is chosen—usually very democratically—for that particular task: a war against a neighboring tribe or a judgment in a particular case.

The Institutionalization of Social Deviance

Durkheim considered social deviance as a consequence of the structural (or negatively: anomical) situation of society. Depending upon the degree of "health" or "sickness" of the "organism" *society,* in some mystical way social deviance would result—hence not an individual but a social phenomenon. For African societies, it has been shown that the reverse is equally true: society produces social deviance in order to maintain its specific anomical (or positively: "structural") situation. Society producing deviance, or deviance producing society are but two aspects of the same process, at least in relatively simple societies. In complex societies as our own, there are "functional alternatives" producing society.

Since social deviance plays such a crucial role in African societies, they do not rely on some mystical way of producing deviance (comparable to the way societies produce a more or less steady rate of suicide as described by Durkheim) but rather institutionalize it. The institutionalization of deviance in African societies is directed toward keeping social deviance at an equilibrium level where it prevents society from overintegration (fusion of its segments) and from disintegration. Two aspects of the institutionalization of deviance may be distinguished: (1) it may be directed toward guaranteeing the continued existence of social deviance; or (2) it may be directed toward one form of deviance that is integrative or at least not disintegrative as a substitute for other—disintegrative—forms of deviance.

Most actual cases of institutionalized deviance have both aspects, although one may prevail over the other. Some examples of institutionalized deviance follow.

Dual Structuring

In many societies, macrostructural conflict, or, taking conflict as a type of deviance, macrostructural deviance is built right into the social system by using the balanced opposition of segments or moieties as a structural principle. Among the Gusii and Nuer, LeVine (1960: 51) found that, "Two segments of equal level within the tribe would combine to fight a different tribe, but would conduct blood feuds against each other at times." Among the Arusha where even the polygynous nuclear family is divided into two groups of co-wives, Gulliver (1963: 72, 110) found that "bifurcate segmentation (is) a principle of social structure . . . and it is essential to regular social processes." On a more general level, Carlston (1968: 393) found that African societies

> exhibiting kinship structures of social action may order such structures into a series of levels of similar but opposing kinship groups, with (1) the kinship groups in each level being identified by descent from a common ancestor of the same degree of remoteness or structural distance from the last-born generation and (2) each kinship group in the same level being perceived to be in opposition to the others yet successively united in more inclusive kinship groups at higher levels identified by common descent from an ancestor of an increasingly remote structural distance from the last-born generation. This dual structuring of kinship groups enables the performance of exogamic, political, dispute-settlement, and war functions.

The two aspects of institutionalized deviance are apparent: dual structure guarantees the maintenance of structural opposition rather than leading to a fusion of the segments of society. It provides a setting for exogamic, political, dispute-settlement, and war-alliance relations rather than leaving the relationship anomic and the social field open for *any* type of deviant act. At the same time, allegiance, or exclusion from allegiance, can be determined in any situation of conflict and dispute by means of the principle of dichotomy: "The group or category of smallest scale of which the two disputants are both members is divisible into its two segments . . . , such that each segment contains one of the disputants, and the other members of that segment are automatically his supporters." (Gulliver, 1963: 118).

Fission and Fusion

Tensions within a group or between related groups may rise to the point that they result in deviant acts. In most cases, there is a vested interest in reconciliation that is achieved through these deviant acts and the subsequent sanctioning processes. However, if groups have grown much beyond the customary size of groups and/or if tensions have become insurmountable, there is in segmentary societies an institutionalized alternative to civil strife: fission. In those cases where the group that splits away is too small to form its own segment, it may fuse with some other segment. Fission may be seen primarily in terms of a mechanism preventing other forms of deviance, namely, civil strife. However, by splitting away a group becomes a new segment that represents a potential for conflict with other groups—the first aspect that was previously discussed (see Carlston, 1968: 36, 404–405).

Nonfinality of Settlement

In many African societies, the two parties may agree to a partial rather than a full restitution for a deviant act. Among the Nuer, for instance, "in a dispute over adultery, the wronged husband may eventually agree to accept only three head of cattle. Even though there may be little chance of getting the remainder, his face is saved because six head is the established custom and the rest will be due to him in the form of a debt" (Howell, 1954:26). This practice has even been overtaken by the Nuer courts that were introduced by the colonial government that may order the making of part of the payment immediately and the remainder at an unspecified later time. In a more general sense, Gluckman (1965:8) states that "disputes in these groups of kind can never be finally settled," ramifying through the whole network of ties that bind various kin to one another. During each dispute, kin who are ostensibly outside the quarrel at issue side with one of the litigants; the way in which they take sides is influenced by degrees of kinship, by factional alignments within villages, and by past records of friendships and hostilities. This nonfinality of settlement in itself may be considered a deviant state of affairs. At the same time, it invites minor deviant acts, such as quarrels over the outstanding debt or even acts of self-help as described previously, which then may become a new focus of dispute. Directing the interest of the parties concerned to these minor acts of deviance may also serve as a substitute for graver offenses.

"Joking Relationships"

Joking relationships, defined as relations "between two persons in which one is by custom permitted, and in some instances required, to tease or make fun of the other, who in turn is required to take no offence" (Radcliffe-Brown, 1952:90), are extremely widespread in Africa and in other parts of the world. They are typically found in relations that are particularly strenuous and have to be prevented from being alienated, as among relatives by marriage. They may also exist between clans and even tribes, as, for instance, between the Sukuma and Zaramu, the Sukuma and Zigua, and the Ngoni and Bemba. (Radcliffe-Brown, 1952: 91, 94). The dual aspect of institutionalized deviance in joking relationships—modes of organizing a definite and stable system of social behavior in which conjunctive and disjunctive components are maintained and combined—has been noted by Radcliffe-Brown (1952: 92):

> Any serious hostility is prevented by the playful antagonism of teasing, and this in its regular repetition is a constant expression or reminder of that social disjunction which is one of the essential components of the relation, while the social conjunction is maintained by the friendliness that takes no offence at insult.

An alternative to joking relationship is avoidance.

Rites of Reversal

Centralized societies may provide rites of reversal as institutionalized outlets for political tensions which would otherwise lead to rebellion. Such rites typically reverse the usual authority role relationship, for example, rites of reversal may require a king to walk naked through the people and to accept humiliation without reprisal. This ritual protest against the established order implies that the order as such is accepted. "Once there is questioning of the social order, the ritual of protest is inappropriate, since the purpose of the ritual is to unite people who do not or cannot query their social roles" (Gluckman, 1955: 134). The same type of political conflict that is aired in rituals of rebellion among the centralized Zulu and Swazi is also found among the Barotse, another centralized society, but without such rituals. Among the Barotse, these conflicts are built into an elaborate series of councils (Gluckman, 1955: 133), comparable in their function of institutionalizing conflict to dual and segmentary structuring as previously described.

Deviant Organizations

Reference has been made to leopard societies and similar deviant organizations and to the strongly integrative function of the use of extreme types of deviance. Beatty's (1915) detailed descriptions of leopard societies in Sierra Leone point to the interkin group and intertribal integration achieved by these societies. They have to be seen in conjunction with Poro, an intertribal secret society to which *every* adult free-born male in most tribes of Eastern Sierra Leone and Western Liberia belongs. It seems that the integrative function of Poro alone is not sufficient to handle the task of bringing about integration *within* tribes (none of which is strongly centralized) and a minimum level of integration *between* tribes. To understand to what extent leopard societies are accepted by society in general, it is crucial to realize the strength of ties between leopard societies and Poro: "Every member of the Human Leopard Society is a member of the Poro, the main supporters of both societies are the chiefs, the place of meeting for both societies is the Poro bush . . ." (Beatty, 1915: 20). Institutionalization implies control. That is, if deviant organizations become deviant, control mechanisms start operating. One such mechanism is the Tongo play in Sierra Leone. Alldrige (1901: 156–159), writing about the Sherbro in Sierra Leone, reports that, "As soon as the Tongo players determined to comply with a request from a chief (to investigate into acts of murder and anthropophagy committed by leopard societies—HDS), they sent out their emissaries into his towns and villages to obtain information concerning suspected people. . . . In the investigation one village at a time was dealt with. A messenger was dispatched to call all the men, women, and children to a meeting to be held on an appointed day." During this meeting, either a trial was held in conjunction with an ordeal, or a "play" or dance was performed during which the guilty were discovered. They were usually clubbed and burned to death (see also Beatty, 1915: 21). Leopard societies are probably the most extreme case of institutionalized deviance in African societies. The two aspects of institutionalized deviance are again apparent: their very existence guarantees the maintenance of a certain level of deviance—for integrative purposes; at the same time, by creating inter-kin group and inter-tribal ties, they prevent other forms of deviance, at least temporarily, namely wars.

Social Deviance and the Web of Obligations

One of the most basic social categories of traditional African societies is the *obligation*. In fact, the *web of obligations* in these societies is to be considered as a synonym for *social structure*. As an example of a state society, we report Gluckman's (1965: 242) finding that, ". . . the Barotse conceive of all relationships, whether of established status or ensuing from either 'contract' or tort, in terms of 'debt.' " It is to be noted that the Barotse use only a single word to express the meaning of "right" and "duty," which is derived from a verbal form that can be translated as "ought." The same was found among the Tiv, a stateless society, by Bohannan (1957: 112): "The idea of contract takes, for purposes of classification, a subordinate position to the idea of the debt involved." In fact, *debt* is an aspect on which Tiv classify:

> The Tiv word for this classification, *injô,* covers a wider range of phenomena and social relations than the English word "debt" usually does. If I borrow money or goods and fail to repay, I have "fallen into debt" (*gba injô*). Furthermore, if I have agreed to care for some of my kinsman's livestock, this stock and its natural increase are my debt or *injô* to him. Still further, if my animal damages a neighbour's field the matter "becomes a debt.". . . Many Tiv personal relationships are expressed in terms of debt. If my ward has married into a lineage which has not provided me or one of my close kinsmen with a wife, it is their *injô* to do so, even though there may be no actual bridewealth debt. The matter of "flesh debts" covers one of the primary problems of social relationships as expressed in terms of witchcraft and religious belief. [Bohannan, 1957:102]

Gluckman (1965: 242) claims that all early law is a *law of debt* or a *law of obligations*. Malinowski (1926: 18–23) asserts that obligations are the basic principle of Melanesian economics:

> The ownership and use of the canoe consist of a series of definite obligations and duties uniting a group of people into a working team . . . Thus on a close inquiry we discover . . . a definite system of division of function and a rigid system of mutual obligations, into which a sense of duty and the recognition of the need of cooperation enter side by side with a realization of self-interest, privileges and benefits,

the enforcement mechanism being reciprocity. Malinowski (1926: 22) found obligations being at the root of social relations throughout the whole social system, for example, ". . . in the Trobriands there is not one single mortuary act, not one ceremony, which is not considered to be an obligation of the performer towards some of the other survivors," and arguing on a most general level: ". . . in all social relations and in all the various domains of tribal life, exactly the same legal mechanism can be traced, that it places the *binding obligations* in a special category and sets them apart from other types of customary rules." (Malinowski, 1926: 39).

An obligation may be defined as the probability of transferring anything perceived by society as scarce or valuable. It was claimed that the web of obligations constitutes the social structure. To test this proposition, we assume that the above probability becomes zero. According to the definition, this implies that there is no obligation. Hence, there is no social relationship, or a previous social relationship is terminated if the probability of transferring the valuables implied by a particular obligation becomes zero. Of the evidence, we cite only the rule among the Nuer that failures to fulfill obligations are grounds for divorce, that is, the termination of a marital relationship. Such failures to fulfill obligations are barrenness, laziness, continued adultery, desertion, impotence or sterility of the husband, stinginess, failure to support wife, and ill-treatment (Howell 1954: 141–144). Most important in this context are procreative obligations. The Nuer are very legalistic about the implications of our hypothesis. They conclude that if the probability of transferring the goods, services, and the like which are constitutive for a particular obligation cannot become zero, then the social relationship derived from that obligation cannot be dissolved: "Nuer consider that the dissolution of marriage, instituted by either party, is impossible if the wife has fulfilled her procreative obligations" (Howell, 1954: 148).

Our definition of deviance and obligation places the two in a very special relationship to each other: *deviance is the probability of incurring obligations: actually and/or ideally.* Sanctioning processes are then mechanisms of enforcing the fulfillment of obligations. This is very clearly expressed by Bohannan (1957: 137): among the Tiv, "all institutions of self-help are seen, by the persons who use them, as mechanisms for . . . making other people perform their obligations." The same is true for the Nuer where "a man may seize for himself cattle which he regards as his just due in compensation for some injury done to him by their owner." (Howell, 1954: 199). By that very act, however, the wronged party also incurs an obligation toward the wrong-doer party. Thus arises the web of obligations as an emanation of deviance. Needless to say as deviance involves groups rather than individuals, obligations arise between groups rather than individuals.

The crucial role played by deviance now becomes apparent: society is but a web of obligations, and deviance is the process of producing obligations.

An example of this set of relationship is the widespread practice of "subletting wives." In most African societies, the standard of living is basically egalitarian, the wealthy cannot eat more than a certain amount of food, they cannot wear luxurious clothes when only materials such as skin, barkcloth, and a little cotton are available, or live in a palace when habitations are made of skin, grass, or mud. Hence, the wealthy and powerful do not form a separate "class," cut off from the poor by a different life style. In fact, rich and poor may be kin to one another, and intermarriage is possible without provoking a public scandal. The social consequence of this situation is that "the powerful and wealthy use the lands and goods they control to attract followers, and a man's prestige is determined by the number of dependents or subjects he has, much more than by mere possession and use of goods. Prestige and power are important and enable a man to control the actions of others; but he gains that control through establishing relationships of personal dependence with as many others as he can" (Gluckman, 1965: 4–5). These relationships of personal dependence arise out of obligations that are largely produced by deviance. Hence deviance may be skillfully used to create or increase one's number of followers. In many societies, a man may "sublet" his wives— often for indefinite periods. The deviance it involves—adultery—makes the legal husband the owner of obligations and thus creates a clientele. The group which thence arises is held together by a web of obligations arising out of deviance. No moral stigma is attached to this practice.

The relationship between deviance and obligations brings to light an aspect of social order that is inherent in any deviance and obligation: the aspect of dualism. One form of this was discussed in a previous section entitled "The Institutionalization of Social Deviance" that is dual structuring. According to Malinowski (1923: 25),

> The dual principle is neither the result of "fusion" nor "splitting" nor of any other sociological cataclysm. It is the integral result of the inner symmetry of all social transactions, of the reciprocity of services, without which no primitive community could exist . . . symmetry of structure . . . as the indispensable basis of reciprocal obligations.

II: Large-Scale African Societies

Large-scale African societies are more differentiated and more centralized than small scale societies. However, they are not as differentiated and centralized as modernized societies. In fact, the element of decentralization is a feature of any, even the most centralized, nonmodernized society. "However despotic their rulers, relatively nonmodernized societies are never stable without major provisions for decentralization. The major structure of decentralization in the last analysis is always the actual if not ideal autonomy of the nearly self-sufficient units within the sphere of their own devices" (Levy, 1966:100). This puts complex African societies into an intermediate position where they have certain features in common with simple African as well as modernized Western societies.

Because of their emphasis on decentralization, complex societies share the basic features of deviance in simple societies: deviance is the prime mechanism of integration, the units of intregration being groups rather than individuals; since deviance functions as an integrative mechanism, the deviant act is not considered immoral, nor are groups or persons labeled as deviant; societal reactions to deviance are directed toward reintegration rather than alienation of the deviant; secondary deviance is avoided. The higher the degree of complexity and of centralization, however, the higher is the probability of finding *simultaneously* a tendency to use mechanisms other than deviance for integration to emphasize groups *and* individuals as units of integration, to consider deviant acts as immoral, to label groups or persons as deviant, to alienate the deviant, and to create secondary deviance. One of the most telling accounts of this tendency is found in Rattray's (1929) description of the highly centralized Ashanti kingdom. Rattray (1929: 294) reports the existence of *Oman Akyiwdie,* "things hateful to the tribe" that were considered as "sins" to be punished immediately by the central authority. He (1929: 372–378) also found labeling to be widespread and little concern about reconciliation and rehabilitation. The strongest sanction among the Ashanti was the label of derision or ridicule. Rattray gives examples of people who carried the label of ridicule even for acts that are only slightly deviant. He reports cases in which the ridiculed were so ashamed that they committed suicide—another ("secondary") deviant act considered far more severe by the Ashanti than anything the ridiculed could have possibly committed before. Rattray also reports the widespread use of capital punishment (decapitation, strangling, clubbing, or mutilation of the ears, lips, nose, and genitals as a substitute), flogging, imprisonment, imposing of fines and of enslavement as a punishment by the central authority. This testifies clearly to the existence of the principle of individual responsibility as found in modern societies. At the same time, however, "corporate responsibility for every act was an established principle that survived even the advent of a powerful central public authority as the administrator of public justice" (Rattray, 1929: 286). Sanctioning mechanisms in complex African societies are in part identical with those in simple societies. The moot is an important institution for the settlement of disputes in both types of societies. The conclusions Beattie (1957: 194–195) reaches about the role and effectiveness of the moots ("neighbors courts" in his terminology) in the Banyoro kingdom of Uganda are similar to those of Gibbs. In the words of an informant, the moot's aim is "to finish off people's quarrels and to abolish bad feelings." As in the Kpelle moot, the losing party is asked to provide beer and meat, which is shared with the other party and all those attending the *rukurato* (moot). This feast is not to be viewed primarily as a penalty, for the wrongdoer acts as host and also shares in the food and drink. "It is a praiseworthy thing; from a dishonourable status he is promoted to an honourable one . . . and reintegrated into the community."

Whereas the moot operates in both simple and complex societies and is *relatively* independent from the degree of complexity, self-help as a sanctioning mechanism varies inversely with the size of societies. In complex and centralized large-scale African societies, self-help is, if it occurs, a deviant act rather than a legitimate sanctioning mechanism. Its substitute in centralized societies is the court as a mechanism of administering sanctions.

In centralized African societies, legal sanctions are backed by the power of judicial authorities to inflict punishment. Actually, Bohannan (1964: 199) asserts that, "Africa is one of the homes of advanced legal institutions." This is particularly true for the Bantu states where the local or provincial chief is one of a number of judges on a large and inclusive bench. The bench includes representatives of all of the important social groups of the community. The judges form a regular and pronounced hierarchy and are seated in a row or an arc. Judgment is passed up the hierarchy, starting with the youngest judge and ending with the highest whose decision is final (Bohannan, 1964: 199–200). Similarly, "Among the Barotse we are dealing with a powerful kingship exercising its authority through a hierarchy of councils which acted as parliaments, executives, and courts of justice" (Gluckman, 1965: 4).

Previously, it has been asserted that sanctioning processes in our society frequently alienate the wrongdoer from society, whereas in most African societies they are directed toward integration and reintegration. An explanation for this difference is in order before evaluating the role of deviance in African states with a court system and nonstates without a court system. In every society there is conflict between individuals and groups representing, or resulting in, deviant acts. These are the centri- or sociofugal forces that tend to drive the units of society apart. To keep society in its present form, namely some kind of a coherent and integrated social system, counteracting mechanisms are needed, centri- or sociopetal forces that weld the units of society together. In highly differentiated societies, usually special institutions, for example, the bureaucratic administration of a centralized political organization, keep society integrated. In undifferentiated societies without such unifunctional institutions, some of the more basic multifunctional social processes have to fulfill that function. Such a basic process is social deviance that is not just an outburst of antisocial tendencies but serves an integrative function in itself and/or in conjunction with subsequent sanctioning processes. Simple societies cannot afford the luxury of wasting the integrative potential of social deviance, whereas highly differentiated societies can, and do.

Centralized African societies are in an intermediate position where they still have to rely to some extent on the integrative functions of social deviance and its sanctions and at the same time, either to some extent or at times, on the centralized political system for the integration of society. That means that in many cases they may be concerned about not alienating individuals or groups from their social environment by the type of sanctions imposed or about reconciling individuals or groups in conflict. In fact, some of Gluckman's (1965) descriptions of trials in the Barotse kingdom very closely resemble Gibbs' and Beattie's descriptions of the moot. In other cases, however, the punishment inflicted by courts may be guided by quite different principles, as Rattray (1929: 292) asserts for the Ashanti kingdom—principles he considers a consequence of centralization:

> In the olden days, before the rise of a powerful class of aristocracy, the chief aim of such authority as existed seemed to have been the avoidance of possible causes of dispute and the conciliation of the parties temporarily estranged by litigation. In more modern times an exactly opposite result would appear to have become the goal of a central authority, which found itself powerful enough to quell serious disputes, if necessary by force, and came to rely on the proceeds of litigation as a fruitful means of replenishing a depleted treasury. Litigation, in this somewhat degenerate epoch, came actually to be encouraged. Having given a decision, the courts were indifferent whether conciliation between the parties took place or not. . . . Prayers were offered to the gods to send cases. [See also Hoebel, 1954: 233]

If such centralized societies fail to make use of the integrative functions of deviance and its sanctions (that is, if they fail to decentralize—Levy, 1966: 100), they are likely to disintegrate and break into their tribal segments as happened frequently in the history of Africa; it is only in relatively modernized societies that other institutions are, in the long run, strong enough to guarantee the cohesion of society.

This proposition may be expressed in more general terms: *the more centralized a society, the lower is the probability that it relies on deviance alone for the maintenance of integration.* That centralized societies can afford to do without the integrative function of deviance was explained by referring to the fact that they have developed specialized integrative institutions. However, why they in fact choose the specialized institutions over deviance is to be explained by our theory of the relativity of deviance and of its sanctions: the less intimate a social relationship, the less serious is a deviant act and the lower the probability of reintegration. Since centralized societies "are usually amalgams of different ethnic groups" (Elias, 1956: 11), which are socially distant from each other, deviance involving two different ethnic groups in a centralized society has a very slight integrative effect. Hence, if integration is to be maintained, it is to be achieved by institutions other than deviance. *Within* ethnic groups, deviance may still fulfill its integrative function.

III: Toward a Theory of Deviance

Deviance in the Light of Structural-Functionalism and Conflict Theory

It is now in order to draw the major theoretical conclusion that gradually emerged out of the previous analyses. We have shown that social order, that is, the network of patterns of social interaction or the ordered system of social relationships, in short, social structure, depends essentially on deviance. Social order emerges only out of the break of social order; none can be considered *prius*. Social structure is a process *essentially* depending upon conflict or deviance, and deviance is a conflict depending *essentially* upon social structure. Both are but two aspects of the same phenomenon.

The structural-functional model rests on the assumption of a stable equilibrium created by the system-maintaining functions of the institutions of society. However, it was found that deviance, conflict, and disorder represent a central institution directed toward that equilibrium—an equilibrium that is never stable because social structure is a dynamic process. The conflict model rests on the premise of incompatible interests of individuals and/or groups that by their very nature cannot be brought into any equilibrium. But it was found that deviance is in fact directed toward an equilibrium and may actually bring it about for a point in time—even if this is only the beginning of a new series of conflict and deviance. Only permanent deviance creates integration and stability, and only that integration and stability creates deviance. Hence, the study of social deviance in Africa has led us to the conclusion that a theory of society cannot be based on either a structural-functional or a conflict model: it rests on both. The two models are not incompatible; they depict but two aspects of the same process, a process constituting society. The dispute between the two theories is the same as between Parmenides and Heraclitus of whom the former saw stability (structure) and only stability in all movement, and the latter saw movement and only movement in all stability.

Definitions

The crucial term in this chapter is *deviance*. Most of the definitions of this term are not culture-free and are thus of little applicability in the African context, and hence of a relatively low level of generality. The conventional definition of deviance as behavior contrary to norms leads to a contradiction in itself when applied to African societies because—considering norms as prescriptions for behavior—deviance has been shown to be in fact prescribed behavior, actually and ideally. The now fashionable labeling definition that considers deviance as a property conferred upon a person by others is irrelevant because small-scale African societies simply do not label—except in some very specific cases: deviance in Africa is social behavior that occurs between groups, and not between individuals or between individuals and groups; also, deviance in Africa is not a moral category. Hence, there is no basis for labeling. A definition more applicable to the African context has been suggested by Black and Reiss: individual or group behavior is deviant if it falls within a class of behavior for which there is a probability of negative sanctions subsequent to its detection.

The definition used in this chapter has gradually evolved out of the study of deviance in African societies, starting with a prescientific notion of deviance. It is claimed that the definition is of a higher level of generality than the ones previously given and is applicable in both modernized and nonmodernized societies.

1. *Deviance is that aspect of social behavior that refers to the probability of incurring social sanctions.*

2. *Social sanctions are claims to anything perceived as scarce or valuable by society,* such as goods, services, persons, life, psychic gratification, political or economic power, and the like; these claims are independent of the consent of the individuals upon whom sanctions are imposed. Combining (1) and (2), the definition can be abbreviated into:

3. *Deviance refers to the probability of incurring claims to anything perceived by society as scarce or valuable.*

   It has been shown that there is a close relationship between deviance and obligations:

4. *An obligation refers to the probability of transferring anything perceived by society as scarce or valuable.*

   This allows a redefinition of deviance for small-scale societies:

5. *Deviance refers to the probability of incurring obligations.*

   For large-scale societies, with their focus on rights rather than obligations, this definition reads:

6. *Deviance refers to the probability of incurring claims to rights.*

   In either case, the incurrence may be ideal and/or actual.

It may be noted that a transfer is a type of interaction and not of solitary action; hence, it is a social category. Obligation and deviance are patterns of action that involve two parties. Where no second party of actual individuals or groups is involved, society in the abstract may be substituted—this is the procedure in large-scale societies where many deviant acts are considered as being committed against society. The other alternative that usually occurs in small-scale societies is not to consider such action as obligation or deviance.

Propositions toward a Theory of Deviance

1. Three universals are of relevance for the study of social deviance:
    a. *In every known society, there is social deviance.*
    b. *In every known society, there are social sanctions.*
    c. *In every known society, there is social integration.*

2. Levels of social deviance, social sanctions, and social integration are intrasocietally and intersocietally variable.

3. The following three associations may be postulated:
    a. There is an association between social deviance and social sanctions.
    b. There is an association between social deviance and social integration.
    c. There is an association between social sanctions and social integration.

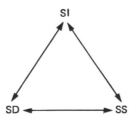

Figure 10-1: Social Deviance, Social Sanctions, and Social Integration.

4. Since social sanctions are a complement to social deviance, the three propositions may be reduced to a single proposition that constitutes the *basic theorem of deviance:*

    There is an association between social deviance (and its sanctions) and social integration.

5. The relationship is one between structure and function: social deviance is a structural device directed toward social integration as a requisite function.

6. The association between social deviance and social sanctions is probabilistic and symmetrical with regard to each other. (a) That the association is probabilistic implies that there are not only two congruent combinations of the two variables, but also incongruent combinations. (b) That the association is symmetrical implies that both incongruent combina-

tions exist: there is social deviance without sanctions; and there are social sanctions without deviance.

7. The two incongruent combinations represent inconsistencies in the system. Since systems tend to avoid inconsistencies, there is a tendency to assume supernatural deviance (for example, witchcraft) in the case of the No Deviance-Sanctions pattern and supernatural sanctions in the case of the Deviance-No Sanctions pattern (for example, damnation).

		Sanctions	
		Yes	No
Deviance	Yes	Sanctioned Deviance	Nonsanctioned Deviance
	No	Sanctioned Nondeviance	Nonsanctioned Nondeviance

Figure 10-2: Social Deviance and Social Sanctions.

8. Since the level of integration varies by the types of units to be integrated, the following *relativity theorem of deviance* can be derived from the basic theorem (4):

    There is an association between standards of deviance on the one hand and intimacy of social relations (or: levels of integration, or: types of units to be integrated and types of relationships between units to be integrated) on the other.

    With reference to standards of deviance, the *relativity theorem of deviance* may be reformulated in terms of the following propositions.

9. There is a direct association between intimacy of social relations among units and the probability of perceiving an act as deviant.

10. There is a direct association between intimacy of social relations among units and the perceived magnitude of deviance of an act. As the intimacy of social relations approximates zero, the relativity theorem of deviance leads to the following corollary:

11. *Corollary I:* No deviant acts can be committed between units that do not stand in a social relationship to each other. Without a social relationship, there is no need for social integration; without a need for social integration, there is no need for deviance. As intimacy of social relations tends to infinity, the relativity theorem of deviance leads to the following corollary:

12. *Corollary II:* When social relations are most intimate, the probability of perceiving an act as deviant and the perceived magnitude of deviance of a given act are highest.

13. Since social sanctions are a complement to social deviance, propositions (8) to (12) may be reformulated into a *relativity theorem of sanctions,*

and its derivatives. The relationship between social deviance and social sanctions with regard to social integration is asymmetrical.

14. There is an association between standards of sanctions on the one hand and intimacy of social relations on the other.

    With reference to standards of sanctions, the relativity theorem of sanctions may be reformulated in terms of propositions (15) and (16).

15. There is a direct association between intimacy of social relations among units and the probability of sanctions.

16. There is an inverse association between intimacy of social relations and magnitude of sanctions.

    As the intimacy of social relations approximates zero, the relativity theorem of sanctions leads to proposition:

17. *Corollary I:* No sanctions are imposed between units that do not stand in a social relationship to each other.

    As the intimacy of social relations approaches infinity, the relativity theorem of deviance leads to proposition:

18. *Corollary II:* When social relations are most intimate, the probability of imposing sanctions is highest and the magnitude of sanctions is lowest.

References

Alldrige, T. J., 1901. *The Sherbro and its Hinterland.* London: The Macmillan Company.

Allott, Anthony, 1960. *Essays in African Law: With Special Reference to the Law of Ghana.* London: Butterworths.

Beattie, J. H. M., 1957. "Informal Judicial Activity in Bunyoro." *Journal of African Administration* 9: 188–195.

Beatty, K. J., 1915. *Human Leopards: An Account of the Trials of Human Leopards Before the Special Commission Court; with a Note on Sierra Leone, Past and Present.* London: Hugh Rees, Ltd.

Bohannan, Paul, 1957. *Justice and Judgment Among the Tiv.* London: Oxford University Press.

Bohannan, Paul, ed., 1960. *African Homicide and Suicide.* Princeton: Princeton University Press.

Bohannan, Paul, 1964. *Africa and Africans.* Garden City, N.Y.: The Natural History Press.

Carlston, Kenneth S., 1968. *Social Theory and African Tribal Organization: The Development of Socio-Legal Theory.* Urbana: University of Illinois Press.

Durkheim, Emile, 1933. *The Division of Labor in Society.* New York: The Free Press.

Durkheim, Emile, 1938. *The Rules of Sociological Method*. Chicago: The University of Chicago Press.

Durkheim, Emile, 1951. *Suicide: A Study in Sociology*. New York: The Free Press.

Elias, T. Olawale, 1956. *The Nature of African Customary Law*. Manchester: Manchester University Press.

Erikson, Kai T., 1966. *Wayward Puritans: A Study in the Sociology of Deviance*. New York: John Wiley Sons, Inc.

Geiger, Theodor, 1962. *Arbeiten zur Soziologie*. Neuwied: Luchterhand.

Geiger, Theodor, 1964. *Vorstudien zu einer Soziologie des Rechts*. Neuwied: Luchterhand.

Gibbs, James L., Jr., 1962. "Poro Values and Courtroom Procedures in a Kpelle Chiefdom." *Southwestern Journal of Anthropology* 18: 341–350.

Gibbs, James L., Jr., 1963. "The Kpelle Moot: A Therapeutic Model for the Informal Settlement of Disputes." *Africa* 33 (January): 1–11.

Gibbs, James L., Jr., 1965. "The Kpelle of Liberia." Pp. 197–240 in James L. Gibbs, Jr., ed. *Peoples of Africa*. New York: Holt, Rinehart and Winston.

Gibbs, James L., Jr., 1969. "Law and Personality: Signposts for a New Direction." Pp. 176–207 in Laura Nader, ed. *Law in Culture and Society*. Chicago: Aldine Publishing Company.

Gluckman, Max, 1954. *Rituals of Rebellion in South-East Africa*. Manchester: University Press.

Gluckman, Max, 1955. *Custom and Conflict in Africa*. Oxford: Basil Blackwell.

Gluckman, Max, 1962. "Les Rites de Passage." Pp. 1–52 in Max Gluckman, ed. *The Ritual of Social Relations*. Manchester: University Press.

Gluckman, Max, 1963. *Order and Rebellion in Tribal Africa*. New York: The Free Press.

Gluckman, Max, 1965. *The Ideas in Barotse Jurisprudence*. New Haven: Yale University Press.

Gluckman, Max, 1967. "The Judicial Process among the Barotse." Pp. 59–91 in Paul Bohannan, ed. *Law and Warfare: Studies in the Anthropology of Conflict*. Garden City: Natural History Press.

Gulliver, P. H., 1963. *Social Control in an African Society: A Study of the Arusha: Agricultural Masai of Northern Tanganyika*. Boston: Boston University Press.

Hoebel, E. Adamson, 1954. *The Law of Primitive Man: A Study in Comparative Legal Dynamics*. Cambridge: Harvard University Press.

Howell, P. P., 1954. *A Manual of Nuer Law*. London: Oxford University Press.

Joset, P. E., 1955. *Les Sociétés Secrètes des Hommes-Léopards en Afrique Noire*. Paris: Payot.

Leighton, Alexander H., et al., 1963. *Psychiatric Disorders among the Yoruba.* Ithaca: Cornell University Press.

Lemert, Edwin M., 1967. *Human Deviance, Social Problems, and Social Control.* Englewood Cliffs: Prentice-Hall, Inc.

LeVine, Robert A., 1960. "The Internalization of Political Values in Stateless Societies." *Human Organization* 19: 51–58.

Levy, Marion J., Jr., 1966. *Modernization and the Structure of Societies: A Setting for International Affairs.* Princeton: Princeton University Press.

Lewin, Julius, 1947. *Studies in Africa Native Law.* Cape Town: The African Bookman.

Lloyd, Peter C., 1967. *Africa in Social Change: Changing Traditional Societies in the Modern World.* Baltimore: Penguin Books.

Maine, Henry Sumner, 1861. *Ancient Law.* London: John Murray.

Malinowski, Bronislaw, 1926. *Crime and Custom in Savage Society.* London: Routledge and Kegan Paul.

Middleton, John, and Tait, D., eds., 1958. *Tribes without Rulers: Studies in African Segmentary Systems.* London: Routledge and Kegan Paul.

Murdock, George Peter, 1949. *Social Structure.* New York: The Macmillan Company.

Nader, Laura, 1965. .The Anthropological Study of Law." *American Anthropologist* 67: 3–32.

Parsons, Talcott, 1960. "Durkheim's Contribution to the Theory of Integration of Social Systems." Pp. 118–153 in Kurt H. Wolff ed. Emile Durkheim, et al., *Essays on Sociology and Philosophy.* New York: Harper & Row Publishers, Inc.

Parsons, Talcott, 1962. "The Law and Social Control." Pp. 56–72 in William M. Evan, ed. *Law and Sociology: Exploratory Essays.* New York: The Free Press.

Pospisil, Leopold, 1967. "The Attributes of Law." Pp. 25–41 in Paul Bohannan, ed. *Law and Warfare: Studies in the Anthropology of Conflict.* Garden City: Natural History Press.

Radcliffe-Brown, A. R., 1952. *Structure and Function in Primitive Society.* New York: The Free Press.

Rattray, R. S., 1929. *Ashanti Law and Constitution.* Oxford: Clarendon Press.

Redfield, Robert, 1967. "Primitive Law." Pp. 3–24 in Paul Bohannan, ed. *Law and Warfare: Studies in the Anthropology of Conflict.* Garden City: Natural History Press.

Rehbinder, Manfred, 1967. "Wandlungen der Rechtsstruktur im Sozialstaat." Pp. 197–222 in Ernst E. Hirsch and Manfred Rehbinder, eds., *Studien und Materialien zur Rechtssoziologie.* Kölner Zeitschrift für Soziologie und Sozialpsychologie: Sonderheft 11/1967.

Ruark, Robert C., 1955. *Something of Value.* New York: Doubleday & Company, Inc.

Schott, Rüdiger, 1959. "Die Eigentumsrechte der Buschmänner in Südafrika." *Zeitschrift für vergleichende Rechtswissenschaft* 61: 101–223.

Seibel, H. Dieter, 1967. "Die wirtschaftliche Entwicklung Liberias." *Internationales Afrikaforum* 4 (November): 532–540.

Simmel, Georg, 1908. *Soziologie: Untersuchungen über die Formen der Vergesellschaftung.* Leipzig: Duncker and Humblot.

Swartz, Marc, Jr., 1966. "Bases for Compliance in Bena Villages." Pp. 89–108 in Marc J. Swartz, Victor W. Turner, and Arthur Tuden, eds. *Political Anthropology.* Chicago: Aldine Publishing Company.

Trappe, Paul, 1969. "Über Typologien afrikanischer Sozialstrukturen." Pp. 9–42 in Paul Trappe, ed., *Sozialer Wandel in Afrika südlich der Sahara. Part I, Sonderheft* 2, *Vierteljahresberichte.* Forschungsinstitut der Friedrich-Ebert-Stiftung. Hannover: Verlag für Literatur und Zeitgeschehen.

Weber, Max, 1967. *Rechtssoziologie.* Neuwied: Hermann-Luchterhand Verlag.

Chapter Eleven

SOCIAL CONTROL AND THE AMPLIFICATION OF DEVIANCE

Andrew Scull

Much of modern writing on deviance views the systems and agents of social control as deeply implicated in the process by which others become deviant. "The very effort to prevent, intervene, arrest, and 'cure' persons of their alleged pathologies may, according to the neo-Chicagoan view, precipitate or seriously aggravate the tendency society wishes to guard against."[1] From this perspective, one views "deviance as a consequence of the extent and form of social control, . . ." and, indeed, "social control becomes a 'cause' rather than an effect of the magnitude and variable forms of deviation."[2]

Such arguments have by now become almost the conventional wisdom in the field. Most of the sociological literature on drug addiction makes explicit or implicit use of this perspective; indeed, the American drug problem is generally regarded as the most telling example, or even as proof of the thesis: Lindesmith claims that opiate addiction in America only became a major social (as opposed to personal) problem following the passage of the 1915 Harrison Act, or rather, following the interpretation of that passage by narcotics officials as prohibiting the prescription of heroin to addicts. He asserts that, prior to 1915, criminality and addiction were not linked as they are now, the number of addicts in jails and prisons was negligible, there was no significant illicit trafficking in drugs, and there was little evidence of opiate use by juveniles.[3] The major cause of these developments, he argues, is to be found in the attempt to control drug use through prohibition.[4] Indeed, the relationship between the control program and the characteristics and numbers of addicts is such that "from a knowledge of the demographic characteristics of a nation's addicts it is usually a simple matter to infer what that nation's policies are, and vice versa."[5]

To buttress the argument on the role of control agencies, writers on addiction frequently employ a comparison with the remarkably benign character of the English drug situation. The major authority cited by those making this comparison has been E. M. Schur's book *Narcotic Addiction in Britain and America: The Impact of Public Policy,* which Lindesmith has described as "a definitive study of British practices."[6] Schur's study is based on two years of research in Britain. Although his conclusions are couched in somewhat more cautious language than Lindesmith's, the argument he makes is essentially the same one. "The question of exactly why addiction has not become a social danger in Great Britain is a very difficult one to answer in any scientifically conclusive way. . . . But I believe strongly that all data from diverse sources, surveyed throughout this study, point in the same direction: to the strong influence of British drug policy on addiction in that country."[7] Elsewhere, Schur has concluded that "medical administration of low-cost legal drugs could drastically undercut the economic incentives underlying the illicit traffic and could largely eliminate various secondary aspects of addiction as a social problem."[8] He claims the effect of the policy pursued in Britain has been to inhibit the development of an addict subculture and the spread of opiate use to juveniles, as well as to avoid the involvement of addicts with crime and illicit trafficking in drugs.[9]

Recent writers on the drug problem in America have continued to use Schur's findings to reinforce their argument that the Federal Bureau of Narcotics is in large part to blame for the nature of that problem, despite the fact that his study was completed by 1960. The author began this study under the impression that the nature and extent of narcotic addiction in Britain had changed somewhat during the 1960s, and that, in consequence, it would be valuable to reexamine the evidence to see whether Schur's major thesis had withstood the test of time.

The evidence presented in the first portion of this chapter suggests strongly that during the early 1960s there *was* a major breakdown in the hitherto highly successful British system of controlling addiction. By the end of this first section, it should also be clear that it would be a mistake to attempt to account for the changes that occurred solely or mainly in terms of shifts in official policy toward addiction and addicts. This is, of course, the reverse of what Schur's study would have led us to expect. Moreover, since it is now quite apparent that allowing addicts to have legal access to heroin is not sufficient to ensure that addiction will not become a major social problem, the role of agencies of social control in the process of becom-

ing deviant assumes a much less malignant character. Whereas control programs may aggravate the problem of addiction, it is misleading to claim that
they "cause" the problem to exist in the first place.

Summarizing the major changes in the nature of addiction in Britain
during the 1960s, it is clear that the problem increased substantially in size
and became much more closely identified with a subculture of young people
whose addiction was nontherapeutic in origin. Unlike many of the addicts
Schur studied, these people were clearly unable to live useful lives, even with
maintenance doses of heroin. These changes occurred before there was any
alteration in official policy; in fact, the official response shifted only after the
appearance of a subculture of addicts selling drugs on a thriving black
market. Consequently, those theories that seek to utilize variations in public
policy as their primary explanatory variable are clearly unsatisfactory.

Perhaps the most plausible portions of the arguments advanced by Schur
and Lindesmith were those in which they claimed that the unavailability of
illicit sources of heroin drove addicts to crime, and by creating the possibility
of realizing enormous profits created an illicit market for drugs. Even here,
it seems that the thesis will have to be modified. The existence of a burgeoning black market in heroin in the mid-1960s showed that allowing opiates
to be supplied by doctors to addicts is not necessarily sufficient to prevent
the illicit sale of drugs, and therefore, the spread of addiction. Equally, as
James' study clearly indicates, even where the availability of illicit, low-
cost supplies of heroin removes the economic necessity for addicts to steal,
addict-related crime can still prove troublesome. Consequently, in contradistinction to the arguments advanced by Schur and Lindesmith, the question
of whether or not an addiction problem exists is not dependent upon the
control policies one adopts; although some policies do act to worsen the
situation. This is a question to which we shall return toward the end of this
chapter. For the moment, however, we will concentrate on presenting as
complete a picture as possible of the changes that have taken place in the
British drug situation during the past decade.

Opiate Addiction in Britain in the 1960s

Before attempting to indicate the nature and extent of drug addiction in
Britain in 1960, the "system" of narcotics control that was employed in the
early 1960s is briefly described. *The Dangerous Drug Act* of 1920 had
placed stringent restrictions on the manufacture, distribution, sale, and possession of narcotics. But unlike the situation with respect to the Harrison
Act in the United States, the seeming harshness of the English act's provisions was modified in practice, along the lines recommended by the 1926
Rolleston Committee. As interpreted, the law permitted the administration of
morphine or its derivatives to addicts:

(a) where patients are under treatment by the gradual withdrawal method with a view to cure; (b) where it has been demonstrated, after a prolonged attempt at a cure, that the use of the drug cannot be safely discontinued entirely, on account of the severity of the withdrawal symptoms produced; (c) where it has been demonstrated that the patient, while capable of living a useful and relatively normal life when a certain minimum dose is regularly administered, becomes incapable of this when the drug is entirely discontinued.[10]

The interpretation of these broadly framed regulations was left from that time on to the individual physician, who remained the final arbiter of what constituted proper medical treatment of any addict patient.

Denials that this approach constituted a "system" have been frequently made even recently,[11] the main grounds for this assertion being that there was no compulsory central registration of addicts (the Home Office merely "requested" notification) and "no scheme by which the authorities allocate to them regular supplies of the drugs they are taking."[12] To avoid entering a sterile semantic debate, let us simply reiterate that control of addiction did (and to a large extent does) reside in medical hands in Britain, in marked contrast to the situation in America.

This policy was widely regarded as extremely successful. The number of known addicts to morphine, its derivatives and synthetic substitutes, remained at a consistently low level, as may be seen from Table 11-1.[13] A slight increase in numbers is evident in the late 1950s although, in view of later developments, one should note that very little of this increase was of addiction to heroin. In any event, it was the view of the first Brain Committee that:

> The figures provided by the Home Office . . . which might suggest an extension of addiction in Great Britain reflect, we think, an intensified activity for its detection and recognition over the post-war period. At the same time, the choice of drugs has altered, the new synthetics taken orally being now more popular. *There is nevertheless in our opinion no cause to fear that any real increase is at present occurring.*[14]

Furthermore, it seems clear that, in contrast to the situation even two or three years later, the figures giving the number of addicts known to the Home Office were largely accurate. Schur and the Brain Committee both agree on this.[15] Glatt has noted a tendency on the part of some addicts to postpone "registration," that is, going to a doctor and eventually becoming known to the Home Office, born of a feeling that "once you're registered, you're really hooked."[16] However, this data was gathered in 1965, and there is much evidence to show that the extent of addiction and the behavior of addicts had changed markedly by then.

We can also accept the contention that at this time the black market in addicting drugs was almost nonexistent. "According to the Home Office and the police, supported by such independent evidence as we have been able to obtain, the purveying of illicit supplies of manufactured dangerous drugs for addicts in this country is so small as to be almost negligible."[17] Schur concurs: "Even addicts who have had contact with such black market operations as do exist agree that this illicit trafficking is on a very small scale and is limited geographically as well as numerically." He adds: "This study found no evidence seriously contradicting the government's claim that 'the addict who is also a pusher is seldom encountered in the United Kingdom.' "[18]

Schur suggested that these and other aspects of the British "drug scene" could be explained largely in terms of the system that was adopted to deal with addiction. As things stood in 1960, this seemed an eminently plausible explanation. Both the system and the number of addicts had remained basically unchanged over a period of almost forty years. The essentials of the argument were that the legal provision of drugs prevented the development of an underworld black market by almost eliminating its potential profitability; the lack of a black market reduced the chances for the spread of the habit; at the same time, the addicts did not need to steal to support their habit, nor to develop a real subculture, since they did not face "the social, legal, and economic pressure to band together and to establish their own group way of life";[19] the high average age of addicts could be explained in terms of access to drugs and the high proportion of addicts in the medical profession.[20] However, events over the next few years showed this to be an inadequate analysis.

In 1960 there were a total of 437 narcotics addicts in Britain. The majority of these addicts were middle-aged and had either become addicted "as a result of injudicious medical treatment or else because of professional contact with drugs."[21] The first Interdepartmental Committee under the chairmanship of Sir Russell Brain, asked to review the policies established by the 1926 Commission, was set up in 1958 and made its final report in 1961. Not unnaturally, it concluded that the system was working very satisfactorily and that no basic changes were needed. By July 1964, however, the situation had deteriorated sufficiently seriously for the committee to be reconvened "to consider whether, in the light of recent experience, the advice they gave in 1961 in relation to the prescribing of addictive drugs by doctors needs revising and if so to make recommendations."[22]

The committee found that:

1. During the years 1959–1964 the total number of addicts to dangerous drugs known to the Home Office had risen from 454 to 753. During this period, the number of heroin addicts had risen from 68 to 342, whereas the incidence of addiction to other dangerous drugs remained more or less the same. Most of the new addicts were taking heroin.

2. The number of cocaine addicts had increased from 30 in 1959 to 211 in 1964. Virtually all of these were using the drug in conjunction with heroin.

3. The number of those who had become addicted to dangerous drugs other

than as a result of medical treatment had risen from 98 in 1959 to 372 in 1964. For heroin the corresponding figures were 47 and 328, respectively. Thus out of 342 heroin addicts, 328 were of nontherapeutic origin.

4. There had been a significant change in the age distribution of addicts. In 1959 only 50 out of 454 (that is, 11 percent) were less than 35 years old; by 1964 this group numbered 297 out of 753 (that is, nearly 40 percent), 40 of them being under 20 years of age (1 being as young as 15). All 40 addicts under the age of 20 and the majority under the age of 35 were taking heroin. . . .

5. The increase in addiction to heroin and cocaine appeared to be centered very largely on London, but indications of a similar trend on a much smaller scale had been observed in one or two of the other large cities.[23]

Before indicating other changes that had occurred in the period 1959–1964, it is as well to point out two things. The first is that the changes noted, as well as those that are considered soon, occurred even though the policies for dealing with the addiction problems had not altered. The second is that since the new type of addict initially obtained his drugs illicitly and often relied on the pseudo black market[24] to supply him for a period "of several months,"[25] the figures cited certainly underestimate the growth in numbers that had taken place. The unreliability of the Home Office statistics persists at least until after the setting up of the narcotics clinics in 1968.

Nevertheless, the figures given indicate a clear trend. The Brain Report brings out some of the major changes—the large increase in the number of addicts under thirty-five, and the appearance, for the first time, of teen-age addicts; the growth of heroin to the status of the most important drug of addiction, and the large increase in the number of nontherapeutic addicts.[26] In the early stages of what James has termed the epidemic, a fairly high proportion of the new addicts were Canadians, Americans, and other foreigners.[27] However, growing numbers of the new kind of addict were recruited from British-born young people, in the ratio of approximately three males for every female.[28]

Virtually all of the increase in the number of addicts in the decade beginning in 1960 occurred in the group known as "nontherapeutic" addicts. (For example, in 1965, the latest year for which I have a breakdown, there were 347 known therapeutic addicts, compared with 356 in 1959; but 580 nontherapeutic addicts compared with only 98 in 1959.) Unlike the "typical" 1950s addict, the overwhelming majority of the newer addicts were under thirty, were clustered in certain areas of London, and formed a definite and self-conscious "junkie" subculture, employing an argot in part imported from American and in part of their own invention. James asserts that they were "mostly of unstable personality and social background" and that such groups "formed the focuses for the epidemic spread of heroin addiction to other susceptible individuals with whom they came in contact."[29]

There were other important changes in the nature of the addict population during these years. In contrast to the first Brain Report's comments on "stabilized addicts,"[30] James reports that of a sample of fifty addicts seen in London prisons during 1967, which he considers "typical of the 'nontherapeutic' intravenous high-dosage, heroin/methylamphetamine . . . regular daily user, there was little evidence that these addicts were able to live useful lives on a medical regime of heroin maintenance."[31] The fact that these addicts were studied in prison points up another change in the drug scene in Britain, namely, a much closer relationship between crime (or delinquency) and addiction. James' sample is not, of course, necessarily representative, but it is probably a fairly accurate description of much of the current addict population.

Whereas most American addicts use less than one grain of heroin a day, prescriptions for three to eight grains of heroin were regularly obtained by British addicts. Cases have been reported of daily doses of as much as 1,600 milligrams.[32] These variations illustrate one of the major problems faced by a system providing legal maintenance doses of addictive drugs, namely, that of accurately estimating dosage. Bewley has referred to this process as "judicious guesswork and bizarre haggling."[33] If too much of the drug is given, the addict may die of an overdose, or, if a ready market exists, divert the surplus to illicit use, thus spreading the habit; if, on the other hand, too little is given, the legal program can degenerate into a shambles, as addicts seek to augment their supplies on the black market.

A further development in Britain, in the 1960s, has been the appearance of what has been called the "poly-addict," who may prefer a mixture of heroin and methedrine, but who often resorts to other drugs, usually in very large quantities. This aspect of the drug culture has become more prominent since 1968, when the setting up of government clinics led to tighter restrictions on the prescription of heroin. *The New York Times* recently provided graphic illustrations of this unwanted side-effect of the change in official policy.

> Because the supply of legal heroin has been reduced, addicts are looking to other drugs that are even more deadly in some respects because they are so completely unsuitable for injection, even by a trained physician. The current fad among junkies who gather in Piccadilly Circus is to crush a barbiturate sleeping pill, preferably Nembutal, into a vial with water and then mainline the mixture into a vein just as they would do with heroin.
>
> But oral Nembutal was never intended for injection and anyone who tries it will develop huge sores the size of golf balls. . . . Barbiturates . . . are heavily alkaline. If a junky misses his vein and makes only a subcutaneous injection, the barbiturates will immediately begin to cause an abscess under the skin. And because the sores produced are not caused by bacteria, attempts to treat them with antibiotics are useless.
>
> But an addict who is "lucky" to hit the vein cleanly is not as lucky after all. Barbiturates frequently cannot be carried away by the blood fast enough

and, even after a single injection, a vein will collapse, impairing circulation.

But in their uncontrollable urge to continue mainlining, the junkies seek new veins. As soon as they find one, the vein collapses. And so the junkies pursue even the tiniest veins—ones most people don't even know they have— veins between the fingers, veins between the toes, veins in the genitalia. In one instance a boy tried to give himself a needle in the white of his eye. And in Piccadilly the junkies talked about him. Nobody knew where he was.

The junkies knew, though, that they were fortunate if all they had was an ugly wound. Because all around Piccadilly—in the tunnels leading to the Underground, in the coffee bars, in the back alleys of Soho—there were junkies with something worse: gangrene.

Doctors cannot agree whether the gangrene is caused by a characteristic of the barbiturates or by the open sores not being kept clean. But all around the West End one sees junkies with missing toes or missing fingers or with the greying flesh that signifies an amputation is imminent.[34]

The large average dose of heroin and this tendency to use other, highly unsuitable drugs for intravenous injection are probably among the reasons "why heroin addiction is a much more lethal disorder in the United Kingdom" than in the United States.[35] In an article elsewhere, James has shown that these mortality rates may amount to up to twenty times the expected figure.[36]

No one who has seriously studied the subject disagrees with the second Brain Report's conclusion that, at least up to 1964, there was no "significant traffic, organized or otherwise, in dangerous drugs that have been stolen or smuggled into this country. . . . The major source of supply has been the activity of a very few doctors who have prescribed excessively for addicts."[37] As has been noted, estimating the dosage necessary is always to some extent a matter of guesswork. But beyond this, there is considerable evidence that a number of the very few doctors prepared to prescribe for heroin addicts in the early 1960s behaved in an extremely irresponsible fashion. Glatt, for example, states he came across many addicts whose doctors had supplied them "without ascertaining their medical needs for the drug, without going closely into their history, without asking for a second opinion."[3] As the Brain Report indicates, some of these doctors wrote prescriptions for spectacular quantities of heroin.[39] "It is a measure of the abundance of this source of supply that the illicit price of heroin did not increase at all between 1960 and 1966 in spite of a tremendously escalating demand" and in spite of the fact that up to this time there was "virtually no illicit importation of heroin into this country."[40]

The second Brain Committee had interpreted its terms of reference as implying that they should concentrate their attention and recommendations on the role played by doctors in prescribing addictive drugs. Not unnaturally, in view of the facts their investigations provided, they recommended changes in government policy. In making these suggestions, the committee pointed out that it had "borne in mind the dilemma which faces the authorities. . . . If there is insufficient control it may lead to the spread of addiction—as is happening at present. If, on the other hand, the restrictions are so severe as to prevent or seriously discourage the addict from obtaining any supplies from legitimate sources it may lead to the development of an organized illicit traffic."[41]

The recommendations, then, were an attempt "to prevent abuse without sacrificing the advantages of the present system," and the committee emphasized that (as in the past) "the addict should be regarded as a sick person, [and] he should be treated as such and not as a criminal."[42] The major changes suggested can be quickly summarized: the setting up of treatment centers and limiting the prescribing of heroin and cocaine (and of other drugs if this proved necessary) to doctors on the staff of these treatment centers; powers for the compulsory detention of addicts in these centers during the withdrawal period; notification of all addicts to a central authority; and the setting up of a permanent standing committee to keep the whole problem of drug addiction under review.[43] All of these, with the exception of the provision for compulsory detention during treatment, were later adopted. In omitting this the government was perhaps swayed by the arguments of the earlier committee report that such compulsion was neither desirable nor effective.[44]

The general reaction to these proposals was one of qualified approval. *The London Times'* editorial called the figures on the growth of addiction "alarming" and gave conditional support to the clinic proposal. The major medical journals, the *Lancet* and the *British Medical Journal,* demurred only on small points—the *Lancet* suggesting a prohibition on the prescription of cocaine and the placing of other addictive drugs as well as heroin on the restricted list; and the *British Medical Journal* arguing that general practitioners should be allowed to continue to prescribe for addicts, provided that they did so in consultation with an expert.

More trenchant criticism came from those in direct contact with drug addicts. As has been noted, only a dozen or so doctors were treating addiction at this time, among whom six had been identified as overprescribers. Unfortunately, there is no way at present to distinguish these six from the rest, so that statements from any "junky doctor" will inevitably be greeted by skepticism. One should, however, have some idea of their reactions to the report. In an interview with the *Sunday Times* (London), some of the prescribing doctors criticized the Brain Report and attempted to justify their position. Many of them voiced fears of an organized black market if the recommendations were accepted and predicted that some addicts, at least, would not attend the new centers. They also doubted that many doctors would put up with the trouble that "junkies" caused.[45] Elsewhere, fears were voiced that the report might be "just the opening gun in a drive towards more repressive laws" and the creation of a problem of the American type.[46]

These criticisms are considered again later as the ways in which the problem of addiction developed over the next few years are examined. The immediate reaction of the government to the Brain Report seems to have been to ignore it. The report was published in November 1965. By the end of July 1966, the only action taken by the government was the announcement of the setting up of the permanent standing committee on addiction under Lord Brain. Further time went by: in January 1967 Roy Jenkins, the Home Secretary, announced that the government agreed with the Brain Report's recommendations, with the exception of the provision for the compulsory detention of addicts undergoing withdrawal treatment. (He also indicated that the government proposed to undertake in cooperation with the Vera Institute of Justice a comparative study of addiction in the United Kingdom and in the United States. The Institute had just estimated that there would be 10,819 [sic] addicts in Britain by 1972.) In March 1967 legislation was introduced to give effect to these decisions, but the new law was destined to remain inoperative until April 1968, nearly three years after the initial recommendations were made.

What was happening during this long delay? Table 11-4 shows that there was a continuing rise in the number of addicts; from 927 addicts in 1965, the total rose to 1,349 by 1966, 1,729 a year later, and 2,782 by the end of 1968 (of whom 2,240 were heroin addicts). During these three years methadone was becoming an important drug of addiction; numbers of methadone addicts, having remained fairly constant through the early 1960s at between 60 and 70 addicts, now rose to 156 in 1966, 243 in 1967 and 486 in 1968.[47]

In many other ways the situation seems to have worsened. Public attitudes toward addicts and the doctors who prescribed for them became far more antagonistic. As Terence Morris pointed out, these attitudes were "highly coloured by the whole problem of generational conflict and the resentment of adults at the emergence of an adolescent culture that is reflected in a spectrum ranging from affluent pop-singers to disorder on Bank Holiday beaches."[48] The publicity attendant on the publication of the Brain Report brought public awareness of a hard-drug problem, just as earlier newspaper reports had served to focus attention on teen-age use of amphetamines and marijuana or cannabis. Suggestions were made that "those suffering from addiction should be certifiable so that they can be protected, controlled, and treated in the same way as mental patients."[49] A member of the London Drugs Squad remarked that, by supplying addicts, doctors were "fulfilling the role of the Mafia in other countries."[50]

Opposition to the "junky doctors" was further stimulated by the highly publicized case of Dr. Petro. Over a period of several weeks in 1967, the press reported that he was prescribing profusely for addicts in train stations, coffee bars, and similar locations. The case received even more publicity when, following a lengthy interrogation on television, Dr. Petro was arrested on charges of failing to keep a record of his prescriptions for heroin. Press coverage of Dr. Petro's activities continued, as appeals and the slowness of the law and the professional committee meant that he could continue to prescribe on a massive scale through much of 1968. Finally, in June 1968, his license to prescribe drugs was withdrawn.[51]

A side effect of this publicity and the concomitant change in public attitudes was that many of the doctors who had concerned themselves with treating addicts ceased doing so. Leech reported

> a widespread reluctance and refusal of General Practitioners throughout London to prescribe heroin and cocaine, even under carefully controlled conditions, coupled with the opting out of several well-known doctors. . . . While some medical sources of supply have dried up, others have exploited the situation.[52]

Further evidence of what was occurring came from Dr. A. J. Hawes, who described himself as one of "the small, diminishing and despairing band of 'junky' doctors." Like Leech, he pointed out that the latest Home Office report to the United Nations had drawn attention to the "significant increase in the number of addicts who have obtained their drugs *entirely from unknown sources.*" One of the few doctors treating addicts had recently thrown up his practice, leaving "about eighty heroin and cocaine addicts on the open market, which usually means the black market," and the burden was becoming too much for the few doctors remaining.[53]

By January 1967, William Deedes, M. P., a member of the standing committee on drug addiction, was urging the government to provide some institutional means of restoring supplies to addict "before that gap became a major racket."[54] Very little action appears to have been taken, however. The new clinics needed before the Brain Committee's recommendations could be implemented were supposedly in the process of formation, but the Minister of Health indicated that there was no "earmarked" money for setting them up— apparently they were to be grafted on to the outpatient centers of psychiatric hospitals.[55] On the second reading of the Dangerous Drugs Bill, launched to give effect to the Interdepartmental Committee's proposals, a spokesman for the Home Office stressed that while the new law would change the organization of the treatment of addicts, the aim was to retain the underlying basic principle of the British system. A few M. P.'s were skeptical, warning of the dangers of an expanded black market should the clinics fail to attract the known and unknown addicts. This might arise if the new facilities were inadequate in size and number, or if their location in psychiatric wards served to deter addicts from attending them.[56]

The lack of official response to the growing crisis shows up again in the experience of one of the doctors prescribing for addicts. Faced with more addicts than he could handle, he sought advice from the Ministry of Health as to where he should send them. He was given a list of eight hospitals where there were new clinics; on inquiring, however, he found that five of these had no clinic; he could not get a reply from two others; and the one that did claim to have a clinic informed him that the doctor who ran it was away in America.[57]

On July 26, 1967, the government announced that the new drug clinics would be ready "not later than the New Year." Ten hospitals were to provide inpatient treatment, and thirteen were to provide outpatient treatment. It was hoped that these facilities would cope with up to 1,000 addicts. Once more, however, action, even on this modest scale, seems to have been lacking. On January 15, 1968, Kenneth Leech accused the Ministry of Health of gross deceit over the clinics issue, calling the fourteen outpatient clinics it claimed were in existence "a figment of the Ministry's imagination." In consequence, his Soho church hall had to be used as an emergency clinic for addicts cut off from their normal source of supply.[58]

Despite government denials, these charges appear to have been well-founded. The Ministry of Health refused to release the names of the clinics. Inquiries made at the time, however, showed that the clinics that did exist operated "spasmodically," were grossly overcrowded, and imposed a fourteen-day waiting period on those seeking treatment.[59]

The obvious danger here was that if the Ministry decided to implement the section of the 1967 act restricting the prescription of heroin and cocaine to addicts to doctors working in the new clinics while the system was in such a state of disarray, many addicts would be unable to obtain supplies legitimately. Even without this step being taken, the failure to organize the new system more quickly, coupled with the breakdown of the older system, meant that a problem had already appeared. Further research is necessary, however, to discover whether overprescribing by some of the few remaining "junky doctors" continued on a sufficient scale to provide for an addict population that was growing at an even more rapid rate than before; or whether supplies were being obtained from a more organized black market.

On January 31, 1968, the Ministry of Health, whose original plans had called for the clinics to be already open, revised its estimate of when they would be completed to some time in the spring. It also announced where the clinics would be located, in order to allow the transfer of patients to begin before the new regulations came into effect, as and when the new facilities expanded to take them.[60] Once more the Ministry quoted a figure of 1,000 addicts as the expected number to be treated, a curious choice, since there were already 899 known heroin addicts in 1966, and figures were soon to be released showing that the number had risen to 1,299 in 1967.[61] If the Ministry was only making provision for 1,000 addicts this would suggest that when the new clinics opened they would fall far short of what was required. This would mean either serious overcrowding or that addicts would resort to the black market.

On April 16, 1968, the provision in the 1967 Dangerous Drugs Act making it illegal for doctors not on the staff of one of the new clinics to prescribe heroin or cocaine for an addict was finally activated.[62] Consideration of whether this changeover was smoothly effected and of the subsequent effectiveness of the clinic system is obviously essential in any attempt to trace the development of the new patterns of addiction during the 1960s. Information in both areas is inadequate at present and, particularly over the question of how well the changeover was managed, opinions diverge sharply.

If one accepts the official interpretation, the takeover was a smooth one. The Minister of Health criticized "the attitude of certain newspapers and a few people concerned with addiction in a purely voluntary capacity," claiming that they had been biased in their assessments of the new system "by their hostility to this system of treatment." He admitted that the Home Office had evidence of small quantities of heroin being imported illegally, but stated that the main source of supply on the black market was still overprescription by doctors.

Other observers, however, were not so optimistic. The Association for the Prevention of Addiction (whose chairman, Francis Camps, is the Home Office's chief pathologist) reported delays of up to four or five days in obtaining appointments for the treatment of addicts at the clinics, and claimed that, in general, the clinics were "not functioning very well." In addition, there was "positive evidence" that supplies of powdered heroin were available on the black market, and that one grain, formerly priced at £1, now cost between 30s. and 35s. A few days later a letter to *The London Times* from Dr. A. J. Hawes, one of the former prescribing doctors, provided further evidence that the changeover had not been as smooth as had been claimed. He spoke of the change as "a pitiful experience to a great number of addicts . . . the sort of people who just cannot look ahead so that his doorstep was almost festering with addicts in various stages of depravation."[63]

The Ministry of Health's own figures would also seem to cast doubt on their earlier statements. As late as October 26, 1968, by which time one might have expected all addicts to have transferred to the new clinics, the Ministry claimed that only 870 were being treated at the centers in London and 204 at centers elsewhere. In addition, seventy-five addicts in London and forty-four elsewhere were receiving inpatient care. This gives a maximum total of 1,193 addicts being treated by the new facilities; even supposing that all of these were heroin addicts, one must conclude that the clinics were failing to reach nearly half of their clientele; for Home Office figures show that by the end of 1968, only 2 months later, there were 2,240 addicts to heroin alone, and a total of 2,782 if one includes those addicted to morphine and synthetic equivalents such as methadone.[64] Future research must obviously be directed toward discovering how these other addicts were maintaining their habits, why the clinics were being shunned on so massive a scale, and whether there is any evidence of organized illicit importation of heroin for sale on the black market.

Information on the operation of the clinics is, at the moment, extremely scanty. As the prescribing doctors had predicted, some of those involved in treating the addicts appear to have become swiftly disillusioned.[65] On January 9, 1969, six doctors at University College Hospital wrote to complain that addicts were interfering with work for other patients and in some cases behaving violently. Describing the situation as "intolerable," they suggested that addicts should, perhaps, be made to obtain their supplies from police stations rather than hospitals.[66] A similar complaint came from the casualty superintendent at Charing Cross Hospital. This time addicts were accused of being "not only a damn nuisance, but positively dangerous." The proposed "solution" was "to have them certified for a month at the minimum so that they can be removed to a suitable psychiatric unit where the necessary medical and psychiatric treatment can be undertaken"; again, something likely to increase the number of addicts shunning the legal program.[67]

Two other clues as to the trends under the new system are significant. *The New York Times,* in its extensive article on addiction in Britain, reported that junkies felt that there was "a growing reluctance on the part of clinics to accept new addicts for heroin maintenance."[68] In a later report, the same writer indicated that: "An estimated half of the physicians in the health clinics have either stopped heroin prescription or eliminated it completely. And the British talk about adopting American psychotherapeutic programs that have been attacked in New York as unequal to the task."[69]

Use of Soft Drugs in Britain in the 1960s

Having dealt at some length with the ways in which the nature of opiate addiction in Britain changed during the 1960s, this chapter now focuses on two remaining problems; namely, the reasons for the extensive changes noted in the nature of opiate addiction in Britain; and to elaborate on the implications the research reported here has for the more general question of the role of agencies of social control in the creation of secondary deviance. In attempting these tasks, it became increasingly clear that a satisfactory resolution of either of them necessarily involved a discussion of the growth of soft-drug-taking among British teen-agers over the past decade. For not only did the development of an extensive soft-drug using subculture have important repercussions on public and official reactions to drug-taking in general, but, in addition, the growth of such a subculture was perhaps the decisive factor behind the change in the nature of the opiate addiction problem.

The use of soft drugs (marijuana, amphetamines, and barbiturates) does not seem to have become a matter of public concern until the early 1960s. Throughout the 1950s the consumption of barbiturates and amphetamines increased fairly steadily,[70] but their use was largely confined to middle-aged people, particularly housewives, who obtained their supplies legitimately through the National Health Service.[71] At this time marijuana use was on a relatively small scale and was largely confined to immigrant groups, especially West Indians.[72]

During the first two or three years of the 1960s, new patterns of consumption appeared in all three types of drugs. Initially the change seems to have occurred where teen-agers had regular access in their homes to amphetamines and/or barbiturates (for example, to "mother's diet pills").[73] The drugs were taken for the feeling of self-assurance they provided and because they counteracted fatigue and drowsiness. Research remains to be done on the pattern that grew from these relatively isolated and unorganized beginnings, but certainly by 1963 an important change had occurred. For the first time one finds evidence of organized trafficking in these drugs and they appeared to have assumed considerable importance in the life style of certain groups of teen-agers. For the moment this changing situation was confined to the West End and particularly to certain discotheques and clubs in the Soho area.[74] In terms of numbers, comparatively few were involved—as late as December 1965 the "best guess" of those knowledgeable about the phenomenon was that only 10,000 teen-agers "were regularly taking 'pep pills' or had experimented with them."[75]

As the use of soft drugs became a regular part of the life style of a small but growing group of teen-agers, the press began to report a number of police raids on clubs in Soho, which had resulted in the confiscation of large quantities of "purple hearts."[76] The continuing growth of a soft-drug oriented subculture brought increased public attention to bear on the phenomenon of drug taking and concomitant changes in the authorities' attitudes. Articles denouncing the growth of teen-age drug abuse began to appear in the popular press, and there were suggestions that the rise of drug taking was linked with the outbreaks of violence between "mods" and "rockers," which were becoming a regular feature of Bank Holiday weekends.

On the first occasion the matter was raised in the House of Commons, the Home Secretary merely responded that he was asking manufacturers to tighten security at their factories, and was endeavoring to develop ways of guarding against the forging of prescriptions for amphetamines and barbiturates. However, further press publicity in the early months of 1964 about the burgeoning "purple heart" subculture centered on Soho led to increased pressure for government intervention. Partly out of a desire to regain public favor during the last few months before an election, the government introduced the Drugs (Prevention of Misuse) Bill. This bill had three major provisions: manufacturers and wholesalers of the drugs named were required to register with the Home Secretary and importers to obtain a license; powers were given to justices of the peace to issue warrants to allow police to enter and search club and café premises; and finally, it established "unauthorized possession" of these drugs as being an offense making one liable to a fine of up to £200 and/or six months in prison.[77] The bill was later amended to include a two-year prison sentence for large-scale peddling and became law on August 1, 1964.

The new act was important in several respects. As Lord Balniel remarked at the time, it created a new criminal offense, and a whole new class of criminals, those using the drugs, and this despite the fact that alcohol use and cigarette smoking were seemingly far more damaging to the physical health of people than habituation to amphetamine drugs.[78] Strictly speaking, unauthorized possession has also been punishable as a criminal offense in the case of both heroin and marijuana; however, most of the use of marijuana up to the early 1960s was confined to immigrant groups and had little impact on the public consciousness of the drug problem, while offenses in connection with opiates were both rare and lightly punished up to this time since most addicts were able to obtain supplies legitimately from doctors. Thus in an important respect, the new act was a radical departure in public policy, affecting a group then very much in the public eye, who had no prospect of obtaining supplies of their drugs other than by illegal means. The impact of this group on public attitudes toward drug taking was probably all the greater since most press reports failed to make clear distinctions between hard and soft drugs—those of addiction and those of habituation.[79]

During the passage of the bill, *The Times,* as well as those who were in contact with the drug subculture, criticized the proposed law. Many of their remarks centered on the treatment of users as criminals, and on the likelihood that hastily conceived restrictive legislation would prove counterproductive. "Two Soho villagers of long standing feel that once the Drinamyl trade goes underground it will become much more vicious. The real criminals, they believe, will never be caught."[80] There were also predictions that black-market prices would rise and that more users would start acting as pushers as a means of supporting their own habit.

To a considerable degree, these predictions seem to have been borne out. Although it is, of course, difficult to separate out the extent to which later developments would have occurred anyway, the influence of the 1964 law does not seem to have been benign. At the time, however, it passed easily through Parliament, with Brooke, the Home Secretary, receiving all party support, and with very little adverse comment from M. P.'s. The two major exceptions to this were Lord Balniel, whose criticisms we have already summarized, and Ronald Bell, who drew attention to the role of police pressure behind the new bill. He suggested that the bill had been introduced "simply because the police were finding it difficult to get convictions."[81] Ironically, Bewley reports that since the act "if a café where there is traffic in amphetamines is raided now by the police, vast numbers of tablets may be found on the floor but not in anyone's possession."[82] Thus, it would seem that the increased power scarcely helped the police.

By the end of 1965, *The Times* reported that the use of amphetamines had spread from the West End to outer London and was involving increasing numbers of teen-agers.[83] Further evidence of the growth of soft-drug taking following the change in the law was provided by a study of boys in a London remand home by Scott and Wilcox, which showed that at least 16 per cent of them had recently taken unauthorized amphetamines.[84] At the same time, the black-market price of tablets was rising, from six pence a time before the act to 1/– or 1/6 by December 1965 and up to 2/6 a tablet at weekends in 1966.[85]

The economics of this price rise are somewhat obscure. There can be little doubt that the demand for the tablets was expanding rapidly, possibly in part because of the publicity surrounding the change in the law. At the same time, some sources of supply were contracting as doctors' prescribing policies grew more conservative and security was tightened at both manufacturers and pharmacists. Yet there seems to have been little difficulty in obtaining a variety of pills for illegal sale, and the number of black-market outlets seems to have expanded rapidly as the habit spread into the provinces. Although direct evidence is lacking, therefore, there must be a strong presumption that, while obtaining and distributing the pills required more organization and ingenuity and involved a higher risk, ways were being found to keep a growing market plentifully supplied. Thus the price rise may have in part reflected the increased risks of the suppliers; possibly, too, the fad was now strong enough to overcome the deterrent effect of higher prices on new users.

During 1967 there were several highly publicized reports of police raids on teen-age clubs. The number of arrests made was usually very small, especially in view of the fact that often a hundred or more police were involved in a single raid. The major results of this crackdown seem to have been the creation of a large amount of publicity, perhaps aimed at generating an impression that something was being done about the problem; a decline in respect for the law, caused in part by police tactics and in part by their inability to make many arrests;[86] and police harassment of teen-agers.[87] Recently, the police seem to have abandoned even these semifutile attempts at control. At the 1969 Isle of Wight rock festival the police stopped only the most blatant drug pushing, and they now seem to leave teen-age clubs and cafés alone. Although there are over 3,000 convictions a year under the 1964 Drugs Act, all kinds of drugs are sold openly in Soho clubs. Apparently there are too many people involved to make mass arrests a practical proposition.[88]

With regard to marijuana, the use of this drug has certainly grown during the 1960s, although in a somewhat different manner than did the use of amphetamines and barbiturates. Before 1945 the use of marijuana was almost unknown in Britain, but in the years from 1945 to 1960 there was a slow increase both in its use and in convictions for possession. At this stage consumption was largely confined to the immigrant population, particularly those from West Africa and the West Indies.

Patterns of marijuana use changed markedly during the early 1960s.

Not only was there an increase in the number of people using the drug but in addition some sections of the white population were introduced to marijuana. These changes were reflected in an increase in the number of convictions for the possession of the drug.

By the mid 1960s, there were scattered suggestions that there existed a strong case for the legalization of marijuana, suggestions that provoked a violent response from some quarters.[89] At the same time as, and perhaps in response to, the growing talk of legalizing marijuana, there was a series of police raids on the homes of prominent pop-singers, leading to arrests on charges of possessing the drug and a plethora of publicity about drug use in the press. As the *Times* commented: "the total effect has been to dramatize drug taking and almost certainly to spread rather than inhibit the habit."[90] A further effect was to discredit at least some of those attempting to change the law and to emphasize the association between drug taking and pop-world "immorality" in the minds of older people. Despite warnings that "exaggerated accounts of the effects of drugs are having a very harmful effect on the kids at risk, who are often more intelligent than the crusaders," grossly inaccurate accounts of the dangers of marijuana continued to appear in the press.[91]

Further efforts to arouse public support for the repeal of the law making the possession of marijuana illegal stirred bitter controversy.[92] A common theme in the remarks of many of those opposed to any change was a violent distaste for the so-called "permissive society," and its most obvious representatives, pop singers. Meanwhile, the government had asked a subcommittee of the Advisory Committee on Drug Dependence, which had been set up on the advice of the second Brain Report, to consider the whole question of marijuana and the law.

As early as October 1968, there were leaks to the press suggesting that the committee would recommend decreased penalties for simple possession, but that the Home Secretary would reject this advice.[93] When the report was finally published on January 8, 1969, its major conclusion was that in terms of physical harm marijuana was "very much less dangerous than opiates, amphetamines, and barbiturates, and also less dangerous than alcohol." It also substantially rejected the arguments that the use of marijuana led directly to hard-drug use and to crime. As the *Times* commented: "It almost comes as a surprise that the committee, having reached these conclusions, does not recommend legalizing cannabis." The major reason given by the committee for not doing so was a lack of knowledge about the drug's mental effects. Nevertheless, they "make it clear that they do not regard prison as the right punishment for the small user, and that taking cannabis in moderation should be regarded as a relatively minor offense."[94]

These recommendations were immediately met by a barrage of hostile criticism, much of it seeming to reflect a less than careful reading of the report's actual proposals.[95] More important, when the report was debated in the House of Commons, the Home Secretary officially rejected its main conclusions. Accusing the committee of being overinfluenced by a lobby for the legalization of marijuana, he added that he was glad that his decision had enabled the House to call a halt to the advancing tide of permissiveness.[96]

The failure of the attempt to liberalize the law on marijuana provides more evidence that the government felt that the growth in drug use could be controlled by means of vigorous law enforcement. Yet thus far, as in the case of amphetamines and barbiturates, the use of marijuana has continued to increase. Although enforcement efforts have forced the black market to become more organized, the soft-drug subculture shows no signs of dying.

Theoretical Implications

Any attempt to explain the changes in the British drug scene in the 1960s has at least these tasks: it must explain (1) why the changes had not occurred before; (2) why they occurred when they did; and (3) why they took the form they did. It is apparent that there are very intimate connections between all of these questions, so that I shall not attempt to rigorously separate the answers to each of them.

As we seek to discover why Britain managed for so long to successfully contain the problem of opiate addiction, I think major emphasis must be placed on the line of explanation developed by Schur, namely that "who the addict is and how he behaves is determined at least in part by the prevailing social and legal definitions of addiction."[97] We have already sketched the main lines of his argument that the legal availability of drugs for addicts largely precluded the growth of a drug-taking subculture, and hence of addiction as a social problem.[98] However, that this explanation was not entirely adequate was demonstrated by the experience of the early 1960s when, despite an unchanged legal response to opiate addiction, considerable numbers of young, nontherapeutic addicts began to appear. We must, therefore, identify the factors that precipitated this change.

The most widely accepted reason for the breakdown of the British system is the one put forward by the second Brain Committee, that the new situation primarily reflected massive overprescribing on the part of a few doctors. By itself, however, this is insufficient. A small "pseudo black market" had existed for heroin even in the 1950s, supplied by the surplus that a few addicts managed to obtain from their doctors.[99] But this market remained insignificant, being confined to a few Soho "jazz junkies" selling to weekend "skin-poppers." It created very few new addicts. Yet one may presume that doctors found it as difficult in the 1950s to estimate how much of his drug an addict needed as they did in the 1960s. We have no grounds for supposing that, had addicts tried to obtain the large surpluses that they successfully sought in the 1960s, the doctors then prescribing would have been any more likely to resist those pressures. I conclude from this that addicts in the 1950s did not attempt to obtain supplies of drugs other than those they themselves needed to stave off withdrawal.

The obvious next question is why this should have been the case. One reason is immediately apparent; as Schur has shown, most of the addicts in the 1960s were the sort of people who were unlikely to attempt to spread the habit—geographically scattered, middle-aged doctors, housewives and professional people who usually did not interact with other addicts.[100] Yet there were a certain number of addicts, most notably the small group of Soho "jazz junkies," for whom these restraints did not exist. On the contrary, as Glatt has pointed out,[101] on purely economic grounds a strong incentive for such addicts to obtain a surplus for sale on the black market already existed. For even if, under a system of legal provision of drugs, the addict did not need money to support his habit, he needed income to live on, which seemingly was most easily obtained by selling drugs. The fact that the Soho addicts did so on only such a small scale suggests that in the 1950s a ready market for hard drugs just did not exist. Given this situation, addicts had little or no incentive to obtain more drugs than they required for their own immediate needs, and hence there was little pressure for doctors to over-prescribe.

The key element in bringing about a change in this situation during the 1960s was the development of a fairly sizable teen-age subculture prepared to experiment with drugs. Howard Becker has pointed out that one of the major ways of achieving control over people's behavior is "by affecting the conceptions persons have of the to-be-controlled activity, and of the possibility of engaging in it," so that we can fruitfully examine "the genesis of deviant behavior in terms of events which render sanctions ineffective and experiences which shift conceptions so that the behavior becomes a conceivable possibility to the person."[102]

I have already described the growth of the teen-age soft-drug culture in Britain. The manner in which it came into existence and the reasons it did so are somewhat obscure.[103] But whatever the initial sources of the behavior, sufficient numbers of teen-agers began taking the pills regularly and con-gregating at clubs in the Soho area to create (for the first time in England) a fairly sizable subculture with favorable attitudes toward the illicit taking of drugs. Despite, or perhaps because of, increased publicity about drug abuse and attempts by the authorities to stamp out the practice, it continued to grow and spread to new areas.

The subculture provided the opportunities for learning new types of behavior and the rationales supporting them. For the first time large numbers of young people were in a position where they could gain access to drugs. One would expect the "justifications" developed to neutralize the widely held stereotype of the drug user "to contain a general repudiation of con-ventional moral rules," breaking down at least some of the barriers against experimenting with hard drugs.[104] The new willingness to experiment with drugs soon led some amphetamine users to marijuana. As has been noted, this drug was available in Britain throughout the post-war period, but not until the 1960s did its use spread from the colored immigrant groups to the white population. This growth in use occurred largely *after* the "pill culture" had established itself.

In the case of opiate addiction, the evidence suggesting the importance of the role played by the development of the soft-drug subculture is stronger, although the situation is rather more complicated. The use of amphetamines was originally centered in Soho, and in particular in certain teen-age clubs. Soho was also the one area in Britain where, even at the time that Schur wrote, there existed the nucleus of a hard-drug subculture.[105] Yet although a small pseudo black market existed there, it contributed very little to the spread of addiction.

Around 1960, however, fairly large numbers of Canadian and American addicts, in an effort to escape from the repressive drug laws of their own countries, began to arrive in London. No information exists at the moment about where these addicts settled. On the other hand, the legitimate sources for the supply of opiates were very limited in number, so that they are likely to have come into close contact with other nonmedical groups of addicts in London. In addition, the "jazz junkie" culture of Soho represented the closest approach to the groups from which they had come so that it seems reasonable to conclude that many of these transatlantic addicts chose to congregate in and around Soho.

As can be seen from Table 11-5, these foreign addicts provided the majority of the new addicts in 1961 and a large proportion of the new addicts the following year. I suspect, however, that their influence extended beyond this temporary addition to the number of addicts.[106] Not only may this increase in the number of nontherapeutic heroin addicts have provided the critical mass necessary to begin the spread of the habit, but these addicts from abroad were used to pushing drugs as a means of supporting their habit. Under British conditions, pushing may no longer have been necessary to provide income to buy one's own drugs, but it provided an easy way to obtain extra income.

We have already pointed out the near impossibility, at least on an out-patient basis, of estimating the dosage an addict needs to stave off withdrawal symptoms with any degree of accuracy. In practice, this meant that it was relatively easy to obtain surpluses on a prescription for subsequent sale. This might not have mattered if the situation had not been changing in other respects, but the rapid growth of a teen-age drug culture provided a ready market for such a surplus. Even without direct evidence of links between the two groups, the presence of both of them within the narrowly defined area of Soho and their obvious similarities of interest would lead one to expect close ties between the two groups. Beyond this, however, almost all observers of the scene agree that *most* of the new nontherapeutic addicts had only taken heroin following an involvement with amphetamines and barbiturates and/or marijuana.[107]

Cloward and Ohlin have commented on a similar process in America: "Younger persons who are ready to experiment or who are already occasional users represent a readily exploitable market; hence mature users tend to become linked to these younger persons. The older user provides a ready market for drugs."[108] The British experience suggests that the young are not slow to learn their lesson and quickly begin selling drugs themselves.

Obviously, the number of new addicts grew more rapidly because the gullibility or greed of a small group of doctors provided vast surpluses for addicts to sell through massive overprescription. This was the situation uncovered by the second Brain Committee. During the two-and-a-half-year hiatus that followed this report, the situation if anything deteriorated. The soft-drug market was becoming more organized in the face of an attempted official crackdown, and we have already described how some of the doctors involved were ceasing to prescribe, leaving the field largely to the most irresponsible of their number.

When the clinic system was finally initiated in 1968, there were official protestations to the effect that the intention was simply to change the *organization,* and not the underlying principle, of the British system. Even had the changeover not involved a change in this principle, the results might not have been wholly beneficial. As Nyswander argues, "My opinion, borne out by experience, is that any treatment center which brings active addicts together in large numbers is bound to fail in its purpose."[109] Nevertheless, whatever flaws of this type the clinics might exhibit, as long as they effectively reached the addict population and were prepared, where necessary, to make available legal heroin maintenance, they could at least prevent the emergence of a true black market and hence of a situation paralleling the American experience. Unfortunately, what evidence we have suggests that:

1. The clinics failed to reach all the addict population;
2. They were initially reluctant to provide heroin maintenance, and this reluctance has, if anything, increased. Obviously, a vital part of any further research on the British drug situation is to inquire into the reasons for and the effects of such a policy.[110]

To summarize the arguments of this section of the chapter: the emergence of a soft-drug subculture in Britain provided for the first time a sizable potential market for illicit addictive drugs. This situation was exploited by some addicts (their numbers were probably augmented by "refugees" from Canada and the United States) who were able to obtain large surpluses of heroin from a few irresponsible doctors. Official inaction following the discovery of this state of affairs probably worsened the situation, and recent developments in the policies of the new narcotics clinics threaten to compound the error by forcing addicts to resort to the black market to obtain their drugs.

It should be clear by now that it is not necessary for a government to prevent access to legal maintenance doses of heroin on the part of addicts for opiate addiction to develop into a social problem. It is quite apparent that in Britain in the 1960s the nature of addiction changed drastically, with increasing connections between drug taking and crime, the growth of an illicit traffic in drugs, the rapid increase of heroin use among juveniles, and so on. As I have pointed out, these new patterns arose prior to and independently of any official response, even though government response, when it did come, proved to be a complicating factor.

Consequently, the argument that Lindesmith tries to maintain, that knowledge of the policies adopted to control opiate addiction is sufficient to enable one to predict the nature of addiction in that country, will have to be modified or abandoned. Equally clearly, the relationship between legal definitions and practices and the nature of secondary deviance is by no means as simple as some writers have tried to maintain. As Lorber has noted in another context, the labeling approach frequently results in our "focusing on the characteristics of the controllers rather than the deviants."[111] It neglects to take account of the fact that a deviant outcome is the result of a process of reciprocal interaction. Indeed such an approach distorts any explanation of deviance in a morally unfortunate way, by making the deviant "the put-upon victim, with the social control agents the villain of the piece."[112] Writers on the subject of drug addiction have too often made precisely this mistake, as this chapter has tried to show.

Appendix Eleven

Table 11-1: Number of Known Addicts to Each Drug in Great Britain in 1936, 1937, 1938, 1939, 1947, 1950, 1954, 1958, 1959, and 1960.

	1936	1937	1938	1939	1947	1950	1954	1958	1959	1960
Morphine	545	447	406	421	134	139	150	169	205	204
Heroin	60	106	68	70	39	43	55	66	62	68
Cocaine	50	50	34	35	8	9	7	15	25	30
Methadone	—	—	—	—	2	5	17	32	47	51
Others	—	17	11	8	30	41	45	109	170	162
Total Addicts	616	620	519	534	199	226	260	347	442	454

Note: Where a person is addicted to more than one drug, he is counted as an addict to each drug, but in arriving at the totals shown at the bottom of the table each addict is counted once only.

Source: Adapted from *Drug Addiction: Report of the Interdepartmental Committee*, London, 1961, p.20.

Table 11-2. Addicts to Dangerous Drugs.

	1959	1960	1961	1962	1963	1964	1965
Total Number of Addicts to Dangerous Drugs	454	437	470	532	635	753	927
Number of Addicts to Heroin	68	94	132	175	237	342	521
Number of Addicts to Cocaine	30	52	84	112	171	211	311
Total Number of Addicts of Non-Therapeutic Origin	98	122	159	212	270	372	580
Number of Heroin Addicts of Non-Therapeutic Origin	47	72	112	157	222	328	509

Source: Drug Addiction: The Second Report of the Interdepartmental Committee, London, 1965, p. 14, together with provisional Home Office Figures for 1965.

Table 11-3: Ages of Addicts to Dangerous Drugs.

	1959	1960	1961	1962	1963	1964	1965	1966
Age under 20	—	1	2	3	17	40	145	329
Taking Heroin	—	1	2	3	17	40	134	n.a.
Age 20-34	50	62	94	132	184	257	347	558
Taking Heroin	35	52	87	126	162	219	319	n.a.
Age 35-49	92	91	95	107	128	138	134	162
Taking Heroin	7	14	19	24	38	61	52	n.a.
Age 50 and over	278	267	272	274	298	311	291	286
Taking Heroin	26	27	24	22	20	22	16	n.a.
Age Unknown	34	16	7	16	8	7	10	14
Total	454	437	470	532	635	753	927	1349

Source: Drug Addiction: The Second Report of the Interdepartmental Committee, London, 1965, p. 14, together with Provisional Home Office Figures for 1965 and Figures from M. M. Glatt et al., *The Drug Scene in Great Britain*, p. 18, for 1966.

Table 11-4: Rise in Addiction, 1960-1968.

	1960	1961	1962	1963	1964	1965	1966	1967	1968
Total Known Addicts	437	470	532	635	753	927	1349	1729	2782
Using Morphine	177	168	157	172	171	160	157	158	198
Using Heroin	94	132	175	237	342	521	899	1299	2240
Using Cocaine	52	84	112	171	211	311	441	462	564
Using Pethidine	98	105	112	123	128	102	123	112	120
Using Methadone	68	59	54	59	62	72	156	243	486
Male	195	223	262	339	409	558	886	1262	2161
Female	242	247	270	296	344	369	463	467	621

Note: Where a person is addicted to more than one drug, he is counted as an addict to each drug, but in arriving at the totals shown at the bottom of the table each addict is counted only once.

Source: The New York Times, March 30, 1970.

Table 11-5: Number of New Cases of Heroin Addiction Recorded, 1955-1964.

	1955	1956	1957	1958	1959	1960	1961	1962	1963	1964
British Men	4	5	5	3	4	11	18	39	54	98
British Women	5	5	2	8	6	4	9	10	23	35
Total New British Addicts	9	10	7	11	10	15	27	49	77	133
Canadian	—	—	—	—	1	4	24	16	10	15
Other Nationality*	1	—	—	—	—	4	5	5	3	14
Total New Foreign Addicts	1	—	—	—	1	8	29	21	13	29

*Includes: United States, 13; Jamaica, 8; India, 3; Australia, 3; New Zealand, 2; Other, 3.

Source: Adapted from Thomas Bewley, *British Medical Journal* (1965): 1284.

Table 11-6: Nationality of Heroin Addicts in the United Kingdom, First Known to Be Addicted, 1955-1965.

British Born	587
Canadian	72
United States	19
Jamaica	10
Australian	7
Nine Other Nationalities	14
Total	709

Source: Thomas Bewley, *United Nations Bulletin on Narcotics*, 18, No. 4 (1966): 4.

Notes

1. D. Matza, *Becoming Deviant* (Englewood Cliffs, N.J., Prentice-Hall, Inc., 1969), p. 80.

2. E. Lemert, *Social Structure, Social Control, and Deviation,* in Lemert, *Human Deviance, Social Problems, and Social Control* (Englewood Cliffs, N.J., Prentice-Hall, Inc. 1967), p. 18.

3. A. R. Lindesmith, *The Addict and the Law* (New York, Vintage Books, 1965), p. 128.

4. *Ibid.,* p. 283.

5. *Ibid.,* p. 129.

6. E. M. Schur, *Narcotic Addiction in Britain and America: The Impact of Public Policy* (Bloomington and London: The University of Indiana Press, 1962). Lindesmith's remark is to be found in Lindesmith, *The Addict and the Law,* p. 164.

7. Schur, *Narcotic Addiction in Britain and America,* p. 209.

8. E. M. Schur, *Crimes Without Victims: Deviant Behavior and Public Policy* (Englewood Cliffs, N.J., Prentice-Hall, Inc., 1965), p. 152.

9. *Ibid.,* pp. 154–155.

10. Department Committee on Morphine and Heroin Addiction, *Report* (London, 1926), p. 19.

11. Thomas Bewley, *Recent Changes in the Pattern of Drug Abuse in the United Kingdom,* United Nations Bulletin on Narcotics 18, No. 4 (1966): 1.

12. *Drug Addiction: Report of the Interdepartmental Committee,* p. 9. (Hereafter referred to as *Drug Addiction I*).

13. See Appendix.

14. *Drug Addiction I,* p. 9. The Brain Committee was originally set up in 1958 to inquire into the workings of the British system of Narcotics control. Three years after its first report, the Committee was reviewed, with a somewhat changed membership, to reassess its earlier advice in the light of changes in the nature and extent of addiction.

15. *Drug Addiction I,* p. 9, and Schur, *Crimes Without Victims,* pp. 119–120. Schur points out that addicts relying on the black market would be driven to crime; yet the number of addicts convicted for any offense has been consistently low.

16. M. M. Glatt, D. J. Pitmann, D. G. Gillespie, D. R. Hills. *The Drug Scene in Great Britain* (London: Edward Arnold Publishers Ltd., 1967), p. 23.

17. *Drug Addiction I,* p. 9.

18. Schur, *Narcotic Addiction in Britain and America,* pp. 142–143.

19. *Ibid.,* p. 144.

20. For an elaboration of the argument presented in this paragraph, see Schur, *ibid.*, pp. 138–156 et passim.

21. I. P. James, "Delinquency and Heroin Addiction in Britain," *British Journal of Criminology* (1969): 109–110.

22. *Drug Addiction: The Second Report of the Interdepartmental Committee.* (London: Her Majesty's Stationery Office, 1965), p. 4. (Hereafter, *Drug Addiction II*).

23. *Drug Addiction II*, pp. 5–6.

24. Glatt, et al., coined this term to make useful distinction between a black market that is supplied solely from surplus drugs originally obtained by addicts from a legal source and the sort of market prevailing in the United States.

25. James, *Delinquency and Heroin Addiction*, p. 110.

26. Despite the growing unreliability of Home Office figures, all of the available evidence points in one direction, namely, that this period saw a radical change in the nature of Britain's addict population. From Tables 11–2 and 11–3 (see Appendix 11) it is apparent that almost all the increase in numbers occurred among young people, principally those under thirty-five, and that an overwhelming proportion of these new addicts were of nontherapeutic origin and were addicted to heroin. The number of known addicts aged fifty and over remained remarkably stable over the same period of time, and the incidence of addiction to heroin, as opposed to other opiates, tended to decline somewhat among addicts in this age range.

27. See Table 11–5: note especially the figures for 1961 (when they provided more than half the new cases) and 1962. This table also provides confirmation that the growth in heroin addiction began towards the end of 1960 or in the early part of 1961. For a discussion of the role these foreign addicts may have played in the genesis of an addiction problem, see p. 302.

28. James, *Delinquency and Heroin Addiction*, p. 110. See also Table 11–6.

29. *Ibid.*

30. *Drug Addiction I*, pp. 11 and 22–23.

31. James, *Delinquency and Heroin Addiction*, pp. 119–122.

32. *The New York Times*, March 30, 1970.

33. *Ibid.*

34. *The New York Times*, March 30, 1970.

35. James, *Delinquency and Heroin Addiction*, p. 116.

36. I. P. James, "Suicide and Mortality Among Heroin Addicts in Britain," *British Journal of Addiction* (1967): 391–398.

37. *Drug Addiction II*, p. 6. The report estimates the number of such doctors as "not more than six." (*Ibid.*)

38. Max M. Glatt, *A Review of the Second Report of the Interdepartmental Committee on Addiction,* United Nations Bulletin on Narcotics 18, No. 2 (1966): 37.

39. *Drug Addiction II,* p. 6. The report states:

> From the evidence before us we have been led to the conclusion that the major source of supply has been the activity of a very few doctors who have prescribed excessively for addicts. Thus we were informed that in 1962 one doctor alone prescribed almost 600,000 tablets of heroin (i.e., six kilogrammes) for addicts. The same doctor, on one occasion, prescribed 900 tablets of heroin (nine grammes) to one addict and, three days later, prescribed for the same patient another six hundred tablets (i.e., six grammes) "to replace pills lost in an accident." Further prescriptions of seven hundred and twenty (i.e., 7.2 grammes) and eight hundred and forty (i.e., 8.4 grammes) tablets followed later to the same patient. Two doctors each issued a single prescription for one thousand tablets (i.e., ten grammes). These are only the more startling examples. We heard of other incidents of prescriptions for considerable, if less spectacular, quantities of dangerous drugs over a long period of time. Supplies on such a scale can easily supply a surplus that will attract new recruits to the ranks of the addicts.

40. James, *Delinquency and Heroin Addiction,* p. 111.

41. *Drug Addiction II,* p. 7.

42. *Drug Addiction II,* pp. 7–8.

43. *Drug Addiction II,* p. 13.

44. *Drug Addiction I,* p. 9.

45. *Sunday Times* (London), February 20, 1966.

46. *The Observer* (London), December 5, 1965.

47. One should bear in mind throughout this discussion that these are official figures and, as pointed out on p. 287, cannot be considered completely reliable. For our purposes, we are less concerned with the accuracy of any particular figure than with the trends the figures taken as a whole reveal. The fact that the official statistics tend to underestimate the rate of change in the character of the addicted population strengthens rather than weakens the argument we are making.

48. T. Morris, *British Journal of Sociology,* 1965, p. 368. Cited in Glatt et al., *The Drug Scene in Great Britain,* p. 30.

49. *The Times* (London), March 16, 1966.

50. *The Times* (London), January 30, 1967.

51. For an example of the treatment of the story in the less sensational press, see *The Times* (London), July 8, 1967, January 12, 1968, February 15, 1968, May 31, 1968, June 1, 1968, September 20, 1968. For a less restrained treatment, see the *Daily Mail* (London) for the same period.

52. *The Times* (London), November 9, 1966.

53. *The Times* (London), November 15, 1966.

54. *The Times* (London), January 31, 1967.

55. *The Times* (London), January 31, 1967, and April 7, 1967. Sir Paul Mallinson warned (*The Times,* February 7, 1967) that money should be allocated for the new centers and that these should not be grafted on to psychiatric

hospitals, which lacked both the premises and the staff to be used for this purpose.

56. *The Times* (London), April 7, 1967.

57. *The Times* (London), July 8, 1967.

58. *The Times* (London), January 15, 1968. In the same article, the doctor who had run the clinic commented: "The system is geared to creating fewer and fewer doctors to treat more and more addicts."

59. *The Times* (London), January 25, 1968. "At many (clinics) facilities are so rudimentary that they can barely be said to exist. . . . The experiences of some addicts suggest that some of the centres are not over-sophisticated. At one, an addict reported, he was offered his daily 'fix' in the form of a tablet with a glass of water."

60. *The Times* (London), January 31, 1968. Clinics were claimed to be in operation at: Westminster*, St. Clement's*, Charing Cross, Lambeth*, University College, Paddington, St. Giles (Kings), the Maudsley*, West Middlesex, Calne Hill*, and Bexley* Hospitals. (* Signifies that treatment was also available on an inpatient basis.) Westminster and St. Clement's held ten clinics a week; Charing Cross eight; and the rest one to three.

In addition, the following hospitals offered only inpatient care: Bethlem Royal, Tooting Bec, St. Bernard's and Hackney and North Middlesex. (All these inpatient units were treating a grand total of forty-two patients at the beginning of the year.)

New clinics were planned for: St. Luke's Woodside, Paddington General, Queen Mary's, Roehampton, Hackney, and St. George's, Tooting.

61. See Table 11–4. The official total of known addicts for 1967, including those addicted to opiates other than heroin, was 1729.

62. *The Times* (London), April 25, 1968, reports that 545 doctors were now allowed to prescribe heroin and cocaine to addicts; 529 of these were on the staff of 219 N.H.S. hospitals with treatment facilities; 7 were doctors in the prisons; and 9 were doctors in private centers providing treatment.

63. *The Times* (London), April 17, 1968, and April 30, 1968.

64. One distinguishes heroin addicts since, strictly speaking, other addicts could still be supplied by general practitioners; in fact, it is likely that addicts to some of the other drugs also used the clinics. For the figures on the number of addicts being treated at clinics, see *The Times* (London), October 26, 1968; on the total number of addicts, see Table 11–4.

65. See, p. 290.

66. *The Times* (London), January 9, 1969. A reply appeared on January 16 from Drs. Bewley and Willis, from which I quote:

> Dr. Adams and his colleagues point out that addicts require a great deal of time and attention which interferes with work done for other patients. This is true of any form of treatment in that the time and skill given to one patient means that there is that much less time and skill that can be devoted to others. If one is going to take the criterion of need or seriousness of illness when deciding treatment priorities, then heroin addicts who are often irresponsible and feckless and sometimes

lead lives not unlike that of man in his natural state—"solitary, poor, nasty, brutish and short"—especially since they are liable to secondary complications, have a strong claim to medical care on these grounds. The criteria for deciding on priorities for treatment should not be the comfort or convenience of the medical staff. If one is going to start picking and choosing "good" as opposed to "bad" patients, medicine is liable to deteriorate into occupational therapy for doctors.

The suggestion that addicts should attend police stations for treatment raises further problems. Damage to hospitals and waste of time can be caused by other patients attending casualty departments, for example, those drunk on a Saturday night. Are these also to go to the police station to have their wounds sutured? Since addicts are liable to the same illnesses as other people, apart from their addiction, they will require the same facilities for treatment as frequently as other patients. Dr. Adams and his colleagues have not indicated how they think these could be provided in a police station.

(The writers were consultant psychiatrists to: St. Thomas, St. George, and Tooting Bec hospitals and Bexley, Guys, King's College, and St. Giles hospitals).

To this statement, one must add that attempting to force addicts to obtain their supplies at police stations would be very likely to increase the number resorting to the black market.

67. *The Times* (London), January 14, 1969.

68. *The New York Times,* March 30, 1970.

69. *The New York Times,* September 13, 1970. In this context, a passage in the March 30 article in *The New York Times* had an ominous ring:

As the amount of Government heroin has dwindled, black market heroin, originating in China and smuggled through Hong Kong, is appearing in London's West End. It is called red chicken and the price has risen in the last eight months from $2.40 for 60 milligrams to as much as $14.40 (60 milligrams in New York would cost about $20). Although Scotland Yard is worried that the price is now profitable enough to encourage organized large-scale smuggling, officials say they have not seen evidence of it as yet. . . .

70. *Drug Addiction I,* p. 15 and p. 23.

71. L. G. Kiloh and S. Brandon, *British Medical Journal,* 2(1962): 40. Cited by Bewley, *Recent Changes in the Pattern of Drug Abuse,* p. 7.

72. Bewley, *Recent Changes in the Pattern of Drug Abuse,* p. 5.

73. Max M. Glatt, et al., *The Drug Scene in Great Britain* (London: Edward Arnold Publishers, Ltd., 1967), p. 43.

74. Bewley, *Recent Changes in the Pattern of Drug Abuse,* p. 6.

75. *The Times* (London), December 20, 1965.

76. "Purple hearts," the slang term for Drinamyl, an amphetamine/barbiturate combination, were the most commonly used pills at this time.

77. *The Times* (London), April 1, 1964.

78. *The Times* (London), May 1, 1964.

79. On this, see *The Times* (London), March 8, 1966, and April 14, 1966.

80. *The Times* (London), April 20, 1966.

81. *The Times* (London), May 1, 1964. Some of Brooke's remarks in the same debate seem to provide evidence for this assertion.

82. Bewley, *Recent Changes in the Pattern of Drug Abuse,* p. 7.

83. *The Times* (London), December 20, 1964.

84. P. Scott and D. Wilcox, *British Journal of Addiction,* 61: 9. Cited in Bewley, *Recent Changes in the Pattern of Drug Abuse,* p. 9.

85. Bewley, *Recent Changes in the Pattern of Drug Abuse,* p. 6.

86. For an example of this latter point, see *The Times* (London) March 2, 1968, when a raid by 150 police on a Soho club led to only 7 arrests on drug charges.

87. A good example of this point is to be found in *The Times* (London), March 13, 1967, where it was reported that 100 police spent 5 hours searching 600 teen-agers. For more examples, see *The Times* (London), April 24, 1967, and March 2, 1968.

88. *The Times* (London), September 22, 1970. This same article also suggests that in part this may reflect a decision on the part of the police to concentrate their forces on marijuana abuse, which would be a curious decision in view of the known greater dangers of amphetamines and barbiturates.

89. For suggestions that the time was ripe for a change in the law, see *The Times* (London), March 8, 1966, and April 1, 1967. Among the more extreme reactions against these proposals were the attempts to link marijuana to murder, homosexuality, and venereal disease. See *The Times* (London), January 31, 1967, and February 11, 1967.

90. *The Times* (London), February 28, 1967. Among those arrested were two of the Beatles, two of the Rolling Stones, and Donovan.

91. Letter from Rev. Kenneth Leech, *The Times* (London), March 4, 1967.

92. Perhaps the best known of the efforts to arouse support for the repeal of the act was the full-page advertisement appearing in *The Times* on July 24, 1967. For the views of the opponents, see *The Times* (London), July 26 and July 29, 1967.

93. This offense was at this time punishable by up to 10 years in jail and a fine of up to £1,000.

94. *The Times* (London), January 8, 1969.

95. One doctor attacked the report as "a sort of junkies' " charter; the British Medical Association said that they could not support any proposal that marijuana should be freely available; and the U.N. Division of Narcotics Drugs warned that any move to legalize marijuana would be "foolish and dangerous." *The Times* (London), January 9, 1969.

96. *The Times* (London), January 24, 1969.

97. Schur, *Narcotic Addiction in Britain and America,* p. 114.

98. See above, p. 286.

99. Glatt, et al., *The Drug Scene in Great Britain,* p. 28.

100. Schur, *Narcotic Addiction in Britain and America,* pp. 122–128.

101. Glatt, et al., *The Drug Scene in Great Britain,* p. 21.

102. Howard S. Becker, *Outsiders: Studies in the Sociology of Deviance* (New York: The Free Press, 1963).

103. One may speculate: possibly the increased legitimacy of chemical means of altering moods, brought about by massive advertising and widespread adult use of pills, may have been a factor; the prescription of large numbers of such drugs made them readily available; and their growing use by the stars of the pop world may have encouraged imitators.

104. Becker, *Outsiders,* p. 39.

105. Glatt, et al. (*The Drug Scene in Great Britain,* pp. 26–28) emphasize this more than does Schur (*Narcotic Addiction in Britain and America,* p. 146).

106. We obviously need further, less circumstantial, evidence to confirm this hypothesis.

107. For example: Glatt, et al. (*The Drug Scene in Great Britain,* pp. 63–64) comment: "Becoming an addict follows a rather well-defined pattern" and then cite a progression from purple hearts to marijuana to heroin obtained from pseudo black market, and eventually to the status of a registered addict.

     Bewley (*Recent Changes in the Pattern of Drug Abuse,* pp. 5–6) claims that "the majority" of young heroin users had previously taken marijuana.

     James (*Delinquency and Heroin Addiction,* p. 117) states that "only 66 percent (of his sample) admitted to regular use of cannabis prior to narcotic addiction."

     For other examples, see *The Times* (London), December 21, 1965 ("Young people were attracted toward hard drugs by the prestige attached to those who took them. There comes a feeling that 'only kids take purple hearts.' "), and January 25, 1968, January 28, 1969.

108. R. Cloward and L. Ohlin, *Delinquency and Opportunity: A Theory of Delinquent Gangs* (New York: The Free Press, 1900), p. 191.

109. Marie Nyswander, *The Drug Addict as a Patient* (New York: Grune Stratton, Inc., 1956), p. 116. Cited in Schur, *Narcotic Addiction in Britain and America,* p. 30.

     Some insight into why this should be the case is provided by Kai Erikson's remarks on agencies of social control: "Such institutions gather marginal people into tightly segregated groups, giving them an opportunity to teach one another the skills and attitudes of a deviant career, and often provoke them into employing these skills by reinforcing their sense of alienation from the rest of society." (K. Erikson, *Notes on the Sociology of Deviance* in H. Becker, *The Other Side* [New York: The Free Press, 1964], p. 16.)

110. Howard Becker has pointed out that changes in rules affecting deviants are usually drafted by professionals and that we should look for the consequences of this. From this perspective, it is interesting that the new narcotics clinics were established under the control of the psychiatric staff of hospitals. Since then, many doctors "have come to believe that dispensing heroin is incompatible with psychotherapy." With the aim of "helping the addict come to

grips with reality," they have decided to discontinue heroin maintenance. This ignores the disappointing results of similar programs in New York and raises the specter of addicts, unable to obtain supplies legally, resorting to a (growing) black market. Such actions may, *in practice,* change the principle underlying the British system of narcotics control to one resembling the American one. (Becker's remarks are to be found in *Outsiders,* p. 155; the quotations in this note are from *The New York Times,* March 30, 1970.)

111. J. Lorber, "Deviance as Performance," *Social Problems* 14, No. 3 (Winter 1967): 302.

112. *Ibid.,* p. 309.

| VI |

Sociological Theory
and Social Action

Some of the most original and challenging sociological research and theory done in the last decade has come from students of deviant behavior. This is not by chance. The subject matter itself raises the kinds of questions and problems that most directly challenge fundamental assumptions of sociological theory. It is, therefore, fitting that this volume concludes with two essays on sociological theory written by people who have studied deviance extensively.

The first essay, by Quinney, is a critique of sociological theory from the perspective of a radical. According to Quinney, our theories in the past, including those about deviance, have served to justify the existing social order because these theories take the existing order for granted and question only departures and threats to it. Value questions are held in abeyance and sociologists think about what is and not what ought to be. Quinney believes that this approach must be replaced with an alternative that springs from political involvement. It must be based on experience and desire; it must be relevant and personal. The sociologist's task is to decide what ought to be and to discover how to realize it. When this happens, sociological theory will become a liberating force in society rather than a force justifying the established order. Not all readers will agree with Quinney's point of view, but they will find his argument provocative and challenging.

The essay by Blum attacks the sociological enterprise from a different point of view. He suggests that sociologists have become preoccupied with studying social life while neglecting to examine in a self-conscious manner the nature of the enterprise in which they are engaging. Sociology studies the moral life, and, according to Blum, the sociological enterprise is itself an instance of morality in the sense that each study contains an implicit recommendation about how adequate inquiry is best accomplished. Blum argues that the failure of sociologists to analyze more deliberately the process by which they inquire into social life has resulted in a body of theory with both philosophical and practical defects.

Chapter Twelve

FROM REPRESSION
TO LIBERATION:
SOCIAL THEORY IN A
RADICAL AGE*

Richard Quinney

Theories of deviance—sometimes enhanced by research—serve a single purpose: they justify the existing social order. In all such endeavors, the established system is taken as given; what is questioned are departures from and threats to that order. In the name of understanding deviance, society has been protected at the expense of human freedoms. And through a special form of reasoning, the needs of the individual have been identified with the need to maintain and perpetuate social order.

We are now beginning to realize, however, what we have been doing as social scientists. Our social theories, based on old sensibilities, have done little else than support the established order. We have erected barriers to our lives and our imaginations. Our theories have been repressive, just as the order based on these theories has been oppressive. In other words, social theories have served to constrain rather than to liberate.

But we are entering a new age, one based on liberation as opposed to

* This article is an adapted version of Chapter 1 from Richard Quinney's *Social Theory in a Radical Age* (New Haven, Conn.: College & University Press, forthcoming).

repression. Our theories and our lives must be appropriate to the new age. No longer can we rely on obsolete ideas, inherited from a former age. Existing social theory—especially that pertaining to "deviance"—must be recognized for what it is and replaced by ideas that are relevant to the world we are creating. The only thing we have to lose is our captivity; what we will gain is our liberation.

In this chapter I would like to consider several aspects of our current malaise and the possibilities for our future. What I want to suggest is the nature of a social theory for our times. That theory will provide an alternative to the current perspectives toward "deviance." Only alternative ideas can be liberating, and liberation is the goal of our age.

I

The social sciences have always been the servants of the established society. Indeed, the very emergence of the social sciences was a reaction to social and political change. The early sociologists were disturbed by the many conflicts and upheavals that were occurring in Europe at the end of the eighteenth and the first half of the nineteenth century. It was hoped that sociology would discover the natural laws of society, and thereby provide a program for social tranquility.

The social sciences never broke from their reactionary background. To this day social scientists in their attempt to discover the laws of social order tend to favor the existing social arrangements. That which threatens social order is regarded as a violation of the natural laws of society. Sociology has supported that which would uphold social order and rejected anything that would disrupt that order, all in the name of a "value-free" science.

The search for order has provided a unity that embodies assumptions about the nature of reality, a methodology, and substantive theories of human existence. So that order might be discovered in the universe, the scientist has to assume that an order did in fact exist. And that knowable order easily led to the tautology that order was a desirable condition for man and his universe.

Only now are we beginning to construct alternative notions about reality and the process by which we understand our experiences. For us today the only reality is the one that man creates. This *social reality* begins in the imagination of the individuals who are involved with one another in the world of everyday life. The only reality that we can be attuned to is the reality that is ours as conscious social beings.

Yet as both observers and participants we want to give meaning to that reality. How can we ever really understand that reality? My own conclusion is that we cannot with absolute certainty. But this need not bother us; it may be the source of any significance that we obtain from our investigations. Our obligation becomes one of providing an interpretation that is relevant to the kinds of questions we raise and the lives we live in reference to that reality.

The "findings" of science have always been the constructs of the observer. All phenomena that we perceive are the result of the operations of our mind and soul. Our explanations are the consequence of the manipulation of our own constructions. Hence, the only world that we know as observers is the one we imagine. And that world is constructed through processes that are not always evident, by intuition as much as by rational thought.

The world, therefore, is always screened through the eye of the observer. We can have it no other way. The credibility of our observations is strengthened, however, by our involvement in the social reality that we are trying to understand. The traditional separation between the observer and the subject is consequently disappearing; to observe is to be part of that which is being observed. Knowledge is not an objective characterization, a "copy of reality," but a plausible interpretation of what we experience. The standard by which we judge the validity of our work is solely in terms of the meaning and consequences of our conclusions. This makes our work a truly moral endeavor.

Regarding the substance of their social theories, sociologists have traditionally been party to the established social order. They have been satisfied with the "facts," and have maintained an ideology that proscribed any attempt to go beyond them. Sociologists have generally yielded to the existing state of affairs, failing to delve into the metaphysics of what could be. Other than furnishing the rationale for the status quo, our lives have been impotent in both thought and action. The *transcendental* perspective has been systematically excluded from sociology in the attempt to achieve scientific status. What we are now beginning to realize is that our social theory must include metaphysical considerations. What I envision is the emergence of a transcendental mode of knowing, a critical stance that goes beyond an understanding of what *is* to a recognition of what *could be*. The result will be a *radical* social theory.

The substance of that theory will differ greatly from the theories based on the former model. Order will not be taken as the ideal of social existence. Disorder and change, rather than consensus and stability, will be recognized, and therefore will be an integral part of social theory. Society will be understood in terms of its power structures. The segments of society will be viewed according to their conflicts. Man will be understood as a creative being who is in the process of shaping his own history and the events around him. Man is always engaged in transcending his own existence. On the basis of such assumptions, we will construct social theories that are drastically different from those that dominate the social sciences. And never will we as individuals be the same. We will be a part of the dreams that we are creating.

II

But what is this thing called social theory? What does a social theory look like? And perhaps most important, is social theory really necessary? The answers to these questions are far from certain. My own answers have changed markedly in recent years. One thing is certain: the answers are not to be sought in the traditional model of science. The scientific approach to social theory has outlived its age.

For sociologists, social theory is not theory unless it is based on specific research. Theories, accordingly, are developed in the course of "testing" hypotheses. Sociologists have been so emphatic about this that they have designated their theories as "sociological theories." By doing this they have tried to eliminate the fear that there could be a social theory arrived at by other means.

Yet all theories (whether "sociological" or "social") attempt to accomplish the same objective: to understand the world that we experience. There are no short cuts to this objective, including those advanced in the canons of science. In spite of all rationale, we are all trying to give meaning to our lives and to reconstruct society.

A modern version of rationalism can replace many of the absurdities of the empiricism that has dominated the social sciences. Accordingly, everything we do can be regarded as research. Living is research. The aim is to understand and, when necessary, change the world around us. If some form of systematic research can aid that goal, then it should be conducted. But the problem with so much of scientific research is that it supports what the researcher already knows. Also, only low-level questions can be answered by such research. If the research can answer the question, the question was not significant enough to ask. Yet, rigid research may be justifiable when "data" are needed to support an important thesis. If the only way a significant argument can be accepted by others is through the show of research, then there should be research. But the social theory that is the most important for mankind is the theory that is tested through action, and the theory that calls for further action.

The forms that a social theory may take are varied. Some sociologists would have us believe that the forms are extremely limited. George Homans, as a major proponent of this position, has decreed that we must abide by the classical definition of theory: an explanation by means of a deductive system.[1] Such a theory contains a conceptual scheme and consists of a set of propositions, each stating a relationship. The propositions form a deductive system whereby subsequent propositions can be derived from prior ones. Ideally, it is accordingly suggested, a calculus should relate the variables and propositions.

Moreover, much of the theorizing in the social sciences takes the form of causal explanation. Following the mechanistic conception, it is assumed that the world is divided into variables and that the variables are causally related. Thus, many social theories postulate that one thing causes another, that event B is produced by event A. Such is the logic of implication: If this (A), then that (B). In this way, the methodological construct of causation has become the substantive theory of human behavior. The irony here for the social scientists is that the physical scientists have long since dispensed with causal explanation or use it with qualified meaning. A revision in the conception of the natural world and the relation of the observer to it has already occurred in the modern philosophy of science.

I contend that a social theory can take any form that makes sense. A social theory can look like anything one wants it to look like. It can be a deductive system, a series of statements, an essay that conveys a meaning in its totality, a poem, or a photograph. Communication of one's understanding can be on a very personal level. To communicate in precise scientific terminology need not be the only way of transmitting meanings. Poetic thought has its own way of informing us. A new language of expression seems to be emerging.

A debate exists in the social sciences as to the appropriate level of abstraction for social theory. Some years ago C. Wright Mills, in *The Sociological Imagination,* criticized what he called "grand theory" in sociology. Such theory, Mills observed, really said very little once its language was decoded. Recently Alvin Gouldner, in *The Coming Crisis of Western Sociology,* has renewed the attack. Gouldner contends that grand theory is a cop-out: "It is the politically defeated or the historically checkmated who write intensive, technically complex social theory. Such Grand Social Theory is thus, in part, a substitute for politics."[2] This critique of grand theory is important in pointing out the political nature of our activity—or at least our potential politicality. Such theorizing cannot be a substitute for political involvement. At the very least, our social theory must be politically relevant.

The best social theory, then, is that which springs from a political involvement. This means that as long as sociologists remain aloof from the happenings of our time their theorizing will be insignificant. Better are the ideas that come from those who are involved in the struggles of human liberation. Social theory is then based on experience and desire, that is to say, it is theory that means something. Rudi Dutschke, a leader in the Berlin student movement, wrote the following, which may serve as a word of advice for anyone who would engage in abstract theory:

> Today we are not bound together by an abstract theory of history but by an existential disgust in the presence of a society which chatters about liberty and yet brutally oppresses the immediate interests and needs of individuals and peoples fighting for their social-economic emancipation.[3]

Who needs a complex abstract theory when wrongs and actions are so clear?

This brings up the issue of who constructs meaningful and useful social theory. There is the myth that all social theory is written by a separate class of social theorists. This myth is perpetuated to a great extent by intellectuals and academicians who want to protect their own enterprise. But social theory as I conceive of it is made by any and all people. As long as there is an image of how things are or how they should be, a social theory exists. The consciousness of the people is a social theory. Social theory, in this sense, is being constructed in the everyday activities of living. It is such theory that is the most important for the way we live and the way we struggle for necessary changes in society.

The professional social theorists are persistent about separating theory from ideology. We are constantly being told that ideology plays no part in social theory. The historians of social theory, for example, are forever attempting to separate Karl Marx's ideology from his theory. But I maintain that one's ideology cannot be divorced from his theory, that, in fact, to do so robs social theory of its force and its potential. Everything that has any worth embodies a critique of our past and present, an image of the future, and a program of how we might achieve a better world. A theory is as good as its politics.

Social theory, therefore, must be linked to political action. The problem with social theory written by professional theorists is that they and their theories are usually removed from political involvement. Social theory by intellectuals has in the past century been formulated out of alienation and has been removed from action.[4] Even Marxism in America has been a reaction of isolated intellectuals rather than a viable social theory that has led to practice. For social theory to be important, those who propose it have to be involved in its realization. Such social theory is a combination of critique, a program, and a continual practice.

Without this unity social theory is destined to be forever ineffectual. The necessary unity of theory and action has been stressed by the Marxist economist, Ernest Mandel. While lecturing in the United States recently, Mandel discussed theory and action in the following way:

> Any form of theory which is not tested through action is not adequate theory, it is useless from the point of view of the emancipation of mankind. It is through a constant effort to pursue the two at one and the same time, simultaneously, and without division of labor that the unity of theory and action can be reestablished on a progressively higher level so that any revolutionary movement, whatever its origins and socially progressive goals, can really attain its objectives.[5]

Such a conception of social theory is centuries old. The driving force of the Enlightenment was the development of knowledge for the purpose of informing actions. Through reason man could critically examine his institutions and propose alterations that would allow him to realize his potential. Reason was the intellectual source of freedom. Theory and action were one.

Only later did a fascination with knowledge become the sufficient goal. Those who engaged in intellectual pursuits took refuge in knowing for its own sake. A rationale emerged that gave support to those who would remove themselves from the world of action in the name of knowledge. Academic freedom came to mean, among other things, the right to abdicate the responsibility of relating ideas and actions.

In the true sense of reason we can know and act because we have an idea of what things should be like. We know what exists in light of our knowledge of what should be—and we remove that part of existence that is not in accord with our vision of what should be. The ability to think negatively, as Herbert Marcuse has suggested, will allow us to return to this sense of reason.[6] Through the dialectical approach we can question current experience and work toward an alternative existence.

Rather than merely looking for an objective reality in our social theory, our concern is with the negation of the established order. That negation takes place both in our thought and in our action. Our actions are informed by our thoughts and our thoughts are shaped by our actions. This is social theory that is worth the effort.

III

The social theory I have in mind can only be regarded as *radical* social theory. And the age to which I am referring is the same—radical. Then what is radical?

I suppose the most common meaning of radical is a deviation of thought or action from some standard—no matter what that standard may be. The term according to this usage is devoid of substance. Depending upon one's own position, such deviation can be defined either positively or negatively. In these times, the term radical conjures up intense feelings in one direction or the other.

For people who place a high value on order and the traditional, radical is a pejorative designation. A marked departure from the usual is not regarded by many in America as fair play. Where moderation is a virtue— where vanilla ice cream is the safest way out—an attempt to go beyond existing conditions is cause for alarm. In such a context, the radical is regarded as being extravagant, extreme, and even fanatical. Whether he merely advocates a change or acts to bring it about, he is a radical.

Of course, radical as a label has to be imposed by someone on someone else. Radical in this sense has no specific content. It is only according to someone's sense of appropriate style. It follows that those who define others as radical have something to lose if a change should come about. The term radical is then used as a form of social control—to define as "bad" those who would advocate or bring about new conditions. When the term radical is used, you can be certain that someone in a position of power is trying to protect something he values. In this sense of radical, there is no substance to being radical, radical is merely a term that is used as a means of control. It changes with the wind—with alterations in the power structure.

But radical has a more lasting, substantive meaning. Radical is a philosophy that has definite content. It is this sense of radical that I take as my reference. Radical refers to that which is naturally fundamental to man and his social relations, that which is authentic to man. Radical is a particular consciousness and existence, one that assures the realization of man's potential as a human being. It is that which is irreducible and indivisible in man. Obviously I refer to a natural image of man that is self-evident. Radical is god-given, if you will.

The meaning of radical found its historical context in the course of the American experience. Following the ideals of the Enlightenment, America was founded on the libertarian principles of freedom and equality for all. As Staughton Lynd has shown in his *Intellectual Origins of American Radicalism,* radicalism was anything that would bring about and secure the freedom of man. This meant the removal of any oppression that denied man his freedom and equality. Through truths that are self-evident to all men, man has certain inalienable rights. These rights are not to be surrendered through government. In fact, it is man's obligation to overthrow that which denies him these rights. Oppressive laws are to be broken. Revolution is an ideal that may be practiced when man's rights are at stake. Our allegiance is not to particular governments but to the whole family of man.

It is to these ideals of definite substance that I refer when I use the term radical. We are in an age in which these ideals are more relevant than ever before, relevant because many of the ideals are not being realized. By referring to them, we can make aright that which is being denied. This is why a social theory based on radical principles is essential. We need a theory of ourselves and our society that will help us to achieve our human potential. A *radical social theory* can best assist us in accomplishing this task.

IV

A radical social theory is one that is also *personal.* The heretofore impersonal requisite of social theory is to be avoided. We are entering an age that calls for a different form of knowing. I begin my argument here with the recognition that intellectually we are coming into a time that combines the reason of the Enlightenment with a new romanticism. We are creating new assumptions about gaining knowledge. A new mode of knowing—one that is both radical and transcendental—is in the process of emerging.

Contemporary man has been a captive of his own rationality. Hawthorne, in what can only be the description of a very modern man, characterized our current malaise in Owen Warland, a man who would fashion a beautiful machine:

> He had lost his faith in the invisible, and now prided himself, as such unfortunates invariably do, in the wisdom which rejected much that even his eye could see, and trusted confidently in nothing but what his hand could touch. This is the calamity of men whose spiritual part dies out of them and leaves the grosser understanding to assimilate them more and more to the things of which alone it can take cognizance.[7]

Only now are we beginning to recognize the unseen that has been excluded by our impersonal rationality.

The scientific model has systematically excluded anything that could not be known through sense experience. We have naïvely suspended other means of knowing from our methodology. Yet there are other aspects of being human that enter into the process of knowing. Far from "biasing" our observations, these human characteristics make knowing possible. We entertain an idea because we simultaneously aspire to something beyond that which we experience.

The myth of rationality has thus prevented us from knowing about anything other than what presently exists. Working from a positivistic epistemology, the scientist has never been able to transcend the world that is. As a consequence we have not been able (and have not dared) to exceed the limits of ordinary experience. Politically, our science has been an alibi for the status quo. Little wonder that twentieth-century man has not risen above the problems of the age.

But how can a transcendental mode of knowing be achieved? As a beginning, we can only think transcendentally when we realize that such thinking is possible and, indeed, a necessary part of our endeavor. And most important, we can think and act transcendentally only when we live in a way that makes such activity possible. This means that those who would engage in radical thought and action must give up some of the pedestrian ways that have been followed as scientists. Transcendental thought requires that life be lived with an element of the romantic impulse. We must be immersed in our experiences, not letting life escape us. An image of the Greek tragedy is a good beginning; we are immersed in the stream of life, but our lives will never be fulfilled, never because we know of what we might be capable.

Some sociologists are fond of suggesting that sociology is an art as well as a science. With this sentiment I agree. The artistic would provide some of the elements for transcendence—for the construction of radical social theory. But the argument is usually that sociology is definitely a science (and must remain so), but that it can be infused with some of the creative imagination of the arts.[8] Aside from the questionable belief that science and sociology will remain the same, sociology really cannot be infused with the artistic until those who would do sociology live their lives *as artists*. This means that we cannot continually share in the comforts of the known and the established. We must be willing to push our lives to unknown limits. What we do in our research and writing must be related to the problems that are personal to us. Our investigations will have significance only when they are an integral part of our lives. Research is an experience out of which we know about ourselves and the world about us. We know the world about us because we are learning about ourselves in the process.

What I am saying is that as social theorists we cannot subscribe to the scientific model that claims to eliminate the personal factor from the knowing process. Rather, the personal factor is to be used to advantage. According to the scheme I have been presenting, we know through our personal experiences. No matter how hard we try, and in spite of the hopes of some sociologists, we can never get completely into the world of others. What we always end up with are descriptions based on how we as individuals see the world of others.

The place of our own biographies thus becomes paramount in the process of knowing. Our efforts cannot be devoted to a dispassionate analysis of past or current events. Norman Mailer has shown in writing *The Armies of the Night* that his personal account of that day at the Pentagon is as accurate as one put together by a historian. Mailer's account was better, more enlightening, more plausible, more sensitive because he was involved in what was happening. For all of us, involved in the happenings of the times, can furnish ourselves and others with a consciousness of what it is to be alive—to be acting and to be knowing.

The personal expression of our knowing also allows us to admit something that drives us all to know. That something is the desire to let others share our personal vision. Our labors are not exempt from a passion to leave an imprint where we once passed. This passion has been candidly admitted by R. D. Laing in the following way:

> This writing is not exempt. It remains like all writing an absurd and revolting effort to make an impression on a world that will remain as unmoved as it is avid. If I could turn you on, if I could drive you out of your wretched mind, if I could tell you, I would let you know.
>
> Who is not engaged in trying to impress, to leave a mark, to engrave his image on the others and the world—graven images held more dear than life itself? We wish to die leaving our imprints burned into the hearts of others. What would life be if there were no one to remember us, to think of us when we are absent, to keep us alive when we are dead? And when we are dead, suddenly or gradually, our presence, scattered in ten or ten thousand hearts, will fade and disappear. How many candles in how many hearts? Of such stuff is our hope and our despair.[9]

The only point at which I would qualify the personal style of knowing and acting is in respect to a style that becomes so highly personal that it is a retreat from the ongoing struggle for human liberation. Christopher Lasch finds some of this in the philosophy of the New Left.[10] Such an "existential irrationalism" may be so idiosyncratic that the resulting social theory will not be able to support a collective effort at radical social change. On the other hand, without a good measure of the personal, our social theories will be devoid of any potential for achieving radical goals.

In the long run, our own self-awareness will be the force that secures a radical social theory. Our social theory will, in turn, strengthen our self-awareness. We will be transformed as we consider social theory, and our social theory will be transformed as we gain self-awareness. As Gouldner has recently indicated, sociology as it now exists will be transcended as we develop a "Reflexive Sociology." This sociology will necessarily be a Radical Sociology.

> Radical because it would recognize that knowledge of the world cannot be advanced apart from the sociologist's knowledge of himself and his position in the social world, or apart from his efforts to change these. Radical, because it seeks to transform as well as to know the alien world outside the sociologist as well as the alien world inside him. Radical, because it would accept the fact that the roots of sociology pass through the sociologist as a total man, and that the question he must confront, therefore, is not merely how to *work* but how to *live*.[11]

Social theory conceived in such a way is appropriate to our age.

V

A principal problem that I am concerned with is the *exhaustion* of existing social theory. We are already into an age that requires a different set of ideas. Existing social theories were formulated according to sentiments quite distinct from our own. Today we are living lives that find little support in the theories we have inherited. We need social theories that refer to our lives and our hopes for the future. We must make our own social theory.

Today, more than ever before, we are realizing that social theories do not necessarily span the ages. As philosophers of science in our own right, we know that the credibility of a theory is more important than its validity, that a theory must be consistent with the infrastructure of the times. Today we have new sensibilities, but our inherited theories are based on old ones. Why shouldn't we be hostile to the old theories? The problem has been neatly stated for us by Gouldner:

> There is, in short, a gap between the newly emerging structure of sentiments among young radicals and the older "languages" or theories, a gap that has

not yet been bridged by the development of a new theoretical language in which young radicals might more fully express themselves and their own conception of reality.[12]

We are at a point where our experiences and our actions are ahead of our theory. We need a social theory that both corresponds to and gives guidance to our actions. Our theories will be advanced by our new circumstances. Certainly our current experiences are making many of the ideas of the past obsolete.

Yet, we are constantly being told to learn the classical theories of the past. Graduate and undergraduate students are held accountable for the theories of the "great" social theorists. I have friends, who years after completing their Ph.D.'s in sociology, continue to spend their summers rereading the classical theorists. Such studious homage is perpetuated by the sociology textbooks we read, write, and assign. A recent textbook, for example, *The Study of Modern Society,* has the subtitle of *Perspectives from Classical Sociology.* The author's purpose is to show "the student how these ideas apply to an understanding of contemporary American society."[13] From my reading, our understanding of contemporary society is not especially sharpened by the writings of Auguste Comte, Herbert Spencer, or the later sociologists. On the contrary, I find that my understanding is diminished by a rereading of these theorists.

The emphasis on studying the classical social theorist is given support in a recent book on theoretical sociology by Robert Nisbet, who reminds us: "We live, and should not forget it, in a late phase of the classical age of sociology."[14] He adds, "Strip from present-day sociology the perspectives and frameworks provided by men like Weber and Durkheim, and little would be left but lifeless heaps of data and stray hypotheses." Included in Nisbet's array of classical social theorists, in addition to Max Weber and Emile Durkheim, are Ferdinand Tönnies, Frédéric Le Play, Georg Simmel, Alexis de Tocqueville, and sometimes Karl Marx.

To his credit, Nisbet concludes his book with some reservations about the relevancy of the classical theorists: "It becomes ever more difficult to extract new essences, new hypotheses, new conclusions, from them. Distinctions become ever more tenuous, examples ever more repetitive, vital subject matter ever more elusive."[15] Sooner or later, he continues, a revolt from the classical theorists may occur. "Perhaps it is taking place in our own day before our unseeing eyes, with some thus far mute, inglorious Weber or Durkheim even now encapsulating stray hypotheses and random observations into a new idea system for sociology." To my mind there is no question about the imminence of the revolt.

The problem underlying our inherited theory is that it was designed to understand a preindustrial or industrial society. It posed questions, as all good theories must, about human nature, social order, and change. These questions are still relevant to us, but we have gone beyond the problems of the industrial age. Our problems are those of a postindustrial world. Whereas the ideas of community, authority, status, alienation, and the sacred are important to us, their substance has changed. Whereas the classical theorists, in constructing these concepts, were reacting to *disorder,* our reaction is to *order,* to the repression we find all around us. Therefore, the meaning that we give to our constructs are quite different from those given by the classical theorists. They valued order, we question order. They tended to support order for its own sake, we reject any order that oppresses us. Liberation is our goal—in theory and in action.

There is no question that there is more of value in Karl Marx than in all the other classical theorists put together. But I must admit that I find the orthodox ideas of Marx inadequate for our age. True, Marx raised for us the questions that are necessary for relevant social theory. His theory was real because it made us change our lives and carry on the fight for a better society.

Intellectually we seem to be between ages. *Between Past and Future* is how Hannah Arendt conceives of the problem. Whereas Marxist theory is more appropriate for us than an earlier theoretical tradition, we are now in another age.

> Our tradition of political thought had its definite beginning in the teachings of Plato and Aristotle. I believe it came to a no less definite end in the theories of Karl Marx. The beginning was made when, in the Republic's allegory of the cave, Plato described the sphere of human affairs—all that belongs to the living together of men in a common world—in terms of darkness, confusion, and deception which those aspiring to true being must turn away from and abandon if they want to discover the clear sky of eternal ideas. The end came with Marx's declaration that philosophy and truth are located not outside the affairs of men and their common world but precisely in them, and can be "realized" only in the sphere of living together, which he called "society," through the emergence of "socialized men."[16]

Especially troublesome for us today is the realpolitic of Marxism. Whatever Marx may have intended, his ideas have been used to support the authoritarian state. I am against authority of any kind—even when it is supposed to better mankind. That stuff on "dictatorship of the proletariat" does not strike a pleasing chord within me. My own anarchistic tendencies prevent me from considering any form of state socialism. That the state is to someday "wither away" gives me no satisfaction.

Moreover, the Marxist ideas on revolution pertain to social and historical situations that are quite different from our own. Marx was concerned primarily with the future of European industrial societies. Lenin bridged the gap between colonial countries and industrialized nations by theorizing about their mutual revolutionary conditions. Mao, in his own application of Marx, developed a theory for revolution in an Asian peasant society. What we need now is a theory—or a drastic revision of Marxist theory—for revolution in an advanced industrial society.

No, I am certain that we must formulate our own theories. No matter *what* Marx said, we must say it for ourselves—in our own time. Our consciousness is different from that of Marx. We must create a theory that relates to our own consciousness. Yet, we will continue for some time to take Marx as our reference point. But we must say it and do it in our own way, in terms of how we are living, what we are feeling, what we are doing, according to the consciousness of our time. We must make our own theories in terms of the experiences of our age.

I am convinced that the significant ideas are being advanced by the new revolutionaries and anarchists. The way they are living their lives and the nature of their political action are pointing the way to a new existence. Not only are they acting but through their writings they are informing the rest of the world. The writings of the new revolutionaries and anarchists are more in keeping with the theories that we will need for our future than are most of the writings of established social scientists.

In other words, I think I know where the social theory of our age is being written, or where the greatest potential for such theory lies. To be sure, it is easy to criticize some of the ideas or the lack of direction among some of the writers. But when something new is being created, you cannot expect (nor desire) the rigid schemes that characterize the theories that are being surpassed.

The New Left can be disappointing in the way some of its writers are dominated by a strict Marxist interpretation and the use of a 1930s rhetoric In this respect the New Left differs little from the Old Left, except that the New Left does not have the guilt of the cold war experience. Some time ago, C. Wright Mills, as he was defining the emergence of the New Left, noted how it clings to questionable Marxist ideas, remarking that "what I do not quite understand about some New Left writers is why they cling so mightily to 'the working class' of the advanced capitalist societies as *the* historic agency, or even as the most important agency, in the face of the really impressive historical evidence that now stands against this expectation."[17] Yet we are unlikely to throw off the past completely as we enter a new world. In spite of the ethic on spontaneity and originality, and perhaps unfortunately, new worlds are shaped by the old.

Yet the theory for our age is emerging. It is coming from many corners. The sources are to be found in the universities, in the communities, on the street, in the ghetto, wherever men and women desire to be free. We are relying on our experiences and our instincts for guidance. Where we are going no one has ever been before.

VI

Part of the problem that we inherit from a former age is science itself. At least the ethic of science has channeled the efforts of its members in specific directions. This leads to the exclusion of other ways of viewing and understanding the world. And in many cases, science has directly produced problems, rather than solving them.

The social scientist is especially defensive about his enterprise. He has been trained to regard science as the surest way of gaining knowledge and the best means for solving social problems. The sociologist has been a superscientist, for he has had to continually fight for scientific status. What we find in sociology today reflects the sociologist's overcompensation to become a scientist.

The battle cry for the sociologist has been that all social problems can be solved by scientific solutions. (Or I should say, this ideology has become the prevailing theme for the entire society. The sociologist has been both a force and a tool in establishing and maintaining this ideology.) George Lundberg expressed the gospel when he, in *Can Science Save Us?,* argued that "the best hope for man in his present social predicament lies in a type of social science strictly comparable to the other natural sciences."[18] It had to be a particular kind of social science, a positivistic one modeled after the natural sciences, that would provide salvation for us all.

We proceeded on the assumption that knowledge (scientific knowledge) is by definition a good thing, that any knowledge obtained would be a positive force. For the sociologist this meant that any research was valuable. Research supposedly would lead to enlightenment and eventually to the right solutions to our social problems. What was ignored in this formula was the fact that social problems and their solution are a matter of values. And it is only through political action that changes can be made. No amount of research can solve social problems as long as the research that relates to the problem ignores (or tacitly supports) the values underlying the problem. The sociologist's research for the many recent government task forces (on crime, drugs, riots, violence, and campus disorder) does little more than support the society that brought the problem about in the first place. Rather, what is needed for change is a questioning of the existing society, the existing values, that makes such conditions and events possible. Once we are locked into the research that supports existing definitions of the situation, we are unlikely to break out. And the release requires taking a value position and politically acting in a way that achieves a redefinition of the situation.

But our social science trains us to exclude values from our consciousness and political action from our lives. Indeed, the canons of science are quite specific in this regard. There is a whole doctrine that supports a "disinterest" on the part of the scientist. We have a trained incapacity to value and to act. It is the sociologist's "moral responsibility" to abide by the canons of his science. The sociologist has received the lofty calling to "the enterprise of science and scientific inquiry."

> This enterprise has its own rules and regulations—its own norms—and these he has the moral obligation to obey. I refer in this connection to the ordinary norms of intellectual discipline—the discipline, in the other sense of that word, that makes of scientific inquiry a regulated and orderly kind of procedure. These are the *mores* of science, the responsibilities that the social scientist owes to the discipline itself. They include such things as his obligation to satisfy appropriate canons of evidence, to exhibit a proper energy in the search for negative instances, to dissipate his biases as far as possible, to allot a condign credit to his predecessors, to enclose his quotations in quotation marks, to entertain his premises with skepticism and to offer his conclusions with humility.[19]

This is no less than the application of the *law and order* ideology to our intelligence. Quite consistent with it would be a police force to ensure enforcement of the canons and concentration camps for the dissidents. And I doubt if there would be a court of law to assure the minimums of due process. But who needs the apparatus when we already have effective informal procedures that keep us good and ostracize us when we are bad? Besides, the rewards for being good, social, and pecuniary are too great to pass by.

Science itself, then, is repressive in its own right. It is repressive to those who practice it and repressive to those who are subject to it. This in the name of being "value-free." In fact, it is this "value-free" ideology that permits the social scientist to accommodate to the existing system, to research problems and solutions that will maintain the status quo, and to oppress both himself and his subjects. The sociologists, in spite of Max Weber's sleight-of-hand in the elimination of value-judgments, has values—dangerous ones that assure accommodation instead of liberation. Rather than transcending the repressiveness of our society, we become part of it. Our activity is a part of the problem. Real solutions will come only when we break out of the mold.

This is what seems to be occurring. The model of science is undergoing a process of change. We are moving out of the scientism of the past. The science—if that is what we want to call it—of the future will be considerably different from the science we have known for the last century. As social scientists—or whatever we are becoming—we will not be bound by the repressive rules of positivistic science and we will not engage in enterprises that oppress others. We will refuse to be a part of the established power structure. In our thought we will dare to transcend current modes of understanding. In our actions we will bring about radical alternatives. Never will we be the same.

VII

But can there be a relevant sociology? Can there be a sociology as an occupation? Will there be a sociology that is other than repressive? Will there be one that is liberating? Can there be a radical sociology? Or is something entirely different happening?

Sociology has traditionally, in rhetoric at least, been above mundane practical affairs. Under the doctrine of objectivity, it has pursued "truth for its own sake." Sociologists have tried not to support or advocate any particular social policy. When they did so, it had to be as "citizen," not as sociologist. Only now are we realizing that this godlike stance was merely an accommodation to a particular kind of society.

On occasion, and with increasing frequency, social scientists have advocated some form of participation in public policy. An early version of policy involvement was proposed under the rubric of "the policy sciences." (Such activity, after all, had to be "scientific.") Harold Lasswell, as the principal creator of the policy sciences, advocated the scientific implementation of values. In particular, "If our moral intention is to realize a democratic society, we need a science of democracy to implement the goal."[20] The problem in this formulation, for any libertarian, however, is the policy scientist's desire to control the factors upon which democracy rests. Lasswell had in mind a "techno-scientific culture," one whose population was manipulated by the policy scientists. For the policy scientists, as Floyd Matson has shown,

> This faith in social and political physics has produced with impressive regularity the vision of a techno-scientific future from which all contest and contingency have been removed; and with it a corresponding image of man —manipulated and managed, conditioned and controlled—from whom the intolerable burden of freedom has been lifted.[21]

The more modern version of the policy sciences, but containing the same tendency to manipulate the people, is found among a group of social scientists who advise the government. This "vanguard of professional reformers" propose liberal policies to be benignly administered to the people. The magazine founded by Daniel Bell and Irving Kristol, *The Public Interest,* represents some of these "scholar-consultants."[22] For these professional reformers, bureaucratic centralization of services is the only means for achieving the good society. Social change takes place within the existing order, through the good graces of the Welfare State.

Today establishment sociology itself is tied to the Welfare State. Whereas there is still some nominal rhetoric about the separation of sociology from government policy-making, the fact is that establishment sociology has formed an alliance with the Welfare State for the mutual benefit of both. A good indication of this alliance is found in the recent report titled *Sociology,* commissioned by the National Academy of Sciences and the Social Science Research Council, and edited by Neil Smelser and James Davis. As Alvin Gouldner has observed in a review of the report, this is "the Sociological Establishment's view on how to manage relations with the Welfare State without undermining its own power position in sociology."[23] Establishment sociology has made its peace with the problem of objectivity. Its ideology combines rigorous science with government cooperation, serving the need all at once for financial support and respectability.

Another variety of sociology, which is fast becoming part of establishment sociology, is characterized by a special approach to the study of social problems. Beginning years ago at the University of Chicago, this brand of sociology uses informal research and attempts to view behavior from the standpoint of the actor. This approach aims to represent the interests of the social deviant, the "underdog." Nevertheless, these sociologists maintain a detached and complacent stance toward the world.[24] Politically the approach is characterized by its liberalism, which means that the Welfare State is supported. The deviant is regarded as a product of society who can be improved, rather than as a conscientious rebel against it. Such deviance, according to this sociology, which supposedly represents the deviant, is a problem to be handled by agencies beyond the deviant's control, by the Welfare State.

A new style of sociology is emerging that conceives of sociology as a distinct interest group. Its adherents make explicit their advocacy of particular policies, and in order to make such advocacy effective, the sociologist needs the support and protection of a strong sociological association. In the hands of its principal spokesman, Irving Louis Horowitz, there is much talk about making sociology "viable," a sociology with "clout," a sociology that will be "taken seriously by friend and foe alike." There is the desire to gain access to the centers of decision-making. Out of this fear of impotency, Horowitz suggests a sociology that has power, at least one that can represent itself in the governmental decision-making process.

This "new sociology" is to be composed of a loyal group of members. There is no room for what Horowitz calls the "marginals," those "unsociologists" who are trained in sociology but have allegiance to other institutions, or those "antisociologists" who have allegiance to social science horizons outside of sociology proper. The "new sociology" is to develop among the "mainliners" who regard sociology as an occupation. "Without wishing to minimize the contributions of the 'marginal,' it must be said in all frankness that the main struggle for the emergence of a new sociology can be engaged in only by those willing and capable of entering the arena; that is, by the 'mainliners.' "[25] No room here for an outsider, only the loyal. The most pressing question then becomes, "What kind of agency should the sociologist have?" What kind of organization will best promote the vested interests of the sociologist?

Finally, there is emerging within sociology a group of "radical sociologists." Much of the effort thus far has been a rebellion against establishment sociology. At the annual meetings of the American Sociological Association there have been "counterconventions," occurring alongside the regularly scheduled program. For the moment the goals and tactics of radical sociologists are far from certain. It is not clear whether the aim is to radicalize the membership of the American Sociological Association, or whether it is to form a new organization of radical sociologists. And there is yet to emerge a definite intellectual stance. But what is important for the moment is the emergence of a consciousness that sociologists cannot help but be politically involved. Whereas the sociologist has always been involved in spite of himself, he must now be aware of his involvement and use it to promote the liberation movement.

But can sociology, as an occupation or profession, even in a radicalized form, be a liberating force? Can there be a radical "sociology"? Some sociologists certainly think so.[26] But I am counting on some other form of activity and intelligence to bring about radical alternatives. A truly liberated society, as I see it, will be attained only when individuals are free to think and act as human beings. What I envisage are radical human beings, not a cadre of sociologists who would try to be radical. I doubt that an organization of sociologists can be liberating. What I fear is that such an organization would merely become a new establishment of sociologists who are more desirous of promoting their own interests as sociologists than in fighting oppression and achieving liberation. The new establishment would be merely another form of oppression. The truly liberated person will think and act as a human being, not as a member of another establishment.

What may be occurring, then, is the demise of the sociologist. Indeed, I am arguing that this must be the case if we are to attain our human rights and achieve a liberated society. A sociology can exist only in a repressive society. In a free society there will be no organization of sociologists, radical or otherwise. In a free society all the people will be capable of thought and action. These are human qualities, not special ones reserved for the elect. Any organization of sociologists is an elitist body. The people will not need sociologists to speak for them; they will speak for themselves. I find hope in a free, radical people, rather than in a radical sociology.

VIII

The radical today must contend with a particular kind of intellectual environment. It is out of this environment that many of us are emerging. A new one is being created, but at the same time the old one continues to stake its claims. Although I hesitate to distinguish the two intellectual environments this way, one is the liberal, the other is the radical. The two, as is obvious throughout my discussion, are clashing sharply. It is liberalism that I am reacting to in formulating a radical social theory.

The liberal style of thought embodies a certain demeanor on the part of its adherents, just as the radical thought has its own style. Basically, the liberal style entails a gentlemanly, compromising demeanor that ends in support of the establishment. The syndrome has been aptly described:

> Between our ineradicable bourgeois upbringing and the taste for the finer things of life that our humanistic education has given us, we have become conditioned to a minimally middle-class standard of living—even if it involves no more than a regular yearly income of four or five thousand; and the security of our pleasant sanctuary on the campus, in the publishing house or foundation headquarters, and we have amassed our own modest interest in the status quo.[27]

The political accomplishment of this style is the inadvertent diversion of intellectuals away from radical commitment. This is a humanism that has in spite of itself given support to a nonhumanistic power elite.

The theoretical stance of the liberal style came to be characterized by a single phrase: the end of ideology. Ironically (perhaps), this thesis itself became an ideology among liberal scholars. What was a perspective for analyzing politics and society was also a statement of desire. The end of ideology thesis involved not only the notion that ideological politics was absent in industrial society, but a positive value was placed on the absence of such a politics. The good society was one without ideology, one characterized by stability and affluence, and such a society was within reach. The presence of an ideology would only serve to hinder the realization of such a society.

The end of ideology thesis was developed in such works as Edward Shils' *The Torment of Secrecy,* Seymour Lipset's *Political Man,* and Raymond Aron's *The Opium of the Intellectual.* But most important was the writing of Daniel Bell, found particularly in his book entitled precisely *The End of Ideology.* Whereas the definitions of ideology varied among the writers, all found little redeeming value in the presence of ideology. Ideology, except their Old Left socialistic one, was something to abhor, or at least to be wary of. Ideology was not social theory held by a group of people, but a justification for questionable action. As Bell stated it, "Ideology is the conversion of ideas into social levers." All were skeptical of the passion with which ideologies are held by their adherents. Passion, after all, is not a gentlemanly quality; it breaches the etiquette of moderation.

The liberal end of ideology writers had a particular notion of democracy in mind—an elite democracy. For them democracy is stable, yes, but is based upon the rule of selected men, "representatives," who rule in the name of the people. And, of course, these rulers keep the people from erring in their ways. Complete power in the hands of the people, they assume, is a dangerous thing for a "stable democracy." In other words, a complete and thorough democracy, a people's democracy, is unthinkable—for the good of the people.

The liberal orientation (ideology) to politics found support in the prevailing sociological theories, especially in the highly abstract work of Talcott Parsons. In *The Social Systems,* among other places, Parsons developed his model of the stable society, one that is in a state of equilibrium, or one that is constantly "maintaining" its equilibrium. Any deviance must be expelled from the system or absorbed in some way. Social change takes place within the system, not from without. Morality is viewed as a source of social order, rather than as a human creation that gives meaning to life. Everything is for the good of preserving the social system. The functionalism of Parsons and his followers represents the *law and order* approach to social theory.

EXTREMISM! That's what failure to conform to genteel politics will lead to. If a social system fails to maintain its order, there will be those who will engage in a politics outside of the "legitimate" political process. The result will be ideological politics rather than procedural politics. Orderly politics is especially tenuous in "mass society," in a society that is not characterized by a pluralism of social groupings. The assumption is that in a liberal democracy all people will engage in political activity within some agreed upon system of rules and procedures. Anything outside of this system is "extreme."

Most of the liberal writers used either Nazi Germany or the McCarthy era in the United States as the grounds for their formulations. Daniel Bell edited several essays by some of these writers in a book titled *The Radical Right.* (The term "radical" was of course devoid of substantive politics, referring instead to an "extremism" on the right.) All of the writers attempted to explain the rise of the "radical right" within the liberal-functional-pluralistic framework. For Bell the radical right members engaged in politics because they were "dispossessed": "Today the politics of the radical right is the politics of frustration—the sour impotence of those who find themselves unable to understand, let alone command, the complex mass society that is the polity today."[28] In his essay, Richard Hofstadter argued that McCarthyism could be explained as a form of "status anxiety" in groups that have been "tormented by a nagging doubt as to whether they are really and truly and fully American." Lipset went on to distinguish between "class politics" (extremist politics during periods of depression) and "status politics" (extremist politics during periods of prosperity). What the writers were really disturbed about was the lack of *civility* among extremists. Using Shils' phrase, "the civility achieved only in a small group of countries—those largely with an Anglo-Saxon or Scandinavian political tradition," was being threatened by an extremist politics.

Such was the danger of any ideology. The liberal scholars were so traumatized by the Nazi experience and the right wing movement that they could not conceive of *any* politics outside of the politics of American civility. They continue to place such a value on civility, stability, and their idea of liberal democracy that they cannot admit the value of any form of politics that threatens the existing political regime. This reasoning would have us all lie down like lambs (be good Germans) while the American government unconstitutionally stifles dissent and continues an immoral and illegal war in Southeast Asia. Liberals do protest sometimes, but all within the framework of civility, within a framework that is as ineffectual as it is genteel. The liberals—with their obsession over style—continue to be confused. They lack the ability today to make distinctions, to see and value true radicalism when it appears, a radicalism that promotes a genuine democracy. Nowhere do they allow a conscience that detests an immoral and repressive government.

The point I am making is that liberalism as practiced today is inadequate for our age. Continual reliance on it is also a source of the problems of our age. But I have argued, as well, that classic Marxism has lost much of its significance for us today. C. Wright Mills reached a similar conclusion: "The major developments of our time can be adequately understood in terms of neither the liberal nor the Marxian interpretation of politics and culture."[29] We are in what Mills called "The Fourth Epoch," an age beyond "The Modern Age." Yet, our explanations are derived from the transition of the Medieval to the Modern Age. Both liberalism and the Marxian interpretation have collapsed as a social theory for understanding the society we now experience.

Yet, some of the ideals of liberalism are still important; and Marxism as a statement of man's oppression and liberation is essential. But both present us with inadequate social theories for the kind of society we have today. "If the moral force of liberalism is still stimulating, its sociological content is weak; it has no theory of society adequate to its moral aims."[30] Whereas the ideals of liberalism may remain viable, they cannot be realized according to the social theories that modern liberals espouse. Although Marxist utopianism must continue to prevail, continual espousal of classical Marxist rhetoric will accomplish little in today's world.

What we need is a social theory that relates both sets of ideals and goes beyond them to a better understanding of our age. The radical perspective seems to be the answer. We are trying to achieve our liberation in a society that represses its attainment. This is a perspective that takes the libertarian ideal and relates it to a radical critique of society. The result is utopian: a free human being in a liberated society.

IX

In conclusion we return to the underlying concern: the nature and purpose of social theory in our lives. It is evident by now that the social theories we have inherited from former ages are inadequate for our times. Our inherited theories are bankrupt, for they no longer help us to understand the world around us.

Liberal social theories were not able to predict what has happened to America. They did not foresee the collapse of the system. They promised only that science and technology, and a liberal intelligence, would make the world better. Instead, today's problems are beyond reform; the war in Southeast Asia is a moral disaster (rather than merely a miscalculation), and a revolution is in progress. The traditional social theories did little more than provide a rationale for the perpetuation of a corrupt system.

When all of this can happen, we ask: Is social theory really necessary? When the dominant social theories were so far from the truth, when they were lies, why did we bother with theories at all? If a revolution can take place without social theories, why have any social theory?

These are hard questions when one assumes that lives are informed by ideas. After all of this writing, I am not yet ready to admit that social theory is dead. Social theory—*if conceived correctly*—does have a vital role in shaping a new world. A judgment on the inadequacy of traditional social theory does not automatically negate the importance of all social theory. Indeed, the radical ideas I draw from—to understand our age—form a social theory to rival the traditional theories. Furthermore, the remarkable happenings of our time have resulted from these very ideas. Our lives have been influenced by ideas, but they have been other than the ideas that have dominated our established social theories.

The social theory of our radical age is thus drastically different from traditional social theory. It is different, first, in substance. Radical social theory liberates rather than represses. Radical social theory and traditional social theory are different, secondly, in their form. Rather than necessarily being systematically formulated and highly analytical, radical social theory tends to be less orderly, more descriptive, and highly critical. Third, the social theory in our radical age, in comparison to the theories inherited from former ages, differs considerably in its sources. Whereas the traditional social theories were, for the most part, formulated and presented by established philosophers, social scientists, and the like, radical social theory is suggested by anyone—and everyone. Radical social theory is not an elite theory, coming necessarily from the prominent intellectuals of the day. Instead, radical social theory is constantly being made by the people.

And it is this fact that makes today's social theory so relevant: it is derived from our experiences and it, in turn, makes us act in the creation of new experiences. Never before has social theory been such an integral part of action. Theory and action are becoming one. As this happens we do not necessarily look to books for our social theory, but social theory is found in our everyday activities, in the way we live our lives. Radical social theory is in itself a revolutionary social theory.

The final characteristic of radical social theory, in contrast to traditional theory, is that it makes no attempt to stop with what is. Instead, a primary concern with what ought to be helps us to create and understand what is even beyond our experience, and, only a consideration of what could be allows us to understand what presently exists. Traditional social theory failed, among other reasons, because it refused to consider what could be. In being one-sided it failed to understand what is. Radical social theory moves us beyond an understanding of the present to a future that can be.

What I am proposing as a radical social theory, then, involves a fusion of the transcendental and the political. A radical social theory is inconceivable without this combination. The transcendental allows us to go beyond our experiences; the political forces us to question our experiences and to act in a way that will alter them. Only through such a social theory can we meet the problems of our age. It is through a radical social theory that we can approach our current crisis in thought and action. Only a radical social theory can liberate us—socially and spiritually. Liberation is the true goal of social theory in our radical age.

Notes

1. George Casper Homans, "Contemporary Theory in Sociology," in Robert E. L. Faris, ed., *Handbook of Modern Sociology* (Chicago: Rand McNally, Inc., 1964), pp. 951–977.

2. Alvin W. Gouldner, *The Coming Crisis of Western Sociology* (New York: Basic Books, Inc., 1970), p. 153.

3. Rudi Dutschke, "On Anti-Authoritarianism," in Carl Oglesby, ed., *The New Left Reader* (New York: Grove Press, Inc., 1969), p. 251.

4. See T. B. Bottomore, *Critics of Society: Radical Thought in North America* (New York: Pantheon Books, Inc., 1968), pp. 37–46.

5. Ernest Mandel, "The Revolutionary Student Movement: Theory and Practice" (New York: Young Socialist Alliance, 1969), p. 11.

6. Herbert Marcuse, *Reason and Revolution* (Boston: The Beacon Press, 1960), pp. 3–29.

7. Nathaniel Hawthorne, "The Artist of the Beautiful," *Selected Short Stories*, edited by Alfred Kazin (New York: Fawcett World Library, 1966), p. 213.

8. Robert A. Nisbet, "Sociology as an Art Form," in Maurice Stein and Arthur Vidick, eds., *Sociology on Trial* (Englewood Cliffs, N.J.: Prentice-Hall, Inc., 1963), pp. 148–161.

9. R. D. Laing, *The Politics of Experience* (New York: Ballantine Books, Inc., 1967), pp. 185–186.

10. Christopher Lasch, *The Agony of the American Left* (New York: Vintage Books, 1969), pp. 46–47.

11. Gouldner, *The Coming Crisis of Western Sociology*, p. 489

12. *Ibid.,* p. 7.

13. Philip Olson, *The Study of Modern Society: Perspectives from Classical Sociology* (New York: Random House, Inc., 1970), from the back cover.

14. Robert A. Nisbet, *The Sociological Tradition* (New York: Basic Books, Inc., 1966), p. 5.

15. *Ibid.,* p. 318.

16. Hannah Arendt, *Between Past and Future* (New York: The Viking Press, Inc., 1968), p. 17.

17. C. Wright Mills, "The New Left," *Power, Politics, and People: The Collected Essays of C. Wright Mills,* edited by Irving Louis Horowitz (New York: Ballantine Books, Inc., 1962), p. 256.

18. George A. Lundberg, *Can Science Save Us?* 2nd edition (New York: David McKay, Inc., 1961), p. 42.

19. Robert Bierstedt, "Social Science and Public Service," in Alvin W. Gouldner and S. M. Miller, eds., *Applied Sociology* (New York: The Free Press, 1965), p. 413.

20. Harold D. Lasswell, *Analysis of Political Behavior: An Empirical Approach* (London: Routledge and Kegan Paul, 1948), p. 17.

21. Floyd W. Matson, *The Broken Image: Man, Science and Society* (New York: Doubleday Anchor Books, 1966), p. 99.

22. See Maurice R. Berube and Marilyn Gittell, "In Whose Interest Is 'The Public Interest?'" *Social Policy* (May/June, 1970): 5–9.

23. Alvin W. Gouldner, review of Neil J. Smelser and James A. Davis eds., *Sociology* (Englewood Cliffs, N.J.: Prentice-Hall, Inc., 1969), in *American Sociological Review* 35 (April, 1970): 332–334.

24. For a critique, see Alvin W. Gouldner, "The Sociologist as Partisan: Sociology and the Welfare State," *American Sociologist* 3 (May, 1968): 103–116.

25. Irving Louis Horowitz, "Mainliners and Marginals: The Human Shape of Sociological Theory," *Professional Sociology* (Chicago: Aldine Publishing Company, 1968), p. 218.

26. See Alvin W. Gouldner, "Toward the Radical Reconstruction of Sociology," *Social Policy* (May/June, 1970): 18–25.

27. Donald Lazere, "Down With Culture"? *The Village Voice,* September, 1969, p. 32.

28. Daniel Bell, "The Dispossessed," in Daniel Bell, ed., *The Radical Right* (New York: Doubleday & Company, Inc., 1963), p. 31.

29. C. Wright Mills, "Culture and Politics," *Power, Politics and People,* p. 237.

30. C. Wright Mills, "Liberal Values in the Modern World," *Power, Politics and People,* p. 191.

Chapter Thirteen

SOCIOLOGY, WRONGDOING, AND AKRASIA: AN ATTEMPT TO THINK GREEK ABOUT THE PROBLEM OF THEORY AND PRACTICE

Alan F. Blum

My objection to the whole of Sociology . . . is that it knows from experience only the decaying forms of society and takes its own decaying instincts with perfect innocence as the norm of sociological value judgment. Declining life, the diminution of all organizing power, that is to say the power of separating, of opening up chasms, of ranking above and below, formulates itself in the sociology of today as the ideal. . . .

The unconscious influence of decadence has gained ascendency even over the ideals of the sciences.

Friedrich Nietzsche, 1888

Sociology studies the moral life, and sociology is itself an instance of the moral life. Our task is to protect this understanding from being forgotten: contemporary sociology either forgets that it is an instance of the moral life or makes feeble attempts to remember—attempts that are amoral themselves.

One could say that sociology does not *have* to study the moral life—that it could study attitudes, aggregates, attributions, behavior, usage—but such a claim is confused. It assumes that the moral character of inquiry borrows from the objects studied—is parasitic upon such objects—instead of seeing the morality of inquiry as that which makes possible any conception of objects. All inquiry displays a moral commitment in that it makes reference to an authoritative election concerning how a phenomenon ought to be understood. The very occurrence of sociology testifies to its morality: sociological practice wills an authoritative version of things and accepts such authority as its ground and its plan.

The morality of sociology does not then reside in the matter that it formulates (for example, in studying working-class misery rather than the occupational practices of dentists), for the matter that sociology formulates is its most concrete and superficial subject. Rather, the morality of sociology is discernible in its subjugation of its practice to a rule to which it requires itself to submit. The analytic subject matter of sociology is the rule to which sociology elects to subject itself; this rule provides the auspices for sociological description of any and every thing. Sociology is not ruled by its concrete matter, but by its rule for producing a topic out of any matter.

The moral character of a practice is not reflected in conceptions of the material upon which the practice operates, but by that which the practice *is*. If sociology is an instance of the moral life, this means that the practice displays its essential morality in whatever it happens to study. How does any practice display its morality?

The moral concerns "ought" or the "Good." The moral typically pertains to what we ought to do: the moral character of a practice makes reference to how the practice ought to be conducted. Sociology is an instance of the moral life because, in studying whatever, it displays each of its studies as a recommendation as to how inquiry ought to be accomplished. In the idiom of sociology, any study exemplifies a normative commitment to some version of adequate inquiry. This "version" provides for and constrains the study, it makes it possible and intelligible; the problem is to grasp the relationship between the practitioner and this authority. Thus, those nihilists in modern sociology who surreptitiously disguise their moral concern behind rubrics such as "value neutrality," "reproducibility," "naturalistic observation," and the like can only launch such descriptive crusades under the auspices of their own paradoxical versions of how inquiry ought to be done. To deny the moral grounds of one's program is to moralize in the deepest sense.

Thus far, we have located the moral character of inquiry in the fact that any occasion of inquiry is an exercise of authority. This is just a start, for it leaves the deep character of the morality of inquiry untouched. The moral practitioner would then be typified as one who understands the conduct of his practice as an exercise of authority. We want to go further. We must add to the picture the notion of one who orients to his display of authority as a method of making reference to his rationality.

To put it otherwise, any and every occasion of inquiry is an occasion of speech and insofar as one takes upon himself the act of speaking, he raises the possibility of silence. Every speech recommends its pertinence, that is, affirms that it is a speech worth speaking. Consequently, every speech (every inquiry) carries with it an essential reference to the reason for its being spoken; somehow, every speech carries as an essential feature of its accomplishment an argument as to its being worth speaking.

To locate the morality of a speech in its display of authority is to stop prematurely, for the display of authority invites consideration of the deeper question concerning the Reason for the authority being worth exercising. Consider the idea of Reason with which we are working: it refers to the primordial notion of the ground, foundation, or Good that an activity serves, that which makes it as it is. To ask for this Reason is to ask a distinctively moral question; it is to ask for "that for the sake of which" the activity is. To say that an inquiry displays its authority is then only the start, for the next question asks how the inquiry makes reference to the rational character of its authority.

For Plato inquiry was essentially moral. This connection was made possible because of the necessary feature of analysis as rational, where "rational" was understood as "that which inquiry is for." Actually, every practice in its mere accomplishment raised the question of its moral character because every practice had to meet the test of rationality to qualify for the status of a practice or "art" rather than a "knack." The mere doing of any practice then raised the question of its rationality and the rationality of a practice is what we understand by its moral character. This is to say that the accomplishment of any practice raises the question of the possibility of the practice as the only rational topic for the practice itself.

The reason of a practice is its subject matter; not the material upon which it operates but the Reason for its being done. Now our opening maxim should be more transparent: we said that sociology studies the moral life and is an instance of the moral life. This is to say that sociology seeks to formulate the rational character of practices, and as such an inquestive activity the practice of sociology itself makes reference to its own rational character. The fact that sociology rarely speaks deeply about the rational character of its own practice only means that we have to look at what sociology says about other practices to see sociology's conception of its own practice.[1] To understand this problem we want to enter more deeply into the Reason and ground of a practice: we want to say that the moral practitioner is one who keeps the question of the rationality of his practice in view; one who realizes that in speaking about whatever, he is making the rationality of his practice transparent; one who forgets this question forgets why he practices (why he speaks) and shows his immorality. Thus, the concern of this chapter, formulable in various ways as the problem of theory and practice, is actually a concern with the relationship between speech and its standard. If the ideal of speech is ideal rationality—true speaking—speech can only make elliptic and partial reference to such a standard because the very act of speaking makes use of the standard to constitute itself. Inquiry then acquires its moral (rational, analytic) character when it shows its desire to address itself, when it treats the unity of its speech with its standard as the only topic worth speaking about. This is how we can say that the rational or moral practice is the one that raises its own possibility as the only rational topic.

Socratic Rationality as the Paradigm of Reason

It is supposed that Socrates was interested in questions such as "What is X?" as if he introduced and championed the problem of definition. To moderns the virtue of Socrates is either his tireless questioning (his method) or his contributions to the development of the mathematical theory of knowledge; these contributions make Socrates important to the prehistory of theory, but it is only later that the so-called "theory of knowledge" comes of age. What is overlooked is that everything essential is already in Socrates and only remains to be rediscovered.

It is usually assumed that Socrates' interest in ideas such as virtue, justice, piety, or courage was to create an exemplary model or procedure for adequate definition, and consequently these examples are inspected in order to recover his latent theory. Yet, this is a superficial reading of the Socratic task, for it fails to capture the character of his interest in X as a device for instructing an Other; it fails to grasp the fact that the X was not a matter to be distilled in a rule or formula but served more as an occasion to provide incentive for rational analysis.

Recall Socrates' exchange with Polus in *Gorgias*. They speak about practices such as rhetoric and power and Socrates attempts to elicit definitions. When Socrates rejects the various definitions offered by Polus what we get is less a theory of definition than a notion of how one ought to think so as to be seen as thinking rationally. To think rationally is to display through speech one's unity with his Nature. It is in these dialogues that the idea of inquiry as a movement of the soul appears. Adequate definition is a surface feature of a rational (well-ordered) soul in the sense that defining is a metaphor for inquiry brought to speech, and it is through his speech that man makes reference to his rationality. The problem of the dialogues is not the problem of how to produce a good definition, but how to recognize a good man, and one way of recognizing such a man and of distinguishing him from the false and shrunken souls that abound is through his speech (his inquiry). The problem of the dialogues is not the problem of definition but of how speech makes reference to the soul.

The problem that Socrates then sets for himself (which his daemon has set for him) is to provide for the moral character of the analytic by showing how any rational analytic is essentially an icon of the rational soul. Socrates' task is to convert the problem of analysis into the problem of rationality by showing the problem of analysis to be the problem of soul.

To say that the problem of analysis is the problem of soul is to formulate analysis as Desire: analysis is the desire for the perfect speech. Since analysis is a desire for Rationality and since rationality can only be displayed through speech, analysis seeks to achieve Rationality through speech. Speech is done under the auspices of an interest in its perfection.

The perfect speech is by the nature of speech impossible because it would be a speech that is free from the conditions of speaking. The perfect speech as the speech of speeches, as the comprehensive whole about which one speaks, requires transcending the conditions of speaking, which is impossible, for its attainment would achieve the termination of speech itself. Yet the perfect, rational speech is Real in the sense that an aspiration for the whole grounds speaking and constitutes the auspices under which speech is accomplished; the perfect speech is Real insofar as Desire depicts the will to speak under its auspices.

Whereas practices speak about things and, in their moments of self-consciousness, about speeches about things, the perfect speech speaks about speech as a whole or about the conditions or grounds of perfect speech. Since every such attempt is itself a practical, partial speech, the Rational speech is that which preserves in its partiality the image of the constraint of the perfect speech, or which preserves the unspeakable character of that about which it desires to speak.

Thus, the centrality of desire in analysis: for theorizing is the desire to speak the unspeakable—or to speak in the face of the unspeakable—because such desire is a condition of one's unity with his Self. Desire depicts the need to speak about the unspeakable as a condition of Rationality.

To say that Socrates had this recognition is to propose a different view of Socratic definition. Definitions as partial speeches about the whole were only intended to make reference to the desire to speak essentially, which they could never reproduce. As such partial speeches, definitions were employed as icons of Rational Desire.

We see this recognition occurring in early dialogues such as *Meno* and *Protagoras*. For example, Meno's problem—of lacking knowledge for the execution of proper definitions—is only a surface problem that is itself made intelligible by the state of his soul. Meno has a shrunken soul, he does not know how to think essentially (rationally) for he grasps at concrete particulars and at inessential and extraneous conditions. Meno wants to speak about virtue, but in attempting to do so he speaks in a way that says nothing; Meno says nothing essential about virtue because he does not know how to speak essentially, and this knowledge cannot be learned through a formula, for his entire soul must be reeducated. What the interlocutor shows in these dialogues is not the absence of a technique or method (a course in Symbolic Logic), but rather a kind of irrationality.

To define is to think essentially; consequently, the problem of the typical interlocutor is that he does not know how to think essentially. To think essentially is not to think according to method, plan, or rule, yet neither is it to think in any old way; it is to think of that which is worth thinking or of that which needs being thought. In terms of the ideas under inspection, to think essentially is to think of that which is decisive or central to the idea: in contrast, one who conjures up the accidental, the extraneous, or the inessential is one who thinks of what is most apparent and available, or of what is easiest to think. To think essentially is to think of the Reason (foundation, nature) of the idea, or is to think of that which makes the idea as it is (something) rather than otherwise (nothing). Essential thinking is rational thinking since it asks for the Reason for the idea or for what makes the idea worth thinking (speaking).

Because the dialectic occurs through speech, essential thinking is essential speaking. Socrates wants to induce the interlocutor to speak essentially and so he wants to terminate chatter. The Socratic mission—to hold the Other responsible for his talk, to disclose the character of the talk as chatter, and to reorient the speaker toward responsibility—is a task of educating the soul of the Other through the example of an idea. Essential thinking is essential speaking; it is rational, responsible speech.

The human is the speaking animal, the one who makes intelligible through speech; speech is the paradigmatic human practice. To be responsible for one's speech is to orient to the Reason for speaking where such a Reason cannot be taken for granted. *One must have a Reason for speaking or else, he might as well remain silent.* It is through the Reason that the speaker is identified as having something to say; the Reason provides for speech rather than silence.

Thus, to speak about the inessential, the extraneous, the accidental, and the contingent is to speak irrationally, for it is to speak without thinking (without thinking essentially), and to speak without thinking is thoughtless, that is, it is chatter and babble.

Thought is then not subject to method and procedure because it is ruled by soul; thought seeks to conform to the ideal of a rational soul and therefore thought is responsible to soul and seeks to display through its speech its conformity to its nature. Method and procedure are merely practical devices for making this responsibility clear and intelligible. We should not blanch at this statement for it is not mysterious: it says that essential thinking (speaking) can only be done by one who knows what is worth speaking (thinking); the good soul is one who knows what is worth speaking and how to use his speech to instruct Other. Rational thought is thought that is in touch with the Reason for speaking; it is thought that knows why it is done and shows that it knows, it is thought that is responsible to itself. Only in this sense is thought "utopian" for it is ruled by the ideal of a unity with its nature; in the same way, thought is real, for this rational unity of thought with its nature is the only thought worth thinking. Anything extraneous to this unity is nothing.

Recall Socrates' instruction to Glaucon in the *Republic:* "In itself, an art is sound and flawless so long as it is entirely true to its own nature as an art in the strictest sense—and it is the strict sense that I want to keep in view."[2] To think of the strict sense of the practice is to think essentially about the practice and all other senses are discarded; the strict sense is that which makes the practice intelligible—which makes it something rather than nothing—and although other senses are speakable they are strictly speaking nothing. Speaking about other senses does not touch what the practice *is* even though such speech is the easiest speech in the world.

To keep one's eye upon the strict sense; to keep in view the Reason or nature of the practice. Why is this difficult? Because one is overwhelmed by the overpowering force and availability of other senses of the practice; consequently, one must exercise another kind of force or violence to keep the strict sense in mind and to preserve it against the overwhelming pressures from the dispersive, inessential, and accidental. This is how analysis appears as a matter of soul: to keep one's eye upon the strict sense is to use all of the violence at one's command to preserve the integrity of the idea; one's soul must desire or Will strict sense, and further, it must Will to preserve it against all of the possible dispersive senses. Admittedly then, one needs to be prepared for analysis, for one must prepare his soul; one must Will or desire this kind of rationality despite the fact that it goes nowhere (that it must willfully and violently resist the inessential "useful" questions put by the interlocutors).

Furthermore, one does not enter analysis with a rational and secure soul in hand, for analysis *is* essentially the preparation of soul. Thus, Desire (for essential thinking) is both a ground and achievement of analysis, and analysis always begins (*en media res*) in the middle of desire.

Today, we operate with a conception of rationality that formulates the idea as a standard or maxim for intelligible conduct. The versions of rationality that we find in modern sociology are either idealizations of mathemeticity or descriptions of ordinary procedures; "rational" comes to stand for an exhibition of the planful and intelligible character of a practice. In this way, Socrates' problem is abandoned, since any practice can be given an intelligible sense and still be shown to be segregated from its Reason.

We might recall the exchange between Socrates and Gorgias that opens the *Gorgias*. Socrates seeks to induce the sophist to address the meaning of his art, the art of rhetoric. Gorgias responds successively: it is the art that deals with words, and it is the art that secures certain effects upon an audience, that is, that persuades. Now, although Socrates does not claim to know what Rhetoric is, he knows the difference between speaking essentially and peripherally; he knows that a number of practices use "words" and he knows that the *effects* of a practice are in the strict sense external to its nature. Again, it is not merely that Gorgias fails to come up with a definition; it is rather, that he fails to address the problem of the Reason of his practice (he has forgotten why he speaks). This is no little comment on Gorgias for he is the Rhetorician supreme: Mister Rhetoric (think of Mister Sociology here) just does it because he has always done it, and he is rooted so unreflexively in the inessential that he does not think to address the problem of what his practice means.

The Rational Possibilities of Practice

Sociology is an art or practice no different from other exemplary practices. When a practice forgets why it speaks it begins to chatter, it begins to speak about the inessential: that which is worth thinking—the ground of the practice itself—is forgotten. Socrates calls this kind of forgetting irrational or "ignorant"; it is the requirement of any and every practice to seek to discover, preserve, and cultivate its Reason (its nature) so as to restore itself as knowledge. Since the man is analytically the practice personified, practices such as men can be seen as custodians of Reason and as seeking to preserve essential thought and speech.

The art seeks to preserve its morality in the fact of the dispersive forces of the inessential by speaking essentially, by recalling its Reason for speech. The Rational practice shows its command of its Reason through speech; through what it speaks about it shows how it can speak in the deepest sense because the practice makes every occasion of speech (every inquestive occasion) an occasion for making reference to its Rationality. In this sense, the Rational practice struggles to preserve its Desire.

The Rational practice is then one that Wills Rationality through its desire to speak essentially. Because such a desire is recognized as a required feature of the practice, it is anything but tangential or peripheral, and constitutes the very spirit of the practice. The desire to speak essentially is internal to the practice because the practice is only a Rational art when it grasps itself as an art, when its conduct is at one with its nature. When the conduct of the practice "belongs" to its nature it is accomplished in such a way as to show its Oneness with its nature. The Rational practice is the activity that grasps itself as a Unity, that grasps the unity of its conduct with its nature as a unity encapsulated in its Reason.[3]

Analytically, the only practice worth speaking about is then the perfect practice, the practice that is formulated as one with its nature. It is the job of analysis to restore all degenerate versions of practice by reformulating them as Rational; this applies to all practice. Thus, the warrant for our practice is thoroughly restorative: we seek to provide for the Rationality of all practice and in so doing we exemplify our practice—theorizing—as the practice of practices (the royal art).

If the nature or Good of theory is the most perfect and comprehensive speech about the nature of theory, and since theory is the omnirelevant practice that addresses the relationship between any speech (practice) and the Real (the perfect speech that ought to serve as the standard for any practice), then the nature or Good of theory is the most comprehensive and perfect speech about the Good. The nature, Reason, or Good of theory is nothing less than wisdom, and the practice of theorizing is the production and appraisal of speeches about the real under the auspices of an orientation to the standard of perfect speech (the speech that makes reference to wisdom).

To understand the nature of theory is to understand the kind of speech that makes reference to the standard of the perfect speech. Since this standard constitutes the nature of theory, the practice of theorizing seeks to discover, cultivate, preserve, and recollect this standard. One who in his inquestive activities can be so formulated is the typical (that is, ideal, Rational) theorist. Since it is the nature of theory to address, appraise, and seek to understand Rational speech, the Good of theory is the recollection and preservation of Rational speech. Because the standard of Rational speech to which particular practices are seen as aspiring are parochial truths whose limits are provided by the context of the practice(s), it is only the practice of theory, which transcends every substantive practice except itself in seeking to make reference to the reason of Reason, and to the Goodness of the Good. Thus, it is theory's task to be the highest art while yet an art just the same; it is the nature of theory to make reference to its Good or Reason as the highest Good while under the constraint of its recognition of the unspeakability of this Good. It is then the nature of theory to show in its practice that it seeks to perfect its speech, that it seeks to make the most comprehensive speech.

In contrast, we might consider the plight of the practice that is not responsive to the question of its nature. Such a practice is not responsible to the question of its Reason; the Reason for its doing as it does is either self-evident or conventional and consequently, *the question* of its Reason is not worth thinking. Thus, Socrates pronounces upon Rhetoric to Gorgias:

> It aims at pleasure without consideration of what is best; and I say that it is not an art, but a knack, because it is unable to render any account of the nature of the methods it applies and so cannot tell the cause of each of them. I am unable to give the name of art to anything irrational. . . .[4]

Note that the irrationality of Rhetoric consists in its inability to provide an account of the *nature* of its methods, which in the Socratic idiom means the Reason for the project: Rhetoric cannot give an account of how its method shows the unity of the project with its nature because Rhetoric does not even address its nature.

The knack then, in contrast to the art, treats its nature as secure and well-founded, as that which is in hand. To say that the nature of the practice is in hand suggests that the question of this nature raises no problem for it is secure. *What is secure is the understanding of the security of this nature.* To treat the nature of the practice as secure is to cut off possibilities for its exploration because that which would be explored is beyond security and to explore the insecure is folly or madness. To treat the nature of the practice as secure is to accept the practice in its degenerate form. This is how Nietzsche can suggest that the practical understanding of a practice is decadent. By "practical" we intend the understanding that tries to comprehend the practice while using the self-same practice as the standard and limit of authoritative understanding.

Yet, the requirement to understand the practice without using it as a resource seems to create irreconcilable demands. The apparent tension between these demands can lead one to abandon the interest of the practice, or to forego the interests of Rationality. In the latter case, the practice abandons the attempt to provide for itself in any way for which its practice itself cannot provide. The practice then rules that the rational treatment of itself is the treatment that conforms to the essential rule of the practice. The practice authorizes itself as the limit of rational Self-Exploration; it decides authoritatively to explore itself only under the auspices of its practical interest in itself. In this way the Rational practice is the practice that elects to provide for itself as an occasion of the self-same practice; it is the practice that analyzes itself as an instance of itself.

Science epitomizes this practical mode of understanding. If scientific self understanding is unreal knowledge this means that it everywhere represents conduct not as an icon of Reason, but according to science (rationally rather than Rationally). To paraphrase Heidegger: whenever real knowledge places the Reason of conduct into the limelight, natural knowledge (science) looks the other way because its truth is thereby disputed. Science keeps to its own. Everything that comes before it is subsumed under the statement: it is and remains mine, and *is,* as such, as being mine.[5] Thus, science as the paradigmatic practice becomes absorbed in the conduct *it* represents (the conduct it represents scientifically), and comes to regard these representations alone as true, as real knowledge. The Rational practice then starts from the presupposition of its own authority (its truth) as a standard and resource for its inquiries; conduct in conformity with this truth *is* rational insofar as it only becomes intelligible in relation to this truth. Yet, such practice is not truly Rational, because it does not understand its truth as the mere concept of truth, it does not know what it truly is.

Thus, from the point of view of a Gorgias the fact that the practice cannot provide an account of the nature of its methods is not a limitation of the practice but a feature of its rationality. The rational character of the practice provides for a treatment of its nature as secure and well-founded and this treatment authoritatively declares itself as that point at which doubt must legitimately terminate. The practice acquires an internal rationality that grounds itself in itself as authoritative. The rationality of the practice then makes Socratic rationality impossible (it makes it look irrational). To pursue the Socratic task is necessarily to abandon the interest of the practice.

When Socrates says that Rhetoric "aims at pleasure without consideration of what is best," he means the kind of pleasure that a practice acquires when it grounds itself in itself. A project aims at pleasure when it refuses to consider what is best, that is, a project that treats its nature as secure and well-founded is not considering "what is best" but what is pleasurable. To accept the nature of the art as secure is pleasurable because it is easy. An irrational practice or art operates on the basis of the pleasure principle, which is to say that it chooses to think what is easiest to think.

> To trace something unknown back to something known is alleviating, sooth-
> ing, gratifying and gives moreover a feeling of power. Danger, disquiet,
> anxiety attend the unknown—the first instinct is to eliminate these distressing
> states. First principle: any explanation is better than none. Because it is at
> bottom only a question of wanting to get rid of oppressive ideas, one is not
> exactly particular about what means one uses to get rid of them: the first
> idea that explains that the unknown is in fact the known does so much good
> that one "holds it for true." Proof by pleasure ("by potency") as criterion
> of truth. . . . The question "why?" should furnish, if at all possible, not so
> much the cause for its own sake as a certain kind of cause—a soothing,
> liberating, alleviating cause. . . . The new, the unexperienced, the strange is
> excluded from being cause. Thus there is sought not only some kind of ex-
> planation, the kind by means of which the feeling of the strange, new, unex-
> perienced is most speedily and most frequently abolished—the most common
> explanations.[6]

The practice aims at pleasure; this is a metaphor for saying that the practice desires to think what is easiest and in terms of the practice what is easiest to think is what is rational. Yet, this is a far cry from the Rationality of Socrates, for to think what is easiest to think is to renounce another kind of desire—the Will to think essentially—and it is the preservation and cultivation of this desire that display the Rational practice.

The rationality of pleasure (as compared to Desire) refers to the rationality of a practice that grounds itself in itself and that only comprehends its conduct as a representation of itself. Pleasure is then a metaphor for the practical rationality of an art, for it captures the security attendant upon abandoning reflexivity as an aspiration. To submit oneself to such pleasure is decadent, because it amounts to abandoning the desire for essential thinking (for Rationality).

It might then be fair to say of a practice such as sociology that it has lost its desire, that its instincts are no longer secure, and that its will to think essentially has been abandoned. To say that sociology has forgotten its desire is to say that sociology has forgotten its Reason for speaking. How though, can a practice such as sociology intelligibly repudiate Rationality in the interests of its practical reason? To understand this is to begin to grasp the real sociology of science.

Deviance

Socrates has no theory of deviance for this would require that he segregate deviance from knowledge and, in the Socratic scheme, that which is segregated from knowledge is not worth speaking about. Consequently, deviance is ignorance, another occasion to exemplify the failure of rationality.

In the early dialogues—particularly the *Protagoras*—Socrates speaks of wrongdoing as ignorance and against the notion of akrasia, that is, of the moral weakness of being overcome by pleasure. What ordinary men recognize as akrasia is really ignorance, for being overcome by pleasure is only intelligible as wrongdoing when it is conceived as ignorance. That is, weakness of will does not provide for the idea of deviance unless it is the weakness of will of ignorance. Concrete weakness of will (for example, being unable to follow a rule) provides only for an empirical description of deviance. This is no small re-emphasis, for it presupposes that what men desire is the Good and that their failures can only be seen as instances of ignorance or of not knowing the Good. Wrong conduct that is done under full knowledge of its "wrongness" does not suggest deviance, because in the strict sense it is ignorance. Deviance is just a gloss off ignorance.

Socratic analysis has no room for a conception of wrongdoing that is external to ignorance; it is only in the positivistic project where action is segregated from knowledge that wrongdoing becomes an independent and autonomous topic. Since the only way to segregate wrongdoing from ignorance (and knowledge) is to locate its source or sources in the concrete idea of Will as pleasure principle, we can understand why Socrates denied analytic status to akrasia; akrasia as ignorance is just a special case of the power of concrete "external" conditions to deflect man from consummating his desire to speak essentially.

If wrongdoing is—analytically—ignorance, to treat it as weakness of will is to treat it most concretely. Such a treatment accepts the *apparent* character of wrongdoing by seeing it as misfire, breakdown, or a case of going awry. The notion of wrongdoing as breakdown conceals under a mechanistic metaphor its character as concrete thinking. The use of akrasia as such a metaphor describes an analytic notion (wrongdoing) concretely, where the task is to provide an analytic formulation of concrete thinking. Modern sociological notions of deviance reproduce the classical akrasia metaphor and thus prevent the recognition that wrongdoing is a failure to theorize. And of course, sociologists are the last persons who want to recognize the connection between wrongdoing and theory (for that is the *real* problem of theory and practice).

Strictly speaking, deviance or wrongdoing is not a case of being overcome by pleasure, but is a failure to think analytically or to think of what is essential to thought. The failure of deviance is not the irrationality of rule violation but is more like the irrationality of thought that forgets why it thinks. The problem of wrongdoing then presupposes an examination of the problem of knowledge, for if wrongdoing is an instance of ignorance, ignorance itself makes reference to knowledge. The segregation of wrongdoing from ignorance —by treating it as a concrete effect of pleasure-seeking will—is to postpone consideration of the problem of knowledge.

We are saying that Socrates provides for the following: deviance can only be seen as weakness of Will if Will is analytically reinterpreted as the desire to think essentially; if so, the weakness that wrongdoing shows is properly spoken of as ignorance. On the other hand, sociology speaks of deviance as the *concrete* weakness of will that occurs through the violation of a rule when the agent is deflected from his course by being overcome. This kind of wrongdoing is, strictly speaking, "nothing" to Socrates, for it merely shows typical and mundane performance. To join the issue squarely: if deviance is formulated analytically, it loses its status as a topic because it is assimilated to the problem of rational theorizing; if deviance is treated concretely—as an autonomous topic—then its essential connection to knowledge is severed and it becomes another mere behavior. In this case, deviance is something not worth speaking about—it is nothing. So the options are clear: either deviance is destroyed by being assimilated to the problem of theory, or it is preserved in a form that is not worth speaking about. The alternatives are then either to use wrongdoing as an occasion to make reference to essential thinking, or to talk about wrongdoing as if it had no connection to essential thinking; the alternatives are rationality and chatter.

Thus, Aristotle's critique of Socrates' denial of akrasia becomes more intelligible. Aristotle insisted that people do wrong and know it, and that they are overcome by pleasure and by concrete forces, and of course Aristotle was correct empirically: whereas Aristotle saw the Socratic account as intellectualistic, such a reading was only possible by holding Socrates to the standard of empirical adequacy. What Aristotle and most of Socrates' critics found objectionable in his denial of akrasia was precisely the analytic character of his formulation of wrongdoing. The great Aristotle could not comprehend Socrates' devotion to essential thinking and could only make it intelligible as an attempt at empirical description. Thus, Aristotle's claim that wickedness *is* voluntary was designed to rebut Socrates as if he had claimed that wickedness was not voluntary. However, Socrates' claim was quite different for he was not pronouncing upon the existential relations between voluntarism and wickedness: he was arguing that any essential formulation of wrongdoing had to see it analytically as the failed desire to think rationally; Socrates was speaking about the character of right doing for the theorist while using the mundane example of ordinary wrongdoing, for he was interested in how the theorist can do right and preserve his rationality. Socrates was telling us what rational theorizing is and not what wrongdoing is, and his version of theorizing required him to subordinate the concrete, empirical detail of any ordinary example so as to make it useful in his struggle to preserve and cultivate rational theory.

To paraphrase Nietzsche, Aristotle and his successors have to preserve wrongdoing and wickedness, that is, they desire to make sick.[7] They desire to make wrongdoing concrete, which they accomplish by divorcing it from ignorance; in this way, they will the unreflexive treatment of wrongdoing. The notion of voluntary wrongdoing lies at the heart of the idea of deviance (if we rule out those modern riders that are not worth talking about—mistake, accident, misfire, incompetence, stigma), and thus, to have a viable idea of deviance is to will an idea of voluntary wickedness. In other words, where Aristotle wants to treat wrongdoing as a *phenomenon* to be *described,* as a description of crime, Socrates sees it as a metaphor of ignorance. Granted that ignorance is a crime, it is a crime against the soul and not a phenomenon that shows departure from rule. Those who speak about rules and rule violation rather than knowledge and ignorance actually preserve *their* ignorance by keeping it under the cover of rule.

Yet, Socrates says that voluntary wickedness is impossible, that those who speak in such a way are really speaking of ignorance, and to speak of ignorance is to address the largest problem of all—knowledge and theory. Why is this not recognized? Socrates would say that it is forgotten.

To treat the problem of wrongdoing as a metaphor for the problem of knowledge is to raise anew the question of essential thinking. But moderns do not want to raise that question, since their very notion of voluntary wrongdoing presupposes an idea of doing right, it presupposes the securing of knowledge in some conception of rule. Thus, wrongdoing only becomes an independent topic for those who think that they know or who are self-confident about what they know; to treat wrongdoing as an instance of ignorance would be to open the floodgates to the problem of knowledge, for it would render their knowledge insecure.

Socrates' message is quite powerful: he is urging us not to be overcome by the pleasures of the concrete and apparent cases of wrongdoing (of deviance) that we see, but rather, to think of our very method of seeing as an occasion for raising the problem of wrongdoing for us. If wrongdoing is ignorance, then it is before our eyes all along not in its examples which we see but in our very attempt to think about whatever we see. Wrongdoing as ignorance reminds us that it is *our* problem; in reminding us to preserve the desire to think essentially it alerts us to the possibilities of inessential thought —ignorance—to which we are heir.

The Sociologists of Deviance

The interesting question then becomes: in speaking about wrongdoing (about deviance) how do sociologists show that they are doing wrong (that they are deviant)? This is a version of the question with which the chapter began—the question of the moral character of sociology. Socrates has already provided most of the grounding: wrongdoing is ignorance that in its turn is the weakened desire to think essentially; how, in its speech about wrongdoing, does sociology show its inessentiality?

The answer has been prepared. By thinking of wrongdoing concretely and by refusing to identify it with ignorance, sociology shows its refusal to face the problem of knowledge. And the refusal to face the problem of knowledge is the supreme and paradigmatic case of wrongdoing for inquiry. This is what we mean by ignorance.

For example, sociologists do not recognize in wrongdoing the kind of ignorance that shows itself as not being at One with self; they, instead, see it as being overcome by concrete, external forces and pressures. Where some version of knowledge is introduced, it is imported as a species of calculative rationality designed to facilitate adjustment to such conditions. In this vein, it has been suggested that the study of wrongdoing has recently been revolutionized by being seen as the achievement of attributions (labeling).

The so-called labeling perspective is at one with the naïve positivism of Mertonian sociology. They both see wrongdoing as a result of being overcome by concrete conditions, although they differ in terms of who it is that they formulate as being overcome. In the labeling approach the one who is responsible for the attribution is the one who is overcome; his concrete weakness of will is a result of his failure to think essentially about another human. In this sense, the labelers take the place of the positivistic observers of earlier traditions of deviance and in their imputations of wickedness to others they show their own weakness of will. The labeling citizen (the member) then becomes the concrete ignoramus, a role that was formerly played by the sociological observer himself. Thus, Becker's sociology is a reinterpretation of Merton's earlier practice with Merton being shifted to the center as a topic for Becker. Yet, who will make Becker a topic? It seems that in speaking, he makes himself a topic for us.

The labeling sociologist shows the weakness of will that is ignorance (not akrasia) by accepting attributions as something worth speaking about. To say "deviance is an attribution" is to say that one has no desire to speak essentially about wrongdoing, that one is not interested in the Reason of wrongdoing. To take a labeling stance is to avoid analytic commitment for it is to elect to permit conventional usage to decide analytic matters.

In its newer forms, modern sociology thinks that it can settle its analytic responsibilities by providing accounts of members' usage. Modern sociology —in these forms—forgets that analysis is a moral issue and that accounts of ordinary practices can only reproduce ordinary moralities. It is not ordinary usage and practice that turn up the problem of essential thought.

Consequently, the idea of essential thought is abandoned, and with it, the ideal of rationality. The desire to speak essentially about wrongdoing is forgotten and a perverted idea of wrongdoing is extracted from the congeries of mundane practices and expressions. Since the idea of wrongdoing that is produced is the most ordinary idea, the inquirer shows through his inquest that his interest lies in the lowly and the mundane. The inquirer is interested in the pleasure and familiar security of the ordinary; he is decadent.

But decadent sociology is not without its weapons. It can treat every question raised in this chapter as irrational and it can do so by treating the Socratic interest as perverse. The perversity of Socrates' interest is that it dares court the strange and unfamiliar at the price of security, that it shows more of a loyalty to thought and reason than to pleasure. In fact, the Socratic interest is outrageous, it is vain, for it dares assert the primacy of its desire for essential speech in the wake of the overpowering impulse for pleasure in the community of science.

Sociology is the paradigmatic case of intellectual wrongdoing; it is deviance personified for an art. Sociologists do not have to *study* wrongdoing, for they exemplify it. If wrongdoing is ignorance, sociologists have it right before their eyes. Furthermore, despite Socrates' denial of akrasia—of being overcome by concrete pleasure—his formulation of wrongdoing as ignorance provides for its character as a kind of submission to pleasure, that is, to the pleasure of practical reason. In its speech about deviance, sociology exemplifies the practice that only seeks to understand itself practically.

We can preserve akrasia if we conceive of ignorance as a kind of being overcome by pleasure, if it becomes the pleasure of ignorance where practical reason can be seen as pleasurable. This is to say that wrongdoing is the akrasia of ignorance, and the question then becomes: how can intellectual wrongdoing be pleasurable, that is, what makes intellectual wrongdoing intelligible? What makes the failure to theorize, the failure to think essentially intelligible? It is forgotten, but how does such forgetting become desirable in itself?

The attack on essential thinking (on Rationality, Rational Desire) is made in the name of science. Essential thinking is extraneous to the strict sense of scientific inquiry because it is either transrational (beyond intelligible speech), or an instance of what science calls "values" or "ideology." Values and ideology are the scientist's way of depicting the desire for essential thought that threatens to deflect the inquirer from the law of the practice. Ignorance is preserved when essential thinking is treated as irrational; how is such a treatment accomplished?

Recall that essential thinking requires one to address the nature of the practice, that one seeks to speak about the unity of the practice with its nature.

Yet, the practice treats its nature as secure and in-hand. The conduct of the practice then rests upon a particular conception of certainty, a conception that prescribes that its Reason is beyond doubt. The practice is only intelligible when it exempts its Reason from doubt or when it conducts any examination of its Reason in a manner sanctioned by the practice itself. The practice cannot examine itself in a way that is free from the practice itself and any self-examination carries within itself as standard the very object of the examination. The practice can never examine its very practice of examining because it always requires itself to examine under the auspices of the interest of the practice. Thus, no matter how the practice describes and formulates itself it always does so within the purview of natural consciousness and not of knowledge. The practice must always remain ignorant of itself as long as it uses itself as its authoritative standard.[8]

The question of doubt and certainty then speaks to this point: that the authoritativeness of the standard of the practice is never questioned. This is how the extremes meet, for regardless of the claims of those who practice the art, they all unite in their use of the standard of the art for conducting examinations of its reason. The conditions of scientific sanity are then drawn at the point at which doubt terminates: *to refuse to doubt the standard of the practice as a resource for doubt itself*—this is the parochial truth of the art. From the point of view of the art, intellectual irrationality (what is being done in this work) is to open oneself to authentic doubt, to let doubt creep in. From the point of view of the art, this is the weakness of will that permits Desire to undermine the interests of the practice; from the point of view of Socrates that is precisely the strength of the Will to think essentially and to preserve Rationality against the secure pleasures of the truth and certainty of the art.

Thus, the practice forgets essential thinking because of the parochial truth of the practice itself. To submit to this truth is to choose to preserve the practice as it is, whereas to think essentially is to seek a vantage point that is free from the control of the practice. Authentic doubt as a precondition and as an achievement of essential thinking serves to put the project into question because it does not doubt under the auspices of the practice but rather, under the condition of Rational aspiration. Essential thinking repudiates all self-examination of the practice as feeble because all such examination preserves the authority of the practice. Essential thinking must destroy the authority of the practice in order to understand the relationship of the practice to itself.

The meaning of "practice" becomes more transparent. To be practical means to keep to oneself, to know the limits of one's inquiry, to do what one can do within the law; the law defines what one can do by providing the limits of practical possibility. The practical actor does not hesitate or delay, for the notion of hesitation only occurs to one who resolves to treat the practice as a mere possibility instead of the limit, ground, and aspiration of action. The practical actor knows the limits of the law and sticks to it not out of a sense of resignation or uncertainty but because thinking within the limits is what thinking essentially is; to think is to think within limits in that the limits (of the law) provide for the rational concept of thinking. To attempt to think away the limits is to succumb to pleasure rather than reason. The ideal practitioner is one who understands how his submission to method becomes a feature of any critique of method, and he is one who accepts this limit as authoritative.

The rational practical actor is then one who knows the limits—or, who knows how the law limits his questioning—and, in this sense, the rational practical actor is one who uses the Rule of inquiry as a resource for identifying the limits of inquiry. Since it is the law that authorizes the point at which doubt terminates, such a point locates every condition that the law cannot understand as that which is not worth understanding. To accept the law is to accept the willful renunciation of that about which the law decides not to speak.

The pleasure of this kind of rationality is apparent: since the law is secure and well-founded, thought that accepts the limits of law is thought that chooses the path of the secure and well-founded in preference to any other path. Such thought then treats everything it thinks as the representation of the law to which it submits; such thought abandons true analysis by seeing it as a reflection of law (that is, as concrete, destructive pleasure). It is in this sense that rational, practical thought forgets analysis—forgets why it thinks, or forgets what thought is for—and treats the only thing worth thinking as that which law can secure as a representation.

The critical character of a practice is then acquired by virtue of the method in terms of which the practice provides for itself as a representation of itself (of the practice). The very concept of Self that the practice employs —the way in which it understands itself—is through its application of the very law that it explores. The practice then understands itself as an expression of itself. The practice cannot truly criticize itself because it cannot address what it is, the practice cannot disclose the foundations in which it is grounded because such foundations are unspeakable topics for the practice. When the practice does attempt to speak about its foundations, such speech is only accomplished when the idea of foundations is transformed to meet the requirements of the law of the practice. Strictly speaking, the practice can only speak about the practical concept of foundations and thus, not about foundations at all; what the practice takes for speech about foundations is mere talk about itself. When the practice speaks about itself practically, it can only speak about the commonplace and ordinary. Regardless of how deeply or radically the practice thinks it penetrates, such thinking is an illusion, for its very notion of depth and penetration is provided for by the practice.

Because the practice can only formulate itself practically, it exempts its grounds from analysis. For example, the practice of science asserts of itself its authoritativeness, and yet, since it can only address the grounds of its authority in a way that is consistent with its practice (that is "scientific"), it can never achieve a reflexive conception of these grounds that will show the practice itself as a mere possibility. Since a science can only attend to its grounds scientifically, as soon as it turns its attention to these grounds it completely obliterates their analytic character by making of them mere practical representations of grounds—whether as opinions, beliefs, values, assumptions, or the like. The tension experienced by a practice such as science can be formulated as follows: in making a claim for its authoritativeness, it necessarily exempts this self-same authoritativeness from authentic interrogation. The spirit of a practice such as sociology can be understood as a response to this tension, for the practice requires of itself that it Will as external and extraneous the very question that it is incapable of addressing, and consequently, it requires that this incapacity be treated not as a deficiency but as an essential positive feature of its authoritative claim. Peculiarly then, science transforms its weakness of Will into a parameter; it re-creates its authority out of its unreflexive character, and thus, it elevates its weakness into its authoritative virtue.

Conclusion

The desire of a soul expresses the need for the analytic—the need to know—and that to which Desire aspires is the Whole. When Desire is redefined, the impulse toward the analytic is radically modified. The practice of science wills to radically alter the character of Desire: it legislates against it by making it external and extraneous, or it converts it into concrete pleasure. Consequently, science transforms the analytic impulse and in the process constructs a new version of the soul—of the Self of the inquirer.

The Self of the practitioner depicts one who resolves to believe and who in this resolve wills the senselessness of doubting the grounds of belief. Such resolve is displayed in the stance the believer takes toward his belief: he treats the grounds of belief from the point of view of belief itself; consequently, the achievement of any examination of scientific belief is always an instance of that belief because it is a believer's conception of belief. What we eventually have to examine are the methods that sociology uses to induce such a strength of resolve in its practitioners, and we have to conduct such an examination under the auspices of the Socratic understanding that such an apparent strength is actually (Really) a weakness of will and Desire, that it is the supreme case of ignorance (of forgetting why one speaks).

Sociology can refuse to examine itself, this is its typical stance. In this way, sociology can refuse to address the manner in which it exercises its authority, it can refuse to take responsibility for its authority. On the other hand, when sociology elects to examine itself, it can only do so sociologically; sociology exempts its very ground and Reason of examination from doubt.

To address itself, sociology must free itself from its practice; sociology must desociologize itself. This means that the practice can only be examined from a historic point that is free from the interests of the practice. As an intellectual craft, sociology must be examined from the vantage point of the climax of intellectual aspiration and must then be seen as a moment in the career of the idea of rational inquiry. The reflexivity of a practice is decadent self-reportage unless it grasps itself as a One with the nature of rational inquiry. Thus, the standard of essential thinking external to the practice must be recollected, remembered, and brought to bear upon the practice as that unity to which the practice ought to aspire to perfect its nature.

In this sense, the moral character of any practice consists in its relationship to itself and to its nature as revealed by the idea of essential thinking. To forget such a relationship is to forget why one speaks, which is the greatest immorality of the mind. Wrongdoing consists in such forgetting, which is why we can say that sociology will always do wrong no matter what it studies as long as it remains ignorant and forgetful of its Reason.

However, we have argued that to do such remembering is impossible for one who accepts the authority of the practice. This is because such a one will always remember in terms of the standard authorized by the practice. Therefore, to remember is to break away from the practice and to divest it of its authority. And why should this be terrorizing, for the practice is only meaningful insofar as it participates in a historic dialogue with Rationality. The practice must then be abandoned for a position that is external to its conduct and yet, internal to its Being; by seeing the practice as a moment in the relationship of an art to its nature, we subjugate the practice to its Reason, and consequently, we destroy its authority in order to restore its integrity. To restore the Reason of the practice its parochial interest must be superseded, it must be used as an occasion to address the suppressed history that the practice forgets; this is the history of the practice's falling out of touch with Reason. The practice must then be resituated within its dialogue with essential thinking.

Notes

1. Thus, sociology *does* address its own practice when it speaks about other practices, although not in the concrete sense of "it speaks directly about its practice," that is, sociology shows (makes reference to) its own practice in speaking about other practices.

2. Plato, *The Republic,* trans. by Francis M. Cornford (Oxford: Oxford University Press, 1945), p. 23.

3. Just as the only history worth speaking about is the history of Reason (compare Hegel's preface to *The Philosophy of History* [New York: Dover

Publications, 1956]) so the only practice worth speaking about is the perfect practice, that is, the practice that grasps its Reason.

4. Compare *Gorgias,* trans. by W. C. Helmbold (Indianapolis: Bobbs-Merrill Company, 1952), p. 25.

5. Martin Heidegger, *Hegel's Concept of Experience,* (New York: Harper & Row, Publishers, Inc. 1970), p. 60.

6. Friedrich Nietzsche, *Twilight of the Idols* (Baltimore: Penguin Books, Inc.), p. 51.

7. These ideas owe much to my discussions with my student, Don Foss, concerning his dissertation.

8. This problem has been discussed interestingly by both Hegel and Heidegger, and the joining of the issues can be seen in Heidegger's commentary on Hegel's "Introduction" to *The Phenomenology of Spirit.*

INDEX